THE ESSENTIAL GUIDE TO
SPEAKING
PUBLICLY, PROFESSIONALLY, AND PERSONALLY

*A Customized Version of Public Speaking: Choices for Effective Results,
Sixth Edition, by Gail E. Mason, Mark J. Butland, and John J. Makay*

Kendall Hunt
publishing company

Professor Caffie J. Risher

Chapters 2–10 and 12–15 from *Public Speaking: Choices for Effective Results,*
Sixth Edition by Gail E. Mason, Mark J. Butland, John J. Makay. Copyright
© 2012 by Kendall Hunt Publishing Company. Reprinted by permission.

Cover:
Images on right © Shutterstock, Inc.
Image on left Courtesy of Shawn Roberts and K.I.S.H. Home, Inc.

Kendall Hunt
publishing company

www.kendallhunt.com
Send all inquiries to:
4050 Westmark Drive
Dubuque, IA 52004-1840

Copyright © 2014 by Kendall Hunt Publishing Company

ISBN 978-1-4652-5981-3

Printed in the United States of America

DEDICATION

Dedicated to the memory of Dr. James McCarthy who, in undergraduate class, stated that I should consider teaching Public Speaking because I would be perfect at it!

First, I want to acknowledge my grandmother, Jessie Mae Simmons who distinctly and prophetically named me, Caffie; my favorite aunt, Effie McClam; and my family.

Thank you Sue Saad and Sara McGovern for your important contribution. I am grateful for your expertise.

Next, special acknowledgment to my mentors and friends: Professor Alyson Schumer; Dr. June West; Dr. Patricia Kuchon; Mr. James Marken; Dr. James Hutton; Professor Emeritus Elaine C. Harrington; Ms. Amryl Ward; Mrs. Barbara Rubel; PCCC's Public Speaking Adjunct Faculty; and a big round of applause goes to my students who have taught me how to teach and President Steve Rose, Vice-President Jacqueline Kineavy and former English Department Chair, Linda Bakian who believed in me and gave me the opportunity to teach at Passaic County Community College. I am forever grateful!

BRIEF CONTENTS

CONTENTS

PREFACE

This text offers theory and practical skills that present public speaking as an art form for transactional communication between speaker and audience.

The goal in writing this text is to prepare students to become effective public speakers in various speaking situations they may encounter in their lives. Whether they are presenting in a professional capacity, speaking as a community leader, offering a tribute to a retiring colleague, eulogizing a friend, delivering a commencement address, or sharing views as a concerned citizen, students will learn how to deliver an effective message to the audience.

This text is comprised of four parts:

Part I: Public Speaking Essentials

Part II: Preparing a Speech

Part III: Types of Presentation Speaking

Part IV: Presenting a Speech

Chapter 1: History of Public Speaking

This chapter focuses on the history of public speaking and its role in expanding freedom and democracy.

Student Learning Objectives

- Students will be able to explain the roots of public speaking, including the ancient study and practice of rhetoric
- Students will be able to identify the ways in which public speaking played a role in the emergence of democratic movements from the Enlightenment to the Twentieth century
- Students will be able to explain the roles that significant individuals have played in the history of public speaking

Chapter 2: Public Speaking and the Challenge of Communication

This chapter focuses on public speaking as a valuable activity that influences career and community success. The basic elements of the communication process are outlined and defined to provide the foundation for growth and understanding.

Student Learning Objectives:

○ Students will be able to explain at least five benefits of public speaking in their lives

○ Students will be able to describe public speaking and the communication process

○ Students will be able to identify and explain the five steps for preparing to speak

Chapter 3: Ethics in Public Speaking

An essential element of every speech, ethics is defined and explained through guidelines to promote speaker credibility. Points for avoiding unethical practices are also discussed.

Students Learning Objectives:

○ Students will be able to understand ethics

○ Students will be able to describe ethos and speaker credibility

○ Students will be able to explain how to develop ethical speaking habits

○ Students will be able to avoid unethical practices

Chapter 4: Listening and Critiquing Speeches

As crucial as the skills for speaking are to a presenter, just as important are listening skills to understand how listening helps improve public speaking. In this chapter are eight steps promote fine-tuning listening skills. Criteria for speech evaluation are also discussed.

Student Learning Objectives:

○ Students will be able to explain the difference between listening and public speaking

○ Students will be able to define listening and other communication activities

○ Students will be able to understand the importance of good listening skills

- Students will be able to understand and reflect on how to listen to a speech
- Students will be able to explain reasons audiences stop listening to a speech
- Students will be able to describe the four stages of listening to a speech
- Students will be able to identify and explain the eight steps for fine-tuning listening skills
- Students will be able to critique speeches
- Students will be able to use technology to provide feedback
- Students will be able to engage in self-evaluation

Chapter 5: Being Audience-Centered

Knowing your audience is the key to presenting a successful speech. This chapter discusses how to adapt to different audiences and situations. It explains how to create a speaker-audience connection by incorporating humor, encouraging participation, and quickly getting to the point of your speech.

Student Learning Objectives:

- Students will be able to identify their audience
- Students will be able to identify and explain how to adapt to different audiences and situations
- Students will be able to explain how to create a speaker-audience connection

Chapter 6: Research and Preparing Supporting Material

Research is the raw material that forms the foundation of public speaking. This chapter will help you develop an effective research strategy and provides guidelines for their chapters to support your speech.

Student Learning Objectives:

- Students will be able to describe how a speaker can develop a research strategy
- Students will be able to explain how speakers support their speech
- Students will be able to describe five functions of support materials
- Students will explain why support materials are needed in their speech
- Students will be able to document information accurately in their speech

Chapter 7: Organizing and Outlining Your Ideas

Organizing a speech helps the audience follow your points and understand your message. This chapter concentrates on developing the body of your speech, including selecting, supporting, and organizing your main points. It also discusses how to create effective outlines and notes to best serve you as you present.

Student Learning Objectives:

- Students will be able to specify the importance of organizing a speech
- Students will be able to identify and explain the benefits of organizing the body of the speech
- Students will be able to understand how to create unity through connections
- Students will be able to construct and edit notes and outlines

Chapter 8: Introducing and Concluding Your Speech

This chapter offers introductions and conclusions approaches in relation to how your speech can make a lasting impression. It discusses how to engage members of the audience at the beginning of a speech so that they will want to listen, and then how to remind your audience at the end of what you said and why it was relevant. Techniques and suggestions including common pitfalls for introductions and conclusions are offered.

Student Learning Objectives:

- Students will be able to define the functions of introductions
- Students will be able to explain how to introduce the same speech in different ways
- Students will be able to identify and explain five guidelines and suggestions for introductions
- Students will be able to describe common pitfalls of introductions
- Students will be able to discuss the functions of conclusions
- Students will be able to recognize the value of developing memorable conclusions

Chapter 9: Informative Speaking

The intent of an informative speech is to communicate information and ideas in a way that your audience will understand and remember. Presented are different types of informative speeches as well as, goals and strategies for informative speaking. This chapter explores the ethics of informative speaking.

Student Learning Objectives:

- Students will be able to differentiate between the three genres or classification of speeches, informative, persuasive, and commemorative (special occasion)
- Students will be able to select and practice the different types of informative speaking
- Students will be able to describe and explain five goals of informative speeches
- Students will be able to identify goals, guidelines and strategies for effective informative speaking
- Students will be able to apply the ethics of informative speaking

Chapter 10: Special Occasion Speaking

Beginning with general guidelines for special occasion speeches, this chapter discusses how to effectively present common situations wherein a brief speech is appropriate. This chapter also addresses introductory, presentational, acceptance, commemorative, keynote, and after-dinner speeches.

Student Learning Objectives:

- Students will be able to identify and explain the seven general guidelines for special-occasion speeches
- Students will be able to list and describe specific guidelines for speeches of introduction, presentation and acceptance
- Students will be able to select, develop and deliver commemorative speeches
- Students will be able to select, develop and deliver keynote speeches
- Students will be able to specify guidelines for speeches of presentation
- Studetnts will be able to specify guidelines for speeches of acceptance

Chapter 11: Successful Interviewing Techniques

This chapter examines the practical application of two kinds of communication situations that are widely used and invites you to be an active participant in the process.

Student Learning Objectives:

○ Students will be able to explain the various types of open and closed ended questions that are used in interviews

○ Students will be able to describe and explain how interviews are structured

○ Students will be able to prepare, plan, and participate in a structured interview

○ Students will be able to conduct an information-gathering interview

Chapter 12: Persuasive Speaking

Persuasion is intended to influence choice through appeals to the audience's sense of ethics, reasoning, and emotion. This chapter explores the goals of persuasive speaking and discusses elements, reasoning, appeals, and arguments as well as the ethics of persuasive messages.

Student Learning Objectives:

○ Students will be able to describe how to analyze the audience in persuasive speaking

○ Students will be able to explain how to build the elements of persuasion

○ Students will be able to identify and explain the goals, aims, and claims of a persuasive speech

○ Students will be able to explain types of persuasive claims

○ Students will be able to explain how to organize persuasive speeches

○ Students will be able to explain the ethics of persuasive speaking

Chapter 13: Language

It is important to remember to consider how words affect your listeners. In this chapter, we identify characteristics of spoken language and provide guidelines for using them more effectively. Addressed are also pitfalls, which are aspects of language, that a speaker should avoid. The use of humor is also discussed.

Student Learning Objectives:

○ Students will be able to identify characteristics of spoken language

○ Students will be able to discuss guidelines for language and style

○ Students will be able to describe language pitfalls

Chapter 14: Delivery and Communication Apprehension

The ability to communicate information, persuade, and entertain the audience is influenced by the manner in which you present yourself to your audience. This chapter discusses methods of delivery and offers specific strategies for vocal delivery and physical delivery so your message is favorably enhanced by the way you convey it. Additionally a focus on communication apprehension and strategies you can use to control it is presented in this chapter as well.

Student Learning Objectives:

- Students will be able to list the four methods of delivery
- Students will be able to describe the aspects of vocal delivery
- Students will be able to explain the aspects of physical delivery
- Students will be able to recognize communication apprehension and learn strategies to avoid it

Chapter 15: Presentational Aids in an Electronic World

Exploring the different types available and offering criteria for their use and display, this chapter focuses on the benefits of using presentation aids. The decision to include an aid should be based on the extent to which it enhances your audience's interest and understanding. Guidelines are presented for determining what to incorporate and how to use it.

Student Learning Objectives:

- Students will be able to explain the nature of presentational aids today
- Students will be able to use the various types of presentational aids with maximum comprehension and clarity
- Students will be able to describe the types of technology-based presentational aids
- Students will be able to explain effective use of presentational aids

Student Oriented Pedagogy

Because we recognize the importance of assessing student learning, included are features that facilitate student learning and tools that help instructors measure learning outcomes.

- **Chapter Outlines** serve as a map to guide students through the content of the chapter and focus on key points.
- **Bold-faced Key Terms** throughout the chapter include clear definitions for each term.

○ **Real-world Examples and Strategies**, including international examples, illustrate chapter theories and concepts, as well as help students apply those concepts in their own work.

○ **Questions for Study and Discussion** encourage students to further explore the concepts they learned in the chapter.

○ **Glossary of Terms** serves as a helpful reference tool at the end of the text.

Instructional Online Enhancements

Both students and instructors have access to online content that is integrated chapter by chapter with the text to enrich student learning. The web access code is included on the inside front cover of the textbook.

Look for the web icon in the text margins to direct you to various interactive tools.

Student Web Content

● **Poll Questions** draw students into the subject matter of the chapter by asking questions relevant to students and the chapter theme.

● **Video** brings the chapter content to life, clearly illustrating theory by showcasing actual student speeches.

● **Interactive Video Exercises** reinforce chapter concepts by incorporating   chapter content with an actual speech example to illustrate the application of the concept.

● **Applications** offer real-world scenarios to key terms so students can apply them effectively.

● **Interactive Flashcards** reinforce definitions of key terms.

Instructor Web Content

● **Chapter Outlines** highlight central ideas for each chapter and can serve as lecture notes.

● **Activities and Worksheets** further explore chapter content and can be made accessible to students.

● **Extensive Teaching Tips** enhance the textbook content to aid student understanding.

● **Comprehensive Test Bank** offers several different types of questions to better assess student comprehension

ABOUT THE AUTHOR

Caffie J. Risher is Assistant Professor and Coordinator of the Public Speaking program at Passaic County Community College in Paterson, New Jersey. Caffie conducts workshops, seminars and webinars to help coaches, speakers, entrepreneurs, and the clergy with their public, professional and personal speaking and communication goals. Caffie is a graduate of Fairleigh Dickinson University with a BA in Communications; Seton Hall University with a MA in Corporate and Public Communication; and a M.Div. degree in Theology from New Brunswick Theological Seminary. Caffie has taught more than 3,000 students on both the undergraduate and graduate level during her tenure at several colleges, universities and seminaries, grading over 10,000 speech presentations. Professor Risher is a member of the National Communication Association (NCA) and the New Jersey Communication Association (NJCA). For more information about Professor Caffie J. Risher's training, consulting and coaching services, visit: http://ewilliams-associates.com.

Part

I

PUBLIC SPEAKING ESSENTIALS

Image © Everett Collection, 2013. Used under license from Shutterstock, Inc.

Chapter

1

"Speech is power: speech is to persuade, to convert, to compel."

Ralph Waldo Emerson

Chapter 1: History of Public Speaking

This chapter focuses on the history of public speaking and its role in expanding freedom and democracy.

Student Learning Objectives:

○ Students will be able to explain the roots of public speaking, including the ancient study and practice of rhetoric

○ Students will be able to identify the ways in which public speaking played a role in the emergence of democratic movements from the Enlightenment to the twentieth century

○ Students will be able to explain the roles that significant individuals have played in the history of public speaking

HISTORY OF PUBLIC SPEAKING

Key Terms

Civic Responsibility   Oratory   Philosophes   Rhetoric
Declamation   Persuasive speech

Ancient Speech and the Roots of Democracy

In the modern world, we can broadcast our opinions from any venue: while standing on a street corner or in a public park, by speaking up at town or city meetings, or on our own podcasts and YouTube videos. In fact, we are so used to this right that we take it for granted. It is often hard to remember that the right to speak in public was not always enjoyed by the majority of people. While skilled orators have been valued in societies around the world for thousands of years, public speaking was once a right reserved only for priests, kings, and other leaders in the ancient world.

Image © Panos Karas, 2013. Used under license from Shutterstock, Inc.

All of that changed during the era of the ancient Greek republic in the late sixth and early fifth centuries B.C.E. At that time, one of the earliest forms of democracy emerged in Athens. In that system, adult male Athenian citizens who had completed their military training had the right to vote and participate in the Assembly, the governing body. In the Assembly, eligible members discussed and decided the important issues that would affect all of the people of Athens, as well as listened to legal grievances and made legal judgments. Therefore, it was expected and required that all voting citizens would participate in the dialogues necessary to help make decisions; public speaking was an important part of that responsibility.

To provide guidelines for these responsibilities, the great Greek philosopher Aristotle (384–322 B.C.E.) established some of the basic and essential rules for public speaking in his treatise *On Rhetoric*, which many scholars regard as "the most important single work on persuasion ever written" (Berquist, et.al, 2009). Rhetoric is the art of **persuasive speech**, and Aristotle explained that rhetoric was the "faculty of discovering the possible means of persuasion in reference to any subject whatever."

Aristotle argued that in order to be a persuasive speaker and win others over to a specific point of view, the speaker must recognize that there are three fundamental persuasive elements in an effective speech:

Glossary

Persuasive speech Public speaking meant to influence the way people think about a given subject.

1. **Ethos**: the credibility or believability of the speaker, which helps convince listeners that the argument is valid.

2. **Logos**: the use of logic in the speech, which must be structurally solid and backed up by evidence.

3. **Pathos**: the emotional appeal of the speech, which can be used to reach the heart of the listener.

These three elements, Aristotle argued, were the root of all successful public speech. Students learned how to use these elements so that they could take their place in the Assembly when they were eligible, and therefore participate in the governance of Athenian society.

The great Roman orator Cicero (106–43 B.C.E.) took Aristotle's study of rhetoric further when he outlined **The Five Canons of Rhetoric**. The Five Canons, or rules, include:

1. **Invention**: The process of deciding on a topic and the appropriate arguments to support it.

2. **Arrangement**: The different components of an argument organized to achieve success.

3. **Style**: The manner in which the argument is delivered. This can include word selection, imagery, and metaphor.

4. **Memory**: The methods orators use to remember their speech and make it memorable for the audience.

5. **Delivery**: The manipulation of speech, including pitch and volume, as well as physical gestures that engage the audience during the speech.

In both Ancient Greece and Rome, the right to speak in public was not universal, but the study of rhetoric and the basic guidelines for effective speech were being established. Over time, rhetoric would grow to include not merely the practice of persuasive speech, but also its role as a primary means to establish greater freedom and democracy in various societies.

The Use of Rhetoric in the Medieval Church

Following the collapse of the Roman Empire, Europe entered a period of reorganization in which the Christian church became the single most dominant power. Appropriately, rhetoric became one of the principle tools the church used to spread its message. St. Augustine (354–430 C.E.), also known as Aurelius Augustinus Hipponensis, was a Roman teacher of **oratory** who converted to Christianity and became one of the earliest Christian leaders. In order to teach priests how to spread the Christian

Glossary

Oratory A form of eloquent public speaking.

BTW!

In the Middle Ages, the new universities focused on two branches of study based on the five senses: the *Trivium* and the *Quadrivium*. The Trivium, or "three roads," was the foundation of the liberal arts and included grammar, logic, and rhetoric. Once these subjects were mastered, the student could move on to the four subjects of the Quadrivium: Arithmetic, Geometry, Music, and Astronomy. These seven liberal arts of classical study were considered the most essential components of a well-rounded education.

message and win converts, Augustine married the Greek and Roman philosophical traditions, including rhetoric, to Judeo-Christian teachings.

For example, in Book Four of his treatise *On Christian Doctrine*, Augustine borrowed Cicero's dictate that "Wisdom without eloquence is of little use to society, while eloquence without wisdom is frequently extremely prejudicial to it, never of any use." He further argued:

> If those, therefore, who have propounded the rules of eloquence, have been obliged, in the very books in which they have done this, to make such a confession at the instigation of truth...how much more ought we to have no other opinion, seeing that we are sons and ministers of this wisdom?

For St. Augustine, the use of rhetoric in public speech was a necessary tool for Christian leaders interested in spreading Christian values through their teaching, as an instrument of truth.

The Christian tradition of rhetoric was joined by a new emphasis on rhetoric as an essential component of the education offered by the new universities that began to emerge during the Middle Ages. The core education provided by these new institutions was the study of seven fundamental subjects: grammar, logic, astronomy, arithmetic, music, geometry, and rhetoric, which is the art and skill of public speaking. These subjects were all considered necessary to the creation of effective political and religious leaders. While the average man on the street might not be able to declaim his opinions without consequence, speech was beginning to be valued as an important way to build political power and unity.

Glossary

Civic responsibility The duty of citizens in a democracy to participate in governance of their society by voting, debating issues, and volunteering for public office or public service.

Freedom of Speech as a Weapon against Tyranny

During the Renaissance of the fourteenth and fifteenth centuries, the works of the ancient Greeks and Romans were rediscovered, including those that emphasized the importance of rhetoric as part of **civic responsibility**. At the time, the new political form of the nation-state was beginning to emerge and political absolutism began in Europe, as kings and emperors consolidated their powers and established rigid censorship to prevent any dissent. Nonetheless, there were frequent challenges to the tyranny of kings and emperors in the seventeenth century. Popular movements emerged to fight for greater rights, and the use of public speech to challenge older patterns of political rule became more common. In addition, the establishment of colonies in North America introduced a new political culture that would rely on public speaking.

In particular, the English Civil War introduced the right to free speech as fundamental to political freedom.

First a dispute between the king and Parliament, the war culminated in the beheading of the king and the creation of a constitutional monarchy resting on the new English Bill of Rights in 1689. The Bill of Rights included the provision that "the freedom of speech and debates or proceedings in Parliament ought not to be impeached or questioned in any court or place out of Parliament."

THE CIVIL WAR 1642-51 fought between the forces of KING & PARLIAMENT: Pikeman

This meant that the king's authority was limited and no longer absolute; members of Parliament were free to debate, proclaim their opinions, and disagree with the king without fear of retaliation from the monarch. This was an important step in securing the right to dissent through free and public speech.

At the same time, the new colonies in North America that were established in the seventeenth century began to forge their own political traditions with public speaking at the center of governance. The New England colonies, including the Massachusetts Bay Colony (now Boston) and Plimoth Plantation, were largely settled as religious experiments in creating "cities on a hill," or perfect Christian communities. Puritan ministers used their pulpits not only to deliver sermons that contained instruction in Christian values, but also to exercise social control and influence town politics. An effective minister could exercise a significant influence over the community through his public speaking abilities, and anyone interested in entering the ministry or town governance was expected to become an effective public speaker.

In addition, these colonies relied on a new form of political participation called the town meeting. Communities generally paid for and built a town meetinghouse with tax money, and the meetinghouse served as both the primary place of worship as well as a forum for the discussion of issues central to the town's needs. All male citizens could participate in town meetings and, through discussion and voting, establish the laws of the town. Successful governance of a town, and the stability of the town, therefore required that men be capable of speaking in public on the issues of the day. To many scholars, these town meetings were the genesis of American democracy.

The Enlightenment Expansion of Freedom of Speech

Image © Georgios Kollidas, 2013. Used under license from Shutterstock, Inc.

In the eighteenth century, new philosophies that grew from ancient Greek and Roman ideas continued to challenge the power of the nation-states over individuals. The Enlightenment, also known as the Age of Reason, was an era of intellectual growth and change when reformers embraced the use of reason and scientific method over the realm of faith and superstition, and promoted the rights of the individual over the power of absolute monarchs. In particular, the French philosophers known as the **philosophes**, which included René Descartes, Denis Diderot, Jean-Jacques Rousseau and Montesquieu, championed the idea that humans were born with natural rights, including freedom of expression.

Two of the most prominent of the Enlightenment thinkers were John Locke (1632–1704) and François-Marie Arouet (1694–1778), who wrote under the pen name Voltaire. Locke's *Second Treatise on Government* (1690) argued that because all men were born with natural rights, the only just form of government was one formed with the consent and participation of the people. Locke wrote:

> To understand political power right, and derive it from its original, we must consider, what state all men are naturally in, and that is, a state of perfect freedom to order their actions, and dispose of their possessions and persons, as they think fit, within the bounds of the law of nature, without asking leave, or depending upon the will of any other man.

It was therefore obvious to Locke that political participation relied on the right to free speech and that all citizens had an obligation to exercise that right in order to maintain legitimate government.

Image © Nicku, 2013. Used under license from Shutterstock, Inc.

Similarly, the Frenchman François-Marie Arouet was one of the most prominent defenders of freedom of speech during the Enlightenment era. Writing under the pen name Voltaire, he was a witty, perceptive author of plays, poetry, novels, and political essays who advocated for freedom and religion and the separation of church and state, which he felt were among the most important bulwarks against political tyranny and important safeguards of individual liberty. He also emphasized the necessity of freedom of speech, having been subject to extreme censorship and exile due to his writings. He wrote, "We have a natural right to make use of our pens as of our tongue, at our peril, risk and hazard."

All in all, the Enlightenment established an important connection between individual freedom and the freedom of speech. These ideas would provide the spark to two events that helped establish modern democracy: the American and French Revolutions.

Public Speaking in the Era of Revolution

Both the American and French revolutions were products of the Enlightenment's new emphasis on the natural rights of the individual and the need to restrain the power of government in order to preserve and protect those rights. Neither of these revolutions would have been possible without decisive and influential use of public speech by their leaders.

Image © Brendan Howard, 2013. Used under license from Shutterstock, Inc.

The American Revolution was the rebellion of the North American colonies against the King of England and British Parliament. The British Government had habitually practiced "benign neglect" of the colonies, generally letting the colonists govern themselves through colonial assemblies. This meant that the colonies developed a tradition of self-rule, in which residents debated issues and established the laws of their communities without much direction from Great Britain.

However, Great Britain began to exercise more control over the colonies following the French and Indian War. Wanting to recoup some of the expenses of the war, Parliament began to enact a series of taxes: the first, called the Stamp Act, was on all official documents. The Stamp Act created vociferous dissent, and residents began to speak out in meetings, at taverns, in public protests, and in the colonial assemblies. The most famous of these public denunciations of the Stamp Act occurred in Virginia in 1765, when Patrick Henry (1736–1799) announced his opposition to the tax by famously stating, "If this be treason, make the most of it!"

Though the vocal protests against the Stamp Act resulted in its demise, the British Government continued to tax the colonies, and initiated both the Sugar and Tea taxes. Protests and riots ensued, all propelled by the public speeches of dissenting colonists. Clearly, the practice of public speaking had an enormous impact on the colonies. The seeds of revolution were sown in these speeches, and as people heard and read more and more arguments against the taxes, and then eventually against monarchy in general, an independence movement began. The colonial assemblies were replaced by Committees of Correspondence, meetings through which the colonists organized their rebellion against Great Britain. It should be no surprise that the founding documents of the United States of America, the *Declaration of Independence* and the *United States Constitution*, both enshrine freedom of speech as a natural right and the cornerstone of liberty and democracy.

Image © Mike Flippo, 2013. Used under license from Shutterstock, Inc.

Just a few years later, the French Revolution of 1789 took up the banner of revolution by overthrowing the King of France and establishing a republic that also linked freedom of speech to liberty and democracy. *The Declaration of the Rights of Man and of the Citizen* was adopted and featured a strong affirmation of the right to freedom of speech as an inalienable right. Article 11 states:

> The free communication of ideas and opinions is one of the most precious of the rights of man. Every citizen may, accordingly, speak, write, and print with freedom, but shall be responsible for such abuses of this freedom as shall be defined by law.

Glossary

Rhetoric The art of persuasive speech.

Through both the American and French revolutions, the right to speak in public was asserted as a natural right to which all citizens were entitled. However, despite the egalitarian **rhetoric** of these revolutions, public speaking was still only practiced by wealthy, white men. This would change in the nineteenth century.

Reform Movements and Public Speaking in the Nineteenth Century

The spirit of democracy in the new United States was summed up by nineteenth century philosopher Henry David Thoreau (1817–1862), who wrote:

> When, in some obscure country town, the farmers come together to a special town-meeting, to express their opinion on some subject which is vexing the land, that, I think, is the true Congress, and the most respectable one that is ever assembled in the United States.

Image © stockelements, 2013. Used under license from Shutterstock, Inc.

Throughout the antebellum era in the nineteenth century, Americans took their democratic ethos and worked to improve society through a series of reform movements in response to growing social problems and the start of the industrial era. Americans spoke and debated about the need to improve school and other social institutions, fight poverty, and, in particular, attacked the persistence of slavery in the United States. A strong abolitionist movement dedicated to freeing the slaves became the leading reform cause before the Civil War, and public speeches denouncing slavery were at the heart of the abolitionist movement. Among those prominent speakers in the abolitionist fight were Frederick Douglass (c. 1818–1895), a former slave, and William Lloyd Garrison (1805–1879), an abolitionist newspaper editor. Each brought the antislavery message to the masses.

One of the most common forums for public speaking in the nineteenth century was the Lyceum circuit. This movement, named for Aristotle's Lyceum, was a form of adult education that featured sponsored public lectures across the Northeast and Midwest, given by leading intellectual figures in the United States such as Ralph Waldo Emerson, Henry David Thoreau, Daniel Webster, Nathaniel Hawthorne, Wendell Phillips, Abraham Lincoln, and Susan B. Anthony. This format was so popular that between 1840 and 1860, over 3000 public lectures were advertised in New York City; other cities also had frequent public lectures on some of the popular issues of the day, including social and political reform.

Women were among the most powerful reform speakers on the Lyceum circuit, despite the fact that women were discouraged from speaking in public venues, especially to mixed gender audiences. They often focused on topics that reflected their desire to expand their domestic realm into the political arena. For example, women spoke out in favor of temperance, the movement to limit the sale and consumption of alcohol, and reform of social institutions such as prisons and asylums.

However, the most frequent and popular topics that women spoke on were abolitionism, the movement to end slavery, and the women's rights movement that began in the 1940s. Journalist Maria Miller Stewart (1803–1880) was the first African-American to speak in public, as well as the first to speak to a mixed race and gender audience. Sarah (1792–1893) and Angelina (1805–1879) Grimké were two southern sisters who renounced their slave-owning families and are often considered the first female public speakers in the United States. They were very popular speakers on the lecture circuit, but they were also criticized for stepping out of traditional gender roles in order to promote their cause. This led them to join the growing women's movement to fight for gender equality. Lucy Stone (1818–1893) was one of the most prominent advocates for women's rights, and was a popular Lyceum speaker.

Image © Brendan Howard, 2013. Used under license from Shutterstock, Inc.

The art and skill of public speaking was highly prized in the United States during this era. Not only were original speeches an important part of the Lyceum movement, but memorized speeches written by others were also performed by popular speakers. This was called the **declamation** style of public speaking, and it became a way for more people to hear the word of the reformers and politicians of the era if they did not have the opportunity to hear those people in person. Declamatory practice became so widespread that it was taught in American schools. In addition, as the nineteenth century progressed, the American political system began to incorporate public debates more frequently, such as the famous Lincoln-Douglas debates of 1858. This ensured that anyone interested in public service needed to excel at public speaking.

Glossary

Declamation A form of public speaking that is forceful and dramatic.

Image © James Steidl, 2013. Used under license from Shutterstock, Inc.

Image © Dave Newman, 2013. Used under license from Shutterstock, Inc.

Public Speaking in the Modern Era

Throughout the nineteenth century, western democracies began to be shaped more and more by the exercise of free speech. In England, a corner of Hyde Park in London became a popular location for just about anyone with an opinion to stand upon a soap box and speak their thoughts to anyone who would listen. Speaker's Corner has ever since provided a forum for such diverse figures as Karl Marx, William Morris, and George Orwell.

However, the birth of recorded sound, radio, film, and television really expanded the forum for public speaking. Politicians, including dictators such as Adolph Hitler, took advantage of these media to persuade and proselytize their ideologies, no matter how offensive or shocking. Public speaking also became a popular means by which to protest oppressive governments, unfair labor or economic practices, and racial inequality. In the twentieth century, Mohandas Gandhi used public speaking to fight the British rule in India, and Martin Luther King, Jr.'s impassioned demands for racial justice led to some of the most memorable speeches in world history.

In fact, one of the greatest benefits of the new technology was the way that it enabled previously powerless and disenfranchised people to express their demands for justice. One example from the American Civil Rights Movement powerfully illustrates just how important the right to speak in public can be. Fannie Lou Hamer (1917–1977) was poorly-educated, impoverished Mississippi sharecropper who lived under the violent and strictly enforced racial segregation of the American south for her entire life.

In the early 1960s, she joined the civil rights movement's voter registration drive and began to fight against segregation. In 1964, she traveled to the Democratic National Convention with a group called the Mississippi Freedom Democratic Party to protest the fact that Mississippi's delegation only included white citizens. Her testimony in front of the convention's Credentials Committee was broadcast live on television; her powerful voice so effectively challenged the segregation of the Mississippi Democratic Party that it threatened to cause President Lyndon Johnson the nomination. The President quickly moved to silence her by holding an emergency press conference that would run on television instead of her speech. Fannie Lou Hamer's story shows the power that one individual, no matter how lacking in education or wealth, can have through public speaking.

The Future of Public Speaking

The advent of the Internet has dramatically expanded the opportunity for public speaking as well as increased the size and diversified the composition of audiences. In the western world, there are no longer any rules limiting those who can speak in public by gender or race, and it is possible to experience multiple styles and an unlimited number of topics by watching and listening to podcasts, TED talks, homemade YouTube videos, and other online formats. The ancient, rigid formulations of Aristotle's rhetoric have given way to improvisation, spontaneity, and market forces that enable people to market their public speaking endeavors in a way that the ancient world could never have envisioned.

The online expansion of free speech may also break down barriers and limitations to public speaking that exist in other parts of the world. For example, women are either forbidden to speak in public or heavily censored in many places around the world, including in societies that practice Sharia Muslim law such as Iran, or nations with oppressive governments like China and Cuba. Recently, Pakistani schoolgirl Malala Yousufzai, who wrote a blog advocating for greater educational opportunities for girls, was shot by Talibani radicals. She survived and has traveled the world, appearing on television and speaking in public on behalf of girls' and women's rights to education and equal treatment.

Like Fannie Lou Hamer, Malala Yousufzai's story shows that public speaking can be a crucial tool in political persuasion, performance, and education. Public speaking has helped forge democracy and individual rights for centuries, and with the expansion of venues like the Internet, it looks like public speaking will continue to do so well into the future.

Summary

The right to speak in public has not always been available or guaranteed. Over centuries, however, public speaking came to be viewed as an essential component of democratic societies. Beginning in ancient Greece and continuing through the medieval era, public speaking has been the cornerstone of education and political change. New ideas about natural rights led people to use public speaking to fight tyranny and oppression through the English Civil War and the American and French Revolutions. Social reformers in the nineteenth century spoke in public to fight slavery and other forms of social and political corruption, and it has been a valuable tool in the fight for gender and racial equality in the twentieth century. In fact, without the right to speak in public, the Civil Rights Movement and decolonization movements around the world might not have succeeded. Today, new methods of communication such as the Internet have emerged and become more accessible to millions of people. Rather than take the right to speak in public for granted, people in the past and even today use it to continue the pursuit of social, political, and economic justice.

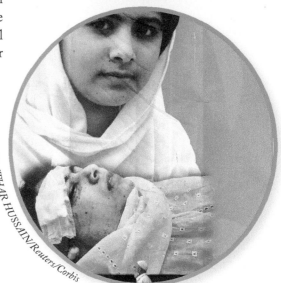

Discussion Starters

1. How did ancient societies contribute to the development of public speaking?

2. How did the Enlightenment help expand the rights of people to speak in public?

3. In what ways has public speaking helped further social change?

4. What barriers have people overcome in the past in order to speak in public?

5. How can one person's voice affect political and social change?

References

Aristotle and Kennedy, George M. *On Rhetoric: A Theory of Civic Discourse.* Oxford: Oxford University Press, 2006.

Berquist, Goodwin, William Coleman, and James M. Sproule. *The Rhetoric of Western Thought: From the Mediterranean World to the Global Setting,* 9th Edition. Dubuque: Kendall Hunt Publishing, 2009.

Eastman, Caroline. *A Nation of Speechifiers: Making an American Public after the Revolution.* Chicago: University of Chicago Press, 2009.

Katula, Richard, A., Director. NEH Landmarks Workshop: The American Lyceum: The Rhetoric of Idealism, Opportunity, and Abolition. LOCATION: Summer, 2011.

Lucas, Stephen E. *The Art of Public Speaking.* New York: McGraw-Hill Publishing Company, 2011.

Murphy, James J. *Rhetoric in the Middle Ages: A History of Rhetorical Theory from St. Augustine to the Renaissance.* Oakland: University of California Press, 1981.

Ray, Angela G. *The Lyceum and Public Culture in Nineteenth Century United States.* East Lansing: Michigan State University Press, 2005.

Scott, Donald M. "The Popular Lecture and the Creation of a Public in Mid-Nineteenth Century America." *The Journal of American History,* Vol. 66, No. 4 (March, 1980).

Walters, Ronald. *American Reformers, 1815-1860.* New York: Hill and Wang, 1997.

Chapter

2

"*Why Speak?*

–To keep a free *society* free.

–To settle differences by talk *instead of* force.

–To alter and promote thought.

–To water and cultivate ideas, hopes, sentiments,
and enthusiasm *in a way and to a degree that
cannot be done while we are separated one
from another.*"

William Norwood Brigance

Chapter 2: Public Speaking and the Challenge of Communication

This chapter focuses on public speaking as a valuable activity that influences career and community success. The basic elements of the communication process are outlined and defined to provide the foundation for growth and understanding.

Student Learning Objectives:

○ Students will be able to explain at least five benefits of public speaking in their lives

○ Students will be able to describe public speaking and the communication process

○ Students will be able to identify and explain the five steps for preparing to speak

PUBLIC SPEAKING AND THE CHALLENGE OF COMMUNICATION

Public Speaking in Your Life

Public Speaking is a valuable activity

Public Speaking influences success in college

Public Speaking teaches critical thinking skills

Public Speaking skills influences career and community success

Public Speaking skills are key to leadership

Public Speaking skills complement technology

Public speaking is part of our Democratic tradition

Public Speaking and the Communication Process

Eight Elements of the Communication Process

1. Sender/Receiver

2. Receiver/Sender

3. Message

4. Channel

5. Feedback

6. Noise

7. Occasion

8. Cultural Context

Five Steps for Preparing to Speak

1. Select and Narrow an audience-centered topic

   Know the speaking assignment

   Understand the audience

   Choose an appropriate topic

   Determine the general purpose, specific purpose, and thesis statement

   Demonstrate ethical behavior throughout the process

2. Develop content through research and sound support

3. Draft the introduction, body, and conclusion

4. Develop language, and presentation aids carefully

   Use plain English

   Remember that writing and speaking are different activities

   Relate your language to your audience's level of knowledge

   Use language for specific effect

   Be culturally sensitive

   Determine where to incorporate technology and presentational aids

5. Rehearse and deliver your speech

Summary

Discussion Starters

References

Key Terms

captive audience	figurative analogy	physical noise	research
communication	immediate feedback	physiological noise	semantic noise
culture	listener	plagiarism	static variables
delayed feedback	literal analogy	psychological noise	voluntary audience
dynamic variables			

Reflect about the time you joined your first online social network. Perhaps it was Myspace, Facebook, or LinkedIn. You were excited about it. You wanted contact with an online audience. You may not have given it much thought, but as you set up your profile, shared information about yourself, and selected pictures to show, you were crafting a message intended to shape how people see and respond to you. It was intentional communication aimed at a desired result.

You have been presenting yourself and your ideas your whole life. At a young age you likely brought interesting treasures to show and tell. Maybe you wanted to share your live bug collection, new kitten, or favorite stuffed animal with your kindergarten classmates. You did not realize that this was a public speaking event; you may not have known what the term "public speaking" meant.

Speaking in front of a group can be personally challenging. And, at the same time, your teachers might have had you speak before your class because public speaking is important. Yet, speaking effectively with an audience can be a powerful experience, and mastering public speaking can propel you in desirable directions.

This book focuses on how you present yourself and your messages in a way that increases the odds of getting what you want in an efficient and ethical way. While the primary focus will be on the more formal presentations, many of the ideas we develop may be applied to other, less formal messages you create and share, such as online profiles, text messages, phone conversations and conference calls, an avatar for your favorite game, or simple face-to-face conversations.

This first chapter lays a foundation for the rest of the book by showing you how important and relevant public speaking is to several aspects of your life. We introduce a model that clarifies the parts of the communication process and how the parts interact to help, and sometimes hurt, our communication effectiveness. Then highlighted are the steps to take to create your first speech.

© Valua Vitaly, 2012. Under license from Shutterstock, Inc.

How do you present yourself on Facebook?

Public Speaking in Your Life

Public speaking can be a *powerful tool* for an effective speaker who wishes to present us with information not known previously, or for the individual who wishes to advocate for a particular position or persuade an audience to take action. As we write this book, the United States is still engaged in military action in the Middle East. In the midst of national and international tensions and military actions, public speaking serves as a powerful force for taking action, resolving disagreements, persuading adversaries, and keeping audiences informed. Power is inherent in effective public speaking—power to communicate facts and emotions, convictions and attitudes, and values and beliefs—in a way that leaves a lasting, and often unequalled, impression on the audience.

Public speaking is also a *creative activity* that includes both mental and physical aspects. The mental aspect involves connecting thoughts and ideas in an original or innovative manner while centering on the audience's needs and interests. Delivering the speech is the physical aspect of the creative process, which includes knowing when to look at the audience, where to pause, where to place emphasis, using appropriate gestures and body movement, communicating ethically, and expressing self-confidence. Effective speakers have learned the *art* of public speaking and are able to design and deliver a speech that resonates with listeners through careful word choice, organization, supporting material, appropriate eye contact, and meaningful gestures. This art is audience centered, and its core is the message.

Public speaking is also a *decision-making process*. While taking your public speaking class, you will have to determine your interests, analyze your audience, decide where to look for information, figure out the best way to organize your information, make decisions about word choice, and decide how to deliver your speech most effectively.

As viewers watch speakers on TV, it's easy to find examples of poor decision making. We watch professional athletes come across poorly on TV because they were unprepared to comment on their performance. Late-night TV comedians, such as Jon Stewart of the *Daily Show*, regularly lampoon politicians for awkward gestures, odd word choice, and lack of logical reasoning.

As authors, our task is to help you think about all the decisions you make when developing and delivering a speech and to guide you to be effective as a speaker and as a listener.

Public Speaking is a Valuable Activity

It is fair to ask what value successful public speaking has in your life. Gaining self-confidence in front of an audience, learning how to make the best use of the time allowed, and being active when given an opportunity to express what you know and how you feel are genuine benefits to be gained from success as a public speaker. Consider these two real-life examples:

① A student proudly announced to her class that what she was learning in her public speaking course had been instrumental in raising her level of personal achievement. She had been asked to help obtain corporate sponsors for her sorority's fundraiser to aid a nearby children's hospital. Her speech to an audience of executives at a local corporation persuaded them to make a contribution of $1,000. A company spokesperson told the student that she gave the best presentation the executives had heard from a college student. Her announcement moved her classmates to applause.

② A young, talented, and ambitious woman on a fast track for advancement in her career at a Washington, D.C.–based trade association was approached by her supervisor, who had given her a glowing job rating. After praising the woman for her performance during the past year, the supervisor explained that he wanted her to begin speaking about the industry to consumer groups across the country. The more specific he became about her future public speaking responsibilities, the more uneasy the woman grew. After several minutes, she said she had rarely given speeches before and that she wanted to avoid this responsibility—even if it meant changing her job. However, after a productive conversation with her boss, she agreed to enroll in a public speaking course taught in the evenings at a nearby college and to join one of the Toastmasters groups in the area. (Toastmasters International is an important self-improvement organization for busy adults who have a need to improve their public speaking skills.)

Public speaking skills are important for success in school, career advancement, and for increasing self-confidence. In the first example, a student reached her fundraising goals and the feedback from the executives and classmates raised, or at least reinforced, her self-confidence. In the second example, we saw how a lack of skills may hinder career growth. Learning to communicate in a public setting is valuable for many reasons, including the six identified as follows.

Public Speaking Influences Success in College

Since you are currently in college, it makes sense to note that the first reason to learn and practice the essentials of public speaking is because they may influence your success in college. Oral presentations in English, philosophy, political science, or environmental science are all considered public speaking events. Normally, part of your grade is based on your presentation skills.

In addition to making presentations in your classes, any involvement in extracurricular activities may also be influenced by your ability to speak in public. If you are comfortable and possess the skills to address an audience, it will be possible to run for student body president, to present your point during an organizational meeting, or to be part of a film criticism workshop.

Image © Andresr, 2013. Used under license from Shutterstock, Inc.

Public speaking skills are important for success and self-confidence.

Public Speaking Teaches Critical Thinking Skills

A second reason for studying public speaking is that it teaches critical think-ing—the application of the principles of reasoning to your ideas and the ideas of others. Generally, teachers of all subjects are concerned that students learn to think critically. Some argue that of all the skills you will learn in college and thereafter, none is more important than critical thinking. *Critical think-ing enables you to evaluate your world and make choices based on what you have learned.* It is the intellectual tool necessary to make critical decisions at work (Do I recommend or discourage a new product line?), at home (Should I encourage my children to learn to read before entering kindergarten?), and in your roles as a consumer and citizen (Should I believe what the auto sales representative tells me or do my own independent research?). The critical thinking skills required to answer these questions can be developed, in part, through public speaking.

Critical thinking skills are used in many ways every time you prepare a speech. When choosing a topic, for example, you may decide that, although a speech describing how to fix a car's transmission would be right for a group of auto mechanics, it would be too technical for your public speaking class-mates. Because gas prices have risen so high, you may decide to persuade your classmates to trade in their old cars for newer, hybrid cars. As everyone in your audience is probably a driver, this topic could be more appropriate.

When researching a speech, you must decide what kinds of supporting material, or evidence, best enable you to express your views and develop your arguments. You use critical thinking skills to build, advance, and assess arguments. And you must make choices about language and expression. For example, think about how you would respond to your classmate who started her speech with the following:

> Most of us have experienced "it" at school or the doctor's office. We have to get a shot. It may be a flu shot or a vac-cine. The shot is given in your arm, your rear-end, or your leg. Some of us do not flinch. Others are slightly anxious; and still others confess this is one of their worst moments in life.
>
> So, how often do you get a shot? Once a year? Less than that? More? How many shots do you think you've had over the last 10 years? 10? 20? 30?
>
> Well, I've had around 11—11,000 that is. I'm an insulin-dependent diabetic. I take three or four shots a day. I also draw blood from my fingers to test my sugar levels at least twice a day. I get bruises on my belly from time to time from poorly placed shots, and if you look closely at my fingertips, you'll see lots of little marks from some 9,000 needle sticks. Welcome to my world.

The way she addressed the class, her language, the use of emphasis, pauses, and her reference to numbers had an impact on her listeners. After reading this introduction, you might think, "Wow! It would be awful to take shots so often" or "I could *never* take shots" or "Yeah. I have asthma. I can relate to someone dealing with a chronic illness." Some students may reflect on their own experiences with injections. Others may think of friends or relatives they know who are insulin dependent. Still others may focus more on the speaker and wonder how it must be to live with a life-threatening disease. If the student had started her speech by explaining what insulin-dependent diabetes is without providing a personal example and engaging the audience, there would be less of an effect on the audience.

Critical thinking is necessary to the development of an effective speech, and it's important in your role as **listener**. A listener perceives through sensory levels and interprets, evaluates, and responds to what he or she hears. Critical thinking skills are essential as you listen to and evaluate the messages of other speakers. As an audience member, your analysis will focus on several factors, including the purpose and organization of the speech; whether the speaker has accomplished his/her goal to persuade, inform, or speak appropriately on a special occasion; and whether he/she has satisfied your needs as an audience member. As your critical thinking skills develop, you will be able to say effectively what you mean as well as assess another speaker's effectiveness.

Public Speaking Skills Influence Career and Community Success

A third reason to study public speaking is that your public speaking skills may influence your success in career and community settings. Upward movement in the corporate hierarchy may depend on your ability to speak to groups at business conferences and at public presentations. Public speaking skills are an essential part of most professional interactions, including sales presentations, campaigns for public office, teaching and training programs, presentation of research findings at conventions, employee recruitment campaigns, and awards ceremonies. People who can speak on their feet, are articulate in meetings, and engage in good conversation have clear advantages. People involved in business, politics, and community activities, and members of the clergy who promote their ideas also promote themselves and what they represent, whether this is their intention or not. Few professionals can avoid public speaking.

In your community, unexpected events may move you into the public arena. For example, in a largely rural region of the Midwest, an international company attempted to acquire scenic land for use as a place to deposit waste materials. Many residents believed this would threaten—if not destroy—much of their rural setting. Citizens left their homes to rally and form a grassroots organization. Through the power of its most effective spokespersons, the organization provided enough resistance to persuade the company to cease its effort to acquire and use the land.

Public Speaking Skills are key to Leadership

A fourth reason public speaking is valuable is that it is a key to leadership. In his book *The Articulate Executive*, corporate communication consultant Granville Toogood (1996) discusses the relationship between effective speaking and coming across as a leader. He advises, "You've got to be able to share your knowledge and information (perhaps even your vision) with other people. It is not in any job description, but you've got to be a translator (explaining the law or technology to neophytes, for example), a teacher, and, eventually, a leader. The only way you can ever be a leader is to learn to speak effectively" (p. 10).

President Barack Obama emerged as an articulate spokesperson from the U.S. Senate, Hillary Clinton became Secretary of State for the United States, Steve Jobs made Apple Computers profitable, and since leaving Washington, Colin Powell has traveled the globe giving speeches on leadership from his perspective. Each of these individuals is a leader who demonstrates considerable public speaking skills. A skill all of these leaders possess is the ability to appear before audiences with well-prepared speeches and deliver them with authority, sincerity, enthusiasm, and self-confidence.

Public Speaking Skills Complement Technology

A fifth reason we find public speaking skills important is that they complement technology. Through Internet access, we can access billions of facts, but those facts may not be as impressive without the added human element. Speeches are supported by computer-generated graphics, supporting material is discovered on electronic databases, and images can easily be projected while a speech is being delivered.

The megachurches in Protestant Christianity rely greatly on graphics and other technology to put forth their message (Wolfe, 2005, p. 76). On entering a large room that can seat approximately one thousand people, individuals may find themselves facing up to six large video screens and a stage with a half-dozen musicians in place. The main speakers have microphones clipped on, replacing the traditional microphone at the pulpit. In the midst of this multimedia and technologically supported stage, the audience is addressed by the main speaker.

Public Speaking is part of our Democratic Tradition

The sixth and important reason public speaking is valuable is that speaking is part of our democratic tradition. The drive for change often begins with the spoken word. Indeed, since the colonial period of America when the First Amendment to the U.S. Constitution guaranteed certain freedoms, public speaking has served an important purpose in our democratic processes and procedures. Citizens have gathered at our nation's Capital to listen to aboli-tionists, suffragettes, and leaders of the civil rights, women's, and gay rights movements. We have witnessed peace marches, Million Man marches, and anti-war protests.

As you speak to your classmates, keep in mind that your speeches are rhetorical opportunities to show your understanding of and commitment to an idea and your ability to communicate your thoughts and feelings to others. If you use your public speaking class as a training ground to develop and refine your skills as a communicator, these learning experiences will serve you well throughout your life. Moreover, the confidence you develop here will allow you to speak forcefully within your community.

Public Speaking and the Communication Process

Communication is the creation of shared meaning through symbolic processes. You communicate your thoughts and feelings to your audience with the intent of generating knowledge and influencing values, beliefs, attitudes, and actions. Often, your purpose is to reach mutual understanding. As you speak in public, you use the shared symbols of communication to achieve a specific purpose.

The speeches you deliver fall into three general categories: *to inform*, *to persuade*, and *to entertain*. Sometimes you may want to share information and create a clear understanding with an audience. Other times you may want your audience to change their attitude and/or follow a different course of action. On special occasions, your task may be to entertain, inspire, or celebrate. Each of these three categories is treated in separate chapters to explain fully what is required for success. No matter what type of speech you deliver, your speaking objective is to elicit a response from your audience by sharing meaning with them.

Eight Elements of the Communication Process

The communication process involves at least eight elements: sender, receiver, message, channel, feedback, noise, occasion, and cultural context. These elements are discussed briefly here but they are explored in more detail throughout the book. Models provide insight into how things work and provide a go-to list when things go wrong. (See Figures 1.1 and 1.2.)

1. Sender/Receiver

Each speaker brings something unique to the occasion. As the speaker, you may have an interesting perception of an issue because of static and dynamic variables. Static variables are those things that remain stable from speaking situation to speaking situation. These include biological aspects such as

Glossary

Communication The creation of shared meaning through symbolic processes.

Static variables Those things that remain stable from speaking situation to speaking situation.

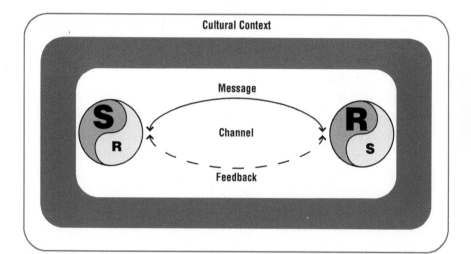

FIGURE 2.1
Communication Model
(Ideal)

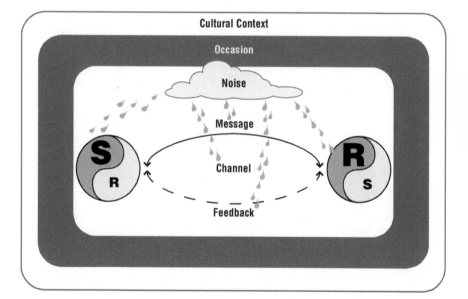

FIGURE 2.2
Communication Model
(Actual)

race, gender, and age. Experience and knowledge are also considered static, because one does not change experience, knowledge, health, and personality based on the speaking situation. **Dynamic variables** are variables that are subject to change. They include decisions you make about a particular speech, word choice, the structure you choose to support your points, and aspects of appearance that are easily changed (clothing, hair, accessories). In your role as a speaker, remember two things:

❶ **Your image makes a statement.** Keep this in mind. The image your audience has of you will be shaped with each comment you make. If you are a member of an athletic team or a frequent performer in plays on campus, your reputation may precede you and determine, in part,

Glossary

Dynamic variables
Those things that are subject
to change.

how your audience responds. However, speaking in front of the class or from your seat as a member of the audience also plays a role in the construction of an image of you and, as a public speaker, you must deal with your audience's preconceived notions. When you speak, your words and style of delivery communicate your involvement with your topic, and your listeners need only a few moments to pass judgment on your confidence, knowledge, integrity, and skill.

❷ **The speaker and the audience both have needs.** The speech is about you *and* your audience. Through the communication exchange, speakers seek from their audience a response that can satisfy certain needs. Depending on the situation, speakers need to be understood, to have influence, to bring about action, to be liked, or to be respected. For example a common practice among financial advisers is to invite clients and potential clients to evening seminars where informative sales presentations are made. The speakers' needs are to produce results in the sale of their financial products and services. After the presentation, the successful speaker will meet the needs of his/her audience, which in this case involves helping clients meet both immediate and long-term financial needs.

In our model, whether you are speaking or are a member of the audience, you are always playing the dual role of sending and receiving messages. As sender, the speaker initiates the message in public speaking. The impact of the speech is affected by whether the receivers find the speaker to be believable, trustworthy, competent, sincere, and confident.

For example, if an audience is receiving a lethal dose of PowerPoint, they will likely send messages of boredom through yawns, murmurs, and possibly nodding off. An effective speaker monitors this audience reaction, or feedback, and adjusts appropriately. In this secondary sense, the sender is also a receiver.

How is an audience's feedback relevant to the speaker?

© AISPIX, 2012. Under license from Shutterstock, Inc.

2. Receiver/Sender

In the communication process, the receiver is the target of the message. In public speaking, the receiver is the collection of individuals gathered to hear the speaker. We underscore the primary importance of the receiver or audience in public speaking situations. An effective speaker focuses on having some meaningful impact on our receivers. Listeners (receivers) bring their own frames of reference, which are influenced by the same variables found in the speaker: race, gender, age, health, personality, knowledge, experience, and so on. These variables influence how the audience responds to a speaker's message.

Although audience members may hear every word a speaker says, they can miss shades of meaning or may attribute meanings that have little or nothing to do with the speaker's intent. Because the potential for misunderstanding always exists, it is critical to plan every speech with your audience in mind. In the classroom, use terms and language your classmates can understand and find engaging but not offensive. Use examples that touch their lives.

Both the speaker and members of the audience share the responsibility of achieving mutual understanding. As such, listening as a necessary skill is mentioned frequently throughout our text. Ron Hoff (1998), a consultant and author on making speeches, explains: "By coming to your presentation, by simply showing up, your audience is expressing a need for help, counsel, wisdom, inspiration—maybe even something that can change its life … If truth be told, the audience arrives on the scene with the ardent hope that the presenter knows something that it does not" (p. 9).

Listening to the speaker and interpreting the speaker's message is the receiver's primary role in the communication process. However, receivers also send messages nonverbally while the speaker presents his/her message. They clap, laugh, yawn, talk to each other, text, frown, and smile. All of these behaviors communicate some message to the speaker. The receiver's feedback is relevant, although one should avoid distracting the speaker. The audience may send cues to the speaker that it is time to wrap up, that the speech is funny, or that something is confusing. The receiver is not a passive participant in the communication process.

3. Message

The message is what is communicated by the speaker and perceived by the audience. Public speaking is a meaning-centered process. Theorists have long recognized that *the essence of the message lies not only in what the speaker intends, but also in the meaning ascribed to the message by the listeners.* A speaker may intend to send a certain message, such as knowledge about a movie. But the speaker may also send an unintentional message, such as superiority or a faulty memory. Likewise, a speaker may choose to send a message via video blog, only to later discover that audiences become bored more easily when watching streaming video.

Though one hundred people may listen to the same speech, each will come away with his or her own interpretation of what the speaker said. While we may share the same language, we do not share identical experiences. Consider the following example:

> Angry students have gathered in a residence hall lounge to hear their protest leader. A meeting was called to express frustrations over a new college ruling declaring two freshmen residence halls off limits to persons of the opposite sex after 9:00 p.m. Violators are to be expelled from the dorm. Most of the residents are in attendance, and the primary spokes-person in opposition to the ruling is one of the residence hall presidents, who is about to learn what it is like to be at the center of a conflict. She states:

"We are here today as responsible adults, although the administration insists on treating us like children; we are here today because we do not want an anonymous college official behaving like our parent. As a matter of fact, our parents never asked for this either. We are old enough and smart enough to know when others have stepped over the line that divides guidance from interference."

As the hall president continued, she called on her fellow students to respect the privacy and personal values of their roommates. Some listeners perceived her remarks as too authoritative, while others questioned why she labeled the school's decision as too parental. The process is one of give and take between a speaker and the audience. While the residence hall president spoke, members of her audience listened to her remarks, attributed meaning to them, and responded based on their own attitudes, values, and beliefs. Near the end of the meeting, a petition was placed on a table in the back of the room, and members of the audience lined up and signed their names.

The need to speak, listen, and respond was important to the speaker and her audience. She responded to the feedback from her audience. *A fundamental task of the speaker's message is to maximize understanding.* Clarity is imperative. You are challenged to make your speech as clear as possible—through your words, lines of reason, and delivery. The message is constructed from your knowledge, feelings, and additional research.

4. Channel

The channel is the medium through which the message is sent. In the previous example, the message was sent from speaker to audience through face-to-face communication. Students could respond nonverbally, displaying disagreement or agreement and understanding or confusion through their facial expressions and body movement. In our wired and wireless society, a speaker's message can be sent by a variety of channels, including a public address system, radio, TV, the Internet, recordings, the use of cell phones, and text messages.

Despite the improved quality of video, we maintain the richest channel for communication is still face-to-face. You are in the same room with the speaker, you have the advantage of experiencing the speaker firsthand. You are in a better position to judge the intangible qualities, including the speaker's honesty, ethical stance, commitment to the topic, trustworthiness, and sincerity. Those qualities can be communicated through eye contact, gestures, and the speaker's voice. When you listen to a speech through a less direct channel, your ability to judge these qualities is diminished.

5. Feedback

In the public speaking transaction, feedback refers to the messages the audience sends back to the speaker. Feedback may be immediate or delayed.

Immediate feedback may range from applause, yawns, laughter, verbal comments, and even boos. A speaker may choose to ignore the feedback or he may change his message in response to the feedback. For example, if the audience looks confused, you may want to slow down, elaborate more fully, or give additional examples. Immediate feedback is difficult for speakers to interpret accurately at first, but with practice, interpreting feedback becomes easier.

Delayed feedback may come in the form of letters, emails, phone calls, formal evaluation, or votes. For example, it was discovered that a politician had plagiarized much of a speech delivered in a local campaign. A report of the incident was noted in the local newspaper, and the politician lightly dismissed his use of someone else's words without acknowledgment. Subsequently, a letter to the editor of the newspaper was sent by an irate citizen. The published letter was a form of delayed feedback.

6. Noise

In an ideal world, noise would not exist. However, the potential for multiple sources of noise exists within every communication transaction. Speakers should not ignore it. Noise is defined as anything that interferes with the communication process. Noise can be physical, physiological, psychological, or semantic in nature.

Physical noise includes anything in the environment that distracts the speaker or listeners. Examples include cell phones going off, the microphone not working well, people talking in class, students kicking chairs or clicking pens, people talking outside the classroom, thunder, noisy cars, heating that kicks on and off, and lights that make buzzing sounds. Physical noise does not actually have to be heard to be considered noise. The classroom may be too cold, the lights may be too dim, the listener may be seated too far from the speaker, or the room may have distracting artwork. Generally, some physical noise always exists and both speaker and listeners are aware of physical noise. To minimize physical noise, we suggest working to filter it out and staying focused on the message.

Physiological noise occurs when our senses fail us in some way. If we have hearing loss or poor vision, for example, we might become frustrated when we cannot hear or see adequately. Likewise, a speaker may grapple with physiological challenges of stuttering, lisping, or tics beyond their control. Maybe the formation of cataracts has diminished the ability to read note cards in the dim lighting often accompanying public speaking. When our senses fail us, typically they are accompanied by another kind of noise as well, that being psychological. Our mind sends us silent, distracting messages of frustration.

Psychological noise exists in the individual's mind. The speaker could be having a bad day and is not happy to be there or it may be near lunch time and the listeners are thinking about how hungry they are. One listener may be thinking about a fight she just had with her boyfriend, and another

Glossary

Immediate feedback Audience response as the speech is performed.

Delayed feedback Audience response after the speech is performed.

Physical noise Anything in the environment that distracts the speaker or listeners.

Physiological noise A result of our senses failing us in some way.

Psychological noise A distraction that exists in an individual's mind.

listener may be thinking about the project that is due next period. Or, the listener may not like the speaker. Understanding psychological noise is more difficult than understanding physical, physiological, or semantic noise. It is easy to tell that the auditorium is cold or that there is too much noise in the hallway. It is not possible to see or hear what affects people psychologically. Sitting in the same row may be one person who is happy to be there, another who is distracted by relationship problems, and a third who is worried about his or her future career.

Semantic noise refers to a disconnect between the speaker's words and the listener's interpretation. This disconnect may result from the use of inappropriate or offensive words, misunderstanding or misinterpretation, or disagreement on the meaning of words. Your professor may use words you do not know, or you may experience cultural differences. Even though Australians, British, and Americans have English as their native tongue, many words cause confusion. (See **BTW: British vs. American English**.)

7. Occasion

The situation for public speaking is often referred to as the *occasion* and is composed of the time, place, event, and traditions that define the moment. Before a speech begins, an audience already has an expectation of what they would like to hear from you. At a recent college commencement ceremony, the usual speakers gave their speeches in the five- to seven-minute range. Then it was time for the invited speaker to present. She spoke for 25 minutes about her background and experience. After about 10 minutes, audience members started shifting in their chairs. After 20 minutes, the audience's

---

BTW!   British vs. American English

Really? We speak the same language? Thanks to *The Septic's Companion Dictionary*, you can see some popular words that have very different meanings depending on whether you reside on the east or west side of the Atlantic Ocean.

To the British, _____ means _____ to Americans.

Biscuit	Cookie	Lorry	Truck
Boot	Trunk	Petrol	Gas
Chips	French fries	Randy (first name)	Horny
Fag	Cigarette	Rubber	Pencil eraser
Fancy	To desire	Smart	Being well-dressed
Football	Soccer	Torch	Flashlight
Lift	Elevator	Zed	Z

www.septicscompanion.com

annoyance was clear to everyone but the speaker. The invited speaker failed to recognize that the commencement ceremony is an occasion designed to focus on the students graduating, not their stamina. She violated their expectations and lost the listening audience because she did not consider the demands of the occasion carefully.

Physical surroundings help define the speaking occasion. As a speaker, you should know in advance whether you are speaking to five people or several hundred and whether you will be speaking from an elevated platform or from an easy chair surrounded by an audience of listeners also seated in easy chairs. Be aware of the order of your speech in the day's events. Are you the first or last speaker? Is your speech scheduled right before or after lunch? Knowing the circumstances of your speech helps you prepare better to meet the needs of the occasion. For example, if your speech is scheduled at the end of the day, a short speech is more appropriate than a long one.

8. Cultural Context

Every speaking occasion operates within a broader cultural context that affects the entire experience. Culture is defined in terms of norms, the rules people follow in their relationships with one another; values, the feelings people share about what is right or wrong, good or bad, desirable or undesirable; customs accepted by the community of institutional practices and expressions; institutions; and language. Culture often determines the common ground between speaker and audience.

As a speaker, one should recognize that cultural differences exist between audiences. As U.S. markets expand throughout the world, Americans need to understand that different countries view speaking situations differently. For example, China is a hierarchical society, and when an American delegation meets with Chinese business leaders, the senior member of a delegation meeting should do the talking. According to their book about business customs around the world, Morrison, Conaway, and Douress (2001) state that senior executives often do the talking: "Junior members do not interrupt and only speak when spoken to" (p. 75). During negotiation meetings in Russia, these researchers claim, Russians "*expect* walkouts and dire proclamations that the deal is off" (p. 319). Regarding Japanese culture, the authors assert that "A persuasive, positive presentation is compatible with Japanese culture—a high-pressure, confrontational approach is not" (p. 229). So knowing the cultural context before developing your presentation is important.

Cultural similarities and differences exist not only between nations, but also between co-cultures that exist within our own population. Therefore, adaptation is necessary. A nearby university hired a new president who was familiar with the corporate culture of a large business organization. When he sought to impose standards from the culture with which he was most familiar, there was considerable opposition to his efforts. At a faculty meeting, one exasperated department chair stood up, faced the new president, and declared: "With all due respect for your new position, you need to

Glossary

Culture The rules people follow in their relationships with one another; values; the feelings people share about what is right or wrong, good or bad, desirable or undesirable; customs accepted by the community of institutional practices and expressions; institutions; and language.

understand that this is a different culture than the one you have worked in, and what you found to be successful rules there are not going to work here." (For more information on co-cultures, see **BTW: Co-Cultures**.)

An effective speaking style in the United States may not be viewed as such by members of a different culture. If we want to be successful speakers, knowledge of our audience's cultural norms is crucial. Failure to adapt can result in a loss of credibility, and prevent you from achieving the purpose of your speech.

In sum, as speakers, we need to be aware of those aspects of communication we have some influence over, and those we do not. Also, it is in the speaker's best interest to address the issue of noise. This may include closing doors, not allowing cell phones, making sure equipment works, being aware of cultural differences, choosing words carefully and thoughtfully, and possibly providing examples for concepts that might be difficult for the audience. While we cannot change things like whether someone in our audience is hungry or battling with distracting thoughts, effective delivery helps minimize some psychological noise.

Finally, do not forget that the eight elements of the communication process are also relevant in a mediated situation, such as a video conference, live streaming of a speech, or recording a speech for later playback. The online speaker or speaker presenting in some other mediated situation needs to create a background conducive to listening, and take care to avoid external noises, such as noises in the hall or construction noise outside. When the channel is mediated, video should be clear, and care should be taken to make sure the speaker can be heard and seen. Taping a speech in your dorm room with all of your "stuff" around can be distracting, just as having a stationary camera might not be effective. We provide more suggestions in our chapter on presentational aids.

BTW!   Co-Cultures

Each country has a dominant culture, although in every culture there are internal contradictions or polarities. According to Samovar, Porter, and McDaniel (2007), *co-cultures* are defined as "groups or social communities that exhibit communication characteristics, perceptions, values, beliefs, and practices that are sufficiently different to distinguish them from the other groups, communities, and the dominant culture" (p. 11).

Co-cultures can be based on race, ethnic background, gender, age, sexual orientation, abilities or disabilities, profession, legality (drug culture or "underworld"), and so forth. These groups used to be called subcultures, but the term co-culture calls attention to the idea of dual members. So, we can be members of a dominant culture and one or more co-cultures simultaneously.

Once you understand the communication process and its elements, you are ready to incorporate your analysis of these elements in your first speech. There are five steps you need to follow when developing any speech.

Five Steps for Preparing to Speak

1 Select and narrow an audience-centered topic.

2 Develop content through research and sound support.

3 Draft the introduction, body, and conclusion.

4 Develop the language of the speech with care.

5 Practice!

I. Select and Narrow an Audience-Centered Topic

A difficult task for students beginning the study and practice of public speaking is selecting a topic. You and some of your classmates may already be thinking of possible topics for all your speeches during this term. Some students find a topic within five minutes of hearing about the assignment; for others, it may take weeks of reflection. This section is designed to make topic selection a productive experience for you.

Know the Speaking Assignment

Before considering topics, *know the constraints of the speaking assignment.* In addition to knowing the general purpose, which is addressed shortly, you need to know the following:

- Time requirements for the speech (3–4 minutes? 4–6 minutes? 5–7 minutes?)
- Time-frame for preparation (one week? one month? six weeks?)
- Type of source materials acceptable (print? Internet? interviews? personal experience?)
- Timeliness of research (last five years? last 10 years?)
- Number of sources required (three sources? five? eight?)
- Note cards (Can I use note cards? How many?)
- Media (Will computer be available? PowerPoint? Multimedia possibility? Smart board?)

Knowing the guidelines for the assignment helps you get started. Whether it's a speech for class, a speech at a fundraiser, or a briefing at work, understanding what is expected of you is the place to begin.

Understand the Audience

As stated throughout our book, public speaking is an audience-centered activity. Your reason for presenting a speech is to communicate your message to others in the clearest, most convincing way. When preparing your speech you must define your audience. *An effective speaker analyzes and adapts to the audience.* This involves finding out as much as possible about your audience in advance, such as their demographics (age, race, gender, religious affiliation, political affiliation, etc.), their level of knowledge about your topic, and their point of view. Critical thinking skills are valuable here as you determine these parameters.

The initial way to approach your responsibility as an audience-centered speaker is to find out as much as possible about the audience. In the chapter on the speaker–audience connection, we discuss audience analysis in depth. Before you gather research or develop main points you should find out the following:

- What does the audience know about me?
- What does the audience know about my topic?
- What are the audience's views on my topic and purpose?
- How do audience members define themselves as an audience?
- How do the setting and occasion influence my audience?
- What other factors might affect how the audience responds?

Outside the classroom, you may become a spokesperson for an issue, a cause, or an organization. Generally speaking, your audience will have some basic information about you. In college, characteristics such as age, gender, race, and level of education are easily known, but you may need to include relevant background information at the beginning of your speech. For example, if you wanted to talk about the problems associated with children of state and federal prisoners and your father worked in the prison system, it would be helpful to note this as you begin your speech.

The amount of supporting material you include and the extent to which you explain or elaborate are influenced by the expertise or knowledge or your audience. If you are speaking to a group of cardiologists on the need to convince pregnant women to stop smoking, you can assume far greater audience knowledge than if you were to deliver the same message to a group of concerned citizens.

The views of your audience should influence your choice of main points, the supporting material, and the way you develop your speech. Attitudes can be more important than information in determining how your audience responds to a message. It's natural to expect some preconceived attitudes about what you are hoping to accomplish.

Audience members may be present at your speech as a result of how they define themselves at that particular moment. At a city council meeting that addresses housing regulations in your community, you might be with several college students attending as tenants of rental property. At another city council meeting, you might gather with other college students because the council is discussing changing the bar entry age in the city. Though the same people might be in the audience, how you identify or define yourselves differs from situation to situation. In one instance, you and the other college students identify yourselves as renters. In the second situation, you are with college students who are interested in expanded entertainment options.

The setting and occasion are important considerations for any speaker. The speech may take place in an indoor gymnasium or an outdoor stadium. The occasion may be a graduation ceremony or a funeral service. It helps a speaker to plan carefully when she or he learns in advance what the general feeling is about the setting and the occasion for the presentation. Members of a congregation during a Christmas Eve service may start to get restless if a member of the clergy drifts off from the main message and begins talking about old family gatherings when his audience is expecting to hear about the story of the birth of Jesus and what this event means in our present day.

Remember, it's harder to reach a **captive audience** (those who are required to attend) than a **voluntary audience** (those who choose to attend). Students who attend a guest lecture on campus simply to obtain extra credit to boost their grade in a class may feel somewhat indifferent, if not bored, while those who chose to attend because of a keen interest in the speech and speaker will feel differently. As a speaker, you need to obtain some helpful information about audience attitudes toward the setting and occasion that will bring everyone together for the speech.

Many factors influence how an audience responds to a speaker. Are you the first speaker of the day? The last speaker? Are you speaking at a convention in Las Vegas at 8:00 a.m.? Were the participants out late? Are you one of six students to give a speech during graduation ceremony? If you have knowledge of any factor that may influence your listeners' attentiveness, you can plan in advance ways to increase the likelihood that they will listen carefully. You can shorten the speech, include more vivid examples, and/or work to make your speech even more engaging.

As time goes by, you get to know your classmates and their concerns. Use that information to create interest and engage their attention. Reflect on the six questions identified above and then adapt your topic, language, support, and delivery based on what you decide. (See **BTW: Audience Analysis** for an interesting story.)

Glossary

Captive audience Those who are required to attend.

Voluntary audience Those who choose to attend.

BTW!

Audience Analysis

In his autobiography, *Jack; Straight from the Gut*, the former chairman of GE for over 20 years, Jack Welch, recalls his first speech to Wall Street analysts: "I had worked on my speech, rewriting it, rehearsing it, and desperately wanting it to be a hit. The analysts arrived expecting to hear the financial results and the success achieved by the company during the year. I gave them little of what they wanted. I pressed on, not letting their blank stares discourage me." In Jack's own words, the speech was a "bomb." This simple oversight of not considering what your audience expects of your message can happen to anyone, including Jack Welch, now famous CEO who is credited for quadrupling GE's worth. (Welch & Byrne, 2001)

Choose an Appropriate Topic

Some instructors may give you a topic while others may provide strict limitations on what you may speak about. If you are allowed to choose, the best place to begin your search for a topic is *yourself.* When the topic springs from your own interests, personal experience, or work experience, you bring to it motivation and information necessary for a good speech.

For example, Courtney found herself preoccupied with choosing the topic for her informative speech. As she reflected on her possibilities, she thought about her two years' experience at a local daycare center before college. She realized she could speak to her classmates about how working at a daycare led to her decision to work with children as her vocation. She felt earning a degree in education would open more doors, and she stressed getting some relevant experience through work or internship before completing a major. Her speech was full of informative, humorous anecdotes, and her enthusiasm made the speech effective.

Perhaps you have a lifelong interest in video games or badminton. Maybe you have some interesting work experience to share with your class, or an amazing travel story, or maybe a life-changing service learning experience. Maybe you have a unique, defining characteristic that you can bring to your audience's attention. One student disclosed his having been born with type 1 diabetes and how it has affected his life. If possible, choose your first speech topic from what you know best.

If no ideas come to you when thinking about a speech topic, try the following. Write down two or three broad categories representing subjects of interest to you, and divide the categories into parts. You might begin, for example, with the broad areas of politics and sports. From these general topics useful lists will emerge.

Politics

1. Campus politics
2. Political corruption
3. Contemporary political campaign tactics

Sports

1. Learning from participation in sports
2. The challenges facing student athletes
3. Why NASCAR races are increasingly popular

As your list of choices grows, you will probably find yourself coming back to the same topic or a variation of it. For example, "Football after college" could be added to "The challenges facing student athletes." Perhaps your brother played college football and then attempted to join a professional football team. You could talk about his experiences, including successes and failures. Now you have your topic.

While choosing a topic you are familiar with is the best place to begin, carefully consider what your *listeners* might want to hear. You may be an Agriculture Management major who is interested in artificial insemination of chickens. Trust us, most audiences do not want to know! Ask yourself if your topic would create murmurs of interests or gasps of horror. If you lean toward the topic less traveled, can you create a motive for your audience to care? What can you tell them early on to convince them of the importance of your chosen topic? Remember, a topic should fit the speaker and audience.

You may know something about your classmates' interests, backgrounds, or group affiliations. You may want to develop a list of general topics by thinking about your audience. For example, in a college classroom, you might consider one or more of the following:

1. Music
2. Politics
3. Current events
4. Hobbies

Once you've thought about general topics of interest to your audience, you add to the list related possibilities:

1. Music
   - Grammy awards
   - Country music
   - Musicals
   - *Glee*
2. Politics
   - Tea Party
   - Unethical behavior
   - Campaign spending
3. Current events
   - Trouble in Libya
   - Trouble in Somalia
   - Social networking and political action
4. Hobbies
   - Collecting
   - Selling on eBay
   - Video games

Once you've developed a list that your audience may have interest in, you can select a few that might be worth exploring in more depth.

Finally, in addition to selecting topics that *you* have interest in or your *listeners* want to hear, you can work to find a topic through **research**. You could ask friends to brainstorm with you for topics, or you can try looking up topics on the Internet. For example, you could search "current events," "top headlines," "sports," or "politics." Broad topics will lead you to other topics. Following are several possible topics:

- Acupuncture
- Biodiesel fuel
- Cyberspace regulation
- Dream analysis
- Education cuts
- Facebook fraud
- Ghosts
- Home schooling
- Joining organizations
- Minimum wage
- Natural foods
- Organ donation
- Prison reform
- Reincarnation
- Surrogacy
- Teacher competency tests
- Volunteering
- World religions
- Zero-tolerance policies

Do not assume, however, that any topic is relevant. Some topics have been used so often, there is not much left to say in the short amount of time you will have. If you are interested in a topic such as "smoking," think about your approach. Ask yourself, Is this something they have heard hundreds of times before, or is there a new or creative approach I can take? If you cannot think of some new approach, then you might want to delete smoking as a topic. If you have a wealth of information, determine what must be left out. If you know about the background of your audience, you can decide what information is most relevant and how much time should be spent on each point.

Determine the General Purpose, Specific Purpose, and Thesis Statement

The time you spend preparing your speech may be of little value if you do not determine what you want your speech to accomplish. Now that you have selected a topic, clarify the general purpose, specific purpose, and thesis statement. How you conceive of each will help you clarify and narrow your topic.

General purpose. There are three general purposes for speeches:

1. To inform
2. To persuade
3. To entertain or inspire

If you want to explain the differences between classical ballet and modern dance, the general purpose of your speech would be "to inform." If you think having a scooter or bicycle on campus is more beneficial to students and the environment than driving a car, your general purpose would be "to persuade." If you hope to make people laugh after eating a good meal, your general purpose is "to entertain." If you want to motivate your fellow graduates at the commencement ceremony, your general purpose is "to inspire."

Keep in mind, however, that it's difficult to deliver a speech that is *only* informative, *only* persuasive, or *only* entertaining. Often, in the perception of listeners, the purposes may converge or overlap. For example, as a speaker informs her audience about options for eating a healthy breakfast each day, some audience members may interpret her speech as an attempt to persuade them to change their daily behavior.

Specific purpose. Once the general purpose is set for your speech, determine the specific purpose. This is the precise response you want from your audience. Specific purpose statements should be expressed as an infinitive phrase that includes the general purpose as well as the main thrust of your speech. The specific purpose also identifies who the intended audience is. Here are two examples of specific purposes:

1. To inform the class of differences between the operations of an on-campus political club and an off-campus political party

2. To persuade the Student Senate that requiring all college students to participate in service-learning projects benefits the student, college, and community

Because the specific purpose identifies the audience who will hear your speech, it guides you in speech preparation. A speech on health care reform given before a group of college students should be constructed differently than a speech on the same topic given before an audience of retirees. Obviously, the second audience has a more immediate need for reform than the first group of listeners.

Following are two specific purpose statements written differently. See if you can pick out which is correct.

Topic 1A: To persuade my audience that the Federal Drug Administration (FDA) should regulate dietary supplements.

Topic 1B: To persuade my audience that the FDA should regulate dietary supplements and print more warning labels on prescriptions.

Topic 2A: To inform my audience of the negative aspects of the Barbie doll.

Topic 2B: To inform my audience of the positive and negative aspects of the Barbie doll.

A specific purpose statement should be written with one goal in mind. With the first topic, "A" is correct. "B" is incorrect, because there are two topics: dietary supplements and warning labels on prescriptions. Also, a specific purpose statement must be clear to all readers. It is possible that "FDA" is not known to all; therefore, it makes sense to spell out the name first and put the initials in parentheses. With the second topic, statement "A" is a persuasive speech that has been falsely identified as an informative speech. With little exception, without presenting both negative and positive aspects, your speech is inherently persuasive.

Thesis statement. While the general and specific purpose statements set the goals for your speech, the thesis statement, or your core idea, focuses on what you want to say. The thesis statement is the central message you want listeners to take with them. It distills your speech to one sentence, summarizing your main idea. A well-defined thesis is critical to your speech's success. The following examples show how one moves from a topic to a thesis statement.

> **Topic:** Study abroad
>
> **General purpose:** To inform
>
> **Specific purpose:** To explain to my class what is involved in the study abroad options available to them at our university
>
> **Thesis statement:** Students interested in earning college credit while studying abroad have several options that differ in terms of academic content, location, length of stay, potential number of credit hours, and cost.
>
> **Topic:** Study abroad
>
> **General purpose:** To persuade
>
> **Specific purpose:** To convince my class that studying abroad would be a life-changing experience
>
> **Thesis statement:** Studying abroad can be a life-changing experience because students gain knowledge in an academic area, face the unfamiliar, and interact with individuals from a different culture.

As you can see, although the topic is "study abroad," there are different aspects of studying abroad that one could address. The above example shows choices for an informative speech and persuasive speech. A speech with the general purpose to entertain could include humorous examples and illustrations of the gaffes, blunders, and errors made while studying in a foreign land.

Remember that your speech has one of three general purposes, which on your outline should be stated in the infinitive. The specific purpose is an infinitive phrase, not a sentence. It should express one goal, not multiple goals. The thesis statement is one idea, and should be stated as one cohesive thought written in one complete sentence.

Demonstrate Ethical Behavior Throughout the Process

A consideration of ethics is important in virtually all aspects of speech development, including, but certainly not limited to, how you approach a topic, where you get information, how you edit or interpret information, word choice, and distinguishing between your own ideas and those that need to be cited. **Plagiarism** involves using other's work, words, or ideas without adequate acknowledgment, according to Plagiarism.org (2011).

Ethics are being discussed within the context of many disciplines, including medicine, psychology, business, and communication. Stories of ethical breaches appear almost daily in the newspapers and online. Unethical behavior in many contexts and situations has heightened our sensitivity to the need for honesty from all sources, including public speakers. Use accurate and current information, rely on sound reasoning, and present a speech that is your own, based on your independent research and views. Remember to cite sources and to quote and paraphrase correctly when you present information or ideas that are not your own.

Glossary

Plagiarism Using another's work, words, or ideas without adequate acknowledgment.

2. Develop Content Through Research and Sound Support

The next step is to research your topic to develop and support your ideas. Each point delivered to an audience should be backed up by research and sound support. Most of your time will be spent on this step.

Research

Now, armed with a focused topic and main points in mind, you are ready to do some research. Before you hit the Internet, though, consider what a time-consuming activity that can be. It is easy to search one topic, check out links to another closely related topic, then follow links to yet another topic, and find yourself engaged in research for an evening but not much closer to preparing your speech. You need a better research plan.

Although you *can* begin your research by seeking out some search engine, we encourage you, even with all the technology available to you, to begin with a visit to your college library. If you are taking an online course from a remote location, this is not possible. And clearly, much research is available to students from the comfort of their own computers. However, the library can be a productive resource for research. You can ask experts for advice, and check out books that may not be available online.

Once there, seek out reference librarians and tell them about your assignment, your topic, thesis, and specific purpose. They will likely have some great ideas and resources at their immediate disposal, including search engines and data bases. Librarians will help you find even more materials that are both relevant and credible. After you drain the reference librarian of all useful information, look around. Could there be a journal article, newspaper story, book chapter, DVD, or audio track of interest? Quickly scan for the facts, statistics, quotations, and expert testimony that relate to your main points. Be sure to take good notes of the source for all

Enlist the help of a librarian when performing your research.

the information you find. You will need to cite sources orally in your speech and may be required to turn in a reference page.

Next in your research plan, consider the benefit of interviewing. Do you know an expert or someone with knowledge or experience on your topic? One student met with a local chiropractor. She outlined her plans for her informative speech and he was enthusiastic. He told her several funny anecdotes involving cracking and popping, let her borrow his expensive model of the human spine, and gave her a myth-vs.-fact sheet to share with her audience.

One warning: Be careful about the credibility of any information you find, and also watch that you don't lose too much time in the process.

Support Your Ideas

Each point made before an audience should be backed up with reliable supporting information and sound reasoning. For example, if you want to persuade your audience that sales tax instead of real estate tax should be used to fund education, concrete evidence will be necessary to support your specific purpose. Later in the book we devote an entire chapter to research and supporting materials, but briefly, we want to point out ways you can provide support.

Use facts. One way to provide support is to use facts. Facts are verifiable. They hold more weight than opinions. If your specific purpose was "To demonstrate how political campaigns have changed dramatically over the last several decades," you might include the following facts:

- In 1960 John Kennedy became the first presidential candidate to use his own polling specialist.
- In 1980 Jimmy Carter campaigned by conference phone calls to voters in Iowa and New Hampshire.
- In 1984 Ronald Reagan used satellite transmissions to appear at fundraisers and rallies.
- In 1992 California Governor Jerry Brown introduced a 1-800 number for fundraising and answering questions.
- In 2007 Hillary Clinton established a website that included video snippets, news reports, an opportunity for blogging, and numerous ways to contribute to her presidential campaign.
- In 2011 Donald Trump tested the waters for a potential presidential run. Through Trump's savvy use of his own and other TV shows in which he made outlandish comments and accusations, he became a colorful part of the national political dialogue.

These facts support the speaker's claim and show how candidates have attempted to reach the masses over time. Do not forget to cite sources as you provide facts.

Provide statistics. A second form of support involves providing statistics. This can offer strong support to your speech. Statistics inform with numbers, and when they are made relevant and understandable to an audience, statistics can startle and convince. In trying to persuade an audience that distracted driving contributes to highway fatalities, a speaker could provide the following statistics, accessed from the U.S. Department of Transportation's website, distraction.gov:

- 20 percent of injury crashes in 2009 involved reports of distracted driving. (National Highway Traffic Safety Administration [NHTSA])
- Of those killed in distracted-driving-related crashes, 995 involved reports of a cell phone as a distraction (18 percent of fatalities in distraction-related crashes). (NHTSA)
- The age group with the greatest proportion of distracted drivers was the under-20 age group. (NHTSA)
- Drivers who use hand-held devices are four times as likely to get into crashes serious enough to injure themselves. (Insurance Institute for Highway Safety)
- Using a cell phone while driving, whether hand-held or hands-free, delays a driver's reactions as much as having a blood alcohol concentration at the legal limit of .08 percent. (unews.utah.edu, 2006)

Keep in mind, however, that your speech should not be a laundry list of statistics. Select carefully only those statistics that you are able to make relevant, interesting, and meaningful. After offering a statistic, summarize what it is intended to demonstrate. Some audience members are easily confused or bored with numbers. By summarizing before you move on, you are less likely to lose them.

Illustrate using examples. A third form of support is examples that illustrate a point or claim. Illustrations, especially detailed and current ones, clarify points and they may leave a lasting impression on your audience. If the purpose of your speech is "To convince the class that voters are influenced by the Internet," you might use the following illustration:

> The use of computers by members of the general public has increased considerably in recent years. Even my 78-year-old uncle Elmer and his friends use their computers for gaming, social networking, and word processing. Elmer meets regularly with a group of friends who, like him, have retired after years of working in a nearby assembly plant. As they developed their computer skills, each browsed the Internet more and began to pay attention to political news and advertisements. This led to new insights on issues of interest to the group, and often served as the subject of their informal

get-togethers leading up to the election. They reported to their friends and family that what they learned from the Internet influenced how they voted.

This example, along with other forms of support such as facts and statistics, demonstrates to the audience the increasing use and effectiveness of the Internet in political campaigns. As an audience-centered speaker, you want to think of the best way to keep the attention of your audience and provide support that is best suited to them. Chapter 5 elaborates on the use of examples.

Include testimony. A fourth form of support is the use of testimony, which involves quoting someone's experience or opinion. Testimony can be a powerful form of support because everyone pays attention to an expert. Courts of law frequently call on the testimony of expert witnesses; televised news programs broadcast the observations of experts on newsworthy stories; and, from time to time, even commercials provide the endorsement of experts rather than celebrities to confirm the reliability of a product or service. So to prove, reinforce, or clarify a point, a public or presentational speaker often quotes or paraphrases statements of a recognized expert on a subject.

Construct analogies. Using analogies is a fifth form of support. This involves making comparisons to clarify or prove a point. Analogies lend support by encouraging listeners to think in a novel way. **Figurative analogies** compare different kinds of things, and **literal analogies** compare similar categories.

If you compare an argument with a sporting event, you are using a figurative analogy, but if you compare one college with another college, you are using a literal analogy. For example, in a speech about studying abroad, a student could use the following figurative analogy.

> Studying abroad is like your first week in college. You're unfamiliar with the environment, you don't know the people around you, and you're not quite sure what to expect. But as the week goes on, you start to make friendships, your environment becomes more comfortable, and you start to get into some kind of predictable routine. Keep in mind, anytime you have a new experience, you'll experience some uncertainty.

Then, the literal analogy:

> Studying abroad is similar to studying at this or any other university. You attend classes and take exams. You have a place to live and dining options. You have to study and you also have free time. The difference is, you're far from home, you aren't familiar with your environment, and people speak a different language.

Glossary

Figurative analogy Drawing comparisons between things that are distinctly different in an attempt to clarify a concept or persuade.

Literal analogy Compares like things from similar classes, such as a game of professional football with a game of college football.

Think of support material as adding interest and texture to your speech. Oftentimes, someone from your audience will recall a story, example, or analogy you offered because of its striking nature. We strive to not only be clear and concise, but to also be colorful as speakers, and the color comes from our use of a variety of support materials that engage our listeners.

3. Draft the Introduction, Body, and Conclusion

If you spend days researching your first speech but little time organizing your ideas, the result is likely to be a speech that fails to present your message in a focused way. To be effective, speeches require an easy-to-follow organizational plan that makes it possible for others to receive and understand your message. As you will see in future chapters, the logical way to organize your speech is to divide it into three parts: introduction, body, and conclusion.

As you draft your speech, lay it out into the three parts. Construct a comprehensive, full-sentence outline and work to tie the sentences into a coherent whole. Then, reduce these sentences to key words and phrases and transfer them onto speaker's notes, which will serve as your guide when you deliver your speech. A well-thought-out, clearly constructed outline and speaker's notes greatly increase the potential for success. The following paragraphs highlight important aspects to consider as you develop your first speech.

Introduction

The introduction should capture the attention and interest of your audience, establish your credibility as a speaker, and preview your speech. You can accomplish these aims in many ways, such as humorous anecdotes or a dramatic or startling statement. For his informative speech, Jesse started with the following:

> You walk into a bar, sit down, and notice something oddly unfamiliar. Where are the beer taps? Where are the liquor bottles? All you see are fish, tentacles, and an assortment of brightly colored items that are not familiar. You've walked into a sushi bar, my friend.
>
> I fell in love with sushi years ago, and so have millions of other Americans. Sushi has become increasingly popular over the past several years, and it has become a major force in the restaurant industry and culinary arts. My passion with sushi began when I started managing a sushi lounge in downtown Memphis called Bluefin. Throughout my three years at Bluefin, I learned quite a bit about the art form of making sushi. To appreciate sushi, it helps to understand its history, the different styles, and common terms and ingredients associated with sushi.

In his introduction, Jesse captures our attention through his vivid description of the bar. He establishes credibility by noting his work experience. Finally, in his last sentence, he presents a preview statement, which lets his audience know what he intends to cover in the body of his speech. He accomplishes the three goals of an effective introduction.

Body

The body of your speech contains your key ideas and relevant supporting material. It's the most time-consuming aspect of speech development. Frequently, speakers work on the body before the introduction, because gaps in logic or information may be discovered as the body is developed. Main points should flow from the thesis statement in some logical pattern. Chapter 7 discusses organizing and outlining your ideas. You have at least five patterns of organization to consider: chronological, topical, spatial, cause-and-effect, and problem–solution. To help your audience follow your ideas and to avoid a disjointed series of points, the body also makes use of transitions. These are well-crafted statements that let our audience know we are moving on to our next point.

Conclusion

Your concluding remarks have three purposes: (1) to reinforce the message, (2) to summarize the main points, and (3) to provide closure in some way that relates your message to your listeners' lives. We focus briefly on creating closure here. Closure may take the form of a quotation, a statement, or a question that reinforces or even broadens the purpose of your speech. The conclusion of a persuasive speech may also describe the specific actions you want your listeners to take. Jesse accomplished the goals of a conclusion this way:

> Now when you walk into a bar and see all the brightly colored fish and seafood, you have a better idea of what you just walked into. With knowledge of the history of sushi, its different styles, and common terms and ingredients; you can steer your palate in the right direction. I urge even the timid to try sushi, and try it more than once to experience the different flavors, textures, and styles. Sushi is not a fad, and sushi will make its way to your neck of the woods soon enough if it hasn't already. Impress your date with a bit of knowledge when you go to the new trendy sushi spot. I bet you'll look like quite the gourmet.

4. Develop Language and Presentation Aids Carefully

An enthusiastic young woman looked out into the audience of almost 1,500 people on her graduation day and was overwhelmed with the spirit that marked this important occasion. A hush fell over the crowd as she began her address as president of the senior class: "You guys are all terrific! Awesome! This has been an awesome four years for us, right? Like, we have really made it! Wow!" As she proceeded, reflecting on the events of the past four years, her comments were laced with slang that may have been suitable for the coffee shop or gatherings with friends, but not for such a special occasion.

The words you choose to convey your message reflect your personality, your attitude toward your subject, occasion, and audience, and your concern for communicating effectively. Words are your primary vehicle for creating meaning. They set forth ideas, spark visions, arouse concerns, elicit emotions, but if not used carefully, produce confusion. The following four guidelines will help you choose your words with care.

Use Plain English

Let simple, direct language convey your message. Your audience should not need an interpreter. You could say "contusion" or "ecchymosis," but most audiences would find the word "bruise" clearer. Also, it's generally best to avoid slang or jargon. (For more information about language, see **BTW: What Are Slang, Cant, Jargon, and Argot?**).

BTW!

What Are Slang, Cant, Jargon, and Argot?

According to Fred Jandt (2009) in his book, *An Introduction to Intercultural Communication*, the specialized vocabulary of subgroups has been called slang, cant, jargon, and argot (p. 354).

○ **Slang** refers to the specialized vocabulary of "stigmatized" groups such as gangs, drug dealers, prostitutes, as well as teen-agers.

○ **Jargon** refers to the technical language of professional subgroups, such as doctors and lawyers.

○ **Cant** refers to the specialized vocabulary of nonprofessional groups such as truckers and construction workers.

○ **Argot** has become more recognized as a term that encompasses all of the above. In other words, argot is the specialized vocabulary of all subgroups.

Remember That Writing and Speaking Are Different Activities

While in a written report the terms "edifice," "regulations," and "in the eventuality of" may be acceptable; in public speaking the words, "building," "rules," and "if" are far more effective. Writing, in general, is a more formal process than speaking. While the spoken word should sound more conversational, we still want you to pronounce words correctly and articulately (avoid "I'ma go now" for "I'm going to go now").

Relate Your Language to Your Audience's Level of Knowledge

If you are describing drug testing in professional sports, do not assume your audience understands such terms as "false positives," "chain of custody," and "legal and individual safeguards." If you use unfamiliar terms in your speech, you should define them to keep the message clear. Recall the audience analysis you have already done and review your words with your intended audience in mind.

Use Language for Specific Effect

Assume you are giving a speech on the plight of America's working poor. Here are two possible introductions:

> Introduction #1: "Although millions of Americans work a full day, they cannot pay their bills or provide for their families."

> Introduction #2: "Millions of Americans come home each day, exhausted and covered with a layer of factory filth or kitchen grease. Their backbreaking labor has given them few rewards: They cannot pay their rent, buy shoes for their children, or eat meat more than once a week."

The first example is not incorrect, but it may be ineffective: The second introduction is more powerful. It paints memorable word pictures. Keep your audience in mind as you choose effective language for communicating your ideas.

Be Culturally Sensitive

Inappropriate cultural references do harm to others and should be eliminated from your speech. Besides, there is always a chance that negative remarks will inflame an audience. At the very least, you will lose credibility. Being culturally sensitive in a global sense includes nationality and race. "Arabs" and "Middle Easterners" are nowhere near synonymous terms. Culture can also refer to regions and groups of people. All Democrats are not liberal, and all Republicans are not conservative. People on welfare are not inherently "lazy," just as people from New York City are not all "brusque." Avoid stereotyping, and avoid making comments about the audience or audience members that may be offensive.

Determine Where to Incorporate Technology and Presentational Aids

You have several decisions to make when it comes to the use of technology. First, not all speeches are enhanced by technology. Some may be too short to warrant its use. Second, PowerPoint should not be the default use of technology. Using PowerPoint to outline the major points of your speech may not be necessary or effective. Third, if you don't have time to practice your speech using the technology, you may be faced with a disastrous series of difficulties. Your flash drive may not work, the setup may not be easy to figure out, and the technology you hope to use may not be available or functioning correctly. Carefully weigh the risks versus the rewards of using technology in this speech.

If you choose to use technology, determine where it will be most effective. For example, in a speech on world population growth, a speaker might begin with a computer-projected image of the current world population count, and at the end of the speech, refer to it again, to show the growth in population over the brief time it took to deliver the speech. In a speech on hurricanes, you may want to show a picture from Hurricane Andrew of a piece of plywood stuck *through* the trunk of a tree (see weathersavvy.com) or a YouTube clip of a hurricane hunter being thrashed by hail.

Using technology could involve something as simple as clicking on a relevant website, using PowerPoint slides, or showing a clip. You might use multiple forms of media, and have music, video, and slides. Whatever you choose, it should enhance your message in some way, and not substitute for content.

5. Rehearse and Deliver Your Speech

How important is practice? Consider what professional speaker and author Bill Bachrach said on the subject: "Practice! Practice by videotaping, audio-taping, or role-playing with friends and colleagues. Be so comfortable with what you are going to say that you don't have to think about it. This frees your thoughts to be totally in tune with your [audience]" (McRae & Brooks, 2004).

Without practicing your speech, it's difficult to know whether the speech flows and the material "works" for you. Sometimes, the outline looks good, and appropriate transitions, main points, and supporting material have been developed, but when you speak aloud, you find that the speech is choppy. You discover your word choice needs tweaking. You may have particularly long words, names of authors, websites, or organizations that you stumble over the first time you try. Practicing reduces such surprises during your speech and, of course, demonstrates to your audience that you are prepared.

Much of what you need to know about practicing is found in the chapter on delivery. The biggest benefit of practicing is that it builds confidence and reduces your nervousness. Keep in mind that practicing allows you to work with your note cards, determine where to pause, and decide when to emphasize certain words and ideas and to think about where it is appropriate to incorporate technology (Welch & Byrne, 2001).

Summary

Public speaking can be a powerful tool that is also a creative activity and a decision-making process. It is a valuable activity that influences success in college, teaches critical thinking skills, influences career and community success, is a key to leadership, complements technology, and importantly, is part of our democratic traditions.

Public speaking is an audience-centered activity that has one of three purposes: to inform, to persuade, or to entertain. To help you understand that communication is a complex process, we discuss the following eight elements of communication: sender/receiver, message, channel, receiver/sender, feedback, noise, occasion, and cultural context. Once you understand the communication process and its elements, you are ready to incorporate your analysis of these elements in your speech.

The last section of this chapter was designed to help you with your first speech. We outlined five steps for preparing to speak; each step involves reflection and decision making. First, reflect on guiding considerations, including committing to excellence and ethical behavior, understanding the audience, and choosing an appropriate topic. Second, narrow and plan your message, including determining the general purpose, specific purpose, thesis statement, and main points. Third, research, support your ideas, and outline. We suggest you use print and online resources as you research, find a variety of support for your speech, including facts, statistics, testimony, and examples. Fourth, develop the language of your speech with care. Consider if and what types of presentational aids will enhance your message. Finally, rehearse and deliver your speech. As you practice your speech, work on nonverbal aspects of delivery, such as eye contact, gestures, and movement. Practice your speech to reduce tension and project enthusiasm and self-confidence.

Discussion Starters

❶ Considering your personal career goals, how are public speaking skills likely to help you in achieving them?

❷ Think of some of the major institutions in society, including government, schools, the judicial system, and organized religion. What role do public speakers play in each of these settings and what do you see as their strengths and their weaknesses?

3 Why is it important to consider the elements of occasion and cultural context when developing your speech? How might your approach to convincing people to vote change based on these two elements?

4 What factors should you keep in mind when choosing a topic and framing a purpose for speaking?

5 How do you think your experience doing research at a library differs from that of doing research in your room on your personal computer? What are the benefits and disadvantages of both?

6 Discuss with members of your class what is understood to be the relationships among a speaker's link to a topic, choice of a purpose, amount of information available, and the needs of the audience.

References

Bradley, B. (1988). *Fundamentals of Speech Communication*, 5th Ed. Dubuque, IA: Wm. C. Brown.

Hoff, R. (1998). *I Can See You Naked: A Guide to Making Fearless Presentations.* Kansas City: Andrews McMeel Publishing.

Jandt, F. E. (2009). *An Introduction to Intercultural Communication: Identities in a Global Community*, 6th Ed. Thousand Oaks, CA: Sage Publications, Inc.

Morrison, T., Conaway, W. A., & Douress, J. J. (2001). *Dun & Bradstreet's Guide to Doing Business Around the World.* Paramus, NJ: Prentice Hall Press.

Rae, C. (2011). *The Septic's Companion: A British Slang Dictionary.* Retrieved July 8, 2011 from www.septicscompanion.com/index.htp.

Samovar, L. A., Porter, R. E., & McDaniel, E. R. (2007). *Communication Between Cultures*, 6th Ed. Belmont, CA: Thomson Wadsworth.

Toogood, G. N. (1996). *The Articulate Executive.* New York: McGraw-Hill, Inc.

Welch, J., & Byrne, J. A. (2001) *Jack; Straight from the Gut.* New York: Grand Central Publishing.

What Americans Do Online: Social Media and Games Dominate Activity. (2010, August 2). Retrieved July 11, 2011 from blog.nielsen.com/ nielsenwire/online_mobile/what-americans-do-online-social-media-and-games-dominate-activity.

Wolfe, A. (2005). *The Transformation of American Religion: How We Actually Live Our Faith.* Chicago: The University of Chicago Press.

Chapter

3

"It is time to start rebuilding the character of the American people. Our greatest leaders came from families whose ethical foundations were built into their very souls."

Billy Graham

Chapter 3: Ethics in Public Speaking

An essential element of every speech, ethics is defined and explained through guidelines to promote speaker credibility. Points for avoiding unethical practices are also discussed.

Student Learning Objectives:

○ Students will be able to understand ethics

○ Students will be able to describe ethos and speaker credibility

○ Students will be able to explain how to develop ethical speaking habits

○ Students will be able to avoid unethical practices

ETHICS IN PUBLIC SPEAKING

Key Terms

Aristotle	extrinsic ethos	innuendos	plain folks
bandwagoning	fallacies	intrinsic ethos	testimonials
dialogic communication	glittering generalities	monologic communication	values
ethics	hidden agenda	name calling	
ethos	information literacy		

As citizens and consumers, we are bombarded by messages each day through print and electronic media. Intense competition exists among these outlets as they strive to be the most watched, read, tweeted, blogged, etc. As media outlets look for bottom-line profits, ethical standards are occasionally bent. Such was the case in 1993 when *Dateline NBC* alleged that some General Motors pickup trucks had a tendency to explode during collisions. It was later revealed that those trucks had been rigged with incendiary devices to assure footage of an explosion. General Motors threatened litigation, which resulted in the on-air admission by journalist Stone Phillips that NBC used the devices without informing the viewers. (For more information, see **BTW:** *Dateline NBC*.)

Ethical violations are not limited to those in the media. Politics, with its mix of power, potential profit, and public service often fosters ethical breaches by officials in powerful positions. One of your authors has lived in Ohio most of his adult life and in 2005 began following a scandal reported in the news that provided details of unethical and unlawful activities by public officials. Ohio has proven to be a vital state in national elections and Tom Noe, a key Republican fundraiser convicted of violating federal campaign law, was the initial subject in a series of stories that reported questionable investments of state funds, the loss of millions of dollars, and a web of cover-up activities. Ultimately, even the governor of Ohio pleaded no contest to charges that he failed to report gifts he received while in office. After

BTW!

Dateline NBC

YouTube link to GM's response to discovering NBC *Dateline's* unethical behavior (www.youtube.com/watch?v=vEkc_DlvN9Y). Is an apology enough? Why do you think the choice was made to "rig" the fuel tanks to explode? Is it ever acceptable to manufacture evidence to demonstrate a fact? If so, should the manipulation be clearly identified up front? If so, does it lose its impact? Does this story make you less trusting of the media in general? What does the media, or speakers for that matter, owe one another in truthfulness? Is this responsibility to truth culturally bound or universal?

hearing and reading about the charges, countercharges, admitted mistakes, and denials, the general public was left with disappointment and cynicism because of these ethical violations.

Unfortunately, scandalous behavior is neither new nor limited to political leaders. Power, status, and money have led to unethical behavior and deceptive speeches throughout history, and public speaking is often a preferred instrument when this sort of abuse occurs. The media plays an important role in investigating unethical behavior and limiting future breaches. For example, during local, state, and national campaigns, the media provides the public with details of sexual misconduct, bribery, poor parenting, and unimpressive military service. No candidate is immune, which leaves the public faced with the dilemma over who is really telling the truth. Ethical violations seem commonplace in media reports, and this suggests that ethics are more important now than ever.

Ethics

Ethics refers to the rules we use to determine good and evil, right and wrong. These rules may be grounded in religious principles, democratic values, codes of conduct, and a variety of other sources. Without an ethical roadmap based on socially accepted values to guide you, you could disregard your audience's need for truth and engage in self-serving deceit, ambiguity, intellectual sloppiness, and emotional manipulation. If you do, your credibility as a speaker is lost as your listeners turn elsewhere for a message—and a speaker—they can trust. Public speaking is a reciprocal process, and audience mistrust can stand in the way of communication. Therefore, an important aspect of being audience-centered is being ethical.

Every time you speak, you risk your reputation. Listeners will forgive many things—stumbling over words, awkward gestures, lack of examples—but if you lie or mislead them, they may never trust you again. For some, maintaining strong ethical standards is second nature. For others, more deliberation is needed. Some speakers rationalize their unethical behaviors so they can continue to misguide their audiences.

Glossary

Ethics The rules we use to determine good and evil, right and wrong. These rules may be grounded in religious principles, democratic values, codes of conduct, and bases of values derived from a variety of sources.

Freedom of Speech

Since the First Amendment to the U.S. Constitution was passed in 1791, American citizens have had a constitutional guarantee of freedom of speech. As a student, you are allowed to interact with your teachers, and you have opportunities to speak before your class about issues of concern. You have the right to support publicly the political party of your choice and you can engage in activities that reflect your social values. As a community resident, you have the right to speak before the city council or the local school board to express agreement or disagreement with their policies. You can write letters to the editor of your local newspaper that support or oppose the president of our nation. With the Internet, you have numerous and highly varied means of communication.

While we live with wide boundaries for speaking, periodically attempts are made to censor both our public and private lives. And as First Amendment lawyer Robert Corn-Revere (2007) notes, the "seemingly simple command" of the First Amendment becomes "exceedingly complex" when applied to electronic media. The difficulty of monitoring the use/abuse of free speech is especially true in this age of blogging, where every second a "citizen journalist" creates a new blog site, adding to the already 37 million existing sites, according to David Sifri (2006), founder of the Technorati weblog data set and link tracker/search engine. Ultimately, limitations to our freedom of speech are decided by the U.S. Supreme Court.

Freedom of expression comes with responsibility. In class, each speaker has the ethical responsibility to communicate accurately with sound reasoning and to decide what is said and best not said. This responsibility requires a speaker to be truthful without hesitation. As listeners, we are also given a responsibility: to respect the opinions of others, even those different from ours.

Freedom of expression is balanced by freedom of choice. In most situations, listeners have the ultimate power to listen or to focus elsewhere. It is the freedom to pursue our individual interests that keeps the freedom of speech of others in check. Yet this is not always a perfect system. There are times when the audience is captive and has no real choice, such as your classroom, when an attendance policy may require students to be there. It becomes the ethical responsibility of the speaker and host (your instructor) to monitor more carefully and on occasion censure inappropriate material on behalf of the captive audience.

We want to emphasize the importance of meeting your ethical responsibilities in any speech you give, whether it is informative, persuasive, or entertaining. We begin by discussing the connection between ethics and public speaking, and then turn to guidelines for incorporating ethical standards in your speeches.

The Ethics and Values Link

Inherent to a discussion about ethics in public speaking is the concept of values and how they ground us. **Values** are socially shared ideas about what is good, right, and desirable. They propel us to speak and act. They determine what we consider important and what we ignore, how we regard our listeners, and how we research and develop a speech. Values are communicated through what speakers say—and fail to say—through delivery, and through responsiveness to audience feedback.

You can speak out against anti-Semitism or remain silent. You can support, through public discourse, the university's right to displace poor families from their university-owned apartments to build another office tower or you can plead for a more humane solution. In a public speaking class, you have a forum to talk about those things you feel are right or wrong, desirable or undesirable. Though you might hesitate to speak out, you may be surprised by how many others agree with you.

Ethos and Speaker Credibility

Ethics receives attention in academic courses but is also a prominent concern in the media, government, and business. It may surprise you to learn that ethics has been systematically studied for over 2,000 years. In his text *Rhetoric*, Aristotle discussed the term ethos, meaning "ethical appeal." In a translation by Lane Cooper (1960), we find that Aristotle defined ethos in terms of the intelligence, character, and goodwill a speaker communicates during a speech:

> Speakers are untrustworthy in what they say or advise from one or more of the following causes. Either through want of intelligence they form wrong opinions; or, while they form correct opinions, their rascality leads them to say what they do not think; or, while intelligent and honest enough, they are not well disposed [to the hearer, audience], and so perchance will fail to advise the best course, though they see it.

Aristotle believed speakers can abuse their ethical relationship with their listeners when they misinterpret information or fail to collect all the information needed to give a complete and fair presentation, and when self-interest leads them to dishonesty and lack of goodwill. For example, a developer comes into a community in the hopes of building a large superstore and, in a public forum, explains how many jobs and how much revenue will be brought to the community. The developer's self-interest in this project may result in her leaving out information, such as the negative impact the superstore will have on employees and owners of the community's smaller businesses, less-than-savory environmental impacts, and potential traffic bottlenecks. As this information becomes available to the audience, the developer may lose much of her credibility.

Notice that Aristotle was also concerned with how well disposed, or liked, the speaker is by the audience. For Aristotle, even if our hypothetical building developer mentioned above had told the whole truth, included the unsavory realities, and then attempted to overcome them, but did so in a demeaning, condescending tone, she would not be successful in maximizing her speaker ethos. Your likability is an important feature and deserves attention along with your speech content.

Since Aristotle's time, scholars have made the distinction between intrinsic ethos and extrinsic ethos. Whereas intrinsic ethos is the ethical appeal found in the actual speech, including such aspects as supporting material, argument flow, and source citation, extrinsic ethos is a speaker's image in the mind of the audience. Extrinsic aspects include how knowledgeable,

Glossary

Ethos Ethical appeal, makes speakers worthy of belief.

Aristotle Ancient Greek philosopher. Lived 384–322 BCE.

Intrinsic ethos Ethical appeal found in the actual speech, including such aspects as supporting material, argument flow, and source citation.

Extrinsic ethos A speaker's image in the mind of the audience.

© Panos Karapanagiotis, 2012. Under license from Shutterstock, Inc.

Aristotle defined ethos in terms of the intelligence, character, and goodwill a speaker communicates during a speech.

trustworthy, and dynamic the speaker is perceived to be. Both intrinsic and extrinsic ethos contribute to a speaker's credibility. Communication theorists McCroskey and Young (1981) tie credibility to the audience's perception of the speaker as an expert, as a person to trust, and as a person with positive and honest intent. If you are too casual, unprepared, or do not provide support for your claims, your credibility may work against you.

Plagiarism and Source Citations

An ethical speaker takes credit for his or her own ideas and, through oral source citation, credits others for their ideas. If you were to find a compelling example that would help you make a point, but that example came from a journal article, you are ethically bound to give oral credit when you use the example. This is achieved by simply saying, "According to [name of author and date of publication] in [name of journal] an excellent example of this is …" and then paraphrase the example. Oral citations are brief but effective in enhancing your credibility by showing you have conducted research and you are honorable enough to give others credit for their work. As public speakers, we orally credit others when we use their ideas, facts, statistics, organizational patterns, testimonies and quotations, stories, examples. When in doubt, give credit. An ethical speaker does not mislead audiences.

Engage in Dialogue with the Audience

Beyond citing sources orally, there are other signs that the speaker may be unethical. Monologic versus dialogic communication tendencies is one clear indicator of ethical responsibility. The least sensitive speakers engage in monologic communication (Johannesen, 1974). From this perspective, the audience is viewed as an object to be manipulated and, in the process, the speaker displays such qualities as deception, superiority, exploitation, dogmatism, domination, insincerity, pretense, coercion, distrust, and defensiveness—all qualities considered unethical.

In contrast, dialogic communication entails an honest concern for listeners' interests. This kind of speech "communicates trust, mutual respect and acceptance, open-mindedness, equality, empathy, directness, lack of pretense, and nonmanipulative intent. Although the speaker in dialogue may offer advice or express disagreement, he or she does not aim to psychologically coerce an audience into accepting his/her view. The speaker's aim is one of assisting the audience in making independent, self-determined decisions" (Johannesen, 1974). Whereas monologic speakers attempt to force an issue, dialogic speakers are interested in creating a fair, honest dialog with their audience. The dialogic speaker does have a goal toward which he/she is attempting to move the audience but is concerned with doing so ethically.

Glossary

Monologic communication From this perspective, the audience is viewed as an object to be manipulated and, in the process, the speaker displays such qualities as deception, superiority, exploitation, dogmatism, domination, insincerity, pretense, coercion, distrust, and defensiveness.

Dialogic communication Demonstrates an honest concern for the welfare of the listeners.

Promoting Ethical Speaking

Dialogic styled speakers use an audience-centered approach, and all decisions made in the development process take the audience into consideration. As you recognize the importance of speaker credibility and project firm ethical standards, we encourage you to reflect on the following four principles of the ethical speaker (Wallace, 1955).

Search

In the context of public speaking and ethics, search refers to putting forth an effort to learn enough about your topic so you are able to speak knowledgeably and confidently. As you speak before your class, realize that, at that moment, you are the primary source of information about your chosen topic. You are responsible for presenting a message that reflects thorough knowledge of the subject, sensitivity to relevant issues and implications, and awareness that many issues are multifaceted. If your search is half-hearted or incomplete, you may not get it right in your speech. In the worst cases, you might mislead others with your words in such ways as to cause harm.

Justice

Justice reminds us to select and present facts and opinions openly and fairly. Instead of attempts to distort or conceal evidence, just speakers offer the audience the opportunity to make fair judgments. The Food and Drug Administration requires the pharmaceutical industry to disclose side-effects of medications in advertising. Daily we hear messages such as "side-effects may include nausea, vomiting, dizziness, rectal leakage, stroke or heart attack, and should not be taken by children under 12, women who are pregnant, or people who have heart problems, liver problems, kidney disease, or diabetes." As a result, the consumer has the opportunity to make a judgment based on known information. Similarly, if someone is considering cosmetic surgery, potential risks are disclosed in addition to the benefits.

Public Motivation

A student may be motivated to give an informative speech on the warning signs of methamphetamine (meth) abuse because of the rise in the number of meth users and meth-related deaths in her community. This is public motivation. Assuming she has reliable information on meth use and meth-related deaths, her motive is to illuminate a public problem. In contrast to public motivation is private motivation. If an instructor tries to convince students to sign up for internships in his department, not because it is a beneficial academic experience, but because as internship coordinator, he gets paid per student, his motivation is private. Keeping such **hidden agendas** is unethical behavior.

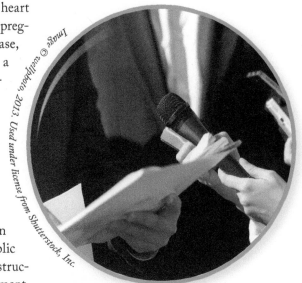

Image © wellphoto, 2013. Used under license from Shutterstock, Inc.

Ethical speakers reveal any personal motives as well as the sources of their information and opinion.

As a speaker, consider whether your motives are personal or reach beyond individual concerns. Ethical speakers reveal personal motives as well as the sources of their information and opinion. Such full disclosure and transparency assists the audience in weighing any special bias, prejudices, and self-centered motivations in a message. Avoid concealing information about your source materials and your own motives because the effectiveness of your message is weakened if they are suspect.

Respect for Dissent

Voltaire (1694–1778), a French writer, historian, and philosopher, is quoted on the first page of this chapter. He writes, "I do not agree with a word you say, but I will defend to the death your right to say it." This quote illustrates the respect for dissent. Respect for dissent allows for and encourages diversity of argument and opinion. It involves seeing a different point of view as a challenge rather than a threat.

The respect for dissent means being open to accepting views different from one's own. This does not mean we have to give in. We can still advocate our position while acknowledging that others may be as firm in their opposition to it. Ideally, in a free marketplace of competing ideas, a healthy debate ensures that truth and wisdom are exposed.

Developing Ethical Speaking Habits

To ensure the above four principles are incorporated into your presentation, consider the following three guidelines and five pitfalls.

Ethical Guidelines

1. Recognize the Power of the Podium

Have you ever watched a commercial and decided you had to have that product? Have you been in church when a minister tells about a needy homeless shelter, and you were compelled to donate at that moment? Have you heard a message about environmental hazards created by plastic bottles and tossed your next empty bottle of water in the recycle bin? These examples illustrate that speaking is an influential activity.

Speakers travel to campuses across the country to address a wide range of issues related to race, ethnicity, poverty, public health, alcoholism, immigration, and national security, to name a few. Some speakers are recruited by organizations on campus; others advertise their expertise in the hopes of being allowed to speak. These people understand the power of the podium. They know they can inform audiences, they can move them emotionally, or they can move them to act.

Some speakers may have national forums through the media or through their positions, such as members of Congress, the military, or even celebrities. Some abuse that power. As speakers, we strive to be aware that we have the power to persuade and the power to pass on information to others—powers that must be used for the common good.

2. Speak Truthfully

Whenever you speak before an audience, be certain of your facts. When your listeners realize your facts are wrong, they will trust you less. For example, if you give a speech on campus thefts and you blame students for the majority of crimes, when, in fact, most thefts are committed by city residents, you will lose credibility with listeners who know the facts.

3. Become Information Literate

When collecting supporting material for a speech, determine whether you are reviewing materials from a credible professional or someone who is simply writing a story, creating a web-based commerce site, or ranting in a blog.

Certain sources have more credibility than others. If you are researching the need for college students to update vaccinations with booster shots, an article in *The New England Journal of Medicine* or *Science* would be preferable to an article in *Newsweek* or *Time*. Although the latter publications are generally reliable, scientific journals are the better choice for this specific type of information. Wikipedia may be informative, but is generally not considered a reliable source on its own, and your instructor may not approve using it as a source.

Information literacy implies consuming information wisely and appropriately. A handy way to ensure your information literacy is found in the acronym PARTS. (For more information, see **BTW: Information Literacy Game**.)

Point of view. Recognize whether there is a point of view or bias. Is the information making every attempt at being objective or is it likely biased to serve a special interest? Even if a source claims to be "fair and balanced," you may not be getting an unbiased view from any one reporter of that organization. Complicating matters more, media personalities play at different times

Glossary

Information literacy
Consuming information wisely and appropriately.

BTW!

Information Literacy Game

University of North Carolina, Greensboro, librarians Scott Rice and Amy Harris have created a fun, interactive way to help you polish up on your information literacy skills. The game allows you to play in groups or individually. Play the game online at library.uncg.edu/game/.

the role of reporter in one instance and commentator in another. Discerning the point of view is critical to consuming information intelligently.

Authority. Consider the credentials of both the author and publisher. Are they recognized as experts and/or leaders in the field? Does the author hold a terminal degree such as Ph.D. or M.D.? Is the publisher a scholarly or reputable news source? The issue of authority is challenging online. The person who is responsible for content on some Web pages and blogs is not always clear. In these cases, it is best to look for independent confirmation in other locations to ensure accuracy.

Reliability. Even if the point of view seems unbiased and the source checks out, consider whether you can believe in the accuracy and treatment of the information. Reliability is related to the credibility, or believability, of the source. For example, recent research has shown that there are health benefits to eating chocolate and drinking a glass of red wine each day. Now, if the wine or cocoa industries commissioned those studies, one might question the reliability of the findings. If the science community came to these conclusions after independent tests, the information has greater credibility. An ethical speaker will look for the most recent, authentic, and unbiased information.

Timeliness. Timeliness refers to how current or up-to-date your information is. In some cases, information as recent as last year may be outdated. Depending on the topic, some information is still timely hundreds of years later. Evaluate how important recent information is to your topic as you gather information.

Consider this: If your specific purpose is to inform your class on the latest technology for diabetes management, a simple search may lead you to the insulin pump. However, by probing a little further and finding more recent information, you should find articles about the insulin inhaler, which has more recently hit the market.

Scope. Scope refers to the extent of your research. Check to see that your research has both depth and breadth. Does the information create an overview or develop a narrow portion of your topic? Determine who the information is intended for, and whether information is too technical and clinical, or too basic. Is it appropriate for a college audience?

Our world is changing rapidly. Old facts are often wrong facts, especially in such volatile areas as public safety, science, and even our civil liberties. As you prepare your speech, take into consideration the need for currency in matters and issues that are relevant now. If you find credible evidence that appears to undermine your position, be honest enough to evaluate it fairly and change your position if warranted. Throughout this process, keep in mind your ethical obligation to present accurate information to your listeners. Here are a few common pitfalls to keep in mind:

Ethical Pitfalls

1. Avoid Purposeful Ambiguity

When we leave out specific detail, we can paint a misleading picture. Choose words carefully to communicate your point. Realize, for example, that references to "hazing abuses" may conjure images of death and bodily injury to some, while others may think of harmless fraternity pranks. Similarly, choose your supporting materials carefully. Ambiguities often stem from inadequate or sloppy research.

2. Avoid Rumors and Innuendos

It is unethical to base your speeches on rumors. Rumors are unproven charges, usually about an individual. By using them as facts, you can tarnish—or ruin—a reputation and convey misleading information to your audience.

Pop culture is rife with rumors. Weekly entertainment magazines are filled with stories about the lives of Hollywood celebrities, many of which are based on rumors. We find out that stars are battling drug and alcohol abuse, or that they are gaining or losing weight. We read that Jen is dating Michael. Oh, no, they just broke up. Wait … they are back together. Now they are married. Oops, they are divorced. She is pregnant. Is it his? Or does it belong to old boyfriend? Every aspect of their lives is reported, frequently without any reliance on facts.

It is also ethically unacceptable to use innuendo to support a point. Innuendos are veiled lies, hints, or remarks that something is what it is not. Innuendo frequently surfaces in the heat of a strongly contested political race. The exaggerated rhetoric of opponents results in observations ranging from misstatements about events to hints about improprieties in the alleged behavior of the political opponent. An ethical speaker avoids any use of rumor or innuendo when preparing a speech.

> **Glossary**
>
> **Innuendos** Veiled lies, hints, or remarks that something is what it is not.

3. Uphold Unpopular Ideas

Speaking in support of the public good implies a willingness to air a diversity of opinions, even when these opinions are unpopular. According to Roderick Hart (1985), professor of communication, we must "accept boat rocking, protests, and free speech as a necessary and desirable part of [our] tradition" (p. 162). Your goal as a speaker can be to encourage the "ideal of the best ideas rising to the surface of debate" (p. 46). Despite the tradition of free speech in Western society, taking an unpopular stand at the podium is not easy, especially when the speaker faces the threat of repercussions.

4. Avoid Hidden Agendas

Consider Joyce, a real estate agent with a home for sale in a suburban community that is suffering from the real estate recession. Many homes are for sale but the market contains too few buyers. Joyce is one among dozens of agents who will find it difficult to make a satisfactory living unless conditions improve. To attract potential homebuyers, Joyce gives a series of speeches in a nearby city, extolling the virtues of suburban life. Although much of what she says is true, Joyce bends some facts to make her real estate seem the most attractive and affordable. For example, she tells her listeners that jobs are available, when in fact, the job market is weak (the rosy employment figures she used are a decade old). Joyce also mentioned that the community schools are among the top in the state, when, in fact, only one in five is ranked above the state average. With her goal of restoring that community to its former economic health, Joyce feels justified in this manipulation.

Do the ends justify the means? While Joyce's intentions were good, her ethics were slimy. As a speaker, you have only one ethical choice: to present the strongest possible legitimate argument, thus allowing each listener to evaluate the argument on its merits.

5. Avoid Excessive and Inappropriate Emotional Appeals

As listeners, we expect speakers to make assertions that are supported by sound reasoning. We expect the speech to flow logically, and to include relevant supporting material. However, some speakers prey on our fears or ignorance and rely heavily on the use of excessive and inappropriate appeals to emotion. To be ethical, emotional appeals must be built on a firm foundation of good reasoning and should never be used to take advantage of susceptible listeners. In our chapter on persuasive speaking, we examine further the nature of emotional appeals. However, following are four circumstances that create ethical concern.

Deception. Your speech creates a need in your audience through deception and requires an action that will primarily benefit you. For example, it is manipulative and unethical to try to convince a group of parents that the *only way* their children will succeed in school is to purchase an educational program that is comprehensive in detail, according to the company you represent.

BTW!

Infomercials or In-for-Fraud?

Tempted by those half-hour commercials to tighten your abs, lose weight, and gain vitality? Be careful. While many pitches lure us with emotional appeals, heightened expectations, and "act now" encouragements, some manipulators want to separate you from your cash. Self-proclaimed "King of Infomercials" Don Lapre (the greatest vitamins in the world) and Kevin Trudeau (natural cures) were both indicted for fraud.

Manipulation. This emotional appeal is aimed at taking advantage of those particularly susceptible to manipulation. A bit of channel surfing late at night will bring the viewer to quite a number of infomercials full of emotional appeals to persuade the viewer to purchase expensive programs that are supposed to lead them to considerable wealth, health, or both. (For more on this topic, see **BTW: Infomercials or In-for-Fraud?**)

Confusion. Emotional appeals are part of a sustained plan to confuse an audience and make them feel insecure and helpless. If, as a community leader, you oppose the effort to establish group homes for the developmentally challenged children by referring repeatedly to the threat these residents pose to the neighborhood children, you leave your listeners feeling vulnerable and frightened. Fear can become so intense that homeowners may dismiss facts and expert opinions that demonstrate developmentally challenged persons are neither violent nor emotionally unstable.

Fallacies. If a speaker realizes his/her logic will not hold up under scrutiny, he/she may appeal to audience emotions to disguise the deficit. Instead of relying on facts to convince listeners, the speaker appeals to the audience's emotional needs. Unethical speakers disguise messages and deceive listeners to achieve their goal, including the following **fallacies**: name calling, glittering generalities, testimonials, plainfolks, and bandwagoning.

Name calling involves linking a person or group with a negative symbol. In a persuasive speech, if your purpose is to convince your audience that abortion is morally wrong, you would be engaging in name calling if you referred to individuals who support a woman's right to choose as "murderers" and "baby-killers." You may believe these labels are truthful, but they are emotionally charged names that will arouse emotions in your audience, and many listeners may tune you out.

Glittering generalities rely on the audience's emotional responses to values such as home, country, and freedom. Suppose the real issues of a campaign are problems associated with the growing budget deficit, illegal immigration, and dependence on foreign oil. If a candidate avoids these issues and argues for keeping the Ten Commandments in front of courthouses, reciting the pledge of allegiance more often, and amending the Constitution to prevent flag-burning, that particular candidate is likely relying considerably on glittering generalities. Although it is acceptable to talk about these latter concerns, manipulating the audience's response so that critical judgments about major issues are clouded in other areas is unethical.

Testimonials can be both helpful and destructive. People who have had their cholesterol levels improve because of a particular prescription medicine may lead others to success. People who love their hybrid cars may help others make the decision to buy one. However, we are bombarded by celebrities touting countless products including shampoo, sports drinks, and phone service because they are paid to do so, not because they have expert knowledge of those products. In most cases no damage is done.

Glossary

Fallacies Appealing to audience emotions to disguise the deficit of the speaker's logic not holding up under scrutiny.

Name calling Linking a person or group with a negative symbol.

Glittering generalities Relying on audience's emotional responses to values such as home, country, and freedom.

Testimonials Statements testifying to benefits received; can be both helpful and destructive.

Years ago, however, Suzanne Somers, an actress who sells health, beauty, and fitness products, created an uproar in the scientific community when she promoted her own diet plan. In addition to the fact that she lacked professional qualifications, her diet plan de-emphasized exercise and she suggested a daily caloric threshold that was dangerous. Since it is well known that any diet or new exercise regimen should be discussed with a medical professional, her testimonial could be damaging.

Plain folks is an effort to identify with the audience. Be cautious when a speaker tells an audience, "Believe me, because I'm just like you." Speakers who present themselves as "plain folks" may be building an identification with their audience appropriately (something speakers often want to do), or they may be manipulating their listeners. One of your authors recalls an incident where an investment adviser conducting a seminar for senior citizens told his audience:

> One main reason I chose this career path is because my own parents, not unlike you gathered here tonight, did not have the opportunities I am offering you. I discovered that they are struggling in their retirement years to make ends meet on a monthly basis. Like you, they worked hard throughout their careers. However, what was available to them to live on when they left their work was modest.

This speaker appeared believable, but in fact, his parents retired with considerable funds acquired from owning a successful business for 30 years. The emotional tactic of using plain folks as an emotional appeal was simply to gain sales.

Bandwagoning is another unethical method of deception. Often listeners are uncomfortable taking a position no one else supports. Realizing this reluctance, unethical speakers may convince their listeners to support their point of view by telling them that "everyone else" is already involved. For example, you may live in a residence hall on a campus where your school's mascot is being threatened with extinction. A rally will be held, and someone on your floor is going door-to-door telling all the residents that "everybody" on campus will be at the rally to support the mascot. Chances are, this is an exaggeration.

As a speaker, try to convince others of the weight of your evidence—not the popularity of your opinion. In the case above, the resident should not be asking everyone to jump on the bandwagon, but should be explaining to people why keeping the mascot is a positive thing.

Avoiding Unethical Practices

After making the commitment to maintain ethical standards as a speaker, you should ensure that your research and speech delivery reflect your com-

---

Glossary

Plain folks An effort to identify with the audience.

Bandwagoning Unethical speakers may convince listeners to support their point of view by telling them that "everyone else" is already involved.

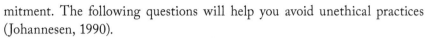

mitment. The following questions will help you avoid unethical practices (Johannesen, 1990).

Research

- Have I used false, fabricated, misrepresented, distorted, or irrelevant evidence to support my arguments or claims?
- Have I intentionally used unsupported, misleading, or illogical reasoning?
- Have I oversimplified complex situations into simplistic either–or, bipolar views or choices?

Delivery

- Will I represent myself as informed or as being an "expert" on a subject when I am not?
- Will I deceive my audience by concealing my real purpose, self-interest, the group I represent, or my position as an advocate of a viewpoint?
- Will I distort, hide, or misrepresent the number, scope, intensity, or undesirable aspects, consequences, or effects?
- Will I use emotional appeals that lack a supporting basis of evidence or reasoning or that would not be accepted if the audience had time to examine the subject themselves?
- Will I pretend certainty where tentativeness and degrees of probability would be more accurate?
- Will I advocate something in which I do not believe myself? (p. 254)

Summary

Because of the many ethical abuses that have taken place in recent years, many have become skeptical about the ethics of public speakers. The U.S. Bill of Rights guarantees freedom of speech. This does not mean that all speech is acceptable, appropriate, or ethical. Ethics is a central part of freedom of speech and ties closely to our personal value systems.

An ethical speaker cites sources when the words spoken are not his/her own, thus avoiding plagiarizing, or using someone else's words. Ethical public speaking is anchored in the values of the speaker, his or her audience, and the larger society. Ethical speakers engage in a "dialogue" with their audience, communicating qualities such as trust and directness, while unethical speakers engage in a monologue as they manipulate their audience for their own profit. Promoting ethical speaking is accomplished by developing the habits of search, justice, public motivation, and respect for dissent. This means that speakers will research their topic, present ideas fairly, make private motives known, and allow for opinions that may conflict with their own.

Ethics is part of every step of speech development. Remember these guidelines: Understand the power of the podium, speak truthfully, and become information literate—know your facts, use credible sources, use current and reliable information, avoid ethical pitfalls, including purposeful ambiguity, rumors, and innuendo, avoiding unpopular ideas, hidden agendas, and using excessive and inappropriate emotional appeals. Unethical speakers disguise messages and deceive listeners to achieve their goal. This is accomplished using a variety of fallacies. Avoid common fallacies, including name calling, glittering generalities, testimonials, plainfolks, and bandwagoning. After committing to being an ethical speaker, you may want to check your research and delivery by asking yourself specific questions that we provide.

Discussion Starters

❶ Why is freedom of speech so important? Are there instances in which citizens should be censured?

❷ How would you define the ethical responsibilities for a public speaker?

❸ Can speakers be ethical and adapt to their audiences at the same time? Does adaptation imply audience manipulation or meeting the audience's needs? What steps can you take to ensure a positive speaker–audience connection?

❹ Who are public speakers you can think of who are not mentioned in this chapter but who you believe have spoken ethically and/or unethically?

❺ What do you believe is an appropriate ethical relationship between self-interest and the needs of the audience?

❻ Consider a current or past election campaign. Can you think of an instance in which a political candidate has used one or more of the fallacies identified in the text?

References

Bruner, B., & Haney, E. (n.d.). *Civil Rights Timeline: Milestones in the Civil Rights Movement*. Info Please. Retrieved August 4, 2011 from www.infoplease.com/spot/civilrightstimeline1.html

Cooper, L. (1960). *The Rhetoric of Aristotle*. Upper Saddle River, NJ: Prentice Hall.

Corn-Revere, R. (2006). *Internet and the First Amendment*. Retrieved from www.firstamendementcenter.org.

Hart, R. (1985). The Politics of Communication Studies: An Address to Undergraduates. *Communication Education, 34,* 162.

Johannesen, Richard L. (1971). The Emerging Concept of Communication as Dialogue. *Quarterly Journal of Speech, 57,* 373–382.

Johannesen, R. L. (1990). *Ethics in Communication.* Prospect Heights, IL: Waveland Press.

McCroskey, J. C., & Young, T. J. (1981). Ethos and Credibility: The Construct and Its Measurement After Three Decades. *The Central States Speech Journal, 22,* 24–34.

Pilkington, E. (2009, January 29). Barack Obama Inauguration Speech. *The Guardian.* Retrieved August 4, 2011 from www.guardian.co.uk/world/2009/jan/20/barack-obama-inauguration-us-speech.

The Y, Share the News. (2010, July 12). A Brand New Day: The YMCA Unveils New Brand Strategy to Further Community Impact. Washington, DC. Retrieved August 4, 2011 from www.ymca.net/news-releases/20100712-brand-new-day.html.

Sifri, D. (2006). *Chinese Bloggers Top 17 Million.* Retrieved May 26, 2006 from www.vnunet.com.

Wallace, K. 1987. An Ethical Basis of Communication. *The Speech Teacher, 4,* 1–9.

Chapter 4

"Spend your leisure time in cultivating an ear attentive to discourse, for in this way you will find that you learn with ease what others have found out with difficulty."

Isocrates

Chapter 4: Listening and Critiquing Speeches

As crucial as the skills for speaking are to a presenter, just as important are listening skills to the audience. Understanding how listening helps improves the process. Eight steps promote fine-tuning your listening skills. Criteria for speech evaluation are discussed.

Student Learning Objectives:

○ Students will be able to explain the difference between listening and public speaking

○ Students will be able to define listening and other communication activities

○ Students will be able to understand the importance of good listening skills

○ Students will be able to understand and reflect on how to listen

○ Students will be able to explain reasons audiences stop listening

○ Students will be able to describe the four stages of listening

○ Students will be able to identify and explain the eight steps for fine-tuning listening skills

○ Students will be able to critique speeches

○ Students will be able to use technology to provide feedback

○ Students will be able to engage in self-evaluation

LISTENING AND CRITIQUING SPEECHES

Key Terms

evaluation   interpreting   reacting/responding   sensing

hearing   listening

Listening and Public Speaking

Two of the first researchers to study listening, Thomas Lewis and Ralph Nichols (1965), wrote that "effective listening and effective speaking are so closely woven together as to be inseparable" (p. 7). In other words, to discuss speaking without a concurrent discussion of listening is not productive. In Chapter 1, our communication model identifies the Sender/Receiver and the Receiver/Sender elements of the model, noting that sending and receiving are simultaneous activities.

One way to improve your chances of successful public speaking is to approach the process from the listening side—that is, to work at developing better listening skills. These skills are essential for two different but complementary reasons. First, by understanding the needs of your listening audience, you are able to develop and deliver speeches that have the greatest chance of communicating your intended meaning. The earliest Jesuit missionaries made it a point to enter new locations and not speak for six months. Instead, they listened. They recognized the importance of understanding the other person's perspective before attempting to educate.

Second, by understanding the factors affecting listening, you are able to monitor your own listening habits, and more effectively evaluate and criticize the speeches of others, including your classmates. A direct relationship exists between the quality of your listening and the quality of your speaking. *Good speakers use what they hear to analyze and respond to the needs of their audience, and to present information in a way that promotes communication.*

This chapter focuses on listening. First we discuss some basics about listening, including defining it, noting how much time we spend listening, and discussing memory and retention. Then we provide reasons people stop listening, the four stages of listening, and tips for better listening. Next, we discuss evaluating speeches, and provide some guidance to help you critique your classmates' speeches. We end the chapter by considering how you might use technology to provide feedback to your classmates after their speeches.

Listening and Other Communication Activities

Glossary

Hearing The physical ability to receive sounds.

Listening and hearing are not synonymous. **Hearing** is the physical ability to receive sounds. The Hearing Loss Association of America reports that, according to recent statistics from the National Center for Health,

36 million Americans, or 17 percent, have some hearing loss. This places hearing loss third in a line of public health issues behind heart disease and arthritis (www.hearingloss.org). So, we shouldn't assume our entire audience will hear us.

Listening is an active process that includes hearing. Many definitions of listening exist, but the International Listening Association defines **listening** as "the attending, receiving, interpreting, and responding to messages presented aurally" (ILA White Pages, 2009). This is a complex process with multiple elements, and *responding* is part of the listening process. We discuss the four stages of listening later in the chapter. But before we discuss listening in further depth, it makes sense to see what role listening plays in our everyday communication. (For more information, see **BTW: Types of Listening.**)

During the day, we spend time listening and speaking, but we also engage in other communication activities. Research conducted on college students (Janusik & Wolvin, 2006) found that listening is the communication activity that consumes the most time. Following are the activities and percentages:

Glossary

Listening The attending, receiving, interpreting, and responding to messages presented aurally.

BTW!

Types of Listening

Lisa Downs, training and development specialist, identifies four primary types of listening: informational, critical, appreciative, and empathic.

○ The goal of informational listening is to accurately receive information from another person. It does not involve judgment or criticism.

○ When engaging in appreciative listening, the goal is to listen for enjoyment or entertainment. It does not involve analyzing or evaluating information.

○ The goal of empathic listening is to understand what the speaker is saying and feeling. This involves making an effort to look at the world through someone else's view.

○ Finally, critical listening involves considering ideas heard from a speaker to decide if the message makes sense. A person using critical listening makes decisions about the message based on logic and evidence, rather than on emotion. An effective listener in a public speaking situation engages in critical listening. The following are four brief tips to help the critical listener:

- Look for evidence to support ideas.
- Consider the source of the evidence.
- Check for logical reasoning.
- Make a special effort to understand what the speaker is saying.

For more information on the types of listening and other listening topics, visit the American Society for Training and Development website at www.astd.org/content/publications/ASTDPress/ListeningSkillsTraining.htm.

- Reading—6 percent
- Writing—8 percent
- Speaking—20 percent
- Listening—24 percent

Within the context of a college student's life, listening, as it applies above, includes interpersonal communication as well as public communication. Other communication activities also consume the college student's life, however. These include the following (listening activities are marked with an asterisk):

- *TV—9 percent
- *Radio—4 percent
- *CDs/Tapes—5 percent
- *Telephone—8 percent
- Email—6 percent
- Internet—9 percent

Total listening-related activities (listening, TV, radio, CDs/tapes, and telephone) account for 50 percent of our daily communication activities (Janusik & Wolvin, 2006). So listening is a critical part of our day, yet little information is provided on how to be an effective listener.

Despite the amount of time we spend listening, our ability to retain what we hear is limited. For more than 50 years, we have known that audiences remember less than half of what they hear. After several days, only about 25 percent of the speech stays with us (Nichols, 1961).

Keeping these facts in mind, reflect on how much you retain from a class lecture. Immediately following the class, you will likely recall half of the material. Without reviewing your notes frequently thereafter, your memory of the lecture will drop dramatically. To counter this natural loss of memory, it is important to develop strategies, like taking and reviewing notes.

The Importance of Good Listening Skills

We listen for entertainment (watching movies, listening to CDs, watching YouTube), and we listen to our professors to understand and retain material, and ultimately succeed in class. We listen to friends so we may develop and maintain relationships. Listening impacts our lives in many ways and, specifically, is related to success. Following are a few interesting research results:

- Listening has been identified as one of the top skills employers seek in entry-level employees as well as those being promoted (AICPA, 2005).
- Listening is tied to effective leadership (Johnson & Bechler, 1998).

○ Confident individuals listen to message content better than individuals who lack confidence (Clark, 1989).

○ Listening and nonverbal communication training significantly influences multicultural sensitivity (Timm & Schroeder, 2000).

○ Effective listening is associated with school success (Bommelje, Houston, & Smither, 2003).

○ Individual performance in an organization is found to be directly related to listening ability or perceived listening effectiveness (Haas & Arnold, 1995).

These brief research results demonstrate some of the long-term positive effects of listening. Good listening may lead to success in school, help a person get a job, result in positive evaluations at work, help with promotion, and result in successful leadership and being seen as culturally sensitive. A poor listener may suffer several consequences in both the long and short term. Among some short-term effects are:

○ Missing a message (not paying attention)

○ Not understanding a message

○ Taking extra time for repetition or clarification

○ Creating a negative impression by appearing disinterested

○ Inability to participate in conversations when you are not paying attention

Each of these short-term effects may not seem terribly problematic, but in the long term damage to personal and professional relationships can occur. For example, when we perceive someone is not listening to us or seems disinterested, it may hurt our feelings or we may feel defensive. We may choose not to communicate with that person again.

On a professional level, we want to make sure the messages we send are interpreted correctly. Having to clarify, repeat, or rephrase takes time away from the task at hand. Poor listeners at the organizational level may get chastised for their ineffective behavior, or colleagues may start to avoid working with someone who does not listen well.

So far, we have shown that listening is an important activity that consumes a large portion of our waking hours. We also know that good listeners are valued in the professional world, and poor listening leads to a variety of negative personal and professional consequences. Next, we provide an opportunity for you to think about your own listening habits.

Reflect on How You Listen

Many people think of listening as a simple task that involves sitting back and giving the speaker your attention. As public speakers, we hope our message and meaning will be understood. As audience members, we may have other things on our minds—distractions, preconceived notions, prejudices, misunderstandings, and stress—and the message we receive may be much different from the message sent. As the following interchange suggests in Table 4.1, listening is more complicated than it appears. The speaker (left column) is an elderly activist from the 1960s. The listener (right column) is a 24-year-old student.

TABLE 4.1	
Speaker	**Listener**
Around 40 years ago, at about this time of year, I—and a whole lot of other committed students—spent a solid week—day and night—in the offices of our college president. Needless to say, we hadn't been invited.	*Here I am again—listening to another speaker who says he stormed his college administration building in the 60s. This must be a popular topic on the college speaking circuit. Maybe this guy will be different from the other three middle-aged radicals I heard, but I doubt it … The least they could do is turn up the air conditioning. It's so hot I can hardly breathe, let alone listen.*
We were protesters and proud of it. We were there because we believed the Vietnam War was wrong. We were there because we believed racism was wrong. We were there because we believed that women should be given the same opportunities as men.	*These guys keep talking about how they know the way and how we're all wrong … I wonder what he does for a living. I'll bet he hasn't saved any lives lately or helped the poor. He probably earns big bucks giving speeches on campus telling us how horrible we are … He looks like he spends a lot of time cultivating his hippie look. He must have slept in those clothes for a week. These guys all look the same.*
Were we victorious? For about 10 years, I thought so. Then something happened. The signs were subtle at first. Haircuts got shorter. The preppie look replaced torn jeans. Business became the major of choice.	*He's harping on the same old issues. Doesn't he know the Vietnam War is ancient history; that women have more opportunities than they ever had—I wish I could earn as much as Rachael Ray … I guess I'll have a pizza for dinner. I should have eaten before I came. I'm really hungry.*
In a flash—it happened that quickly—these subtle changes became a way of life. Campus life, as I knew it, disappeared. Revolution and concern for the oppressed were out, and conservatism and concern for the self were in.	*Of course we're interested in business. Maybe he had a rich father who paid his tuition, but I don't. I need to earn money when I graduate so I can pay back my student loans.*
From the point of view of someone who has seen both sides—the radical, tumultuous 60s and the calm, money-oriented 80s, 90s, and the new century—students of today are really 40-year-olds in 20-year-old bodies. They are conservative to the core at the only time of life when they can choose to live free. I am here to help you see how wrong you are.	*Who does he think he is—calling us conservatives. I'm not a bigot. When I believe something is wrong, I fight to change it—like when I protested against ethnic cleansing overseas and flag burning right here.*
	I wonder when he'll finish. I've got to get back to the dorm to study for my marketing exam. He just goes on and on about the same old things.

Reasons Audiences Stop Listening

You may see a bit of yourself in the speaker–listener example. Maybe this internal dialogue does not occur frequently, but most of us experience this occasionally. Based on the listening facts stated earlier, it is clear that listening is important, and research has shown that we do not retain much of what a speaker says. So, the question remains, Why do we stop listening? There is no single answer to this question, but the following six reasons listed may strike a familiar chord. We stop listening:

❶ When our attention drifts. Listeners drift in and out of a speech, thinking about the heat, their next meal, or an impending exam. Studies have shown that few of us are able to pay attention to a single stimulus for more than 20 seconds without focusing, at least momentarily, on something else.

❷ When we are distracted. Our environment determines how well we can listen. In the speaker–listener example, the heat made it difficult to pay attention. Internal stresses—hunger, unresolved conflict, and concern about exams—are also distractions. With people leaving cell phones on, checking messages, and texting or tweeting during a speech, listeners can be distracted, either because they're creating the distraction or they are near the distraction.

❸ When we have preconceived notions. Before the speaker in the example above opened his mouth, the listener had already decided what the speaker stood for based on the speaker's appearance and on a stereotype of what 60s radicals stood for. Although in this case the listener was right—the speaker's views conformed to the listener's preconceived notions—he/she may be wrong about other speakers.

❹ When we disagree. Although the speaker identified continuing social ills, the listener did not share his concerns. From the listener's point of view, much more was right with the world than the speaker admitted—a perspective that reduced the listener's willingness and ability to consider the speaker's message.

❺ When we are prejudiced or inflexible. Few women earn as much as Rachael Ray. Yet the listener based his/her reaction to the speaker's message on the premise that if one member of a group can succeed, all can. His prejudice prevented him from seeing the truth in the speaker's words.

❻ When we are faced with abstractions and form our own opinions. The speaker never defined the term "conservative." As a result, the listener brought his/her own meaning to the term, equating it with bigotry. This meaning may or may not have coincided with the speaker's intent.

© Yuri Arcurs, 2012. Under license from Shutterstock, Inc.

What causes your attention to drift during a speech?

As audience members, we know our purpose is to listen, think critically, and retain the central idea of the message. But think about what *you* do as you listen and why you stop listening. You may consciously or unconsciously tune the speaker out. You may focus on minor details at the expense of the main point. You may prejudge the speaker based on appearance. You may allow your own emotional needs and responses to distort the message, and so on. Later, we provide specific tips for improving your listening skills, but first, we discuss the four stages of listening.

The Four Stages of Listening

Think back to a time when, in an argument with a family member or friend, you responded with "I hear you!" True, you may have *heard* them. It is possible, however, that you did not *listen* to them. Although listening appears to be instinctual and instantaneous, as noted earlier, it consists of four identifiable stages. We move through these stages every time we listen, regardless of the situation. We may be part of a formal audience listening to a paid speaker, we might be engaged in conversation with a friend, or we might be home alone, listening to "things that go bump in the night." Listening can take place on several different levels, which are characterized by different degrees of attention and emotional and intellectual involvement. At times, we only partially listen as we think about or do other things; other times we listen with complete commitment. The following is an elaboration of the four stages of listening.

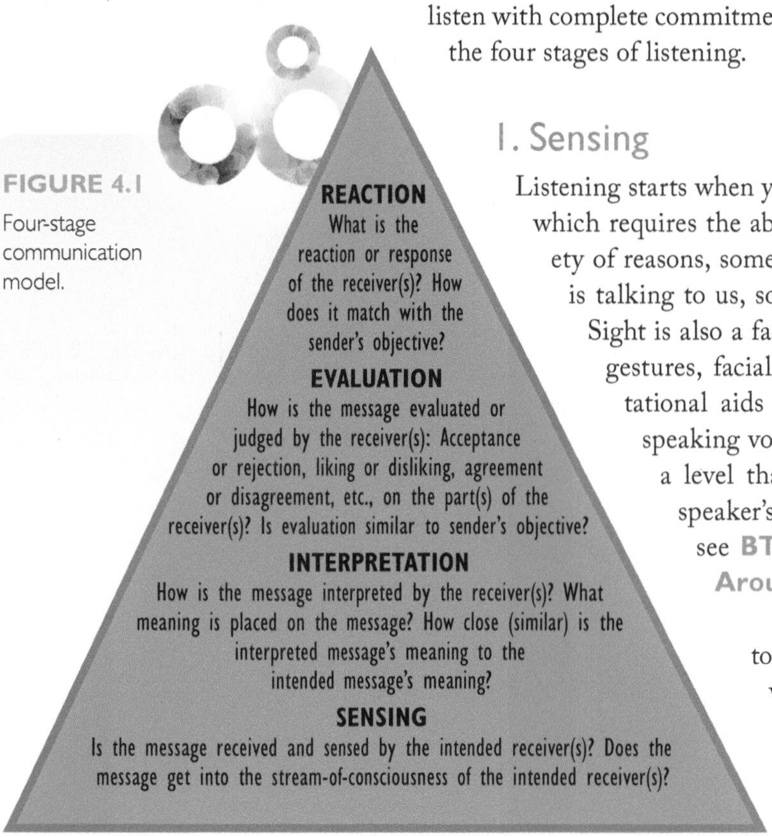

FIGURE 4.1

Four-stage communication model.

REACTION
What is the reaction or response of the receiver(s)? How does it match with the sender's objective?

EVALUATION
How is the message evaluated or judged by the receiver(s): Acceptance or rejection, liking or disliking, agreement or disagreement, etc., on the part(s) of the receiver(s)? Is evaluation similar to sender's objective?

INTERPRETATION
How is the message interpreted by the receiver(s)? What meaning is placed on the message? How close (similar) is the interpreted message's meaning to the intended message's meaning?

SENSING
Is the message received and sensed by the intended receiver(s)? Does the message get into the stream-of-consciousness of the intended receiver(s)?

1. Sensing

Listening starts when you sense information from its source, which requires the ability to hear what is said. For a variety of reasons, sometimes we don't "sense" that someone is talking to us, so we miss part or all of the message. Sight is also a factor with sensing, since the speaker's gestures, facial expressions, and the use of presentational aids communicate intent. Normally, the speaking voice is in the range of 55–80 decibels, a level that comfortably enables us to hear a speaker's words. (For more about decibel level, see **BTW: How Loud Are the Sounds Around Us?**)

As anyone who has tried to listen to a speech over the din of a car siren will realize, obstacles can—and often do—interfere with reception. These obstacles are known to communication theorists as "noise," which was discussed in Chapter 1 as part of the communication model. Physical noise, such as sitting next to someone who has a persistent cough, and environmental annoyances, like uncomfortable chairs, stuffy rooms, cell phone and texting-related distractions, or struggling air-conditioning systems, make concentrated listening nearly impossible.

As we noted in Chapter 1, sometimes a remedy for physical noise is possible. The speaker, for example, can ask the audience to move closer to the front, silence their phones, and resist texting. Audience members can find more comfortable seats. When nothing can be done about noise, work hard to tune out the remaining noise so you can listen to the message.

2. Interpreting

Interpreting messages, which involves attaching meaning to the speaker's words, is also part of listening. As a listener, keep in mind that words have different meanings to different people, and we interpret words based on subjective experiences. Our ability to interpret what we hear is influenced by emotional and intellectual barriers that get in the way of the speaker's intended message.

We may hear specific words that offend us, or we find a statement or message repugnant. These barriers are forms of semantic or psychological noise. Novelist David Leavitt (1989) explains how emotional barriers prevented him from dealing with the topic of AIDS many years ago. A gay man, Leavitt found any mention of AIDS so threatening that he shut off his ability to listen:

> The truth was that AIDS scared me so much I wanted to block it out of my mind. When AIDS came up in a conversation, I'd change the subject. When a frightening headline leaped out at me from the pages of the newspaper, I'd hurriedly skim the article, and, once assured that it described no symptoms I could claim to be suffering from myself, turn the page. Only later ... did I recognize the extent to which I was masking denial with self-righteousness (p. 30).

In this case, the psychological mechanism of denial caused the listening obstruction. A college student who is $140,000 in debt because of loans and maxing out credit cards may consciously "tune out" a classmate's persuasive speech on credit card debt to avoid thinking about the future. A zoning board member might unconsciously stop listening after two of five citizens have spoken in favor of a petition. An expert on public health can hardly sit still while listening to a lecture on lead paint removal. After a few minutes the realization hits that he/she and the speaker have completely different views on removal procedure costs and safety. Instead of listening to the rest of the information, the public health expert fumes over this difference of opinion.

Glossary

Interpreting Attaching meaning to a speaker's words.

BTW!

How Loud Are the Sounds Around Us?

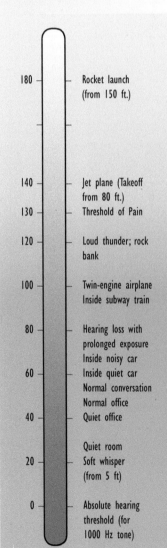

FIGURE 4.2 How loud are the sounds around us?

180	Rocket launch (from 150 ft.)
140	Jet plane (Takeoff from 80 ft.)
130	Threshold of Pain
120	Loud thunder; rock bank
100	Twin-engine airplane Inside subway train
80	Hearing loss with prolonged exposure Inside noisy car
60	Inside quiet car Normal conversation Normal office Quiet office
40	
20	Quiet room Soft whisper (from 5 ft)
0	Absolute hearing threshold (for 1000 Hz tone)

Whether emotional and intellectual barriers are the result of an unwillingness to deal with real-world problems, a refusal to take advice, or a difference of opinion, the result is the same: Listening is obstructed, interpretation skewed, and effective communication prevented.

3. Evaluating

Listening involves evaluating the message. Evaluation requires that you assess the worth of the speaker's ideas and determine their importance to you. It is a mistake to assume that we judge messages solely on their own merits. Research shows that our assessment is influenced by how the message fits into our value system. According to Friedman (1986), there is a "human preference for maintaining internal consistency among personal beliefs, feelings, and actions" (p. 13). We agree with messages that are consistent with other beliefs we have, and we disagree with messages that conflict with our beliefs.

This tendency to agree with ideas that fit our value system and disagree with those ideas that conflict with our value system was first identified as cognitive dissonance by psychologist Leon Festinger (1957). Essentially, the theory argues that we seek internal consistency between attitudes and behaviors. If we do not like a colleague and that person acts badly, we experience consistency between attitude and behavior. If someone we do not like acts in a sincere, friendly manner, we experience inconsistency.

When inconsistency exists, we experience mental stress. To reduce the stress, we are forced to change one or more of our attitudes or behaviors so that the inconsistency is reduced or eliminated. For example, assume you are a school board member who holds a high opinion of the school superintendent, until he angrily tells you to "Shut up!" during a meeting with administrators and other board members. You may experience dissonance because you cannot reconcile your previous esteem for this person with your new feelings of being disrespected.

Dissonance disappears when your overall impression is consistent. In the case mentioned above, you have a choice. You either rationalize the inappropriate behavior and go back to having a high opinion of the school superintendent ("He was under a lot of stress; he didn't mean it") or, you change your opinion of the person ("Someone who behaves this way in a formal meeting should not be leading our district"). Thus, as listeners, we seek information consistent with what we already know; we accept ideas more readily if they are linked to our values and commitments.

To preserve psychological balance, we often reject conflicting ideas and retain our original point of view. This rejection can take many forms, including the following (Friedman, 1986, p. 13):

Shoot the messenger. If you are a member of a college fraternity, you may reject the notion that any group found guilty of a hazing violation should

Glossary

Evaluation Assessing the worth of the speaker's ideas and determining their importance to you.

be banned from campus. You may criticize the speaker as uninformed or as someone who was never in a fraternity like yours himself.

Rally 'round the flag. Listeners who disagree with a speaker's message may seek the support of others who share their point of view—in this case, other fraternity members. Shared support provides comfort and reassurance. However, it does not necessarily mean you are right.

What the speaker says is not what you hear. Although the speaker may focus on hazing violations that put fraternity pledges in physical jeopardy, you hear him say that all violations—even minor infractions—should result in any group being banned.

Convince yourself that the speaker's message has nothing to do with you. Even when opinions collide, you may convince yourself that you and the speaker are talking about two different things. You decide that the issue does not really have any bearing on *your* fraternity because the speaker is giving examples of fraternity mishaps at other schools.

Do not think about it and it will go away. If, as a fraternity member, you took part in several unpleasant hazing incidents, listening to the speech may force you to question what you have done. To avoid the emotional discomfort that goes with this soul-searching, you may unconsciously block messages with which you do not agree.

Although these methods are counterproductive, we all rely on one or more of them at one time or another. It is important to avoid using them excessively, and to recognize the behavior when it happens. Although evaluating does involve judging the speaker's ideas, we need to work on being as objective and open minded as possible. Not all messages are pleasant, nor should we expect to agree with all speakers. However, we should avoid using mechanisms that block out or alter ideas different from ours.

4. Reacting/Responding

Listening involves **reacting/responding** to the speaker's message. Feedback is also part of the listening process. In a conversation, the roles of listener and speaker change regularly. As the listener, you can interrupt the speaker, ask questions, and provide nonverbal cues such as eye contact, touching, or hugging. (For tips on asking questions of a speaker, see **BTW: Tips from a Media Professional**.)

At the mass communication level, you may respond positively to a television series by watching it weekly or by purchasing a product advertised during the commercial. Listeners in a public speaking setting provide feedback in a variety of ways: laughing, smiling, nodding in agreement, cheering or booing, clapping, or questioning the speaker after the presentation. Listeners also provide feedback on a less conscious level, such as yawning, texting, looking around the room, or whispering to the person next to them.

Glossary

Reacting/
responding Providing feedback to the speaker's message.

Effective speakers rely on and encourage feedback from their audience. They watch carefully for messages of approval or disapproval and adjust their presentations accordingly. We discuss audience feedback in our chapter on audience analysis and adaptation.

Eight Steps for Fine-Tuning Your Listening Skills

As a skill, listening is notoriously undervalued. Philosopher Mortimer Adler (1983) uses the following sports analogy to describe why the act of listening is as important as the act of speaking: "Catching is as much an activity as throwing and requires as much skill, though it is a skill of a different kind. Without the complementary efforts of both players, properly attuned to each other, the play cannot be completed." The players involved in the act of communication are speakers and listeners, all of whom have a role in the interaction. In this section, we explain how you can improve your listening skills—and, therefore, the chances of meaningful communication—by becoming conscious of your habits and, when necessary, redirecting your efforts.

BTW!

Tips from a Media Professional

Ed Brodow is a keynote speaker, author, and negotiation guru on PBS, ABC News, Fox News, and *Inside Edition*. When asking questions of a speaker, he provides the following suggestions:

○ **Ask open-ended questions.** Questions that can't be answered with a simple yes or no. "How could we do this?" "What do you think?" Your objective is to get them to talk as much as possible.

○ **Don't ask questions that put them on the defensive.** For example, "Why?" is intimidating. Don't ask, "Why?" Ask, "How come?"

○ **Ask, "What if?"** What if we did it this way?

○ **Ask for their advice.** "What would you suggest we do to resolve this?" Everyone loves to be asked for advice.

○ **Offer alternatives.** "Which way would you prefer?" This demonstrates your respect for the other person.

○ **Ask about their feelings.** "How do you feel about this?" People love to have their feelings validated.

○ **Repeat back what they said.** "Let me be sure I understand what you're saying. You're saying that ...?" This technique prevents misunderstandings and convinces them you really are listening.

To see these tips and for more information about Ed Brodow, his book, and his professional services, visit www.brodow.com.

1. Get Ready to Listen

Preparation is critical, especially when you have other things on your mind. Plan to make the effort to listen even before the speech begins, deliberately clearing your mind of distractions so you are able to concentrate on the speech. This also means turning off your cell phone. In some cases, it may involve having proper "tools" with you, such as pen and paper.

2. Minimize Personal Barriers

This step is more difficult than it sounds, for it involves overcoming emotional and intellectual barriers to listening that we identified in preceding passages. Often, we need help in recognizing our listening "blind spots." As you talk with your classmates about each other's speeches, determine whether the message you received from a speaker was the same message they heard. If it was not, think about what the topic means to you and identify reasons for your differences in interpretation. It may be possible that you are the only one who accurately understood the speaker's message. Sometimes an entire audience misses the point. If a question-and-answer period follows the speech, you can question the speaker directly to make sure you have the right meaning.

3. Leave Distractions Behind

Some distractions are more easily dealt with than others. You can change your seat to get away from the smell of perfume but you cannot make a head cold disappear. You can close the door to your classroom, but you cannot stop the speaker from rattling change in his pocket. Although dealing with distractions is never easy, try putting them aside so you can focus on the speaker and the speech. This task becomes easier when you view listening as a responsibility—and as work. By considering listening as more than a casual interaction, you are more likely to hear the message being sent.

4. Do Not Rush to Judgment

As noted earlier, evaluation is part of the listening process. However, it is important to resist the temptation to *prejudge* speakers. Listeners have the tendency to prejudge topics as well as speakers. You may yawn at the thought-of listening to one of your classmates deliver an informative speech about the "pickling process" or "stage make-up" until you realize that the topic is more interesting than you expected. You may not have an inherent interest in the topic, but that does not mean the speaker cannot be interesting or thought provoking. Some speakers save their best for last. They may start slowly and build a momentum of ideas and language. Your job is to listen and be patient.

© Piotr Sikora, 2012. Under license from Shutterstock, Inc.

By viewing listening as a responsibility, you will be more likely to hear the message being sent.

We demonstrate prejudgment of a speaker when we find ourselves dismissing someone because "she's old," "he's conservative," or "he always dresses funny." As a listener, you have the responsibility to evaluate the content of the speech and not jump to conclusions based on surface speaker characteristics.

5. Listen First for Content, Second for Delivery

Confronted with poor delivery, it is difficult to separate content from presentation. The natural tendency is simply to stop listening when speakers drone on in a monotone, deliver speeches with their heads in their notes, or sway back and forth. However, delivery often has little to do with the quality of the speaker's ideas. Many of the speakers you will hear over the years will be in the position to address you because of their accomplishments, not their speaking ability. While a Nobel Prize–winning scientist may be able to explain a breakthrough in cancer therapy, he or she may have no idea how to make eye contact with an audience. To avoid missing these speakers' points, look past poor delivery and focus on content. In some situations, it is helpful to outline the main ideas as the speaker presents them so that you focus on the ideas instead of the delivery.

6. Become an Effective Note Taker

Each time a professor lectures or conducts a class discussion, you and your fellow students are expected to take notes. After years of note taking, this activity probably seems as natural as breathing; it is something you do to survive (in this case, college). Ironically, this skill often disappears at graduation. Most people do not pull out a pad and pen when listening to a speech in the world outside the classroom. But note taking is as appropriate and necessary for nonstudents as it is for students.

When you listen to a speech at a public event, a political rally, or on TV, taking notes helps you listen more effectively. For example, if your school district plans a referendum, which means registered voters will have to choose "yes" or "no" to raising taxes, being able to take notes allows you to keep track of the purpose of the referendum, how funds will be distributed, and so on. The following suggestions will help you improve your note-taking—and listening—skills:

Taking notes helps you listen more effectively.

- **Create two columns for your notes.** Write "Facts" at the top of the left column and "Personal reactions/questions" at the top of the right column. If the speaker does not answer your questions during the course of the speech, ask for clarification at the end. This is particularly important when the speaker covers something complex, such as a change in insurance coverage, taxes, or city development.

- **Use a key-word outline instead of full sentences to document the speaker's essential points.** If you get bogged down trying to write full sentences, you may miss a huge chunk of the message. At the end of the speech, the key-word outline gives you a quick picture of the speaker's main points.

- **Use your own abbreviations or shorthand symbols to save time.** If you know that "comm" means communication, then use that. If you are not sure whether it means "communication," "communism," or "community," then the abbreviation is not working for you. We have seen students use up and down arrows instead of writing "increase" or "decrease." Develop a system that works for you.

- **Use diagrams, charts, scales, and quick-sketch images to summarize thematic concepts or theories.** Using emoticons may seem trite, but they can express succinctly how you feel about a concept. Drawing a scale may be useful as someone presents the pros and cons of some issue.

- **Use a numbering system to get down procedural, directional, or structural units of information.** Numbering helps organize information, especially if the speaker did not organize the units of information for you.

- **Ask the speaker—verbally or nonverbally—to slow down, if, no matter how quickly you write, you cannot keep up.** Be cautious here. Do not ask the speaker to slow down so you might write full sentences. Instead, ask the speaker to slow down for purposes of general understanding. If you are the only person who is experiencing difficulty, you may want to ask questions at the end instead, or make an appointment to fill in gaps in understanding.

7. Be an Active Listener

As instructors, we have observed that when lecturing to 200 or more students, some appear to believe they cannot be seen. They talk to their neighbors, text friends, slouch low in the seat, put their heads on their desks, or disappear into the hood of their sweatshirt. What these students do not know (surely you are not one of them!) is that we can see you, and we want you to be engaged in the listening process.

As listeners, we can process information at the rate of about 400 words per minute. However, as most people talk at only about 150 words per minute, we have a considerable amount of unused thinking time to spare (Wolf et al., 1983, p. 154). This "extra time" often gets in the way of listening because we tend to take mental excursions away from the speaker's topic. It is natural to take brief trips ("I wonder what's for lunch?") but it can be problematic when they become major vacations ("Wow. Last night when I was talking to Suzy on the phone … and she said … and I thought … and I couldn't believe it when she said … so I said …"). To minimize the potential for taking a lengthy vacation while listening, experts suggest the following techniques:

○ **Take notes to keep your focus on the speech.**

○ **Before the speech begins, write down questions you have about the topic.** As the speech progresses, determine whether the speaker has answered them.

○ **Apply the speaker's comments to your own experience and knowledge.** This makes the message more memorable.

○ **Identify the thesis statement and main supporting points.** This helps you focus on the critical parts of the speech.

○ **Decide whether you agree with the speaker's point of view and evaluate the general performance.** This keeps you engaged by focusing on the message and the speaker.

8. Provide Feedback

Let speakers know what you think. You may be able to provide feedback through the use of questions during or after the speech, and there may be an opportunity to give feedback to the speaker later on a personal level.

Even in a large lecture hall, the speaker is aware of the audience and will establish eye-contact with audience members. As a listener, you can provide nonverbal feedback by leaning forward in your chair, nodding your head, smiling, and frowning when the occasion or your emotions call for it. This kind of participation forces you to focus your attention on the speaker and the speech. Providing feedback at the various stages of a speech is hard work that requires total involvement and a commitment to fighting distractions.

Image © g-stockstudio, 2013. Used under license from Shutterstock, Inc.

How can you provide feedback to a speaker?

Critiquing Speeches

As an audience member in a public speaking situation, you listen to be informed on some topic, to be persuaded to change an attitude or engage in some specific behavior, or to be entertained. Your overall impression may be "I learned something," or "I was not persuaded," or "That wasn't very funny." Your response is not random; you have some reason for your reaction. If you "learned something," perhaps it was because the speaker provided facts or statistics you did not know. If you "were not persuaded," perhaps the speaker used faulty logic or relied on sources that were not credible.

As an audience member, several options exist for providing feedback on the speech. Clapping, laughing, asking questions at the end of the speech, giving a standing ovation, walking out on the speech, and talking to the speaker afterward are all forms of feedback. At a workshop or seminar, you may be asked to provide written feedback for a speaker, and in a public speaking class, you may be asked to give written and/or oral feedback.

When you evaluate speeches, you are engaging in a feedback process that makes you a speech critic. As you consider the elements included in a speech and note the speaker's strengths and weaknesses, you are taking part in a formal process of analysis and appraisal.

Outside the classroom, chances are slim that you would receive a graded critique. Regardless, the point to keep in mind is that criteria are applied each time someone in an audience thinks about a speech, what it means, and what its value may be. As a participant in a public speaking course, you are expected to criticize constructively your classmate's speeches. It is important that you note the *constructive* nature of this process.

Every discipline uses criteria to evaluate something. Chemists use criteria to judge an effective experiment. Psychologists use criteria when selecting participants for their research. Graduate schools use criteria when selecting new students that might include a high GPA, solid letters of recommendation, and adequate previous work experience. Outside of academia, professionals use criteria to evaluate the effectiveness of *something* related to their profession.

For example, jewelers use the "4 Cs" to evaluate diamonds—carat, cut, color, and clarity (gia4cs.gia.edu). Investment brokers use criteria for selecting stock. One source mentions four criteria—earnings, growth potential, ratings, and dividends (eHow.com), whereas another source uses 10 criteria (Klerck & Maritz, 1997). Unlike the standard criteria used in the diamond industry, different sets of criteria are used by different brokerage firms or investment groups.

Public speaking is more like the latter example, where different instructors use different methods to evaluate speeches. Similar criteria are used, but the specifics often differ. Some instructors provide narrative evaluations; others use an intricate rating scale. Some develop a few general categories for evaluation, whereas others identify 20 or more areas to critique. The following section presents criteria we find useful for critiquing speeches.

Five Key Criteria for Evaluating Speeches

As you criticize the strengths and weaknesses of speakers, keep in mind that your comments help your classmates develop as speakers. Your remarks help focus their attention on areas that work effectively as well as areas that need improvement. All speakers need this feedback to improve the quality of their performance.

Before identifying criteria for evaluating speeches, it makes sense to establish a few ground rules about giving feedback through the speech critique process. Feedback should be:

- Timely
- Specific
- Descriptive
- Appropriate

Speakers in both classroom settings and professional settings are helped most when given immediate, timely feedback. In a classroom setting, students may receive written or oral critiques from fellow classmates at the end of the speech or class period. This is certainly helpful. Our memory for detail starts fading immediately after a speech. If feedback is too delayed, lack of memory may impede the feedback process.

A second rule for feedback is to provide specific feedback. It takes little time or effort to say, "Great speech!" or "Funny stories!" or "Huh?" General feedback is less helpful than more focused, directed, specific feedback. Instead of saying, "She was great" or "I certainly did not like his topic," say something like the following:

> "I enjoyed the way she linked her own experiences as a lifeguard to the need for greater water safety," or

> "His discussion of the way accounting students are trained was irrelevant for an audience of non-accounting majors."

Third, feedback should be descriptive rather than evaluative. Researcher Jack Gibbs developed a set of behavioral characteristics that he defined as either supportive or defensive (Tubbs, 2008). When listeners critique speeches, their most productive path of feedback consists of supportive rather than defensive communication. Listeners can create a more supportive environment by providing descriptive comments and suggestions. So instead of saying, "Your reasoning was stupid," you can present something more descriptive, such as, "The statistics you presented for your first point were 10 years old. Is there anything newer out there?" With specific feedback, the speaker could adapt his/her speech the next time.

Finally, feedback given to a speaker should be appropriate. If someone has a facial tic, mentioning that it distracted you is not appropriate. If however, the speaker's hair hung over his eyes to the extent that one could not determine eye contact, a comment to that effect would be helpful. Appropriate also means that a reasonable amount of feedback has been provided. If you can provide two strengths and two weaknesses of a speech, as one listener, that may be sufficient. Providing a crushingly long list of weaknesses would not be appropriate. Too much feedback can be counterproductive. The goal of evaluating speeches is to engage in constructive, manageable feedback.

Five general criteria can be applied to a special occasion speech, an informative speech, or a persuasive speech. We present these with guiding questions that allow the critic to examine both content and delivery. These are *not* presented in order of importance.

❶ Organization
- Was the speech effectively organized?
- Were the general and specific purposes clear and relevant to the assignment?

○ Were the functions of the introduction and conclusion clear (such as gaining attention and previewing)?

○ Were main points clear?

○ Did the speaker use appropriate transitions and internal summaries?

○ Was an organizational pattern clear?

❷ Research/Supporting Material

○ Did the speaker use effective and relevant material to support the thesis statement?

○ Was there evidence of sufficient research?

○ Was supporting material timely?

○ Did the speaker include a variety of supporting material?

○ Was supporting material relevant, helpful, and credible?

○ Were sources integrated into the speech appropriately and cited correctly?

❸ Analysis

○ Was the topic appropriate for the assignment/audience?

○ Was the structure of the speech consistent with the specific purpose?

○ Did the speaker make an effort to analyze the audience and adapt the speech to their needs?

○ Was all evidence presented made relevant and concrete?

○ If used, did presentational aids contribute to the effectiveness of the speech?

❹ Language

○ Did the speaker use clear and accurate language?

○ Did the speaker use various language techniques to engage the listener?

○ Were unfamiliar terms defined?

○ Was language appropriate to the situation and the audience?

❺ Verbal and Nonverbal Delivery

○ Did the speaker appear confident and self-controlled?

○ Did the speaker establish and maintain appropriate eye contact?

○ Were movements and gestures meaningful?

○ Was the quality of the speaker's voice acceptable?

○ Did the speaker pronounce words correctly and articulate effectively?

○ Did the speaker look for and respond to feedback?

○ Did the speaker include relevant emphasis and pauses?

○ Was the speech relatively free of fillers (such as um, er, like, etc.)?

○ Did the speaker use notes effectively?

Use these five criteria as a guide to evaluate your classmates' speeches. When you offer your critique, select a few strengths and a few weaknesses and let the rest go for now. Because student speakers may at times feel vulnerable and defensive in the face of their classmates' feedback, it is important to put them at ease by pointing out *first* what was right with their speech. Then you can offer suggestions for improving their presentation. Instead of saying "Your views on the link between electromagnetic fields and cancer were completely unsupported," you might say: "Your examples were clear and crisp when you talked about how common electric appliances, including coffeemakers, emit potentially dangerous fields." Then you can add, "I don't think you were as clear when you started talking about how these fields can produce changes in body cells. More concrete examples would be helpful." Rather than saying, "Delivery needs work," you could write something more concrete, such as, "You had so much written on your note cards, you didn't look up. Perhaps having less on your note cards would make it easier to look at the class."

Often instructors ask students to use a speech evaluation form similar to the one provided in Figure 4.3. This gives feedback to the speaker on a sliding scale and also gives listeners the opportunity to provide constructive comments.

Using an evaluation form helps you give a speaker constructive criticism. You can change the scale to checks, check minuses and check pluses, or use letter grades, or avoid using a scale altogether. No matter what criteria are used, the goal of evaluating speeches is to provide each speaker with valuable feedback.

Using Technology to Provide Feedback

Traditionally when a speaker is finished, the audience applauds. In some cases, listeners have the opportunity to ask questions. Speakers may also find themselves in situations where feedback response sheets are provided to the audience, and the speaker may read those immediately after the speech or when they are received via the mail. In classroom settings, instructors may provide immediate verbal and/or written feedback, and they may solicit immediate verbal and/or written feedback from members of the class. The amount and structure of feedback varies.

As technology advances, becomes less expensive and more readily available, methods for providing feedback are changing. Student response systems such as TurningPoint are being used in the classroom to engage students. Instructors may include multiple choice questions during a lecture that tests content comprehension, or they may insert opinion questions to gauge the students' attitudes or beliefs about material presented.

FIGURE 4.3 Using a public speaking evaluation form like this one helps you give a speaker constructive and valuable criticism.

Public Speaking Evaluation Form

Speaker: _____ Evaluator: _____ Date: _____

Topic: _____

5 — excellent   4 — very good   3 — satisfactory   2 — fair   1 — unsatisfactory

Rating

Organization

Was the speech effectively organized?   1 2 3 4 5

(effective introduction and conclusion; clear main points; used transitions and internal summaries; pattern related to specific purpose)

Comments:

Research/Supporting Material

Did the speaker use effective and relevant material to support the thesis statement? 1 2 3 4 5

(Evidence of sufficient research; supporting material time, varied, relevant, helpful, credible; sufficient sources; integrated appropriately and cited correctly)

Comments:

Analysis

Were the topic and structure appropriate for the assignment/audience?   1 2 3 4 5

(Clear audience analysis, evidence relevant and concrete; presentational aides contributed to effectiveness)

Comments:

Language

Did the speaker use clear and accurate language?   1 2 3 4 5

(Varied language technique; defined unfamiliar terms; appropriate to the situation)

Comments:

Verbal and Nonverbal Delivery

Did verbal and nonverbal delivery enhance the effectiveness of the speech?   1 2 3 4 5

(Appeared confident, effective eye contact; appropriate gestures and movement; relatively free of nonfluencies; solid pronunciation and diction; good vocal quality; responded to feedback

Comments:

Similarly, a student response system can be used in an academic setting to provide anonymous feedback immediately after the speech. For example, after each speaker concludes, classmates may be asked to identify how effective the speaker's organization was, the extent to which he/she used supporting material, how well the speaker used gestures, movement, eye contact, and so on. Information compiled can be sent immediately to the student.

Positive aspects of the student response system are that all listeners are engaged, and the speaker receives immediate, anonymous, structured feedback from all listeners. Negative aspects are that questions are standardized, responses are a forced-choice of some type, and in depth, immediate feedback does not occur. In a learning environment, anonymous comments can be negative or positive. The instructor, however, can analyze the data from all speakers and check for trends. Perhaps organization is a problem for most speakers in the class, or maybe most speakers do not include sufficient supporting material, and more time needs to be devoted to those aspects of public speaking.

In online public speaking classes, student speeches are often recorded, posted, and reviewed in an invitation-only discussion board. In these cases, students are asked to view and then post feedback on colleagues' speeches. Quickly everyone in class gains from the perspectives of their colleagues. These discussions are particularly fruitful when an emphasis is placed on reinforcing speaker strengths, offering suggestions (as opposed to hammering the speaker over a weak area or flaw), and sharing relevant experiences. When discussions are positive and prosocial, feedback greatly assists speakers as they polish their craft.

Whether in a classroom setting or elsewhere, listeners can also use Twitter, Facebook, blogs, and email to provide feedback. For the speaker, immediate feedback is most useful. Using Twitter is a way to provide quick, concise feedback. Through Facebook and blogging, one can engage many members of an audience within a relatively short time. In whatever form, if the Internet is used to provide feedback to speakers, one needs to remember proper "netiquette." Emails, for example, provide an irreversible paper trail. Once the message is sent, it cannot be retrieved.

When providing feedback via email, being polite and somewhat formal is preferable to being perceived as rude, aloof, or uneducated. Constructive criticism is acceptable; slamming a person is not. Avoid writing in all capital letters. Provide feedback as though you are part of the public speaking process. As such, your credibility is at stake as well. Remember that proper spelling and grammar impact your credibility.

In general, and specifically with social networking sites and blogging, take care not to reveal too much information. Twitter limits your response length, but blogs and Facebook are open ended. Focus on the speaker and the speech, not your own issues and personality. Above all, keep in mind that feedback is meant to identify the speaker's strengths and to encourage improvement.

A Final Note About Self-Evaluation

Just as editing your own writing can be tedious and difficult, so is evaluating your own speech. Often lacking in objectivity, we tend to be hypercritical at times and completely unaware of our errors at other times. This is why critiques from your classmates are so helpful. As you process comments you receive from your listeners, focus on the content, not how it was said or written. Even severe feedback may hold helpful information if you look closely. Try to recognize the important aspects of any criticism, but do not feel you need to attend to every comment.

While our first reaction after giving a speech might be to look at the comments others wrote, we encourage you to first reflect on how *you* think you did. What *do you believe* were your strengths and weaknesses? Did you think you had appropriate organization, adequate research, and effective delivery? Were you fluent? Enthusiastic? What positive aspects of your speech should you keep in mind for the next speech, and what should you try to avoid? Set a few goals for yourself, and view each speech as a learning experience.

Summary

Good listening skills are important for two reasons. First, by understanding the listening needs of your audience, you have a better chance of developing and delivering successful speeches. Second, an understanding of the factors affecting listening enables you to monitor your own listening habits and helps you evaluate the speeches of others. Studies have shown that although we spend a great deal of time listening, most of us are not good listeners. Listening is a complex activity that involves four separate stages: you sense the information from its source through the physiological process of hearing; you interpret the message by attaching your own meaning to the speaker's words; you evaluate what your hear by judging the worth of the speaker's message and deciding its importance to you; and you respond to the speaker's message through feedback.

You can improve your listening skills by preparing yourself to listen, minimizing listening barriers and leaving distractions behind, by not making snap judgments, listening first for content and second for delivery, becoming an effective note taker, being an active listener, and by providing feedback. In speech class use your listening skills to evaluate the speeches of your classmates. It is important to learn the art of constructive criticism in order to encourage the speaker.

Constructive criticism is helpful to all speakers. When you evaluate another's speech, consider addressing five criteria: organization, research and supporting material, analysis, language, and verbal and nonverbal delivery. No matter what technology is used, remember that speakers need constructive feedback.

Listeners can provide immediate feedback through a student response system, or they may provide feedback through emails, blogs, or classroom or Web-based discussion boards. Feedback can also be given through Twitter and Facebook. As a listener providing feedback, we strive to acknowledge the speaker's strengths, indicate areas for improvement by offering specific suggestions, and share our own relevant experiences with the speaker. When done right, mediated feedback can be fast and helpful. After each of your own speeches, spend some time on self-evaluation, reflect on your own strengths and weaknesses, and set goals for future speeches.

Discussion Starters

1. The chapter discusses how much time we spend speaking, listening, reading, and writing. Do you agree with those percentages? How much time do you think students spend on Facebook, using the Internet, texting, tweeting, and talking on cell phones?

2. What role do our emotions play in listening, and how are they related to our ability to think about and analyze a message? Can we suspend our feelings while listening to a speaker? Why or why not?

3. Why is preparation important in listening? How would you prepare to listen to:

   a. a speech on a topic about which you have strong, negative feelings?

   b. a political campaign speech delivered by a candidate you support?

   c. a speech on a crisis that affects your life?

   d. a lecture on a topic that interests but does not excite you?

4. From a listener's point of view, what is the relationship between the content and delivery of a speech? How does a dynamic delivery influence your opinion of the speaker's message? Compare this to your reaction to a flat, uninspired delivery.

5. Why is it common for people to focus on delivery over content? What steps can you take to avoid this bias?

6. After looking at the list of criteria for evaluating speeches, how would you order them by perceived importance if the feedback were for your speech?

7. If you were to provide feedback using some form of new technology, what would you find the easiest? Most helpful to the speaker? Least effective?

References

AICPA. (2005). *Highlighted Responses from the Association for Accounting Marketing Survey. Creating the Future Agenda for the Profession—Managing Partner Perspective.* Retrieved April 8, 2005 from www.aicpa.org/pubs/tpcpa/feb2001/hilight.htm.

Adams, W. C., & Cox, E. Sam. (2010). The Teaching of Listening as an Integral Part of an Oral Activity: An Examination of Public-Speaking Texts. *The International Journal of Listening, 24,* 89–105.

Adler, M. J. (1983). *How to Speak, How to Listen.* New York: Macmillan.

Bommelje, R., Houston, J. M., & Smither, R. (2003). Personality Characteristics of Effective Listeners: A Five-Factor Perspective. *International Journal of Listening, 17,* 32–46.

Botella, C., Gallego, M. J., Garcia-Palacios, A., Guillen, V., Baños, R. M., Quero, S. et al. (2010). *Cyberpsychology, Behavior, and Social Networking, 13*(4), 407–421. doi:10.1089/cyber.2009.0224.

Clark, A. J. (1989). Communication Confidence and Listening Competence: An Investigation of the Relationships of Willingness to Communicate, Communication Apprehension, and Receiver Apprehension to Comprehension of Content and Emotional Meaning in Spoken Messages. *Communication Education, 38*(3), 237–249.

Festinger, L. (1957). *A Theory of Cognitive Dissonance.* Palo Alto, CA: Stanford University Press.

Friedman, P. G. (1986). *Listening Processes: Attention, Understanding, Evaluation* 2nd Ed., (pp. 6–15). Washington, DC: National Education Association.

Haas, J. W., & Arnold, C. L. (1995). An Examination of the Role of Listening in Judgments of Communication Competence in Co-Workers. *Journal of Business Communication, 32*(2), 123–139.

Janusik, L. A., & Wolvin, A. D. (2006). 24 Hours in a Day. A Listening Update to the Time Studies. Paper presented at the meeting of the *International Listening Association*, Salem, OR.

Job Outlook Survey. (2011). National Association of Colleges and Employers (NACE). Retrieved from naceweb.org/press/frequently_asked_questions.aspx.

Johnson, S. D., & Bechler, C. (1998). Examining the Relationship Between Listening Effectiveness and Leadership Emergence: Perceptions, Behaviors, and Recall. *Small Group Research, 29*(4), 452–471.

Klerk, W. G., & Maritz, A. C. (1997). A Test of Graham's Stock Selection Criteria. *Investment Analysis Journal, 45,* 26–33. Retrieved July 27, 2011 from www.iassa.co.za/articles/045_1997_03.pdf.

Leavitt, D. (1989, July 9). *The Way I Live Now. The New York Times Magazine*, p. 30.

Lewis, T. R., & Nichols, R. (1965). *Speaking and Listening: A Guide to Effective Oral-Aural Communication.* Dubuque, IA: W. C. Brown.

Naistadt, I. (2004). *Speak Without Fear.* New York: HarperCollins.

Nichols, R. G. (1961). Do We Know How to Listen? Practical Helps in a Modern Age. *Speech Teacher, March,* 118–124.

Priorities of Listening Research: Four Interrelated Initiatives. (2008). A White Paper sponsored by the Research Committee of the International Listening Association, 1–27. Accessed August 2, 2011 from www. listen.org/Resources/Documents/White_Paper_PrioritiesResearch.pdf.

Timm, S., & Schroeder, B. L. (2000). Listening/Nonverbal Communication Training. *International Journal of Listening, 14,* 109–128.

Tubbs, S. (2008). A *Systems Approach to Small Group Communication.* New York: McGraw-Hill.

Wolf, F. L., Marsnik, N. C., Taceuy, W. S., & Nichols, R. G. (1983). *Perceptive Listening.* New York: Holt, Rinehart and Winston.

Part

II

PREPARING YOUR SPEECH

© Jaimie Duplass, 2012. Under license from Shutterstock, Inc.

Chapter

5

> *"Eloquence not only considers the* subject, *but also the* speaker *and the* hearers, *and both the subject and the speaker for the sake of the hearers."*
>
> George Campbell

Chapter 5: Being Audience-Centered

Knowing your audience is the key to presenting a successful speech. This chapter discusses how to adapt to different audiences and situations. It explains how to create the speaker-audience connection by incorporating humor into your speech, encouraging participation, and quickly getting to the point of your speech.

Student Learning Objectives:

- ○ Students will be able to know their audience
- ○ Students will be able to identify and explain how to adapt to different audiences and situations
- ○ Students will be able to explain how to create the speaker-audience connection

BEING AUDIENCE-CENTERED

adapting

attitudes

audience-centered

beliefs

demographics

ethnocentrism

fixed-alternative
  questions

open-ended questions

psychographics

scale questions

stereotypes

values

At the end of the second week of public speaking, two students approached their teaching assistant, Mr. Wyckoff, and tentatively asserted themselves:

> "Why do you use so many baseball examples?" Liz asked. "I know it's the national pastime and all that, and I realize that the San Francisco Giants just won the World Series, but neither of us *care* for the sport."

> "Yeah," Sarah added, "we don't get all the references, and to be perfectly honest, we lose interest and start tuning you out."

> Mr. Wyckoff, momentarily caught off guard at the realization that the whole world did not share his enthusiasm for the sport, explained, "Oh, I've been involved with baseball since I first played t-ball, and I've umpired for the last 10 years. But thanks for the heads-up. I'll work on variety," adding with a laugh, "assuming there *is* life outside of baseball."

Mr. Wyckoff was able to make adjustments to his lecture by incorporating a variety of examples that related to his audience, and he received more positive reinforcement from his class as a whole.

Whether in a large auditorium, a corporate board room, or a classroom, audiences are usually self-centered. Listeners want to know "What's in it for me?" That is, they want to understand what they can learn from a speech or how they can take action that will, in some way, enhance their lives. If you show your audience you understand their needs and help them achieve their goals, they will want to listen. Being audience-centered and adapting to their needs are critical factors in creating effective presentations. These two concepts are the focus of this chapter.

Know Your Audience

How do you prepare and deliver a speech that will mean enough to your audience to capture their attention and convince them to listen? Begin by learning as much as you can about your listeners so you can identify and focus on their concerns.

Audience-Centeredness

Making your intended audience central in your message formation will result in a stronger, more tailored speech that resonates with your listeners. This is desirable because you can feel and respond positively to the energy and enthusiasm that a receptive and captivated audience exudes. In essence, if you are audience centered, both you and your audience benefit greatly.

Early in your speech, telling your audience what's in it for them and letting them know they were front and center in your mind as you worked on your message is a great way to help establish your credibility, common ground, and build their interest in your topic. Knowing what your audience needs is the first step to being audience-centered.

Audience Analysis

Jon Favreau, who is credited with creating Obama's campaign slogan, "Yes we can," assumed the position of director of speechwriting when Obama took office. Before being hired, the then–presidential candidate asked, "What is your theory of speechwriting?" Favreau admitted:

> I have no theory. But when I saw you at the [2004] convention, you basically told a story about your life from beginning to end, and it was a story that fit with the larger American narrative. People applauded not because you wrote an applause line but because you touched something in the party and the country that people had not touched before. Democrats haven't had that in a long time (Quoted from Richard Wolfe, *Newsweek*, 2008).

Favreau's observation serves to confirm that Obama's approach to the 2004 speech was audience-centered. The speech "touched" people, both at the convention and those watching the proceedings.

In discussing the primaries, Favreau shared his impression of Obama's campaign speech:

> The message out of Iowa was one of unity and reaching out across party lines. We knew we were going to do well with independents, young people and first-time voters. We knew the message was similar to what he said at the 2004 convention.

In creating a message of "unity" and "reaching out across party lines," Favreau identifies the targeted audience characteristics: independents, young people, and first-time voters. Obama's success in the primaries as well as the general election confirms his ability during that campaign to analyze his audience effectively. (For more about Jon Favreau, see **BTW: Are You Like Jon Favreau?**)

This youthful protégé may be more like you than you think. He writes his speeches in Starbucks, often staying up until 3:00 a.m., sipping Red Bulls and espressos. He enjoys playing *Rock Band* in his leisure time and has had inappropriate pictures of him at a party posted on Facebook. He was valedictorian of his college class, a debater, active in student politics and student government, and is a perfectionist. Favreau and President Carter's writer, James Fallows, share the distinction of being the youngest speechwriters in the history of the White House at age 27 (Pilkington, 2009).

Glossary

Demographics Age, gender, race and ethnicity, education/knowledge, group affiliation, occupational group, socioeconomic status, religious background, political affiliation, and geographic identifiers of listeners.

Psychographics The lifestyle choices, attitudes, beliefs, and values of your listeners.

You need not be a presidential speechwriter to understand your audience. All speakers can create a sketch of their listeners by analyzing them in terms of key demographic and psychographic characteristics.

Demographics include age, gender, race and ethnicity, education/knowledge, group affiliation, occupational group, socioeconomic status, religious background, political affiliation, and geographic identifiers. Depending on your general and specific purposes, certain demographics may be more important than others for any given speech.

Psychographics include lifestyle choices, attitudes, beliefs, and values of your listeners. In many cases these are more difficult to ascertain unless the audience is known for their attitudes, beliefs, and values. Information that emerges from demographic and psychographic analyses is the raw material for a successful speaker–audience connection (Woodward & Denton, 2004).

Demographic Analysis

We need a good fit within the various aspects of our speech, such as supporting material, thesis and main points, and audience characteristics. Depending on the speaking situation, ascertaining demographics may be easily accomplished. At your disposal are up to four approaches to determine audience characteristics. First, you may make some assumptions about the audience as a whole. If you were asked to give a speech on patriotism, think about the differences in demographics between the Daughters of the American Revolution and Vietnam Veterans Against the War. We can make certain logical assumptions about each of these audience's demographics; in this instance, that includes age, gender, and group affiliation.

Second, you may have the opportunity to observe the audience in advance and learn first-hand what their demographics are. Third, you could interview someone who knows the audience well. Finally, a fourth strategy involves creating a simple audience analysis survey that you can adapt. Later in this chapter we cover types of questions you might use to uncover demographics. Whether through knowledge of the group the audience represents, direct observation, interview, or survey, it's important to gain insight into your audience before you construct your speech. Ten key demographics are identified as follows.

❶ Age. Try to determine the age of your audience and if there is a large or a small variation in age. Examples and stories you provide need to relate to your audience. Think about how you might foster a feeling of inclusion among all ages present. Ask yourself, "How does my age potentially impact my audience's perceptions of me?" Perhaps certain stereotypes exist based solely on their assessment of your age. If you believe your age may influence their response to you, reflect on how you might make these assumptions work in your favor instead of against you.

One brave student, Vicky, was enraged about proposed tuition increases and decided to speak to the college's board of trustees about the issue. Knowing well that the board was made up of individuals who were on average 30 years her senior, Vicky used examples and illustrations appropriate for their age demographic, including a brief reference to the GI Bill and The Great Society, as well as an impassioned anecdote about a share-cropper family whose son would change the world for migratory farmers: Cesar Chavez. Vicky's message was better received because her audience could identify with her examples. Her tactic was unexpected and appreciated by an audience who thought they were about to hear a whining diatribe with little real substance. Vicky was able to make age-related assumptions work in her favor and serve her ultimate goals for speaking.

When taking into consideration your age and the age(s) of your audience, we suggest the following:

○ **Avoid assumptions about the average age of your audience.** If you are speaking to a group of students, do not assume they will all be in your age bracket. Today, millions of nontraditional students are enrolled in four-year colleges. On any campus, you will meet 40-year-old sophomores seeking a new career or returning to school after their children are grown and 60-year-old freshmen returning because they love learning. Whereas we know that Vietnam Veterans Against the War must fit into a certain age group, to be a member of the Daughters of the American Revolution, a female must be 18 or older. You would need to find other ways to discover the age range of this audience.

○ **Focus on your speech, not your age.** In many cases, there is no reason to bring attention to your age. Doing so may detract from your message. Business consultant Edith Weiner started to deliver speeches to senior-level executives at the age of 23. "I was much younger than people thought I was going to be," said Weiner.

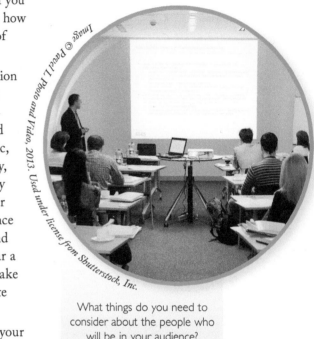

Image © Pavel L Photo and Video, 2013. Used under license from Shutterstock, Inc.

What things do you need to consider about the people who will be in your audience?

"When I got up to speak, they didn't know what to make of me." Weiner's response was to focus on her message. "If I did well in the first three minutes, not only did I surprise the audience, I created fans. Expectations were so low that when I came across as confident and funny and comfortable, the audience was hooked into the rest of my speech" (personal interview, 1989). Her speech may have come across differently if she had apologized for her youth or made excuses.

○ **Avoid dating yourself with references or language.** If you are addressing a group of teenagers on the topic of popular culture, talk about their current favorite rock group, not the New Kids on the Block. If you are addressing a group of middle-aged executives, do not assume that they know what college students are thinking. Avoid purposefully using current terms or phrases that might come off as sounding patronizing and condescending.

❷ Gender. Some topics may have broader appeal to men, in general, while others may be of greater interest to women, in general. One of your authors, Mark, was asked to speak to a group of insurance sales associates. He made a false assumption that the group would likely be nearly all males, when in fact the audience was overwhelmingly female. He adjusted his message to cover a review of the research on women in financial industries and sales while sacrificing a few football analogies. While some of the women might have been interested in football, all were interested in how their gender was performing in their chosen career field. Can you imagine the disaster this would have been if Mark had not adjusted his speech? His sexist assumption could have easily alienated his audience.

Gender role differences do exist, however, and generalizations based on these differences are not necessarily wrong. Therefore, if you are addressing a group of young men who you know are likely to enjoy professional sports, it's fair to use a sports analogy to make your point—not because you are a fan but because talking about the Cleveland Browns or the Dallas Cowboys helps you connect with your listeners.

Consider the composition of your next audience. Is it mixed or is there a majority of males or females? Also, while we do not identify sexual orientation as one of the 10 demographics, it is closely related. Every audience will likely contain members who are gay, lesbian, bisexual, or transgendered. Maintaining this awareness by using sensitive and inclusive language and examples goes a long way toward fostering common ground, inclusiveness, and a more positive response your message. Language sensitivity and inclusiveness are topics that are covered in greater detail in Chapter 9.

Regarding gender, we do suggest that you *structure your speech so you are inclusive.* Avoid unfairly categorizing or stereotyping members of the audience. For example, airlines no longer have "stewardesses," but "flight attendants." "Car salesmen" are no longer only men; that term has been replaced by "sales associates." Departments on college and university campuses are no longer headed by a "chairman" but rather by a "chair" or a "chairperson." For the most part, speakers should avoid relying on the masculine pronoun and find ways to include men *and* women in their audiences.

❸ **Race and ethnicity.** Long ago, the image of the United States as a melting pot gave way to the image of a rainbow of diversity—an image in which African Americans, Hispanics, Asians, Greeks, Arabs, and Europeans define themselves by their racial and ethnic ties as well as by their ties to the United States. Within this diversity are cultural beliefs and traditions that may be different from your own.

Even now, over half a century after the most sweeping civil rights legislation in American history was passed by Congress and signed into law by the President, racial issues and differences spawn controversy. In 2005, Hurricane Katrina devastated much of the southern shoreline of America. Charges were made by a variety of leaders essentially declaring that if the majority of the population of New Orleans had been white, there would have been much greater and quicker efforts to move citizens to safe places with ample food and water. (For more on civil rights, see **BTW: Civil Rights Legislation Timeline.**)

If you deliver a speech on the topic of communication failures and the devastation of Hurricane Katrina, you need take into account the considerable problems faced by black citizens in New Orleans and along the southern shoreline. If you do not, you are likely to fail in achieving your specific purpose for your speech and you will make your presentation unacceptable to some of your listeners. This is not to suggest that you change your views if they are carefully conceived and supported. However, if your topic includes racial and ethnic issues that you fail to acknowledge during your speech, you can expect members of your audience to be offended or dismissive.

While most of us can grasp the concept of race, given that it has a biological basis, understanding ethnicity is somewhat more difficult. A Latino speaker recently noted in his opening comments to a largely Anglo Midwestern audience that he was pleased to be the lone representative from the "real south." His comment brought both laughter and an appreciation for his unique point of view. He made the most of an obvious contrast with his audience (ethnicity) by addressing it quickly and then dismissing it with humor. Notice, though, that he

BTW!

Researchers Brunner and Haney (2007) present a timeline for the civil rights movement starting in 1948 when President Truman signed an executive order stating "It is hereby declared to be the policy of the President that there shall be equality of treatment and opportunity for all persons in the armed services without regard to race, color, religion, or national origin." Following are several other landmark events:

1954–Segregation in schools ends

1955–Emmett Till murdered in hate crime

1955–Rosa Parks goes to front of bus

1964–President Johnson signs Civil Rights Act of 1964

1965–President Johnson requires "affirmative action" in hiring government employees

1967–Interracial marriage ruled legal

1968–End of discrimination in the sale, rent, and financing of housing

1971–Integration via busing is upheld as constitutional

1988–Civil Rights Restoration Act expands reach of nondiscrimination laws to private sector

Read more: Civil Rights Movement Timeline (14th Amendment, 1964 Act, Human Rights Law) — Infoplease.com www.infoplease.com/spot/civilrightstimeline1.html.

Glossary

Stereotypes Related to race, ethnicity, or nationality, even if these groups are not present in your audience.

Ethnocentrism The belief that one's own culture is superior to other cultures.

left it at that. Going too far with racial and ethnic comments can create more tension and discomfort. Noting the obvious is welcomed by audiences, as long as it is handled deftly and with tact.

As you develop your speech, we ask that you avoid invoking **stereotypes** related to race, ethnicity, or nationality, even if these groups are not present in your audience. Even when couched in humor, such comments are deeply offensive and unethical. Appreciation of different people and ways can help you avoid several critical errors in your speech. Any of these gaffes will surely compromise the connection you are trying to create.

Understand also, that **ethnocentrism**, which is the belief that one's own culture is superior to other cultures, comes into play when we express a bias for the way we do things. Unfortunately, some or many individuals who might be identified as ethnocentric have little experience with other cultures. Therefore, an accurate comparison is difficult to make. A speaker should try to avoid being offensive or unfair by examining his/her language usage as well as the examples, stories, and illustrations he/she is contemplating incorporating into a speech.

❹ **Education/knowledge.** Are the members of your audience high school or college graduates, experts with doctorates in the field, or freshmen taking their first course? Knowing the educational level of your audience will aid in the construction of your message. If you're speaking to elementary students about Queen Elizabeth I, you can safely assume they need to be provided with some historical background. But to a group of European historians such information would not be necessary.

Many topics do not guarantee the same degree of audience interest because listeners may believe they've heard all that can be said about a topic. Jenny Clanton (1989), a student at Southeastern Illinois College, skirted this pitfall when she chose to speak on the *Challenger* disaster. She involved her audience through an unconventional approach:

> On January 28, 1986, the American space program suffered the worst disaster in its more than 30-year history. The entire world was shocked when the space shuttle *Challenger* exploded seconds after lift-off, claiming the lives of seven brave astronauts and crippling our ... space agenda. I suppose the oldest cliché in our culture, spoken on battlegrounds and indeed virtually anywhere Americans die, is, "We must press forward so we can say they did not die in vain." Rest assured: They didn't. The deaths of our seven astronauts probably saved the lives of untold thousands of Americans.
>
> For, you see, if the O-rings had not failed on January 28, 1986, but rather on May 20, 1987, the next scheduled shuttle launch, in the words of Dr. John Gofman, professor emeritus at the University of California at Berkeley, you could have "kissed Florida good-bye." Because the next shuttle, the one that was to have explored the atmosphere of Jupiter, was to carry 47 pounds of Plutonium 238, which is, according to Dr. Gofman, the most toxic substance on the face of the earth.
>
> From *Winning Orations of the Interstate Oratorical Association* by J. Clanton. Copyright © 1988 by Interstate Oratorical Association. Reprinted by permission.

Rather than focus specifically on the *Challenger* tragedy, she made reference to it, and then moved to what might have been an even more deadly catastrophe. Ideally, your audience will have some knowledge of your subject matter on which your message will build. It may be more difficult to develop a speech for an audience that has no knowledge of your topic, since they may not have much interest. To determine your audience's knowledge of your topic and desire for additional information, you might explore surveying, interviewing, and observing them.

In addition to determining what type of background information or explanation is needed, another consideration is language. You want to speak *to* your audience, not over their heads or at such a basic level that you sound condescending. We have the following two suggestions that highlight how important it is to analyze your audience's needs:

○ **Do not assume that expertise in one area necessarily means expertise in others.** For example, if you are a stockbroker delivering a speech to a group of scientists about investment opportunities, you may have to define the rules that govern even simple stock trades. Although the more educated your audience, the more sophisticated these explanations can be, explanations must still be included for your speech to make sense.

○ **Be careful about assuming what your audience knows—and does not know—about technical topics.** Mention a server to people who know nothing about computers, and they may be baffled. Define it for a group of computer experts, and they will wonder why you were asked to speak to them. In both cases, you run the risk of losing your audience; people who are confused or who know much more about a subject may simply stop listening.

⑤ Group affiliation. Listeners may identify themselves as members of formal and informal interest groups. An informal interest group generally doesn't require signing up or paying for membership, or making any type of formal commitment. Examples include YouTube watchers, Starbucks customers, and residents of an inner-city neighborhood. A formal interest group usually requires an official commitment, such as signing a membership form or paying dues. Examples include members of Future Farmers of America, the Chamber of Commerce, or a LISTSERV on alternative treatments for Alzheimer's.

Members of your audience may be members of labor organizations or service clubs. Perhaps they volunteer for a local or national organization. They may identify themselves as being Republican, Democratic, Independent, Green, or a member of the Tea Party. Maybe they are active members of the Chinese Student and Scholars Association on your campus. If they belong to any of these groups, these affiliations may well affect choices they make.

If you are addressing members of the Sierra Club, you can be sure the group has a keen awareness of environmental issues. Similarly, if you are addressing an exercise class at the local Y, you can be sure that physical fitness is a priority of everyone in the room. It is important to know something about the group you are speaking to so you can adapt your message to their interest. (For more information about the transition from YMCA to the shortened "Y," see **BTW: "The Y"**.)

Our main suggestion with regard to group affiliation is to *avoid assuming that all members of a group have similar attitudes.* All members of the International Students group on campus do not share the same set of values or beliefs. They represent different countries with different political and religious practices. Their one shared demographic is that they come from a country outside of the United States. While

BTW!

"The Y"

New times, new name. As times change, so to do names and organizational values. Formerly the YMCA (Young Men's Christian Association) and its female counterpart, YWCA, "the name change reflects contemporary ways of talking about the organization. The Y's former logo had been in place since 1967. The refreshed logo, with its multiple color options and new, contemporary look, better reflects the vibrancy of the Y and the diversity of the communities it serves. The new logo's bold, active and welcoming shape symbolizes the Y's commitment to personal and social progress" (*The Y*, July 12, 2010).

our two-party system in the United States classifies individuals as either Democrat or Republican, we know that there are conservatives and liberals in both parties. Knowing group affiliation may help us construct our main points and identify appropriate supporting material. We need to take caution, however, and avoid stereotyping the group.

6. **Occupational groups.** You may find an occasion that involves speaking to a specific occupational group, such as teachers, students, doctors, lawyers, union representatives, miners, or factory workers. Occupational information can often tell you a great deal about listeners' attitudes. An audience of physicians may be unwilling to accept proposed legislation that would strengthen a patient's right to choose a personal physician if it also makes it easier for patients to sue for malpractice. A legislative speaker might need to find creative ways to convince the doctors that the new law would be in the best interests of both doctors and patients.

Knowledge of what your listeners do for a living may also tell you the type of vocabulary appropriate for the occasion. If you are addressing a group of newspaper editors, you can use terms common to the newspaper business without bothering to define them. Do not use job-related jargon indiscriminately, but rather, use it to your advantage.

When conducting your audience analysis, try to determine what your listeners do for a living. The speaking occasion often makes this clear. You may be invited by a group of home builders to speak about the dangers of radon, or a group of insurance agents may ask you to talk about the weather conditions associated with hurricanes. Knowing the occupations of your audience may lead you to decide not only what type of information to include, but what specific statistics, examples, or illustrations would be most effective for the particular group.

© Monkey Business Images, 2012. Under license from Shutterstock, Inc.

Knowing your audience's occupation can give you ideas of how to tailor your speech.

Our suggestion regarding occupational groups is to *avoid too little analysis or too much analysis of the importance of occupational affiliation to your audience members*. When you ask people to describe themselves, what is the first thing they say? It might be "I'm a white female," "I'm a gay activist," "I'm the mother of four young children," or "I'm a lawyer." Some people *define* themselves by their occupation; others view their jobs as a way to feed a family and maintain a reasonable lifestyle. By determining how important the occupational group characteristic is to your audience, you can create an on-target message that meets their needs.

7 Socioeconomic status. Depending on the situation, it may be difficult to determine whether members of your audience earn more than $100,000 a year or less than $30,000. However, this demographic characteristic may influence how you develop your speech and create common ground with your audience. When Rabbi Harold Kushner (2002) talks to groups about his book *When All You've Ever Wanted Isn't Enough*, he learns the group's socioeconomic status in advance. He explains:

> Generally, if I'm addressing affluent business executives, I concentrate on the downside of economic success and on the spiritual nature of affluence. When the group is less affluent, I talk about learning to cope with economic failure and with the feeling of being left behind.

This statement illustrates how one person adapts to his audience based on socioeconomic status. Knowing whether the economic situation has changed recently for your audience or whether there is likely to be another change soon may influence your approach to your topic. For example, when speaking to a group of incoming freshmen at a public university in 2012, it might be wise to spend more time on financial aid than a speaker would have in 2002. Topics such as welfare, socialized medicine, and social security will be approached differently based on whether your audience comes from a wealthy background or one of poverty.

We suggest you be *mindful of your audience's financial status while framing your message*. Giving a speech linking high credit card debt to filing for bankruptcy would need to be adapted to an audience that has no debt. However, those facing financial ruin do not need to hear a "holier-than-thou" lecture on the dangers of credit card debt.

8 Religious background. According to the article "Where We Stand on Faith," many people in the United States consider themselves spiritual and religious (*Newsweek*, September 6, 2005). Suppose your topic is in-vitro fertilization, one of medicine's generally effective techniques to help infertile couples have children. Your presentation goes well, but the faces of your listeners suggest you hit a nerve.

Without realizing it, you may have offended your audience by failing to deal with the potential religious implications of such procedures.

Speakers seldom intend to offend their audiences. However, when it comes to religion, speakers can offend unwittingly. Please consider that *religious beliefs may also define moral attitudes.* When speaking on issues such as abortion, premarital sex, birth control, gay marriage, and gays in the military, we risk alienating our audience. By no means are we suggesting you avoid such topics. However, failing to acknowledge and address the religious beliefs of your listeners when your speech concerns a sensitive topic sets up barriers to communication that may be difficult to overcome.

So, what do you do if you are religious? What if your comments are framed in that specific moral attitude? Explaining your frame of reference and personal biases is ethical and builds rapport, even with those who don't share your convictions. Audiences expect and respect honesty. One student handled her religious frame of reference directly: "Now I am a Christian, and the in-vitro procedure I received was in a Catholic hospital. I understand there are many other ways to look at the ethics of my decision, but I want to put that aside for now and focus only on the process." Where possible, remove stumbling blocks for your audience by being forthright and truthful about your own religious convictions while also communicating tolerance and open-mindedness to other perspectives.

⑨ Political affiliation. In an election year, our interest in political affiliation is heightened. Whether you self-identify as Libertarian, a mainstream Democrat or Republican, or a member of the Tea Party or the Green Party, political affiliation may influence how you respond to a given speaker. If you are fundraising for the homeless, you will probably give a different speech to a group with liberal beliefs than to a group of conservatives. Consider these variations of a message based on political affiliation:

To a group of political liberals

We are a nation of plenty—a nation in which begging seems as out of place as snow in July. Yet our cities are filled with poor citizens who have no food or lodging. They are the have-nots in a nation of haves. I ask for your help tonight because we are a nation built on helping one another escape from poverty. No matter how hard you work to cement your own success, you will never achieve the American Dream if one person is left on the streets without a home.

To a group of political conservatives

It is in your best interest to give money to homeless causes. I'm not talking about handouts on the street but money that goes into putting a roof over people's heads and into job training. In the long run, giving people dignity by giving them a home and training them for productive work will mean fewer people on welfare and lower taxes. Is it a leap of faith to see this connection or just plain common business sense?

Acknowledging political differences has been important in America since its founding. You will not compromise your values when you accept the fact that political differences exist. Rather, you will take the first step in using these differences as the starting point for communication.

We cannot stress enough that *all members of a particular party do not share the same attitudes, beliefs, and values.* Find out how to connect to the diversity of your audience. Your speech as a conservative Republican addressing a group of conservative Republicans will sound different than when addressing an audience that represents the Republican spectrum.

⑩ **Geographic identifiers.** We have a variety of ways to discuss geographic identifiers. One is directional differences, such as north/south or east/west. Think how an audience comprised largely of people from the Deep South might vary from an audience of individuals from the Northwest. A second geographic identifier is upstate vs. downstate. For example, Illinois is divided into two general areas, Chicago and Downstate (everything south of Chicago). This also alludes to the geographic identifier of urban versus rural. You may have an audience that lives in the same community, or you may have an audience that represents a number of communities. A third geographic identifier relates to terrain, such living near mountains, lakes, oceans, or as one of your authors describes herself, living near corn and bean fields and being a "flatlander."

Your authors suggest that understanding geographical identifiers as well as *focusing your message as much as possible on geographical areas of concern will enhance your message's impact and your credibility with your audience.* You may need to adapt your message to accommodate not only differences in language, speech rate, and references, but also specific interests and issues.

Psychographic Analysis

Psychographics refer to the behaviors, attitudes, beliefs, and values of your listeners. Although an analysis of demographic characteristics will give you some clue as to how your listeners are likely to respond to your speech, it will not tell you anything about the speaking occasion, why people have come together as an audience, how they feel about your topic, or about you as a speaker. This information emerges from the second stage of analysis—psychographics—and centers on the speaking situation specifically.

Behaviors. Your lifestyle choices say something about you. Do you walk, bike, drive, or take public transportation to work? Perhaps you avoid driving because walking and biking are "greener" and viewed as healthier. If you choose to be a city dweller who lives in a 22nd-story studio apartment, you probably have less inclination to experience nature than if you opt to live on a 50-acre farm in Vermont. If you put in 12-hour days at the office, your career is probably more important to you than if you choose to work part-time. Behavioral choices are linked to the attitudes, beliefs, and values of your listeners.

Attitudes, beliefs, and values. **Attitudes** are predispositions to act in a particular way that influences our response to objects, events, and situations. Attitudes tend to be long lasting, but can change under pressure. They are often, but not always, related to behavior. If I like vegetables, I am likely to bring a vegetable tray to a party. If I don't like big business, I'm less likely to shop at Walmart. Someone who doesn't care about the environment is less likely to recycle.

Beliefs represent a mental and emotional acceptance of information. They are judgments about the truth or the probability that a statement is correct. Beliefs are formed from experience and learning; they are based on what we perceive to be accurate. To be an effective speaker, you must analyze the beliefs of your audience in the context of your message. For example, if you are dealing with people who believe that working hard is the only way to get ahead, you will have trouble convincing them to take time off between semesters. Your best hope is to persuade them that time off will make them more productive and goal directed when they return. By citing authorities and providing examples of other students who have successfully followed this course, you have a chance of changing their mind-set.

Values are deep-seated abstract judgments about what is important to us. According to Rokeach's (1968) seminal work, we have both terminal and instrumental values. *Terminal values* are those we would like to achieve within our lifetime. These include national security, family security, equality, and freedom. *Instrumental values* help us achieve the terminal values, such as intellect, ambition, self-control, responsibility, and independence. Values separate the worthwhile from the worthless and determine what we consider moral, desirable, important, beautiful, and worth living or dying for.

An audience of concerned students that values the importance of education might express this value in the belief that "a college education should be available to all qualified students" and the attitude that "the state legislature should pass a tuition reduction plan for every state college." If you address this audience, you can use this attitude as the basis for your plea that students picket the State Capitol in support of the tuition reduction plan. Understanding your listeners' attitudes, beliefs, and values helps you put your message in the most effective terms.

Glossary

Attitudes Predispositions to act in a particular way that influences our response to objects, events, and situations.

Beliefs Represent a mental and emotional acceptance of information. They are judgments about the truth or the probability that a statement is correct.

Values Socially shared ideas about what is good, right, and desirable; deep-seated abstract judgments about what is important to us.

Adapting to Different Audiences and Situations

Throughout this chapter and this textbook, you will read the words "it may" or "it might," or "perhaps." We are equivocal because audiences behave differently and have different expectations depending on their characteristics *and* the context or situation. An effective speaker adapts his/her message based on audience characteristics, both demographic and psychographic, and the situation that brings the audience together. A politician may give a speech in New York City, then tweak it before appearing at a gathering in America's heartland. Adapting a speech may be easy or difficult. In your public speaking class, it is important to keep in mind that your teacher is part of the audience. As such, you might need to make a few minor changes to be inclusive.

At a funeral, we know the mood is somber, but depending on the person being remembered and the individuals congregated, there may also be smiles and laughter. The circumstances may call for fond memory of a person's idiosyncrasies, or in case of a tragic death, laughter may be inappropriate. Also, if seven people are giving eulogies, then each one should be relatively brief, but if only two or three are speaking, more time can be allotted to each person. At a political rally, a speech given to an audience that has just seen its candidate soundly defeated would sound different than a speech given by someone on behalf of the winning candidate.

Interest Level and Expectations

Discovering the interest level in your topic and your audience's expectations helps you adapt to your audience. Interest level often determines audience response. High school seniors are more likely than high school freshmen to listen when someone from the financial aid office at the local college discusses scholarships, grants, and financial aid possibilities. People who fly frequently are less likely to pay attention to the flight attendant's description of safety procedures than individuals who have seldom flown. We tend to pay attention to things that are timely and that we know will affect us.

Experienced and successful professionals who speak frequently to audiences around the country collect information that will tell them who their listeners are and what they want and expect from their presentations. Robert Waterman Jr., coauthor of the successful book *In Search of Excellence,* indicates he spends a day or two before a speech observing his corporate audience at work. What he learns helps him address the specific concerns of his listeners (Kiechel, 1987). Waterman achieved success as a professional speaker in part because he assumed little about the characteristics of his prospective audience. To analyze an audience, questionnaires and observation are techniques that can be used successfully.

Accessing Audience Information

To adapt our message to a particular audience within a specific situation, we need to gather information. Three ways to access your audience's demographic and psychographic characteristics as well as their interest level and expectations include creating a questionnaire, observing, and interviewing.

Using a Questionnaire

Public opinion polls are an American tradition, especially around election time. Just about anything is up for analysis, from views on candidates and their issues, opinions on U.S. foreign policy, health care reform, taxes, and legalizing drugs to ice cream preferences and brand recognition.

A questionnaire can determine the specific demographic characteristics of your listeners as well as their perceptions of you and your topic. It can also tell you how much knowledge your listeners have about your topic and the focus they would prefer in your speech.

By surveying all your classmates, sampling every fourth person in your dorm, or emailing selected members of your audience to ask them questions, you can find out information about your audience in advance. These methods are simple and effective. In addition, and depending on the age of your intended audience, online survey creation and response tabulation companies like SurveyMonkey.com now make it easier to poll a group of people via the Internet.

The first step in using a questionnaire is to design specific questions that are likely to get you the information you need. Three basic types of questions are most helpful to public speakers: fixed-alternative questions, scale questions, and open-ended questions (Churchill, 1983).

Fixed-alternative questions limit responses to specific choices, yielding valuable information about such demographic factors as age, education, and income. Fixed-alternative questions can offer many responses, or they can offer only two alternatives, such as yes/no questions. Following is an example of a fixed-alternative question focusing on attitudes:

Do you think all professional athletes should be carefully tested for drugs and steroids? (Choose one)

> Professionals should be carefully tested for drugs and steroids.
>
> Professional athletes should be tested for the use of drugs and steroids in selected sports.
>
> Professional athletes should never be required to test for drugs and steroids.
>
> No opinion.

This type of question is easy to answer, tabulate, and analyze. These questions yield standardized responses. For example, it would be more difficult to ask people, "How many times a week do you eat out?" without supplying possible responses, because you may receive answers like "regularly," "rarely," "every day," and "twice a day." Interpreting these answers is more difficult.

Glossary

Fixed-alternative questions Limit responses to several choices, yielding valuable information about such demographic factors as age, education, and income.

Fixed alternative questions avoid confusion. When asking for marital status, consider providing specific choices. Do not ask marital status if it is irrelevant to your topic.

What is your marital status?

Single

Widowed

Married

Divorced

The disadvantage of using fixed-alternative questions is that it may force people to respond to a question when they are uncertain or have no opinion, especially if you fail to include "no opinion" as a possible response.

Scale questions are a type of fixed-alternative question that ask people to respond to questions set up along a continuum. For example:

How often do you vote?

Always   Regularly   Sometimes   Seldom   Never

If you develop a continuum that can be used repeatedly, several issues can be addressed quickly. For example, you can ask people to use the same scale to tell you how frequently they vote in presidential elections, congressional elections, state elections, and local elections. The disadvantage of the scale question is that it is difficult to get in-depth information about a topic.

In an open-ended question, audience members can respond however they wish. For example:

How do you feel about a 12-month school year for K–12 students?

In response to this question about extending the school year, one person may write, "Keep the school year as it is," while another may suggest a workable plan for extending the year. Because the responses to open-ended questions are so different, they can be difficult to analyze. The advantage to these questions is that they allow you to probe for details and you give respondents the opportunity to tell you what is on their minds. Here are some guidelines for constructing usable questions.

Guidelines for Survey Questions

Avoid leading questions. Try not to lead people to the response you desire through the wording of your question. Here are two examples of leading questions:

Do you feel stricter handgun legislation would stop the wanton *killing* of innocent people?

Do you believe able-bodied men who are *too lazy* to work should be eligible for welfare?

These questions should be reworded. For example, "Do you support stricter handgun legislation?" is no longer a leading question.

Avoid ambiguity. When you use words that can be interpreted in different ways, you reduce the value of a question. For example:

How often do you drink alcohol?

Frequently   Occasionally   Sometimes   Never

In this case one person's "sometimes" may be another person's "occasionally." To avoid ambiguity, rephrase the possible responses to more useful fixed-alternatives:

How often do you drink alcohol?

More than once a week

At least once a month

Less than twice every six months

Never

Ask everyone the same questions. Because variations in the wording of questions can change responses, always ask questions in the same way. Do not ask one person, "Under what circumstances would you consider enlisting in the Army?" and another, "If the United States were attacked by a foreign nation, would you consider joining the Army?" Both of these questions relate to enlisting in the military, but the first one is an open question while the second is a closed question. The answers you receive to the first question have much more information value than the second, which could be answered "yes" or "no." If you do not ask people the same questions, your results may be inaccurate.

Be aware of time constraints. Although questionnaires can help you determine interest, attitudes, and knowledge level, they also take time. If your instructor allows you to pass out a questionnaire in class, make sure it takes only a few minutes to complete. Make yours brief and clear. Ask only what is necessary and make sure the format fits your purpose. Even if there is no structured time in class for a survey, you can still catch students between classes, during group work in class, and by email. Any time spent getting to know your audience helps ensure you are audience centered.

Image © Rawpixel, 2013. Used under license from Shutterstock, Inc.

Why should you always ask questions the same way?

Observe and Interview

You may find that the best way to gather information about a prospective audience is to assume the role of an observer. If you want to persuade your classmates to use reusable bottles, you might watch over a few weeks to see how many students in your class have throw-away (or recyclable) bottles, and how many are bringing reusable bottles to class. Then you could ask students who bring reusable bottles to class how long they've been using reusable bottles and why they do it. You could also interview students who bring recyclable bottles to class to ascertain their attitudes.

If you want to persuade your audience to get more involved with issues on campus, you might attend a student government meeting to see how many students attend (other than those *in* student government), and what types of issues are brought forth. Then you could interview members of the group as well as audience members to find their perceptions of student involvement on campus.

The information you gather from observing and interviewing is likely to be richer if you adopt a less formal style than you used in a traditional audience analysis questionnaire to gather information about your speech topic. By surveying, observing, and interviewing prospective audience members, your message will be well targeted, personalized, and appropriate.

Creating the Speaker–Audience Connection

It takes only seconds for listeners to tune out your message. Convince your audience your message has value by centering your message on your listeners and adapting your message to that specific audience and situation. The following suggestions will help you build the type of audience connection that leads to the message being understood and well received.

Get to the Point Quickly

First impressions count. What you say in the first few minutes is critical. Tell your listeners how you can help them first, not last. If you save your suggestions to the end, it may be that no one is listening. Experienced speakers try to make connections with their listeners as they open their speeches. For example, here is how one CEO addressed falling sales to his employees, "Good afternoon. Sales are down. Profits are gone. What's next? Jobs. I want to see all of you here again next month, but that may not happen. Let me explain how we got here and what we can do." With an opening like that, you can bet the CEO had the full attention of all employees present.

Have Confidence: They want to hear your speech

It happens frequently: Speakers with relatively little knowledge about a subject are asked to speak to a group of experts on that subject. An educator may talk to a group of athletes about intercollegiate sports. A lawyer may talk to a group of doctors about the doctor–patient relationship. When you feel your listeners know more than you do about your topic, realize they have invited you for a reason. In most cases, they want your opinion. Despite their knowledge, you have a perspective they find interesting. Athletes may want to learn how the college sports program is viewed by a professor, and doctors want to hear a lawyer's opinion about malpractice. Simply acknowledging your audience's education or intelligence and mentioning your contribution may be unique and hopefully will help create a bond of mutual respect.

Be of the people, not above the people

We do not want to listen to speakers who consider themselves more accomplished, smarter, or more sophisticated than we are. If speakers convey even a hint of superiority, listeners may tune them out.

When you think about Donald Trump, it is likely you know that he is a multi-millionaire who loves publicity, stars in the television show *The Apprentice*, was a presidential candidate for a nanosecond, and believes that everyone has the right to *his* opinion. "Humble" is not part of his vocabulary.

On the other hand, one of the world's richest men and founder of Facebook, Mark Zuckerberg, demonstrated that he is "of the people" when he gave a speech to a graduating class...of a *middle* school! When Facebook moved its operation to Menlo Park, California in 2011, Zuckerberg reached out to his new neighborhood, by speaking to students and parents at Belle Haven Middle School. Wearing jeans and a t-shirt at the outdoor ceremony, Zuckerberg presented informally a message that was clearly developed for that particular audience.

> "...I just want to share with you guys a few things that I've learned today that I think have enabled me and the people I work with to not succumb to the attitude of 'I can't.' And those things are that everything that is worth doing is actually pretty hard and takes a lot of work. That's one. The second is that you should focus on building great friendships and people that you trust because those really matter. And the third is just do what you love."

Rather than focus on his wealth, or brag about his accomplishments, he constructed a message that made him appear to be an ordinary guy with a meaningful message for the graduates.

Use Humor

Humor can help you connect with your audience and help them think of you as approachable rather than remote. Opening your speech with something that makes people smile or laugh can put both you and your listeners at ease. Consider the opening of Will Ferrell's 2003 speech at Harvard on Class Day (the day before graduation).

> This is not the Worcester, Mass Boat Show, is it? I am sorry. I have made a terrible mistake. Ever since I left *Saturday Night Live*, I mostly do public speaking now. And I must have made an error in the little Palm Pilot. Boy. Don't worry. I got it on me. I got the speech on me. Let's see. Ah, yes. Here we go.

> You know, when Bill Gates first called me to speak to you today, I was honored. ... Are you sure this is not the boat show?

His opening got their attention and made them laugh. Ferrell's humor pokes fun at his message and himself, not his audience. Subject and self-deprecating humor play well; insulting your audience does not. Effective humor should be related in some way to the subject of your speech, your audience, or the occasion. So, starting with a joke that is wholly unrelated to your topic is inappropriate. Also, remember that some of us have difficulty being funny. Others of us do not gauge the audience well. In either of these cases, attempts at humor may end up falling flat or offending. So be careful: Useless or ineffective humor can damage your credibility and hurt your connection with your audience. Yet, when well executed, humor is a powerful tool in your speaker arsenal.

Get Personal

Before management consultant Edith Weiner gives a speech, she learns the names of several members of her audience as well as their roles in the company. During her speech, she refers to these people and the conversations she had with them, thereby creating a personal bond with her audience. Connections can be made by linking yourself directly to the group you are addressing and by referring to your audience with the pronoun "you" rather than the third-person "they." The word "you" inserts your listeners into the middle of your presentation and makes it clear that you are focusing attention on them.

Here is an example of "you language" in a speech delivered by Jeffrey Holland (1988) as president of Brigham Young University to a group of early childhood educators:

> You are offering more than technical expertise or professional advice when you meet with parents. You are demonstrating that you are an ally in their task of rearing the next generation. In all that you do ... however good your work, and whatever the quality of life parents provide, there is no comparable substitute for families. Your best opportunity to act in children's best interests is to strengthen parents, rather than think you can or will replace them. (p. 559)

Content is another way to make it personal. Stories, anecdotes, and examples from your own experience are generally appreciated. But keep in mind, there is too much of a good thing where self-disclosure is concerned. Abide by this rule: If you are not comfortable with it being put in the headlines of the local paper, leave it out of your speech.

Encourage Participation

When you invite the listeners to participate in your speech, they become partners in the event. One of the author's friends, a first-degree black belt in karate, gave a motivational speech to a group of college women at a state university in Michigan. At the beginning of her speech, and to the excitement of the crowd, she broke several boards. She talked about her childhood, her lack of self-esteem, and her struggle to become a well-adjusted businesswoman. She used the phrase "I can succeed" several times during her speech and encouraged her audience to join in with her. By the end of her speech, the group, standing, invigorated, and excited, shouted with her, "I can succeed!"

Another way to involve your listeners is to choose a member of your audience to take part in your talk—have the volunteer help you with a demonstration, do some role-playing—and the rest of the group will feel like one of its own is up there at the podium. Involve the entire audience and they will hang on your every word. While adding participation takes time away from your speaking, it is well worth the investment. And like using humor, you will find it also lightens the mood and sets a favorable tone.

Examine Other Situational Characteristics

When planning your speech, other situational characteristics need to be considered, including time of day, size of audience, and size of room. When speechwriter Robert Rackleff (1987) addressed his colleagues about the "art of speech writing," he offered this advice:

> The time of day affects the speech. In the morning, people are relatively fresh and can listen attentively. You can explain things more carefully. But in the late afternoon, after lunch …, the audience needs something more stimulating. And after dinner, you had better keep it short and have some fireworks handy (311–312).

Room size influences how loud you must speak and whether you need a special microphone.

Rackleff reminded his listeners about the intimate connection between time of day and audience response. The relationship between physical surroundings and audience response is so strong that you should plan every speech with your surroundings in mind.

Management consultant Edith Weiner says there is a vast difference between an audience of six people and an audience of dozens or even hundreds of people: In the first case, says Weiner, "I'm speaking with the audience," but in the second, "I'm speaking to the audience." The intimacy of a small group allows for a speaker-audience interchange not possible in larger groups. Small groups provide almost instantaneous feedback; large groups are more difficult to read.

Room size is important because it influences how loudly you must speak and determines whether you need a microphone. As a student, you will probably be speaking in a classroom. But in other speaking situations, you may find yourself in a convention hall, a small office, or an outdoor setting where only the lineup of chairs determines the size of the speaking space.

If you are delivering an after-dinner speech in your own dining room to 10 members of your reading group, you do not have to worry about projecting your voice to the back row of a large room. If, on the other hand, you are delivering a commencement address in your college auditorium to a thousand graduates, you will need to use a microphone. And keep in mind, proper microphone technique takes practice, preferably in the auditorium in which you will speak.

Learn as You Go

Discovering what your audience thought of your speech can help you give a better speech next time. Realizing the importance of feedback, some professional speakers hand out post-speech questionnaires designed to find out where they succeeded and where they failed to meet audience needs. At workshops, feedback is often provided through questionnaires that can be turned in at the end or at any time during the event. When you are the speaker, you may choose to interview someone, distribute questionnaires randomly to a dozen people, or even ask the entire audience to provide feedback.

Valuable information often emerges from audience feedback, which enables speakers to adjust their presentation for the next occasion. For example, let's assume you delivered a speech to a civic organization on the increasing problem of drunk boating. You handed out questionnaires to the entire audience after your message. Results indicated that your audience would have preferred fewer statistics and more concrete suggestions for combating the problem. In addition, one listener offered a good way to make current laws more easily understood, a suggestion you may incorporate into your next presentation.

Finding out what your audience thought may be simple. In your public speaking class, your fellow classmates may give you immediate, written feedback. In other situations, especially if you are running a workshop or seminar, you may want to hand out a written questionnaire at the end of your speech and ask listeners to return it at a later time. Online survey tools (i.e., SurveyMonkey, SurveyGizmo, Surveyshare) are free and can provide rich feedback for you after your speech. Here are four questions you might ask:

1. Did the speech answer your questions about the topic? If not, what questions remain?
2. How can you apply the information you learned in the presentation to your own situation?
3. What part of the presentation was most helpful? Least helpful?
4. How could the presentation have better met your needs?

To encourage an honest and complete response, indicate in the instructions that people do not have to offer their names in the questionnaire. Remember that the goal of feedback is improvement, not ego gratification. Focus on positive feedback as much as possible and take negative comments as areas for growth.

Your ability to create and maintain a strong connection with your audience is helped by a clear understanding of their demographics and psychographics. Using this information will set you on track for an exceptional experience, for you *and* your audience.

Summary

The most important relationship in public speaking is the relationship between speaker and audience. Being audience-centered means learning everything you can about your audience so you can meet its needs in your topic and your approach. Start by analyzing your audience based on demographics and psychographics. Learn the average age of your listeners, whether they are predominantly male or female, their educational level, and how much they know about your subject. Try to identify members of your audience in terms of their membership in religious, racial and ethnic, occupational, socioeconomic, and political groups. Behavioral choices can tell you a great deal about audience attitudes, beliefs, and values.

Successful speakers define the expectations that surround the speaking occasion. They learn how much interest their audience has in their topic and how much their audience knows about it before they get up to speak. Audience analysis is accomplished through the use of questionnaires based on fixed-alternative questions, scale questions, and open-ended questions. Audience analysis can also be conducted through observation and interviews.

To ensure a speaker–audience connection, show your listeners at the start of your speech how you will help them; have confidence your audience wants to hear you, even if they are more knowledgeable than you. Present yourself as fitting into the group, rather than as being superior to the group. Refer to people in your audience and involve your listeners in your speech. When your speech is over, try to determine your audience's response through a post-speech evaluation, questionnaire, or interview.

Discussion Starters

❶ Why will a speech fail in the absence of audience analysis?

❷ What underlying principles should you use to conduct an effective audience analysis?

❸ What demographic characteristics does this class have in common? Where does this class differ in terms of demographic characteristics?

❹ Why are some demographic characteristics important to the success of your speech in one situation but not so important in another situation?

❺ How are behaviors, attitudes, beliefs, and values related to your next speech topic in the minds of your prospective audience members?

❻ If you wanted to gather information for your topic from members of your class, what do you think would be the most effective way to get responses? How does your answer differ based on the types of questions you want to ask?

References

Brunner, B., & Haney, E. (2007). *Civil Rights Timeline: Milestones in the Civil Rights Movement.* Information Please. Retrieved August 4, 2011 from www.infoplease.com/spot/civilrightstimeline1.html.

Churchill, G. A., Jr. (1983). *Marketing Research: Methodological Foundations,* 3rd Ed. Chicago: The Dryden Press.

Clanton, J. (1988). Title unknown. *Winning Orations of the Interstate Oratorical Association.* Mankato, MN: Interstate Oratorical Association.

Griffin, J. D. (1989, July 16). To Snare the Feet of Greatness: The American Dream Is Alive (Speech). Reprinted in *Vital Speeches of the Day, September 15, 1989,* 735–736.

Holland, J. (1988). Whose Children Are These? The Family Connection (Speech). Reprinted in *Vital Speeches of the Day, July 1, 1988,* 559.

Kiechel, W., III. (1987, June 8). How to Give a Speech. *Fortune,* 179.

Kushner, Harold S. (2002). *When All You've Ever Wanted Isn't Enough: The Search for a Life That Matters.* New York: Random House.

Noonan, P. (1989, October 15). Confessions of a White House Speechwriter, *New York Times,* 72.

Pilkington, E. (2009, January 29). Barack Obama Inauguration Speech. *The Guardian.* Accessed August 4, 2011 from www.guardian.co.uk/world/2009/jan/20/barack-obama-inauguration-us-speech.

Rackleff, R. B. (1987, September 26). The Art of Speechwriting: A Dramatic Event (Speech). Reprinted in *Vital Speeches of the Day,* March 1, 1988.

Rokeach, M. (1968). The Role of Values in Public Opinion Research. *Public Opinion Quarterly, 32*(4), 547–559.

Where We Stand on Faith. (2005, September 6). *Newsweek,* 48–49.

Woodward, G. C., & Denton, R. E., Jr. (2004). *Persuasion and Influence in American Life*, 5th Ed. (pp. 173–174). Long Grove, IL: Waveland Press, Inc.

The Y, Share the Day. (2010, July 12). A Brand New Day: The YMCA Unveils New Brand Strategy to Further Community Impact. Retrieved August 4, 2011 from www.ymca.net/news-releases/20100712-brand-new-day.html.

Chapter

6

"I find that a great part of the information I have acquired was by looking something up and finding something else on the way."

Franklin P. Adams (1881–1960),
writer and columnist

Chapter 6: Research and Preparing Supporting Material

Research is the raw material that forms the foundation of your speech. This chapter helps you develop an effective research strategy and provides guidelines for using various methods to support your speech.

Student Learning Objectives:

- Students will be able to describe how a speaker can develop a research strategy
- Students will be able to explain how a speaker supports his/her speech
- Students will be able to describe five functions of support materials
- Students will explain why support materials are needed in his/her speech
- Students will be able to document information accurately in his/her speech

RESEARCH AND PREPARING SUPPORTING MATERIAL

Develop a Research Strategy

Start (and End) with an Audience Analysis
Assess your knowledge and skills
Search Print and Online Resources
> *Narrow Your Focus*
> *Specific Library Resources*
> *Online Searches*
> *Web Evaluation Criteria*

Interview, If Appropriate

Supporting Your Speech

Five Functions of Support
Forms of Support
> *Facts*
> *Guidelines for Using Facts*
> *Statistics*
> *Guidelines for Using Statistics*
> *Examples*
> *Guidelines for Using Examples*
> *Testimony*
> *Guidelines for Using Testimony*
> *Analogies*
> *Guidelines for Using Analogies*

Documenting Information Accurately in Your Speech

Summary

Discussion Starters

References

Key Terms

accurate	examples	key-word search	secondary sources
analogy	facts	literal analogy	specialized
authority	figurative analogy	objectivity	encyclopedias
coverage	general encyclopedias	opinions	statistics
currency	hypothetical example	primary sources	supporting material

You may feel relief when your instructor approves the topic you have chosen, but your work has just begun. After choosing a topic and developing the general and specific purposes of your speech, it is time to research your topic and search for appropriate supporting material. Starting with what you know is important, but giving a speech based *only* on what you know is not sufficient. To a large extent, your listeners evaluate your speech on the amount and relevance of information gathered and the types of supporting material used.

We live in an information society that produces far more information than we can use. Print resources such as books, journals, magazines, and newspapers are added to library collections daily. Computers give us access to innumerable websites and voluminous databases. As a result of this galaxy of available information, one of your most important jobs will be to decide what is relevant and what is not, what you should incorporate into your speech and what you should discard. Once you have a topic, you need to stay focused on

BTW!

Information Literacy Standards for Higher Education

According to the Association of College and Research Libraries, information literacy forms the basis of lifelong learning. The information literate student:

Standard 1: Determines the nature and extent of the information needed.

Standard 2: Accesses needed information effectively and efficiently.

Standard 3: Evaluates information and its sources critically and incorporates selected information into his or her knowledge base and value system.

Standard 4: Individually or as a member of a group, uses information effectively to accomplish a specific purpose.

Standard 5: Understands many of the economic, legal, and social issues surrounding the use of information and accesses and uses information ethically and legally.

For more information about the standards, performance indicators, and outcomes, view the ACRL website at www.ala.com.

your specific purpose, keep your audience in mind, and search for reliable, credible information that will provide the most effective support for ideas.

In 2009 as President Obama declared October "Information Literacy Awareness" month, he announced:

> Every day, we are inundated with vast amounts of information. A 24-hour news cycle and thousands of global television and radio networks, coupled with an immense array of online resources, have challenged our long-held perceptions of information management. Rather than merely processing data, we must also learn the skills necessary to acquire, collate, and evaluate information for any situation (whitehouse.gov).

Obama's comments relate directly to the purpose of this chapter, which is to guide you through the process of information gathering. (Check out **BTW: Information Literacy Standards for Higher Education**.) Although this chapter is framed within the context of research and supporting material, gathering effective research and supporting material is part of information literacy.

Research provides the foundation for your speech. It enhances knowledge you may already have by giving you the needed tools to expand your thesis statement into a full-length presentation. Your research may include interviewing experts on your topic and locating print and Web-based information, or data you gathered personally. The result of this process is your knowledge of the topic.

Often, research can lead you to deliver a slightly different version of your speech than originally anticipated. As facts emerge you may expand your idea in one place, streamline it in another, or take it apart to accommodate new information. Ultimately, you will piece it together in its final form.

A speech that is well researched is still not complete. You must determine how to use the information gathered most effectively. **Supporting material** is the information used in a particular way to make your case. Supporting material, as we discuss later in this chapter, includes examples, testimony, statistics, facts, and analogies.

For example, if you wanted to inform your class about services available in your community for individuals who are categorized as low income, your research process may lead you to one organization that specializes in debt consolidation, one that offers free or low-cost medical care, another that gives out food for low-income individuals, and yet another that provides children with free school supplies. Having found all of these services, you might decide to include one main point that is stated, "A variety of services are available in our community."

For supporting material, the previously noted agencies provide **examples** of available services. As the types of supporting material vary, you must determine what is most suited to the topic and to your listeners. In a speech about available community services, facts are important because listeners

Glossary

Supporting material The information used in a particular way to make your case.

Examples Support that illustrates a point or claim.

should know how many individuals qualify for specific services as well as how many individuals use these services. Testimony from those who work in the agencies or from those who use their services would provide excellent support for such a speech.

Develop a Research Strategy

Instructors rarely say, "Go! Prepare an informative speech." Instead, they establish parameters regarding appropriate topics, length of speech, minimum number of sources, and types of sources. Before you begin to research your topic, make sure you know the constraints of the assignment as specified by your instructor. No matter how brilliant your delivery, if you haven't met the constraints of the assignment, your speech grade will reflect that. It is important to answer the following questions. What is the minimum number of sources required? How many sources do you need? If you use three issues of *Newsweek*, do they count as one source or as three? Can you use information that is 30 years old, 20 years old, 10 years old, or did your instructor say all material needs to be no more than five years old? Do you need both print and online sources? Does online access to a magazine count as a print source? Can you use all types of print sources? Do you need different types of print sources? Does your instructor allow you to count an interview as a source? Can you use a family member or yourself as a source? Once you know the answers to these questions, you are ready to start the research process.

Once you leave the college environment, constraints still exist. For any speaking engagement, among other things, you need to know the length of the speech, the audience you'll speak before, the audience's expectations in terms of topic/content, and the most effective types of supporting material for that audience. The best-delivered speech will fall short if it is too long, poorly developed, and insufficiently supported.

Whether you are planning to give an informative or persuasive speech, developing an effective research strategy involves the following:

1. **Analyze the audience.** What are the needs, interests, and knowledge level of my audience?

2. **Assess your knowledge/skill.** What knowledge or skill do I have in relation to this topic?

3. **Search print and online resources.** Based on available resources, where and what will I find most useful?

4. **Interview, if appropriate.** Will interviewing someone with personal knowledge or expertise about this topic strengthen this speech?

Each of these aspects can be viewed as research stages. The following section examines each of these stages in detail.

Start (and End) with an Audience Analysis

Throughout this book we stress the importance of connecting with your audience. Before you determine the general or specific purpose for your speech, consider your audience's needs. As explained in an earlier chapter, a careful audience analysis gives you information about who they are and what they value. Understanding your audience helps you develop specific questions that can be answered as you follow your search strategy. For example, suppose you were planning an informative speech explaining prenuptial agreements. You may have some general questions about the topic, such as the following:

- At what age do most people get married?
- What are the statistics on the number of marriages and divorces each year?
- Who benefits financially and who suffers financially as a result of a divorce?
- What happens to property in divorce?
- How expensive is an agreement?
- What issues are addressed in a typical agreement? Is there a "typical" agreement?
- Can people draw up the agreement without legal counsel?

To construct an effective speech that achieves its specific purpose, whether it is informative or persuasive, think about your specific audience. So, if you are working on a speech about prenuptial agreements, consider additional questions such as:

- Considering the age of my audience, how much do they know about prenuptial agreements?
- What do most people feel about prenuptial agreements?
- What might be this audience's greatest areas of concern or interest regarding the topic?

Answering the more specific questions related to your audience helps you determine the depth and breadth of information needed to answer your more general questions. Informally, you may ask students a few questions while waiting before class in the hallway or in the classroom. Your instructor may allow you to ask the class to respond briefly during class, or at the end of class. Perhaps you can survey your class online.

By developing questions based on your understanding of the needs of your audience, you can increase the likelihood of establishing an effective speaker–audience connection. Reflect again on your audience *after* you have gathered information to determine whether you have collected enough material and if it is the right type of material to meet your audience's needs and interests.

Assess your knowledge and skills

Start your research process by assessing your own knowledge and skills. Most likely, you have direct knowledge or experience related to several topics. Your family may own a monument shop or a restaurant, and you grew up exposed to issues related to these professions. Maybe you were raised in a bilingual family. Perhaps by the time you started college, you held one or more jobs, joined a political club, pursued hobbies like video games, or played sports such as soccer or rugby. You may know more about Jackie Chan movies than anyone on campus, or you may play disc golf. Examining your unique experiences or varied interests is a logical starting point for developing a speech.

Having personal knowledge or experience can impact your audience. A student with Type I diabetes can speak credibly on what it is like to take daily injections and deal with the consequences of both low and high blood sugar. A student who works as a barista at the local coffee shop can demonstrate how to make a good latte. Under no circumstances, however, should your research stop with your own personal knowledge or skills. Someone who knows how to make a good latte needs additional research on topics such as coffee shops and how much they make, types of coffee beans and where they come from, how beans are processed, brand names of espresso machines for those who are interested in making their own espresso, fair-trade coffee, and so on.

Choosing a topic on which you have no personal knowledge and skills is not forbidden, of course. However, be aware that speaking about something that is new to you may increase your communication apprehension, and *may* lead audiences to view you as less credible.

Search Print and Online Resources

Once you have assessed your own knowledge or skills, it is time to search print and online resources for other supporting material. The computer provides a rich playing field that also complicates our lives. We have more choices, but we have to work harder to sift through them.

Your search may result in more questions, including the following: What information is most essential to this topic? What will have the greatest impact? How much background do I need to give? Using a variety of sources is advantageous because some sources focus on research whereas others focus on philosophy or current events. Information may be found in regularly published sources or in a one-time publication. Sources target different audiences. We suggest you examine and evaluate materials from a variety of sources to select materials that will benefit you most.

Avoid wasting valuable time floating aimlessly in cyberspace or walking around the library. Instead, if you need direction, *ask a librarian*. Librarians are experts in finding both print and online information efficiently, and they can show you how to use the library's newest search engines and databases.

Image © Andrew F. Kazmierski, 2013. Used under license from Shutterstock, Inc.

If you need direction, ask a librarian. Don't waste time wandering around the library.

With new online and print resources added daily, using the expertise of a librarian can make your job as a researcher much easier.

If you are new to campus, and your instructor has not arranged a library tour for your class, consider taking a workshop on using the library. Your library's home page is helpful. Most college libraries belong to a "live chat" consortium on the Web, where students may contact a librarian 24 hours a day. Also, you can try the Library of Congress online Ask-a-Librarian Service (www.loc.gov) and click on "Ask a librarian."

Narrow Your Focus

It is natural to start with a broad topic. But as you search, the information you find helps you move to a more focused topic, enabling you to define—and refine—the approach you take to your speech. Perhaps you are interested in giving an informative speech about the use of performance enhancing drugs in sports. You must narrow your topic, but you are not quite sure what aspects are most compelling. Choose a search engine, such as Google, Ask.com, Yahoo!, or Bing. Many disciplines have useful search engines, and Google Scholar "provides a search of scholarly literature across many disciplines and sources, including theses, books, abstracts and articles" (scholar.google.com).

Try conducting a **key-word search** on Google for "drugs in sports." This is very general. The key-word search leads you to a list of records that are weighted in order of amount of user access. On February 8, 2011, the Google search led to 80,200,000 hits, whereas on June 22, 2011, there were 186,000,000 results for "drugs in sports," showing that in just over four

Glossary

Key-word search A Web search that leads you to a list of records that are weighted in order of amount of user access.

BTW!

Evaluating Print Sources

According to Raimes (2008), the following questions should be used to evaluate each print source:

○ **What does the work cover?** It should be long enough and detailed enough to provide adequate information.

○ **How objective is the information?** The author, publisher, or periodical should not be affiliated with an organization that has an ax to grind—unless, of course, your topic entails reading critically and making comparisons and assessing other points of view.

○ **How current are the views?** Check the date of publication. The work should be up-to-date if you need a current perspective.

○ **How reputable are the publisher and author?** The work should be published by a reputable publisher in a source that is academically reliable, not one devoted to gossip, advertising, propaganda, or senationalism. Check *Books in Print, Literary Market Place,* or ACQWEB's *Directory of Publishers and Vendors* for details on publishers. The author should be an authority on the subject. Find out what else the author has written (in Google, in *Books in Print,* or at Amazon.com) and what his or her qualifications are as an authority (pg. 122).

months, available information more than doubled. This is both positive and negative. For any given topic, you may have more than a million records or "hits" from which to choose. We suggest you look for valid subject headings, and search more deeply than the first three or four records listed.

Results of the key-word search lead you to many possibilities, including "anabolic steroids." You can discover what they are, how they work, who uses them, how prevalent they are, the different types, drugs banned by the NCAA, and medical uses. Now you have other areas to pursue. Decide what aspects you want to cover that are relevant to the audience and can be discussed effectively within your time constraints. Perhaps you are interested in who uses them. You type, "Who uses anabolic steroids?" This leads you to a website on uses and abuses of steroids. For your audience, you most likely need to define what anabolic steroids are and how they are used and abused. You can continue your research by examining both print and online resources for these specific aspects of performance enhancement drugs. Next, you can develop a specific purpose statement and search for information to support it.

As you search for information, keep three aspects of research in mind: First, recognize the distinction between primary and secondary sources. **Primary sources** include firsthand accounts such as diaries, journals, and letters, as well as statistics, speeches, interviews, questionnaires, and studies. They are records of events as they are first described. According to Raimes (2008), the use of primary sources "can bring an original note to your research and new information" to your listeners (p. 101). Primary sources generally are seen as credible sources but may be more difficult to obtain.

Secondary sources generally provide an analysis, an explanation, or a restatement of a primary source. If the U.S. Surgeon General issues a report on the dangers of smoking, the report itself (available from the U.S. Surgeon General's Office) is the primary source; newspaper and magazine articles *about* the report are secondary source material. Secondary sources may contain bias because someone has interpreted information from the primary source. Both, however, are useful in your search process.

Second, there is a relationship between the length of your speech and the amount of time you must spend in research. Many students learn the hard way that five minutes of research will not suffice for a five-minute speech. We recommend that for every one minute of speaking time, there is an hour of preparation needed. Whatever the length of the speech, you have to spend time uncovering facts and building a strong foundation of support. If you only spend an hour researching your topic, it is likely you have not met the constraints of the assignment. You may have relied too heavily on one source, or you may not have enough sources.

Third, finding information is not enough; you must also be able to evaluate it, and use it in the most appropriate way to achieve your specific purpose. For example, your audience analysis may suggest that specific statistics are necessary to convince your audience. On the other hand, perhaps personal or expert testimony will be most persuasive. Evaluating sources and types of

---

supporting material are discussed later in this chapter. Overall, developing a research strategy is one of the most useful things you will learn in college.

Specific Library Resources

In addition to providing access to computers for online searches, each library houses a variety of research materials, including books, reference materials, newspapers, magazines, journals, and government documents. Microfilm, specifically for archived newspapers, may still be available. If information is not housed in your library, you can electronically extend your search far beyond your campus or community library through interlibrary loan. It may take two weeks or longer to process requests, so planning is especially important when relying on interlibrary loan. The following identifies various library resources, and includes several suggestions for making your library search most effective.

Books. Historically, libraries have been most noted for their collection of books. Many universities built several libraries so students may access large general collections, archived collections, and specific collections. Using the library catalog is essential. Nearly all libraries today have online computer catalogs, which contain records of all materials the library owns. In addition to identifying what books are available and where to find them, an online catalog indicates whether a particular book is checked out and when it is due back. Keep in mind that the library groups books by subject, so as you look in the stacks for a particular book, it makes sense to peruse surrounding books for additional resources.

General reference materials. At the beginning of your search, it may be helpful to start with one or more general reference resources, including encyclopedias, dictionaries, biographical sources, and statistical sources. Most likely, your time spent with these materials will be short, but these resources can provide you with basic facts and definitions.

Unlike some of our experiences in primary school, seldom does a student's research start and end with the encyclopedia. The *World Book Encyclopedia* is helpful if you are unfamiliar with a topic or concept. It can provide facts that are concise as well as easy to read and understand. **General encyclopedias** (e.g., *The Encyclopedia Americana* and *Encyclopedia Britannica*) cover a wide range of topics in a broad manner. In contrast, specialized encyclopedias, such as the *Encyclopedia of Religion* and the *International Encyclopedia of the Social Sciences*, focus on particular areas of knowledge in more detail. Articles in both general and specialized encyclopedias often contain bibliographies that lead you to additional sources.

Encyclopedias are helpful as a basic resource, but they generally are not accepted as main sources for class speeches. Use them to lead to other information. **Caution:** Do not fall into Wikipedia's web of easy access and understanding. Its legitimacy is questionable. Several years ago, Stephen Colbert, host of the TV show *The Colbert Report*, asked his viewers to log on to the

Glossary

General encyclopedias
Cover a wide range of topics in a broad manner.

Specialized encyclopedias
Focus on particular areas of knowledge in more detail.

entry "elephants" on Wikipedia.com to report that the elephant population in Africa "has tripled in the last six months." This online encyclopedia noted a spike in inaccurate entries shortly after the show aired.

Most instructors discourage, if not ban, use of Wikipedia. Although teachers don't want students quoting the encyclopedia, librarians will point out that Wikipedia, like *World Book*, is sometimes useful for getting an overview of the topic, especially if you know nothing about the topic, but information should be verified by a different source.

Dictionaries are helpful when you encounter an unfamiliar word or term. They also provide information on pronunciation, spelling, word division, usage, and etymology (the origins and development of words). As with encyclopedias, dictionaries are classified as either general or specialized. The dictionary is also just a click away. You might try *Merriam-Webster Online* (www.m-w.com). Specialized dictionaries cover words associated with a specific subject or discipline, as in the following: *The American Political Dictionary*, *Black's Law Dictionary*, *Harvard Dictionary of Scientific and Technical Terms*, and *Webster's Sports Dictionary*. Many disciplines use their own specialized terminology that is more extensive and focused, and those definitions are found in their journals and books. **Caution:** Check with your instructor before beginning your speech with "According to Webster's dictionary, the word _____ means ..." As Harris (2002) notes in his book on the effective use of sources, "Generally speaking, starting with a dictionary definition not only lacks creativity but it may not be helpful if the definition is too general or vague" (p. 35).

Biographical sources. Biographical sources, which are international, national, or specialized, provide information on an individual's education, accomplishments, and professional activities. This information is useful when evaluating someone's credibility and reliability. A biographical *index* indicates sources of biographical information in books and journals, whereas a biographical *dictionary* lists and describes the accomplishments of notable people. If you are looking for a brief background of a well-known person, consult the biographical dictionary first. If you need an in-depth profile of a lesser-known person, the biographical index is the better source. Some examples of these sources are *Author Biographies Master Index*, *Biography Index*, *the New York Times Index*, *Dictionary of American Biography*, *European Authors*, *World Authors*, and *Dictionary of American Scholars*. Librarians agree that biography.com is a useful online source for individuals currently famous or infamous.

Statistical sources. When used correctly, statistics provide powerful support. Facts and statistics give authority and credibility to research. Many federal agencies produce and distribute information electronically. The *American Statistics Index* (ASI) includes both an index and abstracts of statistical information published by the federal government. Try also the *Index to International Statistics* (IIS) and the *Statistical Abstract of the United States* (available online at www.census.gov/compendia/statab/). If your library has it, the online source LexisNexis touts itself as providing "content-enabled workflow solutions designed specifically for professionals in the legal, risk management, corporate, government, law enforcement, accounting, and academic markets" (www.lexisnexis.com).

Magazines, newspapers, and journals. Magazines (also known as periodicals) and newspapers provide the most recent print information. Once you identify ideas that connect with the needs of your audience, you can look for specific information in magazines and newspapers. General indexes cover such popular magazines and newspapers such as *Time*, *Newsweek*, *U.S. News & World Report*, the *New York Times*, and the *Chicago Tribune*. Other popular indexes include the *New York Times Index*, *Wall Street Journal*, *Christian Science Monitor*, *Los Angeles Times*, *The Education Index*, *Humanities Index*, *Public Affairs Information Service Bulletin*, *Social Sciences and Humanities Index*, and *Social Sciences Index*.

Journals are serious, scholarly publications that report research conducted by professionals within their fields of study. Newspapers and magazines are differentiated from journals in at least four ways. First, the frequency of distribution is different, with newspapers published daily, magazines published weekly or monthly, and journals published quarterly, monthly, or bimonthly. Second, newspaper and magazine writers are paid, whereas researchers who write journal articles are generally experts in their particular fields and have submitted their work on a competitive, reviewed basis. Third, magazines and newspapers are written for general audiences, whereas journal articles are written for a specific audience. For example, faculty and graduate students in the communication field would be interested in studies conducted on communication apprehension. Fourth, and very importantly, journals focus on original research. Much of the content in a journal is considered to be a primary source because it reports findings from scholarly research.

Government documents. Government documents are prepared by agencies, bureaus, and departments that monitor the affairs and activities of the nation. Documents are issued by the Office of the President, the U.S. Congress, the departments of Commerce, Agriculture, Education, Navy and Army, Indian Affairs, the Veterans' Administration, the Food and Drug Administration, and the FBI.

Through the U.S. Government Printing Office (GPO) one can find unique, authoritative, and timely materials, including detailed census data, vital statistics, congressional papers and reports, presidential documents, military reports, and impact statements on energy, the environment, and pollution. However, it is now archive only, and has been replaced, for the most part, by the Federal Digital System (FDsys).

Overall, a speaker has a wealth of information available at the library. An effective speaker uses a variety of sources, such as books, magazines, and statistics. This requires deep research, more than a quick Google search can uncover. At the library, qualified, expert help is on hand to assist you in your search. Also remember, whether you use print or online sources, you need to evaluate the credibility and timeliness of each source.

Online Searches

As stated earlier, your librarian can lead you to a variety of material. An enormous number of databases exist, and one can approach Web research in many ways. Without help, looking for information on the Web is like upending the library in a football field in the dark and being given a penlight to search for information. The librarian can at least provide you with stadium lights.

Consider using online databases such as ProQuest, InfoTrac, and EBSCO. According to InfoTrac College Edition's website (infotrac. thomsonlearning.com), more than 20 million scholarly and popular articles from nearly 6,000 sources are available to you. The advantage of using this resource is that you may access cross-disciplinary, reliable, full-length articles. It is free of advertising and available 24 hours a day. EBSCO (www.ebsco. com) offers a similar service, and claims to be the most widely used online resource, with access to over 100 databases and thousands of e-journals.

Web Evaluation Criteria

Many students start their research online. Computers can be found everywhere on campus, and it may take only a few steps to access one. Although there is nothing inherently wrong with this, we urge you to proceed with caution. Evaluating the credibility of your online resources is critical. The quantity of information available via the Internet is colossal, and highly respected research can be found as well as pure fiction presented as fact.

Purdue University's online writing lab warns readers to "never use Web sites where an author cannot be determined, unless the site is associated with a reputable institution such as a respected university, a credible media outlet, government program or department, or well-known non-governmental organizations" (owl.english.purdue. edu). Seek information from competent, qualified sources and avoid information from uninformed individuals with little or no credentials. Ultimately, you are accountable for the quality and credibility of the sources you use.

As you access each website, it is important to evaluate its legitimacy as a source for your speech. In Radford, Barnes, and Barr's book on selecting, evaluating, and citing Web research (2006), five Web evaluation criteria are identified that serve as useful standards for evaluating online information.

Evaluate a site's legitimacy as a source before you decide to use it.

Image © wavebreakmedia, 2013. Used under license from Shutterstock, Inc.

❶ Authority. Authority relates to the concept of credibility. As we know, virtually anyone can become a Web publisher. A website that passes this first test contains information provided by an individual, group, or organization known to have expertise in the area.

Questions to guide evaluation include the following:

○ What type of group put up the site? (Educational institution? Government agency? Individual? Commercial business? Organization?)

○ Can you identify the author(s)? (What is the organization or who is the person responsible for the information?)

○ What are the credentials of those responsible?

❷ Accuracy. An accurate website is reliable and error-free. If the site was last updated two years ago and the site is discussing a bill before the legislature, then it is no longer accurate. Millions of websites are also considered *secondary sources*, so the information has been interpreted by someone else. The information may be less accurate. Also, it is relatively easy to take information out of context when it is put online and can be removed at will.

Questions to guide evaluation include the following:

○ Is the information correct?

○ Does the information confirm or contradict what is found in printed sources?

○ Are references given to the sources of information?

❸ Objectivity. The extent to which website material is presented without bias or distortion relates to objectivity. As you examine the material, you want to determine if it is presented as opinion or fact.

Questions to guide evaluation include the following:

○ What is the age level of the intended audience? (Adults? Teenagers? Children?)

○ Is the information on the site factual or an expression of opinion?

○ Is the author controversial? A known conservative? A known liberal?

○ What are the author's credentials?

❹ Coverage. Coverage refers to the depth and breadth of the material. It may be difficult to determine whom the site is targeting. As a result, material may be too general or too specific. Determine if it meets your needs or if critical information is missing.

Questions to guide evaluation include the following:

○ What is the intended purpose of the site? (Educational? Informational? Commercial? Recreational?)

Glossary

Authority An individual cited or considered to be an expert; power to influence or command thought; credible.

Accurate Reliable, current, and error-free.

Objectivity Information that is fair and unbiased.

Coverage The depth and breadth of the material.

○ Who is the intended audience? (General public? Scholars? Students? Professionals?)

○ Is information common knowledge? Too basic? Too technical?

○ Does information include multiple aspects of the issue or concern?

❺ Currency. Currency refers to the timeliness of the material. Some websites exist that have never been updated. Information may be no longer valid or useful. If you look for "Most popular books of the year" and find a site from 2003, that information is no longer current or relevant. Looking at birth rates or literacy rates from the past would not produce relevant information if you are looking for the most recent information.

Questions to guide evaluation include the following:

○ When was the site created?

○ Is the material recent?

○ Is the website updated?

When using these five criteria to evaluate your online information, remember that all criteria should be met, not just one or two of the above. Accurate and current information must also be objective. If critical information is missing (coverage), no matter how accurate and current the information is, it should be eliminated as a source.

Interview, if appropriate

Interviews are useful if you want information too new to be found in published sources or if you want to give your listeners the views of an expert. By talking to an expert, you can clarify questions and fill in knowledge gaps, and you may learn more about a subject than you expected. In the process, you also gather opinions based on years of experience.

Look around your campus and community. You will find experts who can tell you as much as you need to know about thousands of subjects. You can get opinions about the stock market, the effect of different types of running shoes on the development of shin splints, race relations, No Child Left Behind legislation, ethanol, water or air pollution, or curbside recycling.

If you decide to interview one or more people, we offer the following four suggestions:

Contact the person well in advance. Remember, *you* are the one who needs the information. Do not think that leaving one voice message or one email is the extent of your responsibility. You may have to make several attempts to contact the person. Schedule a date and time to interview that leaves you with ample time to prepare your speech.

Prepare questions in advance. An interview is a conversation between two or more people guided by a predetermined purpose. Know the purpose, and make sure you know what topics need to be covered and what information needs to be clarified.

Develop questions in a logical order. One question should lead naturally to another. Place the most important questions at the top to guarantee that they will be answered before your time is up.

Stay within the agreed time frame. If you promise the interview will take no longer than a half hour, keep your word, if at all possible. Do not say, "It'll just take a minute," when you need at least 15 minutes. Build in a little time to ask questions based on the interviewee's answers or for clarification.

After reading this section on research, we hope you recognize that it involves a significant time commitment. It is never too early to start thinking about your next speech topic and where you might find sources. Explore a variety of resources. Ask for help from your instructor or librarian. Make sure you know the constraints of the assignment.

Supporting Your Speech

Imagine a chef with a piece of steak, some cauliflower, and rice; the main ingredients for a dinner special. What the chef does with these raw materials will influence the response of the consumers. The chef decides whether to grill, broil, bake, steam, or fry. Different spices are used for different results. Numerous possibilities exist.

Research you gathered for your speech can be viewed as the raw material. Now you need to determine how to organize and present your information in the most effective way for your audience. It is important to spend sufficient time making choices about how much and what type of supporting material to include in your speech.

Supporting material gives substance to your assertions. If you say that *Casablanca* is the best movie ever produced in Hollywood, you are stating your opinion. If you cite a film critic's essay that notes it is the best movie ever, then your statement has more weight. You may find data that indicate how well the movie did, and a public opinion poll that ranked it as the top movie. These different resources provide support. Just about anything that affirms a speaker's idea in some way can be considered supporting material.

When developing your speech, you have many decisions to make. Consider the following example:

Your public speaking professor asks your class to develop an informative speech addressing the problem of shoplifting. The two following hypothetical versions are among those presented:

Version 1:

> Shoplifting is an enormous problem for American retailers who lose billions of dollars each year to customer theft. Not unexpectedly, retailers pass the cost of shoplifting onto

consumers, which means that people like you and I pay dearly for the crimes of others.

Shoplifting is increasingly becoming a middle-class crime. Experts tell us that many people shoplift just for kicks—for the thrill of defying authority and for the excitement of getting away with something that is against the law. Whatever the reason, 1 in 15 Americans is guilty of this crime.

Version 2:

Imagine walking up to a store owner once a year and giving that person $300 without getting anything in return. Could you afford that? Would you want to do that? Yet that's what happens. Every year, the average American family of four forks over $300 to make amends for the crimes of shoplifters.

Shoplifting is a big cost to big business. According to recent statistics from the National Association for the Prevention of Shoplifting, people who walk out of stores without first stopping at the cash register take with them more than $13 billion annually. That's more than $25 million per day. Their website claims that 1 out of 11 of us is guilty of this crime. To bring this figure uncomfortably close to home, that's at least two students in each of your classes.

Interestingly, shoplifting is no longer a poor person's crime. Hard as it is to imagine, many shoplifters can well afford to buy what they steal. Actress Lindsay Lohan received media attention in February 2011 when she was charged with felony grand theft of a necklace from a jewelry store in Venice, California.

Why do middle- and upper-income people steal? According to psychiatrist James Spikes, quoted in *Ms.* Magazine, shoplifters are "defying authority. They're saying, 'The hell with them. I'll do it anyway ... I can get away with it ...'" Psychologist Stanton Samenow, quoted in *Life* magazine, agrees: "Shoplifters will not accept life as it is; they want to take shortcuts. They do it for kicks."

Although both versions say essentially the same thing, they are not equally effective. The difference is in the supporting materials. Notice, providing supporting material adds depth and breadth to the speech. Listeners are more likely to pay attention when they hear something that relates to their world in some way.

Five Functions of Support

Support should strengthen your speech in five ways. Comparing Version 1 with Version 2 illustrates the value of supporting material.

❶ **Support is specific.** Version 2 gives listeners *more details* than Version 1. We learn, for example, how much shoplifting costs each of us as well as the financial burden retailers must carry.

❷ **Support helps to clarify ideas.** We learn more about the reasons for shoplifting from Version 2. This clarification—from the mouths of experts—reduces the risk of misunderstanding.

❸ **Support adds weight.** The use of credible statistics and expert opinion adds support to the second version's main points. This type of support convinces listeners by building a body of evidence that may be difficult to deny. The testimonies of Drs. Spikes and Samenow are convincing because they are authoritative. We believe what they say far more than we do unattributed facts.

❹ **Support is appropriate to your audience.** Perhaps the most important difference between these two versions is Version 2's determination to gear the supporting material to the audience. It is a rare college student who would not care about a $300 overcharge or who cannot relate to the presence of two possible shoplifters in each class. Also, Hollywood actress Lindsay Lohan's shoplifting is noted in Version 2. Students are familiar with her name, but college students would not be as familiar with an older famous person who has shoplifted, such as Bess Myerson, winner of Miss America in 1945 and actress on several television shows in the 1960s.

❺ **Support creates interest.** Although Version 1 provides information, it arouses little or no interest. Listeners have a hard time caring about the problem or becoming emotionally or intellectually involved. Version 2, on the other hand, creates interest through the use of meaningful statistics, quotations, and an example. When used properly, supporting materials can transform ordinary details into a memorable presentation.

Effective support is used to develop the message you send to your listeners. It is through this message that communication takes place between speaker and audience. In public speaking, you cannot separate the act of speaking from the message the speaker delivers. Supporting your message is one of your most important tasks as you develop your speech.

Forms of Support

Effective speeches generally rely on multiple forms of support. To give your speech greater weight and authority, at least five forms of support can be used. These include facts, statistics, examples, testimony, and analogies. Next, each of these forms of support is discussed, and guidelines for using them are presented.

Glossary

Facts Verifiable and irrefutable pieces of information.

Opinions Points of view that may or may not be supported in fact.

Facts

Nothing undermines a presentation faster than too few facts. **Facts** are verifiable and irrefutable pieces of evidence. **Opinions** are points of view that may or may not be supported in fact. Too often, speakers confuse fact and opinion when adding supporting material to a speech. For example, while it is a fact that Colin Firth won the 2011 Academy Award for Best Actor, it is opinion to state that he is the best actor in Hollywood.

Facts serve at least three purposes:

1. **Facts clarify your main point.** Facts remove ambiguity, making it more likely that the message you send is the message your audience will receive.

2. **Facts indicate your knowledge of the subject.** Rather than say, "The League of Women Voters has been around for a long time," report, "The League of Women Voters was founded in 1919." Your audience wants to know that you have researched the topic and can discuss specifics about your topic.

3. **Facts define.** Facts provide needed definitions that may explain new concepts. In Megan's informative speech on "functional illiteracy," she defined the term in the following way:

> While an illiterate adult has no ability to read, write, or compute, relatively few Americans fall into this category. However, some 30 million Americans can't read, write, compute, speak, or listen effectively enough to function in society. They cannot read street signs, write out a check, apply for a job, or ask a government bureaucrat about a Social Security check they never received. Although they may have minimal communications skills, for all intents and purposes, they are isolated from the rest of society. These people are considered functionally illiterate.

Megan anticipated the potential confusion between the terms illiteracy and functional illiteracy, and differentiated between them. While defining this term for your public speaking class is necessary, if the audience comprises literacy coaches, this would not be necessary.

Guidelines for Using Facts

Carefully determine how many facts to use. Too few facts reveal that you spent little time researching, while too many may overwhelm your listeners. Sometimes, students want to impress their audience, or at least their instructor, with the amount of research completed for a particular speech. The desire to include *all* information may result in a "data dump," where facts are given in a steady stream with little or no connection to the speech or to each other. This overload of information is difficult to process.

To be effective, the number and complexity of the facts must be closely tied to the needs of your listeners. A speech to a group of hikers on poison ivy prevention may include practical issues such as identifying the plant and recognizing, treating, and avoiding the rash. However, when delivering a speech on the same subject to a group of medical students, a detailed explanation of the body's biochemical response to the plant is probably more relevant.

Define terms when they are introduced. The first time you use a term that requires explanation, define it so your meaning is clear. If you talk about the advantages of belonging to a health maintenance organization, define the term the first time it is used.

Make sure your meanings are clear. If words or phrases have different meanings to you than they do to members of your audience, the impact of your speech is lessened. Misunderstandings occur when your audience attributes meanings to terms you did not intend. Think about the following words: success, liberal, conservative, patriot, happiness, good, bad, and smart. Collectively, we do not agree on the meanings of these words. One person may define success in terms of material wealth, while another may think of it in terms of family relationships, job satisfaction, and good health. When it is essential that your audience understand the meaning you intend, take the time to clarify terms.

Statistics

The second form of supporting material is **statistics**: the collection, analysis, interpretation, and presentation of information in numerical form. Statistics give us the information necessary to understand the magnitude of issues and to compare and contrast different points.

Statistics can be misleading. For example, if one were to examine the National League of Baseball (NLB) salaries for 2010, one would find the highest salary went to Alex Rodriguez of the New York Yankees. He earned $33,000,000. However, the average, or mean, salary for the New York Yankees was $8,253,335, and both the mean *and* median salaries were $5,500,000. The lowest salary was just over $400,000 (usatoday.com/sportsdata/baseball). In this case, simply discussing these three statistical measures is not helpful, unless you want to make the point that salaries are not consistent. It might make more sense to discuss the range of salaries or look at a particular group of players' salaries. When using statistics in your speech, it is important to understand what they mean.

Guidelines for Using Statistics

Be precise. Make sure you understand the statistics before including them in your speech. Consider the difference between the following statements.

A 2 percent decrease was shown in the rate of economic growth, as measured by the gross national product, compared to the same period last year.

The gross national product dropped by 2 percent compared to the same period last year.

In the first case, the statistic refers to a drop in the rate of growth—it tells us that the economy is growing at a slower pace but that it is still ahead of last year—while in the second, it refers to an actual drop in the gross national product in comparison to the previous year. These statements say two very different things.

It is critical that you not misinterpret statistics when analyzing the data. If you have questions, refer to a basic statistics text or another source that further explains the data.

Avoid using too many statistics. Too many statistics will confuse and bore your audience and blunt the impact of your most important statistical points. Save your statistics for the places in your speech where they will make the most impact.

Round off your numbers. Is it important for your audience to know that, according to the Census Bureau's daily population projection on August 30, 2011, the U.S. population reached 312,105,211. The figure will have greater impact—and your audience will be more likely to remember it—if you round it off to "just over 312 million (www.census.gov).

Cite your sources. Because statistics are rarely remembered for very long, it is easy for speakers to misquote and misuse them—often in a calculated way for their own ends. As an ethical speaker, you need to make sure your statistics are correct and you need to quote your sources. For example, when talking about the popularity of Girl Scout cookies, you might mention that during peak production of Girl Scout cookies, according to the Little Brownie Bakery website, 4,500,000 Thin Mints are produced each day, and 230,000 pounds of peanut butter are used each week to create Do-si-dos and Tagalongs (www.littlebrowniebakers.com).

Use visual aids to express statistics. Statistics become especially meaningful to listeners when they are presented in visual form. Visual presentations of statistics free you from the need to repeat a litany of numbers that listeners will probably never remember. Instead, by transforming these numbers into visual presentations, you can highlight only the most important points, allowing your listeners to refer to the remaining statistics at any time. For example, in a speech to outline the historical view of the supply and demand of faculty in the social sciences and humanities, a graph displaying the numbers of faculty would be helpful.

Examples

Examples enliven speeches in a way that no other form of supporting material can. Grounding material in the specifics of everyday life has the power to create an empathic bond between speaker and audience, a bond strong enough to tie listeners to a speech and the speaker even after the example is complete.

FIGURE 6.1

A speech to outline the historical view of the supply and demand of faculty can be enhanced by a bar graph.

Examples can be brief or extended, real or hypothetical, and narrative. Although examples differ in length, factual base, and source, their effectiveness lies in the extent to which they support the speaker's core idea.

Examples are brief or extended. Brief examples are short illustrations that clarify a general statement. If you made the following assertion: "Americans are more modest than Europeans," you could support it by using brief examples, such as, "If you take a walk on the beach in Italy or France, you should not be surprised to find women sunbathing topless. Also, many European countries, such as Sweden and Germany, have public saunas that are enjoyed by men and women—who are in the same sauna, sitting naked on their towels."

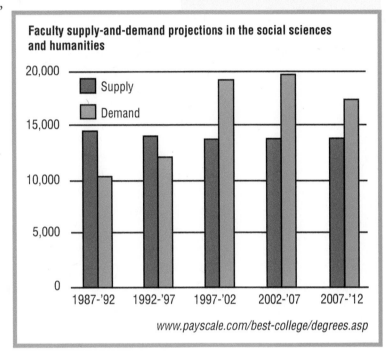

Faculty supply-and-demand projections in the social sciences and humanities

www.payscale.com/best-college/degrees.asp

Brief examples can be used effectively throughout a speech. Your decision to use them depends on many factors, including the needs of your audience, the nature of your material, and your approach.

Extended examples are longer and richer in detail than brief examples. They are used most effectively to build images and to create a lasting impression on the audience, as can been seen in the following excerpt from a speech in 2006 given by Steven Darimont, candidate for sheriff in Coles County, Illinois. When making the point that money is spent unnecessarily on jail food, he stated:

> "Our food budget alone is at $140,000 and we will go over that by $12–15,000 this year. The sheriff has requested that [amount] be raised [an additional] $20,000, to $160,000 next year. The inmates currently get three hot meals a day. An example of this is breakfast: scrambled eggs, toast with butter and jelly, cold cereal with milk, hash browns, fruit, and juice. The Department of Corrections mandates only one hot meal per day, yet we feed three hot meals."

Providing more detail about the budget and the ample food choices creates a greater impact on the listener rather than saying, "We provide three hot meals a day, and we're going over budget."

Because of their impact, extended examples should not be overused or used at inappropriate points. As with other forms of support, they should be reserved for the points at which they will have the greatest effect: in clarifying the message, persuading listeners to your point of view, or establishing a speaker–audience relationship.

Examples are real or hypothetical. Sometimes the best examples are real, and come from your personal experience. By revealing parts of your life that relate to your speech topic, you provide convincing evidence and, at the same time, potentially create a powerful bond between you and your audience. Consider the student who has watched her mother die from lung cancer. The experience of hearing about the diagnosis, discussing treatment possibilities, and making final arrangements while her mother was alive can have a powerful effect on the audience. The words and emotion have great impact because the situation is real, not hypothetical, and the speaker provides a sense of reality to the topic.

Hypothetical examples are useful when you want to exaggerate a point or when you cannot find a factual illustration for your speech. To be effective, they must be tied in some way to the point you are trying to illustrate.

At times, it suits the speaker's purpose to create a fictional or hypothetical example, rather than a real example, to make a point. Although these examples are not based on an actual event, the circumstances they describe are often realistic and thus effective. For example, a student might develop the following:

> Courtney, a 27-year-old, arrived at Springfield Emergency department at 10:30 p.m., after her mother found her lying unconscious and choking on her saliva. At the initial evaluation, the nurse noted the certain symptoms. Courtney's pupils were dilated, her temperature was high, her blood pressure was extremely high, and her heart rate was extremely fast. Doctors immediately ordered fluids to be given to rehydrate her and worked to stabilize her vital signs. Then, she began to show signs of a *heart attack*. She received CPR but about two hours later, she suffered another heart attack. This time, doctors were unable to revive her, and Courtney died. Following a urine analysis, lab technicians discovered she had ingested a lethal dose of *methamphetamine*.

As with the above example, its hypothetical format allows us to distance ourselves somewhat from a terrible situation since we aren't personally connected, but at the same time, we feel the emotional impact because the situation reflects reality.

Glossary

Hypothetical example A fictional example; the circumstances they describe are often realistic and thus effective.

It is important that your listeners know when you are using a hypothetical example and when you are not. Avoid confusion by introducing these examples in a direct way. You might start out by saying, "Imagine that you live next door to a college professor we'll call Dr. Supple," or "Let's talk about a hypothetical mother on welfare named Alice."

Examples can be in narrative form. Narratives are stories within a speech; anecdotes that create visual images in listeners' minds. In many ways, they take extended examples a step further by involving listeners in a tale that captures attention and makes a point—a story connected to the speaker's core idea. Many listeners love a good story, and when the speech is over, the narrative is what they remember. Narratives should have an opening where the characters and the situation are introduced, the action or complication that is the point of the story, and then some type of conclusion or resolution.

Imagine Laura, a person who has traveled significantly, giving an informative speech entitled "The art of shopping outside the United States: Bartering made simple." She might include the following:

> My husband and I were in Morocco shopping with my mother and my aunt. They stopped to speak with a shop owner about carpets and my husband looked around the store. About 45 minutes later, we walked by to see them *still* speaking with the shop owner. Now, though, all three were seated, and they were drinking hot mint tea. We approached the shopkeeper and introduced ourselves. He proceeded to tell us how different my mother and aunt were from most American women. He said that American women will ask the price of something, and he'll throw out some high price. Then the women will offer a significantly lower price. He rejects that but comes down a little bit on his original high price. The American women, usually, will accept his second price, no matter how high! Not these women! My mom and aunt bartered back and forth with the shopkeeper about the price, never giving in! The shopkeeper said he really enjoyed negotiating with them; that they were both friendly *and* insistent. They didn't back down easily, and, according to the shopkeeper, they ended up paying a reasonable price for their carpet.

By their nature, narratives demand that listeners take an active part in linking the story to the speaker's main point. The story moves from beginning to middle to end. Even if the speaker supplies the link after the narrative, audiences still make the connections themselves as they listen.

A narrative can be used anywhere in a speech. No matter where it is placed, it assumes great importance to listeners as they become involved with the details. Through the narrative, speakers can establish a connection with the audience that may continue even after the story is over.

Guidelines for Using Examples

Examples add interest and impact. They should be representative because examples support your core idea only when they accurately reflect the situation. No matter the type of example you use as supporting material, the following three guidelines will help you choose examples for your speeches:

Use examples frequently. Examples are often the lifeblood of a speech. Use them to make your points—but only in appropriate places. When using examples to prove a point, more than one example generally is needed.

Use only the amount of detail necessary. To make your examples work, you want to use only the amount of detail necessary for your audience and no more. The detail you provide in examples should be based on the needs of your audience. If your listeners are familiar with a topic, simply mention what the audience already knows. Interspersing long examples with short ones varies the pace and detail of your discussion.

Use examples to explain new concepts. Difficult concepts become easier to handle when you clarify them with examples. Keep in mind that your listeners might be hearing about complex concepts for the first time. Appropriate examples can mean communicating with or losing your audience.

Testimony

The word testimony may conjure a vision of witnesses in a court of law giving sworn statements to a judge and jury, adding credibility to a case. In public speaking, testimony has nothing to do with the law, but it has everything to do with credibility. When you cite the words of others, either directly or through paraphrasing, you are attempting, in effect, to strengthen your position by telling your audience that people with special knowledge support your position or take your side. Testimony can cite either experience or opinion. Also, short quotations are an effective way to provide testimony.

To be effective, however, testimony needs to be used in its proper context. Purposefully distorting testimony to suit the needs of your speech is misleading and unethical. Be honest to your source as well as your audience. Imagine the following (fictitious) statements *with* and *without* the information in parentheses:

> Michael Crane, head of the local disaster preparedness team, indicated, "The tornado will not have a great impact (if you have found an appropriate shelter)."

> Jenny Smith, director of Sexual Assault Counseling and Information Services said that "Jogging late at night is not very risky for women (who are jogging together in well-lit areas)."

> The local police chief stated, "Crime seldom happens in this town (when a strong police presence is felt)."

Clearly, the statements without parentheses are vastly different from the full statement. To leave out crucial information when providing testimony as supporting material is unethical, and can be dangerous.

Experience as testimony. Experience may be the most credible choice in some cases because someone was "on the scene." For example, if one were to discuss the Egyptian revolution that culminated in February 2011 with President Hosni Mubarak's resignation, testimony of Egyptian nationals would provide great impact. Wael Ghonim, whose "tweets offered both a narrative and a nudge to protesters," would be an excellent source because of his connection to the revolution (CBSnews.com/stories/2011/02/12). Angered by the killing of a 28-year-old Internet activist, who was beaten to death after trying to expose police corruption, Ghonim created a Facebook page with the picture of the dead activist called "We are all Khaled Said." Posted on January 25, 2011, it was instrumental in starting the anti-regime protests and also resulted in his arrest:

> "I was blindfolded for 12 days. I couldn't hear anything. I didn't know what was happening," he said. "I'm not a hero—I slept for 12 days. The heroes, they're the ones who were in the street, who took part in the demonstrations, sacrificed their lives, were beaten, arrested and exposed to danger." (adelaidenow.com, February 8, 2011)

His personal feelings and experiences provide greater impact than a simple description of the situation.

It is possible to use your own testimony when you are an expert. If you are developing a speech on what it is like to recover from a spinal cord injury, use your own expert testimony if you have suffered this injury. Similarly, if you are a female talking about the advantages and problems of being a female lifeguard, cite your own testimony if you have spent summers saving lives at the beach. When you do not have the background necessary to convince your audience, use the testimony of those who do. Remember, that in any speech, it is not sufficient to use your expertise as the sole supporting material. Your personal testimony is only one source. An effective speech uses multiple sources and various forms of supporting material.

Opinion as testimony. In some circumstances, the opinion of a recognized authority may provide the credibility needed to strengthen your argument or prove a point. Jimmy Carter, former president and winner of the Nobel Peace Prize in 2002, was an outspoken critic of the Iraqi War. CBS News (February 9, 2011) quoted him as saying, "I thought then, and I think now, that the invasion of Iraq was unnecessary and unjust. And I think the premises on which it was launched were false" (www. cbsnews.com). While he is clearly stating an opinion, Carter carries a certain amount of credibility

© Reuters/Corbis

Shown here making a statement after receiving the Nobel Peace Prize, Jimmy Carter's opinions carry credibility because of his past accomplishments.

because of his previous position as president of the United States and as a Nobel Peace Prize winner.

Short quotations. A short quotation is a form of testimony, but its purpose is often different. Frequently, short quotations are used to set the tone of a speech, to provide humor, or to make important points more memorable. If you were receiving the MVP award for football at your high school or college, you might start out with something like this:

> Wow. I'm reminded of John Madden's words when he was inducted into the Pro Football Hall of Fame in 2006, "And right now, I don't have, I got like numb, you know, a tingle from the bottom of my toes to the top of my head." Yep. That's exactly how I feel.

Madden's quote is not the most articulate or insightful comment, but it certainly expressed the emotion the football player was feeling, and this quote would set an engaging tone for an acceptance speech.

Sometimes quotations are too long or too complicated to present verbatim. You can choose to cite the source but paraphrase the message. The following is a relatively long quote by activist Judy Heumann, special advisor on disabilities rights for the U.S. State Department under President Obama, in her speech at the International Forum on Independent Living on how education empowers women with disabilities:

Quote:

> We are here today because disabled women still rank at the bottom of every scale that measures progress. Recent studies show that disabled women are among the least likely people to be employed, the most likely to live in dire poverty, and among the people most likely to die young! Studies have shown that strong networks, both national and international, are needed to enable girls and women with disabilities to support each other in their efforts to live independent, productive lives. (DINF.ne.je)

Based on her background and experience, Judy Heumann qualifies as an expert on disabilities issues. If a speaker believed that this quote was an appropriate length for the audience, that it added support, and time was not a factor, the whole quote could be used. However, paraphrasing might be a better choice. Here is another way to use information from her speech.

Paraphrase:

> According to Judy Heumann, the State Department's special advisor on disability rights, disabled women are the most likely people to be unemployed, live in dire poverty, and die young. However, strong support networks can help them lead independent, productive lives.

Paraphrasing is more effective when time is an issue and when getting facts out succinctly is important. Speakers always need to be mindful of the audience and what might have the greatest impact.

Guidelines for Using Testimony

Use only recognizable or credible testimony and quotations. At a time when media exposure is so pervasive, it is easy to find someone who will support your point of view. Before citing a person as an authoritative source, be sure that he or she is an expert. If you are giving a speech on the greatest movies ever produced, it would make sense to quote Roger Ebert, film critic and author of numerous books on the subject of film. However, he would not be the proper choice for a speech on the joys of collecting and trading baseball cards.

As you review expert testimony, keep in mind that the more research you do, the more opinions you will find. Ultimately, your choice should be guided by the relevance and credibility of the source. The fact that you quote Supreme Court justice Elena Kagan in a speech on affirmative action is as important as the quote itself.

Choose unbiased experts. How effective is the following testimony if its source is the *owner* of the Oakland Athletics?

> There is no team in baseball as complete as the Athletics. The team has better pitching, fielding, hitting, and base running than any of its competitors in the National or American League.

If the same quote came from a baseball writer for *Sports Illustrated* you would probably believe it more. Thus, when choosing expert testimony, bear in mind that opinions shaped by self-interest are less valuable, from the point of view of your audience, than those motivated by the merits of the issues.

Identify the source. Not all names of your experts will be recognizable, so it is important to tell your audience why they are qualified to give testimony. If you are cautioning overseas travelers to avoid tourist scams, the following expert testimony provides support:

> According to Rick Steves, travelers should be wary of "The 'helpful' local: Thieves posing as concerned locals will warn you to store your wallet safely—and then steal it after they see where you stash it. Some thieves put out tacks and ambush drivers with their 'assistance' in changing the tire. Others hang out at subway ticket machines eager to 'help' the bewildered tourist buy tickets with a pile of quickly disappearing foreign cash." (www.ricksteves.com)

Without knowing anything about Rick Steves, your readers have no reason to trust this advice. However, if you state his credentials first, you can establish the credibility of your expert. So instead, the speaker could start begin with, "According to Rick Steves, host and producer of the popular public television series Rick Steves' Europe and best-selling author of 30 European travel books, travelers should be wary of ..."

Develop techniques to signal the beginning and ending of each quotation. Your audience may not know when a quote begins or ends. Some speakers prefer to preface quotations with the words "And I quote" and to end quotations with the phrase "end quote." Other speakers indicate the presence of quotations through pauses immediately before and immediately after the quotation or through a slight change of pace or inflection. It may be a good idea to use both techniques in your speech to satisfy your listeners' need for variety. Just do not make quotation signs with your fingers!

Analogies

At times, the most effective form of supporting material is the analogy, which points out similarities between what we know and understand and what we do not know or cannot accept.

Analogies fall into two categories: figurative and literal. **Figurative analogies** draw comparisons between things that are distinctly different in an attempt to clarify a concept or persuade. Biology professor and world-renowned environmentalist Paul Ehrlich uses an analogy of a globe holding and draining water to explain the problem of the world population explosion. The following is an excerpt from a speech delivered to the First National Congress on Optimum Population and Environment, June 9, 1970:

> As a model of the world demographic situation, think of the world as a globe, and think of a faucet being turned on into that globe as being the equivalent of the birth rate, the input into the population. Think of that drain at the base of that globe—water pouring out—as being the equivalent to the output, the death rate of the population. At the time of the Agricultural Revolution, the faucet was turned on full blast; there was a very high birth rate. The drain was wide open; there was a high death rate. There was very little water in the globe, very few people in the population—only above five million. When the Agricultural Revolution took place, we began to plug the drain, cut down the death rate, and the globe began to fill up.

This analogy is effective because it helps the audience understand the population explosion. It explains the nature of the problem in a clear, graphic way. Listener understanding comes not from the presentation of new facts (these facts were presented elsewhere in the speech) but from a simple comparison. When dealing with difficult or emotionally charged concepts, listeners benefit from this type of comparative supporting material.

Keep in mind that while figurative analogies may be helpful, they usually do not serve as sufficient proof in a persuasive argument. Ehrlich, for example, must back his analogy with facts, statistics, examples, and quotations to persuade his listeners that his analogy is accurate—that we are indeed in the midst of a population crisis.

A literal analogy compares like things from similar classes, such as a game of professional football with a game of college football. If, for example, you are delivering a speech to inform your classmates about Russia's involvement in the war in Afghanistan, the following literal analogy might be helpful:

> The war in Afghanistan was the former Soviet Union's Vietnam. Both wars were unwinnable from the start. Neither the Vietnamese nor the Afghans would tolerate foreign domination. Acting with the determination of the Biblical David, they waged a struggle against the Goliaths of Russia and the United States. In large part, the winning weapon in both wars was the collective might of village peasants who were determined to rid their countries of the Superpowers—no matter the odds.

Literal analogies serve as proof when the aspects or concepts compared are similar. When similarities are weak, the proof fails. The analogy, "As Rome fell because of moral decay, so will the United States," is valid only if the United States and Rome have similar economic and social systems, types of governments, and so on. The fewer the similarities between the United States and ancient Rome, the weaker the proof.

Guidelines for Using Analogies

Use analogies to build the power of your argument. Analogies convince through comparison to something the audience already knows. It is psychologically comforting to your listeners to hear new ideas expressed in a familiar context. The result is greater understanding and possible acceptance of your point of view.

Be certain the analogy is clear. Even when the concept of your analogy is solid, if the points of comparison are not effectively carried through from beginning to end, the analogy will fail. Your analogy must be as consistent and complete as in the following example:

> In political campaigns, opponents square off against one another in an attempt to land the winning blow. Although after a close and grueling campaign that resembles a 10-round bout, one candidate may succeed by finding a soft spot in his opponent's record, the fight is hardly over. Even while the downed opponent is flat against the mat, the victor turns to the public and tells yet another distortion of the truth. "My

Glossary

Literal analogy Compares like things from similar classes, such as a game of professional football with a game of college football.

opponent," he says, "never had a chance." Clearly, politicians and prize fighters share one goal in common: to knock their opponents senseless and to make the public believe that they did it with ease.

Avoid using too many analogies. A single effective analogy can communicate your point. Do not diminish its force by including several in a short presentation.

Documenting Information Accurately in Your Speech

Any research included in your speech needs to be cited appropriately to give due credit. A citation is the way you tell your readers that certain material in your work came from another source (plagiarism.org). Some might think that citing sources makes their work seem less original. On the contrary, citing sources helps your listener distinguish your ideas from those of your sources, which will actually emphasize the originality of your own work.

Citing or documenting the sources used in your research serves two purposes. First, it gives proper credit to the authors of the materials used. Second, it allows those who are reading your work to duplicate your research and locate the sources that you have listed as references (www.olinuris. library.cornell.edu).

If you interviewed someone, your audience should know the person's name, credentials, and when and where you spoke with the person. If you use information from a website, the audience should know the name of the website and when you accessed it. For print information, the audience generally needs to know the author, date, and type of publication. Your credibility is connected to your source citation. Expert sources and timely information add to your credibility.

Essentially, all research used in your speech needs to be cited. Otherwise, you have committed an act of plagiarism. According to the *Merriam-Webster Online Dictionary*, to *plagiarize* means:

- To use [another's production] without crediting the source
- To commit literary theft
- To present as new and original an idea or product derived from an existing source
- To steal and pass off (the ideas or words of another) as one's own

Most institutions of higher learning specify what consequences will accrue to the student who plagiarizes. However, not all instances of plagiarism occur within the ivory tower. Following are examples of plagiarism that were considered newsworthy:

- In June 2010, Philip Baker, the University of Alberta's dean of medicine, resigned in the wake of allegations that he plagiarized a speech he gave at a banquet for graduating medical students (www.montrealgazette.com).

- In February 2010, *New York Times* reporter Zachery Kouwe reused language from *The Wall Street Journal*, Reuters, and other sources without attribution or acknowledgment (www.guardian.co.uk).

- An anonymous online poll of more than a thousand students at Britain's Cambridge University found 49 percent admitting that they have passed someone else's work off as their own at some point in their academic career (www.globalethics.org).

- A French writer lost her plagiarism suit against the makers of the George Clooney film *Syriana* with a court in Paris ruling that an author "cannot claim a monopoly on facts of history or current affairs or on political ideas" (www.globalethics.org).

Plagiarism is unethical, and it can result in academic punishment, public embarrassment, or damage to your career. We cannot underscore enough the importance of doing your own work and giving credit to sources. Following are ways to cite sources in your speech. *Consult your instructor*, however, as he or she may have specific concerns.

Example 1:

- **Correct source citation.** In their 2007 book on intercultural communication, researchers Samovar, Porter, and McDaniel argue that travel has extended our sources of diversity because we can now be exposed "to cultural idiosyncrasies in the perception of time and space, the treatment of women and the elderly, the ways and means of conducting business, and even the discover and meaning of truth."

- **Incorrect source citation.** Researchers on intercultural communication argue international travel exposes us to many more aspects of culture than it used to, including observing how people treat women and the elderly, and how they conduct business.

- **Explanation.** We need the date to evaluate the timeliness of the material. We need to know this information was found in a book, as opposed to a TV show, a newspaper, magazine, or other source. We need the authors' names so we know who wrote the information, and so we can find the book. (Remember that if this quote were on your outline, you would need to provide the page number after the quotation marks.)

Example 2:

○ **Correct source citation.** According to a personal interview last week with Diane Ruyle, principal of Danube High School, fewer students are choosing vocational classes than they were 10 years ago.

○ **Incorrect source citation.** According to Diane Ruyle, fewer students are choosing vocational classes.

○ **Explanation.** We need to know why the speaker cited Diane Ruyle. As a principal, she ought to be able to provide accurate information regarding course selection. Adding "than they were 10 years ago" gives the listener a comparison basis. Also, we need to know that this interview was timely; it occurred "last week."

Example 3:

○ **Correct source citation.** According to an Associated Press article published in the *New York Times* on August 9, 2010, "[U]nlike in South Carolina, state laws in Iowa and New Hampshire require officials there to hold the first caucus and primary in the nation, respectively."

○ **Incorrect source citation.** Unlike in South Carolina, state laws in Iowa and New Hampshire require officials there to hold the first caucus and primary in the nation, respectively.

○ **Explanation.** First, if this is published information, it should be cited. Second, since most of us do not know these facts, a citation is necessary. Otherwise, the listener may believe the speaker is making this up. The date provided allows us to check the source and shows us that the information is timely. No author was identified, and since Associated Press articles can be found in many newspapers, it is important to note this was found in the *New York Times*.

Example 4:

○ **Correct source citation.** According to the American Diabetes Association website accessed last week, "Cholesterol is carried through the body in two kinds of bundles called lipoproteins—low-density lipoproteins and high-density lipoproteins. It's important to have healthy levels of both."

○ **Incorrect source citation.** Cholesterol is carried through the body in two kinds of bundles called lipoproteins—low-density lipoproteins and high-density lipoproteins. It's important to have healthy levels of both.

○ **Explanation.** This information is not common knowledge, so it should be cited. Many organizations might include such information on their website, so it is important to note that it came from the American Diabetes Association (ADA). An audience would infer that the ADA is a credible organization regarding this topic. Using the words "last week" suggests current information on the ADA website, which reinforces the timeliness of the material.

In summary, remember that you *do not* need to cite sources when you are reporting your own original ideas or discussing ideas that are commonly held. You *must* cite sources when you are quoting directly or paraphrasing (restating or summarizing a source's ideas in your own words). You must also cite the source of an illustration, diagram, or graph. Providing the date of publication, date of website access, credentials of the source, and/or type of publication where applicable allows the listener to evaluate the credibility of the information. Failing to do so is plagiarism, which is a form of academic dishonesty. Not only may your speech grade suffer, but your instructor is encouraged to report incidents of academic dishonesty to the office on campus that deals with student misconduct.

Summary

Research gives you the tools you need to support your thesis statement. A solid research base increases your credibility. To begin your research strategy, assess your personal knowledge and skills. Then look for print and online resources. The librarian can lead you to valuable sources within the physical library as well as online. You may need to look up information in encyclopedias, dictionaries, books, newspapers, magazines, journal articles, and government documents. When using online resources, it is important to use website evaluation criteria and to question accuracy, authority, objectivity, coverage, and currency.

Supporting materials buttress the main points of your speech and make you a more credible speaker. Among the most important forms of support are facts—verifiable information. Facts clarify your main points, indicate knowledge of your subject, and serve as definitions. Opinions differ from facts in that they cannot be verified. Statistical support involves the presentation of information in numeric form. Because statistics are easily manipulated, it is important to analyze carefully the data you present.

Five types of examples are commonly used as forms of support. Brief examples are short illustrations that clarify a general statement. Extended examples are used to create lasting images. Narratives are stories within a speech that are linked to the speaker's main idea. Hypothetical examples are fictional examples used to make a point. Personal examples are anecdotes related to your topic that come from your own life.

When you use expert testimony, you cite the words of others to increase the credibility of your message. Your sources gain expertise through experience and authority. Analogies focus on the similarities between the familiar and unfamiliar. Figurative analogies compare things that are different, while literal analogies compare things from similar classes. Literal analogies can often be used as proof.

Discussion Starters

1. How important is research in the preparation of most speeches? How can an audience tell if a speech lacks a sound research base?

2. Why is it important that you conduct both an audience analysis and reflect on your own knowledge and skills when it comes to developing your topic?

3. When you are considering information you found on a website, how do you evaluate whether the information you found is appropriate to include as supporting material?

4. How can you best use the services of a librarian?

5. With the idea of a research strategy in mind, how will you determine the types and amount of support you will need to meet the specific purpose of your next speech?

6. Which supporting materials are most effective for clarifying a point and which are most appropriate for proof? Can some forms of support serve both aims? If so, how? If not, why not?

7. In the hands of an unethical speaker, how can statistics and analogies mislead an audience? What is your ethical responsibility in choosing supporting materials?

References

About LexisNexis. Retrieved August 31, 2011 from www.lexisnexis.com/about-us/.

Brook, S. (2010, February 15). *New York Times Investigates Plagiarism Incident.* Retrieved June 20, 2011 from www.guardian.co.uk.

Cookie Fun Fact. Retrieved August 31, 2011 from www.littlebrowniebakers.com/cookies/cookie-fun-facts/.

Ehrlich, P. (1970, June 9). *Speech delivered to First National Congress on Optimum Population and Environment.*

The Face of Egypt's Networking Revolution. Retrieved August 31, 2011 from CBSnews.com/stories/2011/02/12/eveningnews/20031662.shtml.

Google Exec Tells of a 12-Day Egypt Ordeal. Retrieved August 1, 2011 from www.adelaidenow.com/au/news/breaking-news/google-exec-tells-of-a-12-day-Egypt-ordeal/story/.

Harris, R. (2002). *Using Sources Effectively: Strengthening Your Writing and Avoiding Plagiarism.* Glendale, CA: Pyrczak Publishing.

Heumann, J. (1988). *Education: Engine of Empowerment* (Speech). Retrieved August 31, 2011 from www.dinf.ne.jp/doc/english/conf/z20/z20001/z200100.html.

Jimmy Carter Slams Iraq War. Retrieved February 11, 2009 from www. cbsnews.com/stories/2005/07/30/politics/main712910.shtml.

Major League Baseball Salaries: 2011 MLB Salaries by Team. Retrieved August 1, 2011 from content.USAtoday.com/sportsdata/baseball/mlb/ salaries/team.

Obama, Barack. (2009, October). *Presidential Proclamation for Information Literacy Awareness Month.* Accessed October 1, 2009 from www. whitehouse.gov.

Owl.english.purdue.edu. Retrieved June 22, 2011.

Pierse, C., & Simons, P. (2011, June 17). *University's Dean of Medicine Resigns After Plagiarism Accusations.* Retrieved June 20, 2011 from montrealgazette.com.

Plagiarism Incidents Featured in World Press Reports. (2008, November 17). Retrieved June 20, 2011 from www.globalethics.org.

Radford, M. L., Barnes, S. B., & Barr, L. (2006). *Web Research: Selecting, Evaluating, and Citing.* Boston: Allyn & Bacon.

Raimes, A. (2008). *Keys for Writers*, 5th Ed. Boston: Houghton Mifflin Harcourt Publishing Company.

Samovar, L. A., Porter, R. E., & McDaniel, E. R. (2007). *Communication Between Cultures*, 6th Ed. Belmont, CA: Thompson Wadsworth.

The Seven Steps of the Research Process. Retrieved June 20, 2011 from www. olinuris.library.cornell.edu.

Steves, Rick. (n.d.). *Tourist Scams in Europe.* Retrieved August 31, 2011 from www.ricksteves.com/plan/tips/298scam.htm.

U.S. & World Population Clocks. Retrieved August 31, 2011 from www. census.gov/main/www/popclock.html.

What Is Citation? Retrieved June 20, 2011 from www.plagiarism.org.

What Is Google Scholar? Retrieved August 31, 2011 from scholar.google. com/intl/en/scholar/about/html.

Chapter

7

"*Organize, don't agonize.*"

Nancy Pelosi

Chapter 7: Organizing and Outlining Your Ideas

Organizing a speech helps the audience follow your points and understand your message. This chapter concentrates on developing the body of your speech, including selecting, supporting, and organizing your Main Points. It also discusses how to create effective outlines and speaker's notes to best serve you as you present.

Student Learning Objectives:

○ Students will be able to specify the importance of organizing a speech

○ Students will be able to identify and explain the benefits of organizing the body of the speech

○ Students will be able to understand how to create unity through connections

○ Students will be able to construct and edit notes and delivery outlines

Organizing and Outlining Your Ideas

Have you ever had a friend tell you a story, and at some point, you interrupt to say, "Huh? What?" You express confusion over the point of the story, or you don't know the context, or maybe even the people involved? Your friend left something out.

Imagine Professor Plunkett whose unorganized, rambling lessons gallop along, often jumping from topic to topic. Listening to his lecture is like watching a ping-pong ball bounce aimlessly across the table; you never know where the professor will land or what direction his comments will take next. His students—those still awake, that is—often struggle to comprehend what the professor wants them to take away from his message.

The Importance of Organizing a Speech

A good speech flows smoothly and consists of a clear introduction, body, and conclusion. Your listeners should be able to identify these parts of your speech. Also, listeners expect your speech to be logical and organized. A speech that is missing a clear introduction or that has main points unrelated to the introduction will confuse, irritate, or simply turn off your listeners. It doesn't matter if you have gathered astounding facts or if you have incredible quotations to support your points if your speech is not structured logically.

Rather than just starting to write your speech, first consider how best to organize it. If you spend time outlining your ideas, you will discover where you have deficiencies in research, where you have too much information, or where you haven't made appropriate connections from one point to the next. This chapter leads you through organizing the body of a speech step-by-step. We begin with selecting and supporting main points. Next, we present several organizational patterns as well as a template for organizing your main points. You have many decisions to make when organizing, such as the pattern of organization, the number of main points needed, what relevant subpoints to include, and where to put transitions and internal previews. We conclude with a discussion of outlining as a tool to aid you in becoming an organized speaker.

Organizing the Body of Your Speech

The organization of ideas in public speaking refers to the placement of lines of reasoning and supporting materials in a pattern that achieves your chosen general purpose and specific purpose by supporting your thesis. Following a consistent pattern of organization helps listeners pay attention to your message. An organized speech with connected main points helps you maintain a clear focus that leads listeners to a logical conclusion. An organized speech flows smoothly and clearly, from introduction through body to conclusion.

Your introduction and conclusion support the body of your speech. The introduction should capture your audience's attention and indicate your intent. The conclusion reinforces your message and brings your speech to a close. The body includes your main points and supporting material that bolster your specific purpose and thesis statement. The introduction and conclusion are important, but audiences expect you to spend the most time and effort amplifying your main points.

For the body of your speech to flow in an organized, logical way, reflect first on your general purpose, specific purpose, and thesis statement. Your general purpose is either to inform, persuade, or entertain. Since your specific purpose is a statement of intent and your thesis statement identifies the main ideas of your speech, referring to them as you determine your main points prevents misdirection. For example, consider a speech discussing how family pets help children with psychological problems. You might develop the following:

General Purpose: To inform

Specific Purpose: To explain to my class how pets can provide unexpected psychological benefits for children with emotional problems by helping to bolster their self-esteem

Thesis Statement: A close relationship with a family pet can help children with emotional problems feel better about themselves, help therapists build rapport with difficult-to-reach patients, and encourage the development of important social skills.

Your thesis statement indicates your speech will address self-esteem, rapport with therapists, and the development of social skills. This suggests that there are many peripheral topics you will *exclude*, such as the type of pet, pet grooming tips, medical advances in the treatment of feline leukemia, how to choose a kennel when you go on vacation, and so on.

Select Your Main Points

Organizing the body of your speech involves a *four-step process: select the main points, support the main points, choose the best organizational pattern, and create unity throughout the speech.* Before organizing your speech, determine your main points. Main points are the key ideas, or most important issues you

Glossary

Organization of ideas The placement of lines of reasoning and supporting materials in a pattern that helps to achieve your specific purpose.

Introduction Supports the body of your speech and should capture your audience's attention and indicate your intent.

Conclusion Supports the body of your speech, reinforces your message, and brings your speech to a close.

Body Includes your main points and supporting material that reinforces your specific purpose and thesis statement.

General purpose There are three general purposes for speeches: to inform, to persuade, and to entertain or inspire.

Specific purpose The precise response you want from your audience.

Thesis statement The core idea; identifies the main ideas of your speech.

want to discuss with your audience. One way to discover your main points is through **brainstorming**. Brainstorming can occur at any stage of a process, but brainstorming for main points should happen *after* you have gathered sufficient information during topic research.

A best practice is to arrive at *no fewer than two and not more than five main points*. If you add more, you may confuse your listeners, and you may not have time to provide adequate support. All ideas must relate to your general purpose, specific purpose, and thesis statement. The audience analysis you have done previously should ensure your main points are audience-centered.

For purposes of illustration, consider the following:

General Purpose: To inform

Specific Purpose: To describe to my class the causes, symptoms, and treatment of shyness

Thesis Statement: Shyness, which is an anxiety response in social situations that limits social interactions, may respond to appropriate treatment.

Your brainstorming process for the topic of shyness might result in a list of possible main points that include, but are clearly not limited to, the following: symptoms of shyness, shyness and heredity, shyness as an anxiety response, physical and psychological indications of shyness, number of people affected by shyness, shyness and self-esteem, how to handle a job interview if you are shy, treatment for shyness, and what to do when your date is shy.

On reflection, you may realize that several of these points overlap, and others do not relate as much to your thesis statement and should be discarded. So, you make the following list of six possible important points: symptoms of shyness, causes of shyness, treatment for shyness, number of people affected by shyness, shyness as an anxiety response, and shyness and self-esteem.

With six being too many main points to develop, you decide that "shyness as an anxiety response" describes a symptom of shyness and that "shyness and self-esteem" describes a cause. You decide that a discussion of the number of people affected by shyness belongs in your introduction because it is startlingly widespread. Your final list of main points may look like this: symptoms of shyness, causes of shyness, treatment for shyness.

Through this process, you transformed a random list into a focused set of idea clusters reflecting broad areas of your speech. Your main points should be mutually exclusive; each point should be distinct. In addition, each point must relate to and support your thesis statement. We now turn our attention to supporting your points.

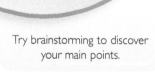

Try brainstorming to discover your main points.

Support Your Main Points

After selecting your main points, use the supporting material you gathered to strengthen each main point. Fitting each piece of research into its appropriate place may seem like completing a complex jigsaw puzzle. Patterns must be matched, rational links must be formed, and common sense must prevail. Each point underneath the main point is called a subpoint (and subsubpoint, and so on). Each subpoint is an extension of the point it supports. If the connection seems forced, reconsider the match. Here, for example, is one way to develop three main points for the speech on shyness. As you sit at your computer, you can expand phrases into sentences. So for now, you can begin to think in terms of the language of your speech. Keep in mind, we are focusing on organization, not the formal outline.

I.   **Main Point 1:** The symptoms of shyness fall into two categories: those that can be seen and those that are felt.

    A. Objective symptoms (symptoms that can be seen) make it apparent to others that you are suffering from shyness, including blushing, dry mouth, cold clammy hands, trembling hands and knocking knees, excessive sweating, and belligerence.

    B. According to psychologist Philip Zimbardo, many shy people never develop the social skills necessary to deal with difficult situations (symptoms that are felt).

    C. They may experience embarrassment, feelings of inferiority or inadequacy, feelings of self-consciousness, a desire to flee, and generalized anxiety. They overreact by becoming argumentative.

    D. Internal symptoms like an unsettled stomach and dizziness make the experience horrible for the sufferer.

II. **Main Point 2:** Recent research has focused on three potential causes of shyness.

    A. Heredity seems to play a large part.

    B. Psychologists at Yale and Harvard have found that 10 to 15 percent of all children are shy from birth. Dr. Jerome Kagan of Harvard found that shy children are wary and withdrawn even with people they know.

    C. Shyness is also the result of faulty learning that lowers self-esteem instead of boosting self-confidence.

        1. When parents criticize a child's ability or appearance or fail to praise the child's success, they plant the seeds of shyness by lowering self-esteem.

        2. Older siblings may destroy a child's self-image through bullying and belittlement.

    D. Shyness is also attributable to poor social skills, due to never having learned how to interact with others, which leaves shy people in an uncomfortable position.

III. **Main Point 3:** Shyness is not necessarily a life sentence; treatment is possible and so is change.

　　A. In a survey of 10,000 adults, Stanford University researchers found that 40 percent said that they had been shy in the past but no longer suffered from the problem.

　　B. People who are extremely shy may benefit from professional therapy offered by psychiatrists and psychologists.

As you weave together your main points and support, your speech should grow in substance and strength. It will be clear to your listeners that you have something to say and that you are saying it in an organized way. (For guidelines on support materials, see **BTW: Is That Supported?**)

Choose the Best Pattern for Organizing Your Main Points

The way you organize your main points depends on your general purpose, specific purpose and thesis statement, the type of material you are presenting, and the needs of your audience. As you develop your main points, consider what you want to emphasize. Assuming you have established three main points, choose how to weight your main points. Three options are possible. First, you may choose the **equality pattern**, which involves giving

Glossary

Equality pattern Giving equal time to each point.

BTW!　　　　　　　　　　　　　　　　　　**Is That Supported?**

The University of Hawaii offers five General Guidelines for Supporting Materials. Use their quick primer to see if your support measures up:

1. Pertinence. Each piece of support should be clearly relevant to the point it is used to support.

2. Variety. The presentation should not rely excessively on one type of support (such as examples) but should instead use a number of forms of support.

3. Amount. The presentation should include a sufficient amount of support (enough to make the ideas presented both clear and compelling to the audience).

4. Detail. Each piece of support needs to be developed to the point that audience members can both understand the item of support and can see how the item backs up the point it is used to support.

5. Appropriateness. Each piece of supporting material should meet the demands that the audience and the occasion place on the kind of material that is likely to be received favorably. A "scholarly" audience, for example, will probably place higher demands on the speaker's sources of information than a "general" audience would. A "graphic" description of a particular topic, while entirely fitting in some occasions, might be out of place in another.

Source: www.hawaii.edu/mauispeech/html/supporting_materials.html

equal time to each point. This means that you will spend approximately the same time on each main point as you deliver the body of your speech.

Using the **strongest point pattern** is a second option. In this case, your first point would take about half of the time you devote to the body of your speech, the second point would be given about one-third, and your final point would receive the least. The advantage to this method is in getting the audience to process, retain, and recall your strongest points. When testing memory, psychologists discovered that, when presented with a list of items, individuals remembered information that was presented either at the beginning of the list *or* at the end. The strongest point pattern, which weighs the first point more heavily than the other points, reflects the phenomenon known as the **primacy effect**. Note there is danger of using this pattern. Our strongest points may also be the most complex and if discussed early in the speech may confuse or turn off the audience.

A third option is to follow a **progressive pattern**. This involves presenting your least important point first and your most important point last. The amount of time given to each is the inverse of the strongest point pattern, so that the last point receives the lion's share of time, the second point receives less, and the first point is the briefest. **Recency effect** suggests people will remember most what they have just processed. Anyone who has heard the phrase "What have you done for me lately?" understands the recency effect. A danger of this pattern is present when we lose our audience by providing weak material first, and in so doing, fail to capture interest.

The pattern for weighting your main points depends on your topic and audience. Based on these three options, keep in mind that your strongest argument does not go in the middle of your main points.

In addition to weighting your main points for emphasis, your information should fit within an overall organizational framework. Many choices exist for any given speech but based on the general purpose, specific purpose, and thesis sentence, one pattern of organization is generally more appropriate than the others. Typically, the right organizational pattern emerges organically as you work with the body of your speech, provided you know in advance what patterns to look for. The five effective patterns of organization to look for are chronological, topic, spatial, causal, and problem–solution. To show how different organizational patterns affect the content and emphasis of a speech, we choose a topic, establish different purposes for speaking, and show how the presentation differs when the organizational pattern is changed.

Chronological Organization

In a chronological speech, information is focused *on relationships in time.* Events are presented in the order in which they occur. When developing your speech chronologically, you might choose to organize your ideas by starting at the beginning and moving to the present, then looking to the future, as in a story, or going step-by-step, as you would if following a recipe.

Glossary

Strongest point pattern You spend the most time in your speech on the first point, less time on the second point, and even less time on the last point of your speech.

Primacy effect The belief that it is the first point in your speech that listeners will most likely remember.

Progressive pattern Progression from least important argument to most important argument.

Recency effect The belief that it is the last point in your speech that listeners will most likely remember.

Topic: The development of the European Union

General Purpose: To inform

Specific Purpose: To inform the class about crucial events that occurred over a 40-year span that influenced the development of the European Union (EU)

Thesis Statement: Although the European Union was formed in 1993, the creation of a coal and steel community, establishment of a common market, and direct elections to the European Parliament were critical events that influenced its development.

Main Points:

I. West Germany, together with France, Italy, and Benelux, signed the Treaty of Paris in 1951 which created the European Coal and Steel community.

II. In 1957 the Treaty of Rome established the European Economic Community, known as the common market to English-speaking countries.

III. In 1979 the first direct elections to the European Parliament were held.

IV. In 1992, with the signing of the Maastricht Treaty, the European Union was created.

Chronological order can also be used to construct a past-present-future organizational pattern. For example, in a speech addressing the development of the European Union, one could present the same topic with a slightly different specific purpose statement that would lead to a different thesis statement and different focus for the main points. Consider the following:

Topic: The development of the European Union

General Purpose: To inform

Specific Purpose: To inform the class how the European Union became a 27-member community that is poised to grow significantly

Thesis Statement: Developed after three important treaties, the 27-member European Union is poised to add another nine countries to its community.

Main Points:

I. Treaties of Paris, Rome, and Maastricht were crucial to the development of the European Union.

II. Currently, the European Union is a community of 27 member states connected both politically and economically.

III. As an indicator of future growth, at least nine countries are potential candidates for inclusion in the European Union.

Past-Present-Future

Using a past-present-future order allows a speaker to provide perspective for a topic or issue that has relevant history and future direction or potential. Notice that in the regular chronological pattern, the three treaties are the main focus of the speech. In the past-present-future pattern, the three treaties would receive much less coverage.

Step-by-Step

Chronological patterns can be used to describe the steps in a process. Here is a step-by-step description of how college texts are produced. Like the other patterns, the process shows a movement in time:

Step 1: The author, having gathered permissions for use of copyrighted material, delivers a manuscript to the publisher.

Step 2: The manuscript is edited, a design and cover are chosen, photos are selected, and illustrations are drawn.

Step 3: The edited manuscript is sent to a compositor for typesetting and set in galley and page proof form.

Step 4: The final proof stage is released to the printing plant where the book is printed and bound.

Spatial Organization

In speeches organized according to a spatial pattern, the sequence of ideas moves from one physical point to another—from London to Istanbul, from basement to attic, from end zone to end zone. To be effective, your speech must follow a consistent directional path. If you are presenting a new marketing strategy to the company sales force, you can arrange your presentation by geographic regions—first the East, then the South, then the Midwest, and finally, the West. So, in a speech on the European Union, one could use a spatial organization pattern to discuss the growth of the EU over time.

I. Six Western European countries joined to establish the European Union.

II. Countries bordering the Eastern Mediterranean are candidates for inclusion in the European Union.

III. As Central and Eastern European countries emerged from dictatorship, they wanted to join the European Union to avoid falling back into the Russian sphere of influence.

Notice the differences between the main points for this speech organized spatially versus chronologically. A speech with the above three points would focus more on the countries involved with the European Union than how the EU came about.

Cause and Effect

With the cause and effect organizational pattern, the speaker can focus specifically on why something happened and what the consequences of the event or action were. The following statements could be developed into a speech that uses a cause and effect pattern:

- Difficult economic times after World War II created the necessity for European countries to work together.
- Alcoholism damages American family life.
- Too much positive feedback in primary school results in young adults being unable to cope with life's problems.
- Fast food is a significant contributor to obesity in America.
- Traveling abroad reduces prejudice.
- Smoking hurts relationships.

Note that in each case, the speaker is trying to provide that something caused something to happen. For example, the effect alcoholism has on family life is that it causes harm. The effect traveling has on people is reducing prejudice. Therefore, traveling is seen as a cause. Some topics have direct links that can be made with facts and/or statistics (Smoking causes cancer) and others have indirect links that must be proved with facts and other forms of support, such as testimony, examples, or illustrations (Smoking hurts relationships).

Problem–Solution Organization

A common strategy, especially in persuasive speeches, is to present an audience with a problem and then examine one or more likely solutions. For example, in a classroom speech, one student described a serious safety problem for women walking alone on campus after dark. He cited incidents in which women were attacked and robbed, and described unlit areas along campus walkways where the attacks had taken place. Next, he turned to a series of proposals to eliminate, or at least minimize, the problem. His proposals included a new escort service, sponsored and maintained by campus organizations, the installation of halogen lights along dark campus walks, and the trimming of bushes where muggers could hide.

Occasionally, speakers choose to present the solution before the problem. Had this student done so, he would have identified how to provide effective security before he explained why these solutions were necessary. Many audiences have trouble with this type of reversal because they find it hard to accept solutions when they are not familiar with the problems that brought them about.

Later in this chapter is an outline of a speech entitled "Revisiting Standard American English." The topic is developed using a problem–solution pattern.

Problem: Requiring speakers and writers to use Standard American English only promotes racism and classism.

Solution: Insist that teachers teach grammar by separating written English and spoken English and study the differences in grammar of both styles in the classroom.

Here the goal is to persuade an audience that a problem still exists and to have listeners agree about how it can be effectively handled.

Topical Organization

The most frequently used organizational system is not tied to time or space, problem or solution, or cause-and-effect, but to the unique needs of your topic. The nature and scope of your topic dictate the pattern of your approach.

If you are delivering an after-dinner humorous speech on the responses of children to their first week of preschool, you can arrange your topics according to their level of humor. For example:

1. The *school supplies* preschoolers think are necessary to survive at school

2. The *behavior of youngsters at school* when they do not get their own way

3. Children's stories of *their lives at home*

4. *The reasons children believe their parents send them to school*

These topics relate to children and their first week at school, but there is no identifiable chronological pattern, so topical order makes sense. When organizing topically, think about how to link and order topics. Transitions can help the audience understand the connections and are discussed in the following section.

Create Unity Through Connections

Without connections, your main points may be difficult to follow. Your audience may wonder what you are trying to say and why you have tried to connect ideas that do not seem to have any relationship with each other. To establish the necessary connections, use transitions, internal previews, and internal summaries.

Transitions

Transitions are the verbal bridges between ideas. They are words, phrases, or sentences that tell your audience how ideas relate. Transitions are critical because they clarify the direction of your speech by giving your audience a means to follow your organization. With only one opportunity to hear your remarks, listeners depend on transitions to make sense of your ideas.

Glossary

Transitions   Verbal bridges between ideas, words, phrases, or sentences that tell your audience how ideas relate.

It helps to think of transitions as verbal signposts that signal the organization and structure of your speech. Here are several examples:

"The first proposal I would like to discuss ..."

This tells listeners that several more ideas will follow.

"Now that we've finished looking at the past, let's move to the future."

These words indicate a movement in time.

"Next, I'll turn from a discussion of the problems to a discussion of the solution."

This tells your listeners that you are following a problem–solution approach.

"On the other hand, many people believe ..."

Here you signal an opposing viewpoint.

The following is a list of common transitional words that reflect the speaker's purpose in using them.

TABLE 6.1 Suggested Transitional Words	
Speaker's Purpose	
1. To define	*that is to say; according to; in other words*
2. To explain	*for example; specifically*
3. To add	*furthermore; also; in addition; likewise*
4. To change direction	*although; on the other hand; conversely*
5. To show both sides	*nevertheless; equally*
6. To contrast	*but; still; on the contrary*
7. To indicate cause	*because; for this reason; since; on account of*
8. To summarize	*recapping; finally; in retrospect; summing up*
9. To conclude	*in conclusion; therefore; and so; finally*
(Makay & Fetzger, 1984, p. 68)	

Internal Previews and Summaries

Internal previews are extended transitions that tell the audience, in general terms, what you will say next. These are frequently used in the body of the speech to outline in advance the details of a main point. Here are two examples:

○ I am going to discuss the orientation you can expect to receive during your first few days on the job, including a tour of the plant, a one-on-one meeting with your supervisor, and a second meeting with the personnel director, who will explain the benefits and responsibilities of working for our corporation.

○ Now that I've shown you that "junk" is the appropriate word to describe junk bonds, we will turn to an analysis of three secure financial instruments: bank certificates of deposit, Treasury bonds, and high-quality corporate paper.

While the first example would be found at the end of the introduction, notice that in the second example, the speaker combines a transition linking the material previously examined with the material to come. Previews are especially helpful when your main point is long and complex. Previews give listeners a set of expectations for what they will hear next. Use them whenever it is necessary to set the stage for your ideas (Turner, 1970, pp. 24–39).

Internal summaries follow a main point and act as reminders. Summaries are especially useful if you are trying to clarify or emphasize what you have just said, as is shown in the following two examples:

○ In short, the American family today is not what it was 40 years ago. As we have seen, with the majority of women working outside the home and with divorce and remarriage bringing stepchildren into the family picture, the traditional family—made up of a working father, a nonworking mother, and 2.3 kids—may be a thing of the past.

○ By and large, the job market seems to be easing for health care professionals, including nurses, aides, medical technicians, physical therapists, and hospital administrators.

When summaries are combined with previews, they emphasize your previous point and make connections to the point to follow:

> Overall, it is my view that cigarette advertising should not be targeted specifically at minority communities. As we have seen, R. J. Reynolds test-marketed a cigarette for African Americans known as "Uptown," only to see it come under a barrage of criticism. What is fair advertising for cigarette makers? We will discuss that next.

Organization plays an important role in effective communication. The principles rhetoricians developed five centuries ago about the internal arrangement of ideas in public speaking have been tested by time and continue

Glossary

Internal previews Extended transitions that tell the audience, in general terms, what you will say next.

Internal summaries Follow a main point and act as reminders; useful to clarify or emphasize what you have just said.

to be valid. (See **BTW: Classic Rhetorical Arrangement**.) Internal previews and summaries help the speaker create meaning with the audience by reinforcing the message and identifying what comes next. Keep in mind that audience members do not have the opportunity to replay or to stop for clarification. Using transitions, previews, and internal summaries are tools a speaker can use to facilitate understanding and reduce the potential for misunderstanding (Clarke, 1963, pp. 23–27; Daniels & Whitman, 1981, pp. 147–160).

Constructing an Outline and Speaker's Notes

Outlining is a time-consuming process, but one that will pay off in a skillful, confident presentation.

Presenting your ideas in an organized way requires a carefully constructed planning outline and a key-word outline to be used as speaker's notes. Both forms are critical to your success as an extemporaneous speaker— one who relies on notes rather than a written manuscript. Your outline is your diagram connecting the information you want to communicate in a rational, consistent way. It enables you to assemble the pieces of the information so that the puzzle makes sense to you and communicates your intended meaning to your audience. Think of outlining as a process of layering ideas on paper so that every statement supports your thesis. It is a time-consuming process, but one that pays off in a skillful, confident presentation (Sprague & Stuart, 1992, p. 92).

Be familiar with the criteria for each speech assignment. Each instructor has his/her own requirements. Some may want to see your planning outline and speaker's notes while others may not. Instead of a planning outline, your instructor may ask you to turn in a full-sentence outline that includes points, subpoints, source citations, and reference pages, but excludes statements about transitions or speech flow. The following discussion is designed to help you develop and, by extension, deliver an effective speech. Your instructor will have specific ideas about the outline and note cards.

BTW!

Classic Rhetoric Arrangement

Classical rhetoricians did sometimes differ on the number or order of a speech's parts, but most used some variation of the divisions suggested in 90 BCE in the text *Rhetorica Ad Herennium* (Willerton, 1999). The manuscript was written in Latin (original Latin terms are included in parentheses), and included: the opening (*exordium*); the background facts (narration); the explanation or definition of terms (*explicatio* or definition); proposition or thesis (partition); the proof for the proposition or thesis (amplification); refutation of opposing arguments (*refutatio* or *reprehensio*); and the conclusion (*peroratio* or *epilogus*) (Horner 1988).

The Planning Outline

The planning outline, also known as the full-content outline, includes most of the information you will present in your speech. It does not include every word you plan to say, but gives you the flexibility required in extemporaneous speaking. An effective outline has four main components: parallelism, coordination, subordination, and division (Tardiff & Brizee, 2011).

Parallelism. On the face of it, parallelism and consistency may sound like the same thing. However, consistency refers to the numbering of sections and points of your outline, whereas parallelism refers to how you construct your sentences. For example, if one point is, "Having a pet gives your children responsibility," another main point *should not* be stated, "When should you *not* have a pet?" Instead, that main point would be phrased something like, "Knowing when to not have a pet is important." Following are a few brief examples:

> **Point 1:** Destroyed are the great redwoods that have survived over the centuries.
>
> **Point 2:** Vanished is the small animal life that used to grow in the great forests of our nation.
>
> **Point 1:** Joining the military will provide specific job skills.
>
> **Point 2:** Staying in the military will provide a stable income.

Parallelism goes beyond phrasing sentences, however. True parallel structure means that your introduction and your conclusion are related. For example, let's say that in your introduction to a speech on world harmony, you paint a picture of how life would be if all people on earth lived together without war or international conflict. With parallel structure, you bring back this picture after the body of your speech, so that you can show your audience that if they did what you're asking them to do (travel, communicate with people from other countries, accept differences, or whatever you propose), this is what life would be like. Using parallel structure is an effective organizational tool and provides listeners with a sense of closure.

Coordination. Coordinate points are your main ideas. We suggested earlier that your speech be composed of three to five main points. Generally speaking, each of your coordinate points should have the same significance, even though, for purposes of an informative or persuasive speech, you may find one point to be your strongest argument or one point to be your most valuable piece of information. In a speech, each coordinate point will require supporting material. In the above example about the military, it can be argued that specific job skills and stable income are two equally significant benefits of being in the military. Finding facts and statistics about these two points is part of your research process for such a speech.

Subordination. Subordinate points support your main or coordinate points. Information in your coordinate points is more general, while information in the subordinate points is more specific. Subordinate points provide relevant supporting material, such as facts, statistics, examples, or testimony. Every speech, and therefore every outline, will have both coordinate and subordinate points. For example, if you were trying to convince college students to buy a scooter, you might include the following main, or coordinate, point with the corresponding subordinate points.

I.   Buying a scooter saves money

    A.   A new scooter costs less than $2,500, which is only a fraction of what a new car costs.

    B.   A Scooter gets between 80 and 100 miles per gallon, thus saving hundreds of dollars each year.

    C.   An on-campus parking sticker for a scooter only costs $5.

Notice that the cost of a scooter, the gas mileage, and the parking sticker costs are all facts that support the idea that buying a scooter saves money.

As you notice in the examples, coordinate and subordinate points are stated as one full sentence that represents one idea. Phrases and incomplete sentences will not state your points fluently, nor will they help you think in terms of the subtle interrelationships among ideas, transitions, and word choice. *Singularity* refers to the notion that each point and subpoint comprises one, separate, but logically connected, idea. A main point should not be "We should all volunteer, and we should require that each person partake in six months of community service before age 21." These are two separate points. A well-constructed planning outline ensures a coherent, well thought-out speech. Using full sentences defines your ideas and guides your choice of language.

Division. Division refers to the fact that points and subpoints are distinct and identifiable on your outline. Each level has at least two points. So if you have a Roman numeral "I," minimally, you will see a "II." If you have a capital "A," minimally, you will see a "B." You should never have just one point or subpoint. Technically, there is no limit to how many main points or subpoints you include on your outline. If you have a large number of points, however, you may want to see if some of them can be combined, making sure you are still developing one fluid idea.

As you develop your outline, check to see how many subpoints you have under each main point. Perhaps you are providing an information overload in one section but you lack support in another area. If you believe that there isn't more than one subpoint under a main point, then perhaps you do not have an adequate main point, and you need to rethink the general structure of your argument.

In addition to addressing the four components of an effective outline, your outline should follow a consistent pattern. In a traditional outline, roman numerals label the speech's main ideas. Subordinate points are labeled with letters and numbers.

The proper positioning of the main and subordinate points with reference to the left margin is critical, for it provides a visual picture of the way your speech is organized. Be consistent with your indentation. The main points are along the left margin, and each subpoint is indented. Each subsubpoint is indented under the subpoint. This visual image presents a hierarchy that expresses the internal logic of your ideas.

In summary, as you construct your outline, check to see that you are following the principles of outlining. Doing so identifies strengths and weaknesses in support and logic, and overall, helps you create an effective speech. The following "boilerplate" suggests the format for a speech.

Name:

Specific Purpose:

Thesis Statement:

Title of Speech:

Introduction

I. Capture attention and focus on topic

II. Set tone and establish credibility

III. Preview main points

Body

I. First main point

   A. First subordinate (sub-) point to explain first main point

      1. First subpoint/supporting material for first subpoint

         a. Subpoint that provides greater details or explanations

         b. Subpoint that provides more details, examples, or explanations to clarify and explain

      2. Second subpoint/supporting material for first subpoint

   B. Second subordinate (sub-) point to explain first main point

      1. First subpoint/supporting material for second subpoint

      2. Second subpoint/supporting material for second subpoint

         a. Subpoint that provides greater details or explanations

         b. Subpoint that provides more details, examples, or explanations to clarify and explain

II. Second main point

   A. First subordinate (sub-) point to explain second main point

      1. First subpoint/supporting material for first subpoint

         a. Subpoint that provides greater details or explanations

         b. Subpoint that provides more details, examples, or explanations to clarify and explain

    2. Second subpoint/supporting material for first subpoint

  B. Second subordinate (sub-) point to explain second main poin

    1. First subpoint/supporting material for second subpoint

    2. Second subpoint/supporting material for second subpoint

III. Third main point

  A. First subordinate (sub-) point to explain third main point

  B. Second subordinate point to explain third main point

    1. First subpoint/supporting material for second subpoint

    2. Second subpoint/supporting material for second subpoint

Conclusion

  I. Summary of main points

  II. Relate to audience

  III. Provide closure/final thought

References (on separate sheet)

Notice the particulars:

❶ Your name, the specific purpose, thesis statement, and title of your speech are all found at the top of the page.

❷ Each section (introduction, body, and conclusion) is labeled.

❸ Each section begins with a Roman numeral.

❹ Each point is not developed identically. In some cases, there are subpoints and subsubpoints. One point may need more development than another point.

Check with your instructor to see if you should have a regular planning outline or a full-sentence outline. A full-sentence outline requires that each point be written as one full sentence. This means no sentence fragments, and no more than one sentence per point.

Include at the end of your planning outline a reference page listing all the sources used to prepare your speech, including books, magazines, journals, newspaper articles, videos, speeches, and interviews. If you are unfamiliar with documentation requirements, check the style guide preferred by your instructor, such as the *American Psychological Association (APA) Publication Manual* (www.apastyle.apa.org) and the *Modern Literature Association (MLA) Handbook for Writers of Research Papers* (www.mla.org). For additional help with the style sheets, check out the home page of the online writing lab at owl.english.purdue.edu.

Check with your instructor to see how detailed your source citations should be in the outline. They should include last name, credentials, type of book (or magazine, journal, Web page, etc.), year/date of publication.

Transitional sentences are valuable additions to your planning outline. They are needed when you move from the introduction to the body to the conclusion of the speech. They also link main points within the body and serve as internal previews and summaries. Put these sentences in parentheses between the points being linked and use the language you may actually speak. When appropriate, include internal summaries and previews of material yet to come.

Here is an example of a planning outline that includes transitional sentences.

Speaker's Name: Corey Schultz

Specific Purpose: To persuade my audience that Standard American English (SAE) should be considered as only one of many acceptable forms of spoken English

Thesis Statement: Since Standard American English (SAE) promotes racism and classism, and is difficult to enforce, it should be only one of many acceptable forms of spoken English.

Title of Speech: Revisiting Standard American English

Introduction

I. It is a common belief shared by almost all Americans that there is only one form of acceptable spoken English, known to linguists as Standard American English (SAE).

    A. An enforced standardization of language is a common occurrence within languages across the world, and is created out of the perception that the natural evolution of language is harmful.

    B. As a result, most grammar is taught without acknowledging a difference between spoken English and written English.

II. Recent research suggests, however, that SAE's prescriptive grammar instruction is not the most ideal form.

    A. Grammar instruction in public education almost exclusively teaches SAE, which has led to the belief that "nonstandard" forms of English like African American Vernacular English, Chicano English, or Southern dialects are somehow incorrect.

    B. This stigma encourages the marginalization of several groups.

(Transition): Because most of us have learned that there is actually one form of "correct" grammar, I see a lot of confused faces in the audience. However, the perpetuation of Standard American English only serves to marginalize racial and socioeconomic groups, and should therefore be considered as only one of many acceptable forms of spoken English.

In this speech, I will examine the problems with the standardization of spoken English, such as its promotion of racism and classism. Next, I will discuss its causes, before finally addressing its solutions.

Body

I.   Initially, Standard English promotes racism and classism.

   A.   According to a recent personal interview with Dr. K. Aaron Smith, author of *The Development of the English Progressive*, mandating the use of Standard English in American classrooms remains the largest, most unapologetic form of racism left in the United States.

   B.   In the 2010 article "Codeswitching: Tools of Language and Culture Transform the Dialectically Diverse Classroom," authors Wheeler and Swords argue that commenting on the invalidity of a student's language indirectly makes a statement about the invalidity of that student's culture.

II.   By not addressing the validity of "nonstandard" English, all students are missing out on unique, important cultural perspectives.

   A.   Many people do not understand that African American Vernacular English, Chicano English, and all other dialects of the language have a structured and complex system of grammar and phonology.

      1.   For example, according to the previously cited interview with Dr. Smith, "aks" is one of the most commonly corrected aspects of African American Vernacular English.

      2.   Aks most likely derived from the Old English verb "acsian," meaning "to ask," was considered standard English until about 1600.

      3.   As "aks" is still maintained in African American Vernacular English, Jamaican English, and many dialects of British English, it isn't wrong, it's only different.

   B.   Failing to open a dialogue with students about differences in dialects and vernaculars teaches students to ignore the important history of language, and teaches students to blindly follow them assuming, that their English is the only "correct" English.

(Transition): While we now understand the problems with the enforcement of Standard American English, it is also equally as important to study its causes.

III.   First, English speakers hold the belief that speech must be formal to be intelligent.

   A.   In 1712, Jonathan Swift wrote *A Proposal for Correcting, Improving and Ascertaining the English Tongue*, in which, among other things, he advocated for the creation of an English Academy literally for the purpose of making the language sound fancier.

      1.   The concept of the double negative, which is something that many students of English struggle with, was instated to reflect the rules of math: Two negatives make a positive.

2. However, if I say, "I ain't gonna do no work," it, in no way, means that I am going to do work.

B. If students learned this history of the rules of grammar, it is possible that the prestige and superiority felt by many speakers of Standard English might be lessened.

IV. Second, many teachers fail to recognize a difference between written English and spoken English.

A. According to Dr. Rai Noguchi in his book *Grammar and the Teaching of Writing*, the growing influence of the oral culture and the accompanying decline of writing complicate grammar instruction.

1. As people read less, they have less exposure to the conventions of writing.

2. Thus, the conventions of writing (as opposed to those of speech) often go unnoticed and must be taught formally in the schools.

B. Similar to how scientists and doctors use specialized language to avoid ambiguity, writing in an academic context should be standardized.

1. This is the reason for grammar instruction.

2. When educators fail to recognize the difference between spoken English and written English, they marginalize specific groups within their classroom.

(**Transition**): Now that we've examined the implications of this phenomenon and looked at the reasons why we enforce standardization, let's look at some solutions to end this problem.

V. Initially, there are several ways in which you can help on a personal level.

A. Don't correct anyone's spoken English.

B. According to the Linguistic Society of America's *Language Rights Resolution*, many of the dialects, vernaculars, and indigenous languages of the United States are severely threatened, which means the cultures that speak those languages are also threatened.

1. Therefore, do not judge speakers (in classrooms or otherwise) based on the way they choose to use language.

2. Also, stand up for those who are unfairly criticized.

VI. There are several institutional changes that should be made.

A. Because the U.S. government has never and *will* never create an institution to control and standardize language, I'm not going to ask you to write your senators.

B. However, it may help to write a letter to your high school principal or English department chair, insisting that teachers teach grammar by separating written English and spoken English, and study the differences in grammar of both styles in the classroom.

Conclusion

I. Today, I have discussed how standardization of the English language is a major problem in society.

II. It's clear that if nothing is done, Standard American English will only continue to marginalize certain cultural and socioeconomic communities.

III. It is important that we, as a society, help end this severely underestimated problem.

References

Language Rights Resolution. Linguistic Society of America. Retrieved from www.lsadc.org/lsa-res-rights.

Noguchi, R. R. (1991). *Grammar and the Teaching of Writing: Limits and Possibilities.* Urbana, IL: National Council of Teachers of English.

Smith, K. A. (2010, September 23). Personal interview at Illinois State University.

Wheeler, R. S., & Swords, R. (2010). Codeswitching: Tools of Language and Culture Transform the Dialectally Diverse Classroom. Workshop on *Developing Writers, Series #5.* Christopher Newport University. Annenberg, 1–19.

A Brief Analysis of the Planning Outline

When applying a real topic to the boilerplate provided earlier, it is easy to see how the process unfolds. Note how transitions work, moving the speaker from the introduction of the speech to the body, from one main point to the next and, finally, from the body of the speech to the conclusion.

Remember, although the word transition appears in the outline, it is not stated in your speech. Transitions help connect listeners in a personal way to the subject being discussed. It also provides the thesis statement and previews the main points of the speech.

Notice that quotes are written word for word in the outline. Also, the preview is found just before the body of the speech. Once stated, the audience will know the main ideas you intend to present. As the outline moves from first- to second- to third-level headings, the specificity of details increases. The planning outline moves from the general to the specific.

Speaker's Notes

Speaker's notes are an abbreviated key-word outline, lacking much of the detail of the planning outline. They function as a reminder of what you plan to say and the order in which you plan to say it. Speaker's notes follow exactly the pattern of your planning outline, but in a condensed format.

Follow the same indentation pattern you used in your planning outline to indicate your points and subpoints. Include notations for the introduction, body, and conclusion and indicate transitions. It is helpful to include suggestions for an effective delivery. Remind yourself to slow down, gesture, pause, use visual aids, and so on. This is helpful during your speech, especially if you experience public speaking apprehension.

Guidelines for Constructing Speaker's Notes

❶ **Avoid overloading your outline.** Some speakers believe that having substantial information with them at the podium will give them confidence and make them more prepared. The opposite is usually true. Speakers who load themselves with too many details are torn between focusing on their audience and focusing on their notes. Too often, as they bob their heads up and down, they lose their place.

❷ **Include only necessary information.** You need just enough information to remind you of your planned points. At times, of course, you must be certain of your facts and your words, such as when you quote an authority or present complex statistical data. In these cases, include all the information you need in your speaker's notes. Long quotes or lists of statistics can be placed on separate index cards or sheets of paper (if allowed in the situation).

❸ **Reduce your sentences to key phrases.** Instead of writing: "The American Medical Association, an interest group for doctors, has lobbied against socialized medicine;" write: "The AMA and socialized medicine." Your notes should serve as a stimulus for what you are going to say. If you only need a few words to remind you, then use them. For example, Therese, who had directed several high school musicals, planned to discuss aspects of directing a high school musical. Her speaker's notes could include the following key words:

- ○ Casting
- ○ Blocking
- ○ Choreography
- ○ Singing
- ○ Acting

Little else would be needed, since she can easily define and/or describe these aspects of directing. However, under the key word "casting," she might include "when to cast," and "how to cast." Relevant quotes or perhaps a reference to a dramatic story would be included in the notes as well.

④ **Include transitions, but in an abbreviated form.** If you included each transition, your notes would be too long, and you would have too much written on them. Look at one of the transitions from the previous speech on the standardization of American English:

> (Transition): Because most of us have learned that there is actually one form of "correct" grammar, I see a lot of confused faces in the audience. However, the perpetuation of Standard American English only serves to marginalize racial and socioeconomic groups, and should therefore be considered as only one of many acceptable forms of spoken English.
>
> In this speech, we will examine the problems with the standardization of spoken English, such as its promotion of racism and classism. Next, we will discuss its causes, before finally addressing its solutions.

Instead of these two paragraphs, your speaker's notes might look like this:

- Confused faces
- SAE marginalizes
- Will discuss problems, causes, solutions

If you practice your speech, these words should suffice as notes. Abbreviate in a way that makes sense to you. Each person will have his or her own version of shorthand.

⑤ **Notes must be legible.** Your notes are useless if you cannot read them. Because you will be looking up and down at your notes as you speak, you must be able to find your place with ease at any point. Do not reduce your planning outline to eight points and paste them to note cards. If you can type your notes, make sure they are 14-point or larger. If you write your notes, take the time to write legibly. Think about this: You may have spent several hours researching, preparing, and organizing your speech. Why take the chance of reducing the impact of your speech by writing your notes at the last minute?

Following is an example of a set of speaker's notes. The transformation from planning outline to key-word outline is noticeable in terms of length and detail. Transitions, delivery hints, and the parts of the outline are emboldened. (For additional suggestions on note cards, see **BTW: More Guidelines for Note Cards**.)

More Guidelines for Note Cards

Additional suggestions can be found from Wisc-Online, an interactive website on the subject (www.wisc-online.com/objects/ViewObject.aspx?ID=SPH3102) and includes:

- Use only one side of your note card.
- Number your note cards.
- Use large letters and dark ink.
- Make sure your note cards have lots of white space in them.
- Limit the number of cards you use.
- Do not read from your note cards; quickly glance at key words.
- Use the same note cards for the speech as those you practiced with.

"Revisiting Standard American English," sample speaker's notes.

Introduction	1

I. Belief in form of English

   A. Common throughout the world

   B. Difference between spoken and written

II. Prescriptive grammar instruction is bad

   A. Belief that "nonstandard" English is wrong

   B. Marginalizes groups

(Look around room. Make eye contact. Slow down.)

(Standard English is racist and classist. We will examine the problems, causes, and solutions.)

Body *(Slow down)*	2

I. Racist and classist

   A. Smith quote on racism

   B. Codeswitching

II. Students miss cultural perspectives

   A. Other forms are legitimate

      1. "aks"

      2. Not wrong, different

   B. Teaches to ignore history of language

(Equally important to understand causes)   3

III. Formal speech = Intelligent speech

    A. Jonathan Swift

        1. Concept of the double negative

        2. "I ain't gonna do no work" ≠ "I'm gonna do work"

    B. Don't know history of rules

IV. No perceived difference between spoken and written   4

    A. Dr. Rai Noguchi quote

        1. Less exposure to conventions

        2. Must be taught formally

    B. Writing should be standardized

        1. This is the reason for SAE

        2. Separate written and spoken English

(Let's look at solutions)   5

V. Personal solutions

    A. Do not correct

    B. Threat to dialect

        1. Do not judge

        2. Stand up for others

VI. Institutional solutions

    A. Do not write to Congress

    B. Write to school

Conclusion	6
I. Discussed problems, causes, and solutions	
II. No change, SAE will always be bad	
II. Help	
(Pause. Wait for applause.)	

A Brief Analysis of Speaker's Notes

Including your specific purpose and thesis statement in your speaker's notes is unnecessary. Speaker's notes follow exactly the pattern of the planning outline so you maintain the organizational structure and flow of your speech. The introduction, body, and conclusion are labeled, although it is possible you might need only the initial letters "I," "B," and "C" to note these divisions. Nonessential words are eliminated, although some facts are included in the speaker's notes to avoid misstatement. Delivery instructions can provide helpful reminders.

The more experience you have as a speaker, the more you will come to rely on both your planning outline and speaker's notes, as both are indispensable to a successful presentation.

Summary

The first step in organizing your speech is to determine your main points. Organize your efforts around your specific purpose and thesis statement, then brainstorm to generate specific ideas, and finally, group similar ideas.

Your second step is to use supporting material to develop each main point. In step 3, choose an organizational pattern. Arrange your ideas in chronological order, use a spatial organizational pattern, follow a pattern of cause and effect, look at a problem and its solutions, or choose a topical pattern. Your final step is to connect your main ideas through transitions, internal previews, and internal summaries.

As you develop your speech, your primary organizational tool is the planning outline, which includes most of the information you will present. The outline uses a traditional outline format, which establishes a hierarchy of ideas. The number of main points developed in your speech should be between two and five. The planning outline uses complete sentences, labels transitions, and includes a reference list.

Speaker's notes, the notes you use during your presentation in an extemporaneous speech, are less detailed than the planning outline. They serve as brief reminders of what you want to say and the order in which you say it. They may include complete quotations and statistical data as well as important delivery suggestions. Speaker's notes are organized around phrases, not sentences, and they use the same format as the planning outline.

Discussion Starters

1. How can you tell an organized speaker from an unorganized one?
2. When do you usually think about how you're going to organize your speech?
3. Why do you think the topical organizational pattern is the most frequently used pattern? Which organizational pattern do you think is used least, and why?
4. If you were going to give an informative speech on "space exploration," think of two organizational patterns that might be appropriate. Now, assume you're going to give a persuasive speech on space exploration. What might be the most appropriate way to organize your ideas? Why?
5. In public speaking, what functions are served by transitions and summaries? Can you think of several effective transitional statements to develop the speech topics from question #4?
6. Review the essential requirements for planning and key-word outlines. Why is it necessary to develop both outline forms, and why are both equally important in extemporaneous speaking?

References

Clarke, M. L. (1963). *Rhetoric at Rome: Historical Survey*. New York: Barnes & Noble.

Creating and Using Presentation Note Cards. Retrieved September 2, 2011 from www.wisc-online.com/objects/ViewObject.aspx?ID=SPH3102.

Daniels, T. D., & Witman, R. F. (1981). The Effects of Message Structure in Verbal Organizing Ability upon Learning Information. *Human Communication Research, Winter*, 147–160.

Horner, W. B. (1988). *Rhetoric in the Classical Tradition*. New York: St. Martin's Press.

Lemonick, M. D. (2007, July 5). How We Get Addicted. *Time*. Retrieved February 15, 2011 from time.com.

Makay, J., & Fetzger, R. C. (1984). *Business Communication Skills: Principles and Practice*, 2nd Ed. Englewood Cliffs, NJ: Prentice-Hall.

Sprague, J., & Stuart, D. (1992). *The Speaker's Handbook*, 3rd Ed. San Diego: Harcourt Brace Jovanovich.

Supporting a Speech. Retrieved September 2, 2011 from www.hawaii.edu/mauispeech/html/supporting_materials.html.

Tardiff, E., & Brizee, A. (2011). Four Main Components of an Effective Outline. Retrieved September 8, 2011 from www.owl.english.purdue.edu/owl/resource/544/01.

Turner, F. H., Jr. (1970). The Effects of Speech Summaries on Audience Comprehension. *Central States Speech Journal, Spring*, 24–39.

Willerton, D. R. (1999, December). *Toward a Rhetoric of Marketing for High-Tech Service*. Published Master's Thesis, University of North Texas. Retrieved August 31, 2011 from digital.library.unt.edu/ark:/67531/metadc2432/m1/1/high_res_d/thesis.pdf.

Chapter

8

> "*The White Rabbit put on his spectacles. 'Where shall I begin, please your Majesty?' he asked. 'Begin at the beginning,' the King said gravely, 'and go on till you come to the end: then stop.'*"
>
> Lewis Carroll's *Alice's Adventures in Wonderland*

Chapter 8: Introducing and Concluding Your Speech

This chapter offer approaches to introductions and conclusions in relation to how your speech can make a lasting impression. It discusses how to engage members of the audience at the beginning of the speech so they will want to listen, and then how to remind your audience at the end of what you said and why it was relevant. Techniques and suggestions, including common pitfalls for introductions and conclusions are offered.

Student Learning Objectives:

○ Students will be able to define the functions of introductions

○ Students will be able to explain how to introduce the same speech in different ways

○ Students will be able to identify and explain five guidelines and suggestions for introductions

○ Students will be able to describe common pitfalls of introductions

○ Students will be able to discuss the functions of conclusions

○ Students will be able to recognize the value of developing memorable conclusions

INTRODUCING AND CONCLUDING YOUR SPEECH

Imagine your classmate is about to give a persuasive speech on intercultural communication, and is mulling over an almost unlimited number of ways to start. Consider the following three possibilities:

○ Bonjour! Parce que ma presentation s'agit d'une question de la communication interculturelle, j'ai decidé de presenter completement en français! D'accord? Bien. La communication interculturelle est un grand probleme dans l'Etats Unis et d'autres nations ont beaucoup souffert. In other words, intercultural communication, or rather, lack thereof, is a huge problem that has plagued America as well as other foreign countries across the world.

○ How many of you have finished your foreign language requirement for college graduation? How many of you feel that you are fluent in another language? Do you realize that it's not unusual for our European counterparts to speak four languages? Intercultural communication or rather, lack thereof, is a huge problem that has plagued America as well as foreign countries across the world.

○ Intercultural communication or rather, lack thereof, is a huge problem that has plagued America as well as foreign countries across the world.

Which beginning do you find most creative? Least creative? Most engaging? Least engaging? Which one would be the easiest to develop? The most difficult? Which is most direct?

As you look at the above examples, a final question comes to mind. Are all three examples acceptable ways to begin a speech? The answer may certainly be yes. The way you begin and end your speech is critical to your overall success. Expending effort on your introduction is time well spent.

This chapter approaches introductions and conclusions in relation to how your speech can make a lasting impression. Two topics are considered: how to engage your audience at the beginning of your speech so they will be motivated to listen to the rest of it, and how to remind your audience at the end of your speech what you said and why it was relevant. For both introducing and concluding your speech, strategies and pitfalls are identified to help you craft your best start and finish.

The primacy/recency effect, explained in the previous chapter, sheds light on the importance of effective speech beginnings and endings. This theory suggests that we tend to recall more vividly the beginning and ending, and less of the middle of an event. When several candidates are interviewing for a job, the first and last candidates have an advantage because the interviewer is most likely to remember more about these two than the others. This theory also holds true for speeches: Your audience will likely recall more of the beginning and ending of your speech than the content in the middle.

The familiar speaker adage, "Tell them what you are going to say, say it, and then tell them what you said," addresses this truth. Beginning and ending a speech well helps your audience remember and, later use, the ideas you present. Let's begin with a closer look at introductions.

Introductions

If done well, an introduction helps your audience make a smooth transition to the main points of your speech, create a positive first impression, and set an appropriate tone and mood for your talk. If done poorly, your audience may prejudge your topic as unimportant or dull and stop listening.

Consider the following example. As part of a conference for a group of business executives, business consultant Edith Weiner was scheduled to deliver a speech on the unequal distribution of world resources—admittedly, a topic with the potential to put her listeners to sleep. She was experienced enough as a speaker, though, to realize that the last thing her listeners wanted to hear at the beginning was a long list of statistics comparing the bounty of North America to the paucities in other parts of the world. Her speech would never recover from such a dull start. The challenge she faced was to capture the audience's attention at the outset.

Arriving at the auditorium early on the morning of her speech, Weiner marked off different-sized sections of the hall to represent, proportionately, the continents. She allotted coffee, pastries, and chairs according to the availability of food and income in each. Then she assigned audience members to these areas according to actual world population ratios.

What happened was memorable. While 30 people in the area representing Africa had to divide three cups of coffee, two pastries, and two chairs, the 17 people assigned to North America had more coffee and pastries than they could eat in a week, surrounded by 40 chairs. As participants took their seats (with those in Asia and Africa standing), they did so with a new perspective on world hunger and poverty, and with a desire to listen to whatever Weiner had to say. She began:

> I wanted to speak ... about a topic most people tire of, but you, being so important to the financial community, cannot ignore. ...
>
> Hunger and poverty aren't comfortable, are they? Neither is bounty when you realize the waste and mismatch of people and resources. ...
>
> (Interview with Edith Weiner, October 10, 1989)

Glossary

Introduction Supports the body of your speech and should capture your audience's attention and indicate your intent.

Edith Weiner's risky introduction grabbed the attention of all audience members in a powerful way.

Functions of Introductions

The emphasis on strong opening comments has long been held as important. In the first century Roman philosopher Quintillian noted that for a speech to be effective, an introduction must do four things (Corbettt & Connor, 1999). Introductions must:

1. Capture attention and focus
2. Provide a motive for the audience to listen
3. Enhance the credibility of the speaker
4. Preview the message and organization

Edith Weiner's introduction was effective because it accomplished each of these objectives, as we shall see.

Capture Attention and Focus

Every experienced speaker knows that the first few moments are critical to the success of the entire speech. It is within these minutes that your listeners decide whether they care enough to continue listening. You want your listeners to think, "This is interesting," or "I didn't know that," or 'That was really funny." The common denominator in each of these responses is piqued audience interest.

Many introductions contain a personalized greeting. This acknowledges the audience and tells listeners that you see the speech as an opportunity to communicate your point of view. William Kamkwamba (2009) was invited to speak before participants at a TED (technology, entertainment, and development) conference to tell how, at 14 years of age, he invented a windmill from scraps in his poverty-stricken country. He began his message in this way: "Two years ago I stood on the TED stage in Arusha, Tanzania. I spoke very briefly about one of my proudest creations. It was a simple machine that changed my life."

Kamkwamba's first appearance at TED two years earlier was unsuccessful because he was too nervous and overwhelmed. At that first speech, his only words were "I tried, and I made it." In his address two years later, he referenced this failure in his introduction, explaining: "Before that time I had never been away from my home in Malawi. I had never used a computer. I had never seen an Internet. On the stage that day, I was so nervous. My English lost, I wanted to vomit. [(Laughter)] I had never been surrounded by so many azungu, white people. [Laughter)]"

Such self-effacing humor and honest, vulnerable explanation created a bond with his audience and piqued their interest in what he would have said two years earlier. Kamkwamba continued with: "There was a story I wouldn't tell you then. But, well, I'm feeling good right now. I would like to share that story today."

As you capture the attention and focus of your audience, you also need to set the mood and tone of your speech. The mood of a speech refers to the overall feeling you hope to engender in your audience. Tone is the emotional disposition of the speaker as the speech is being delivered. Tone is created verbally by the words and ideas you select and nonverbally, by the emotions you communicate.

Imagine observing the following scenario: Angela stood behind the podium beside the closed casket as she delivered the eulogy to tearful faces. Her sentimental message of grief was appropriate in every way except that she delivered it with a smile. The whole speech! The disconnect between her words and facial expressions was unsettling, to say the least. Angela later confessed that she smiled because she wanted to communicate that she was glad to be there and honored to perform such an important duty. Unfortunately, Angela did not create an appropriate tone and mood in her introduction.

Consider the desired mood and adjust your tone appropriately in the introduction. In this way, you ensure that your tone matches your reason for speaking and that your speech creates the desired mood in your audience.

Provide a Motive to Listen

An effective speaker quickly establishes a reason for audience members to listen. Edith Weiner's introduction helped build that critical relationship with her public speaking audience. She wanted her listeners to care about her message. She wanted them to decide from the outset that what she was saying had meaning and importance. Although the introduction also helped make her point with its physical demonstration of world food problems, its primary purpose was to build a psychological bridge that would last throughout the speech. Her well-designed demonstration led her audience to care about her topic because Weiner had effectively related the topic of her speech to something the audience cared about, their own hunger.

The introduction should seek to establish common ground with the audience. By focusing on something you and your audience can share and announcing it early, you help people identify with your topic. When people perceive that your message is meant for them and is relevant to their lives, they will listen attentively.

Enhance Credibility

During your introduction, your listeners make important decisions about you. They decide whether they like you and whether you are credible. Your credibility as a speaker is judged, in large part, on the basis of what you say during your introduction, how you say it, and how you carry yourself.

Edith Weiner (1989) became a credible speaker by demonstrating, in a participatory way, that she understood the problems of world food distribution

Glossary

Mood The overall feeling you hope to engender in your audience.

Tone The emotional disposition of the speaker as the speech is being delivered.

Credibility The extent to which a speaker is perceived as a competent spokesperson.

and that she cared enough about her audience—and topic—to come up with a creative way to present her ideas. Credibility also increases as you identify, early on, what qualifies you to speak about a topic. Weiner might have said, "I want to talk to you about world resources because for several years I have studied how your investments overseas can have important impacts on your future economic well-being." Similarly, Angela, the inappropriately smiling mourner, might have mentioned early on that she was close to the deceased, knew her for 30 years, and thought of her as a sister. Offering an explanation linking you to the topic you are covering helps your audience believe in you and trust your ideas.

Audiences may have an initial sense of your credibility even before you speak. Your introduction is an ideal place to enhance that impression. As we discuss later in the text, you can think of your credibility in terms of your perceived competence, concern for your audience, dynamism, and personal ethics. Put another way, if you know your subject, care about your audience, offer an enthusiastic delivery, and communicate a sense of ethical integrity, your audience's impression of your credibility will likely be positive. The content and delivery of your introduction must maximize these four aspects if you want your audience to listen attentively throughout your speech.

Preview Your Message and Organization

Finally, Weiner used her introduction to tell her audience what she would talk about during the rest of her speech. In a sentence, she previewed her focus. ("I intend to explore several options [for maximizing your role and gain] during the rest of my speech.") This simple statement helped her listeners make the intellectual connections they needed to follow her speech. Instead of wondering, "What will she talk about?" or "What is her point of view?" they were ready for her speech to unfold.

As we said in the opening of this chapter, your audience will recall your message more fully if you tell them what you are going to say, say it, and then tell them what you said. Repeating key ideas helps us recall important information. But the first part, telling them what you are going to say, also provides a preview of the organization you intend to use. If your audience knows the main points you intend to develop in your speech, they are less likely to be confused and distracted. So, an effective introduction might offer a preview statement similar to "Today it is important that we better understand the nature of world hunger, explore creative solutions to this problem, and finally, see if some of these solutions might also be profitable to your business." In this example, the audience learns that there will be three main points to the message.

Here is how Agnes, a student at an international university in Manila, Philippines, started her informative speech on child obesity and junk food at home. The preview statement is italicized:

In July, 2011, McDonald's announced changes to their well-known "Happy Meals" to offer healthier food. Happy Meals target children. United States First Lady Michelle Obama, who has been campaigning against childhood obesity, has commended McDonald's for their action.

Following suit, the National Restaurant Association in the U. S. announced their Kids Live Well program. This means dozens of restaurant chains, including Burger King and Denny's, committed to offering healthier meals for children, too. Great, right? But what about candy, soda, pizza, and other snacks at home?

Changes have been made and are starting to be made across the globe, but many individuals are not taking action here in Manila. More parents need to get involved in this movement because it will better the lives of many children. *Today, I will more clearly define "junk food," discuss the health issues it creates for our kids, and offer easy alternatives to junk food in your home.*

When Agnes finished this statement, her audience had no doubt what her speech would cover. When you preview your message, your audience will listen and understand with increased clarity and will remember more of your message later.

How to introduce the same speech in different ways

Many topics lend themselves to different types of introductions. A startling statement, a dramatic anecdote, a quotation, or a humorous story may each serve as an effective introduction to the same speech. Here, for example, is the same speech introduced three ways:

⑤ Startling statement.

Microwave cooking can be hazardous to your child's health. Children have been burned by opening bags of microwave-heated popcorn too close to their faces. Their throats have been scalded by jelly donuts that feel cool to the touch, but are hot enough inside to burn the esophagus. These and other hazards can transform your microwave into an oven of destruction in the hands of a child. What I would like to talk about today is how dangerous microwaves can be to young children and how you can safeguard your family from accidents.

6 Dramatic story.

Nine-year-old Jenny was one of those kids who managed quite well on her own. Every day she got home from school at 3:30 while her parents were still at work and made herself a snack in the microwave. She had been using the microwave since she was five, and her parents never questioned its safety—that is, not until Jenny had her accident.

It began innocently enough. Jenny heated a bag of microwave popcorn in the oven and opened it inches from her face. The bag was cool to the touch, hiding the danger within. Hot vapors blasted Jenny's face, leaving her with second- and third-degree burns.

What I would like to talk about today is how dangerous microwaves can be to young children and how you can safeguard your family from accidents.

7 Quotation.

Three out of every four American homes have microwave ovens and with them a potential for danger. Louis Slesin, editor of *Microwave News,* a health and safety newsletter, explains how this common kitchen appliance can present potential hazards for young children:

"On a rainy day," says Slesin, "a kid could climb up on a stool, put his face to the door and watch something cook for a long time. It's mesmerizing, like watching a fish tank, but his eye will be at the point of maximum microwave leakage. We don't know the threshold for cataract formation—the industry says you need tons of exposure, but some litigation and literature say you don't need much [for damage to occur]. Children younger than 10 or 12 shouldn't use the oven unsupervised. It's not a toy. It's a sophisticated, serious, adult appliance, and it shouldn't be marketed for kids."

I agree with Slesin, and what I want to talk about today is how dangerous the microwave can be to a young child.

The point of providing these three examples is to demonstrate how differently an introduction can be constructed. Avoid "settling" for an introduction; consider how you might create the most impact.

Developing Effective Introductions

There are many ways to accomplish Quintillion's four functions of an introduction. Following are 10 techniques often used in introductions. You might consider using one or combining several to provide the initial impact you want. This is one area where a little creativity can go a long way. Keep your audience in mind. A few of these techniques may be more appropriate or attention-getting for your specific audience and specific purpose.

Startling Facts/Intriguing Statements

Some introductions seem to force listeners to pay attention. They make it difficult to think of other things because of the impact of what is being said. The effectiveness of these introductions in part, comes from the audience's feeling that the speaker's message is directed at them.

Here is how Lady Gaga began her speech at a rally in Portland, Maine in September 2010 to repeal the military's Don't Ask, Don't Tell policy. After noting that the title of her speech was "The Prime Rib of America" she stated:

> I do solemnly swear, or affirm, that I will support and defend the Constitution of the United States, against all enemies foreign and domestic, and I will bear true faith and allegiance to do the same, and I will obey the orders of the president of the United States and the orders of the officers appointed over me, according to regulations and the uniform code of military justice, so help me God.
>
> Unless, there's a gay soldier in my unit, sir.

© John Ricard/Corbis

Lady Gaga's intriguing introduction to her speech at a Portland rally served to grab the audience's attention.

Starting with this oath served as an intriguing statement, since it wasn't clear initially why she would include it in her speech. Her last statement is startling, and quickly gets to the heart of the issue. In this case, she took the familiar and turned it on its side to arouse audience emotions.

Startling statements often challenge the listener. Instead of revealing the expected, the speaker takes a slightly—or perhaps even a radically—different turn.

Dramatic Story/Build Suspense

Closely related to the startling statement is the dramatic story, which involves listeners in a tale from beginning to end. Shortly after returning from a winter vacation break, Shannon delivered a speech to her classmates that began this way:

> My friends and I were driving home from a day at the ski slopes when suddenly, without warning, a pair of headlights appeared directly in front of our car. To avoid a collision, I swerved sharply to the right, forcing our car off the road into a snow-filled ditch.
>
> It's funny what comes into your mind at moments like this. All I could think of was how Justin Mentell, who used to be on *Boston Legal,* one of my favorite TV shows, died on icy

roads just a month ago. And he was only 27. I thought I was going to die, too, just because of another driver's stupidity and carelessness.

Obviously, I didn't die or even suffer any serious injuries. And my friends are safe, too, although my car was totaled. I'm convinced that we are all here today because we were locked into place by our seat belts. Justin Mentell might have been here, too, had he bothered to buckle up.

Everyone in the audience knew what it was like to be driving home with friends—feeling safe and secure—only to be shocked into the realization that they were vulnerable to tragedy. Audience attention was riveted on the speaker as she launched into her speech on seat belt use.

Quotation and/or Literature Reference

You can capture audience attention by citing the words of others. If you use an appropriate quotation, the words themselves may be compelling enough to engage your listeners. One of the most well-known quotes from Harry Potter was used by a student to introduce the subject of his speech, sarcasm:

"You know your mother, Malfoy? The expression on her face—like she's got dung under her nose? Is she like that all the time or just because you were with her?"

This passage was selected because it is funny, clever, and sarcastic. He set the stage for a lighter look at the harms of sarcasm with this quotation.

Robert Frost, well-known American poet, is frequently quoted from his poem *The Road Not Taken*, particularly, the last three lines:

Two roads diverged in a wood, and I—
I took the one less travelled by,
and that has made all the difference.

The last three lines can be the start of a speech about following your heart, choosing your own path, making your own decisions, not following the crowd.

The two examples above have been used by others to start a speech or make some point. In addition to using the words of a *well-known individual,* you could also cite the words of *a recognized authority* whose reputation enhances your credibility.

Here, for example, is how Toby, a public speaking student, began his speech to capture the attention of his audience. Quoting a knowledgeable public figure, he began:

"Today, 12.5 million children are overweight in the United States—more than 17 percent. Overweight children are at greater risk for many serious health problems." These are the words of your U.S. Surgeon General, Dr. Regina M. Benjamin (OSG, 2011). Dr. Benjamin continues with the following facts:

> Overweight adolescents have a 70 percent chance of becoming overweight or obese adults.
>
> The number of overweight children has more than tripled over the past three decades.
>
> Studies show that nearly 34 percent of children and teens in America are either overweight or at risk of becoming overweight.
>
> Research has shown that parents are often their children's most important role model. If children see their caregivers enjoying healthy foods and being physically active, they are more likely to do the same.

These powerful words from a recognized expert set the stage for Toby to advocate parental involvement in combating the childhood obesity epidemic our nation faces.

In similar fashion, Christopher, another public speaking student, captured his audience's attention when speaking about the nation's health care crisis by stating:

> If a criminal has a right to an attorney, don't you have a right to a doctor? President Obama put it like this: "Everybody here understands the desperation that people feel when they're sick. And I think everybody here is profoundly sympathetic and wants to make sure that we have a system that works for all Americans" (msnbc.com, 2011). Obama sent a clear wake-up call to Congress to get serious about health care reform in America.

Christopher introduces the topic of health care by quoting the words of our president. Although these words could have been uttered by anyone, Christopher establishes credibility at the beginning of his speech by using a recognized authority.

Humor

At the beginning of a speech, humor helps break down the psychological barriers that exist between speaker and audience. Here is how Karen used humor at the start of a classroom speech on the problem of divorce in America:

> Janet and Lauren had been college roommates, but had not seen each other in the 10 years since graduation. They were thrilled when they ran into each other at a college reunion and had a chance to talk.
>
> "Tell me," asked Janet, "has your husband lived up to the promises he made when he was dating you in college?"

"He certainly has!" said Lauren. "He told me then that he wasn't good enough for me and he's proven it ever since."

The class laughed, Karen waited, then:

I laughed, too, when I heard that story. But the fact remains that about half the marriages in our country end in divorce and one of the major reasons for these failures is that one partner can't live up to the expectations of the other.

Humor works in this introduction for two reasons. First, the story is genuinely funny; we chuckle when we hear the punch line. And, second, the humor is tied directly to the subject of the speech; it is appropriate for the topic and the occasion. It also provides an effective transition into the speech body.

Humor *can* work when it's self-deprecating. Rahm Emanuel, mayor of Chicago, was known for his profanity-laced communication. At a commencement ceremony at George Washington University in 2009, he made reference to that at the beginning of his speech:

Congratulations. I also want to thank George Washington University for bestowing this honorary degree. This is actually the second honorary degree I've received this year. Just last week I was awarded an honorary degree for my contribution in the field of linguistics, particularly my work in four-letter words.

Again, humor makes the audience snicker, giggle, or cackle, and it can set the right tone for your speech. Make sure you *can* do humor. At the 2011 Academy Awards, the loudest laughter came when Billy Crystal took the stage away briefly from hosts Anne Hathaway and James Franco, who were *trying* to be funny. If you are not comfortable with humor and elect to force it, both you and your listeners will feel awkward.

Rhetorical Question

When you ask your audience, "How many of you ate breakfast this morning?" you expect to see people raise their hands. When you ask a *rhetorical* question, however, you do not expect an answer. What you hope is that your question will cause your listeners to start thinking about the subject of your speech.

Imagine a speech about the negative effects of snoring. It could start like this:

Have you ever been told you snore? Have you ever had to sleep in the same room with someone who has a loud snore? Have you been told you have a "cute" little snore?

These are all rhetorical questions. The speaker is not expecting someone to answer these questions aloud. The purpose is to get the audience to start thinking about the topic. Hopefully, the speaker has their attention. Then the speaker continues:

> If you don't snore, be grateful. If you do snore, you need to hear this. If you don't snore, but you marry "a snorer," well, good luck! Studies show that married couples argue about snoring as much as they do money; snoring couples have less sex than nonsnoring couples, and over 20 percent of couples regularly sleep apart due to snoring. Ouch! Oh, and there's more. The nonsnorer faces difficulties from sleep deprivation. In the next few minutes I'm going to describe the economic consequences of being sleep deprived, including increased health care costs, automobile accidents, workplace accidents, and decreased job performance.

The speaker linked the rhetorical questions and startling facts to audience, and previewed the main points in her speech. The best rhetorical questions are probing in a personal way. They mean something to every listener and encourage active participation throughout your speech.

Illustrations, Examples, and Anecdotes

Speakers often begin with an interesting comment about the immediate surroundings or some recent or historical event. These openings are even more powerful when the speaker carefully plans these comments. Through the skillful use of *illustrations* ("In the short time I will be talking with you, 150 violent crimes will have been committed in our nation"), *examples* ("Lisa was a young woman from our community whose life was forever altered on January 18th"), and *anecdotes* ("Once, while traveling on the subway, I noticed a shifty looking man carefully watching each passenger enter and leave the car"), speakers gather our attention to them and their message.

Physically Involve the Audience

An example of this technique regularly occurs at sales seminars, where the speaker offers a gift, usually money, to the first person in the audience who will simply leave his/her seat and come to the front to get it. Eventually some brave soul approaches, takes the money, and returns to his/her seat. Then everyone else in the audience realizes they could have had the gift themselves if they had only been willing to act instead of sitting passively.

In a speech about the importance of eating a good breakfast, a speaker could start by asking all students who ate breakfast to raise their hands. Then, the speaker could ask how many of those ate at fast food, or ate eggs or fruit. Depending on how the speaker defined a good breakfast, the questions could lead the speaker to comment that "Only a few of you had a good breakfast today. I hope to make a difference for tomorrow."

Some speakers may ask the audience to yell "Good morning" until they've been loud enough. A speaker talking about the need for exercise may ask the audience to jump up and down for a few moments. At a graduation speech in 2003 at the University of Wisconsin, after thanking the administration, director and movie producer Jerry Zucker involved the audience physically when he started his speech with the following:

> Before I start my remarks, I'd like everyone just to do something for me. Very simply—so everyone can kind of just get to know everyone else—on the count of three, I'd like everyone to turn around and shake the hand of the person sitting right behind you. One, two, three—right now, everybody, please do that.

Relate Personal Experience

Sharing a story or several examples from your past with your listeners can be an effective start. Be sure your personal experiences will not hurt your credibility and that they relate directly to your topic. Recently, a student giving a "speech of presentation" started this way:

> It was the end of my third week of college, and the problem was getting harder and harder to ignore. I, like so many people today, had no idea where to turn, or who to talk to. So, I took to the streets. I walked up 4th, walked around the Courthouse, and then headed due east. Finally, on 9th Street, I found hope again ... In the form of Terry's Clip and Chip Barbershop. You see, my hair had started tickling the backs of my ears, and I was getting that abhorrent ring-around-the-collar phenomenon ...

The student's speech was to present a Small Business award to the barbershop/golf repair shop. He continued to describe his experience as an illustration of why Terry's Clip and Chip deserved the award. It was a humorous beginning with a personal story that related directly to the topic.

Use a Visual or Media Aid

Before the president of the United States speaks, the broadcast feed from the White House shows the presidential seal. This is no accident; it helps to draw attention to the upcoming speech and also helps reinforce the president's credibility. But you do not have to be the president to use this technique. Beginning your speech with an interesting sound recording, visual, or prop is guaranteed to draw attention to the beginning of your speech, too. Showing the world population clock or the U.S. debt clock grabs attention, as would some funny or startling YouTube video. One student brought a garbage bag filled with one week's worth of used diapers for one child to demonstrate how much waste is produced.

Refer to the Situation

Skilled public speakers often begin with a positive comment related to the occasion, the person who spoke before them, the audience, the date, or even the physical location. Each of these may be more appropriate at one time than at another. For example, a commencement speaker at her alma mater might start, "It's hard for me to believe that 25 years ago I sat in those seats listening to the commencement speaker." Or, if an audience was waiting outside in the rain to hear a Democratic candidate who was late, the candidate might start, "I bet there isn't a more committed group of voters than those of you here who have been standing in the rain waiting for me." When you are planning a speech, ask yourself if referencing the event, a prior speaker, the audience, or the significance of this date in history would create interest and gather attention.

Each of these is an option for opening a speech. Keep in mind that your attention-gaining device must relate in some way to your topic or you run the risk of confusing your audience. Your choice should be guided by several other factors. First, consider the mood you are attempting to create. Second, consider your audience's expectations of you and the occasion. Third, consider how much time and resources each approach will require. Finally, consider your strengths and weaknesses—you may not be as strong at joke telling as recalling a powerful story. (For a deeper understanding of how these and other techniques work, see **BTW: Gaining and Holding Attention.**)

BTW!

Gaining and Holding Attention

This is what gains our attention, according to D. Ehninger (1986):

1. **Activity.** Incorporate things that move, flash, blink.

2. **Reality.** Real, concrete, sensual things are more attention-getting than hypothetical, abstract, or mental.

3. **Proximity.** Refer to things that are recent, immediate, or nearby; things that preceded your message—the previous speaker; someone in the audience.

4. **Familiarity.** Draw from what people know; draw from things that are unique or special to them.

5. **Novelty.** People pay attention to things that are new and different.

6. **Suspense.** People pay attention to things that build suspense.

7. **Conflict.** People pay attention to a good fight.

8. **Humor.** People pay attention to things that are funny. Be relevant; use good taste.

9. **The vital.** People nearly always pay attention to matters that affect their health, reputation, property, or employment.

Five Guidelines and Suggestions for Introductions

As you focus on crafting your introduction for your next speech, consider how you can create a strong and effective message. Remember, as in any recipe, no ingredient stands on its own. Attention to each part of the process leads to an excellent final product. After choosing the most appropriate beginning, consider these general guidelines as you prepare and deliver your introduction.

1. Prepare After the Body of the Speech

Your introduction will take form more easily after you have created an outline of the body of your speech. When speakers attempt to create the introduction first, they inevitably rewrite it several times as they continue to change the body of their message. However, some students find that writing the introduction after selecting a thesis and main points helps to "jump start" the rest of the creative process. In either case, the direction and key ideas are in place before the introduction is considered.

2. Make It Creative and Easy to Follow

Whether you are offering a startling statistic or asking a question, keep things simple. When you offer your thesis and even when you preview your main points, look for ways to be concise and straight-forward. Recently, a student beginning his persuasive speech started with his arms open in a pleading gesture, zealously urging the class, "Please! Please I beg of you— stop washing your hands!" He then briefly noted the dangers of too much cleansing and stated his thesis. His enthusiastic approach and startling plea made for a creative introduction that was simple and easy to understand.

Consider your introduction as an invitation to creativity. The more creative your introduction, the more likely your audience will listen to the entire message. One student turned the lectern around on the table so the top sloped toward his audience, climbed up, and perched himself atop with legs dangling, and paused. His audience chuckled at his odd behavior. Then he forcefully announced, "Science has discovered a link between nonconformity and intelligence." His audience roared! His speech about nonconformity and intelligence was well received, but his attention-gaining strategy was risky. Sometimes creativity can backfire. Be sure your strategy suits your occasion and audience expectations of the speaker.

3. Communicate High Energy by Being Well Practiced

The most important part of your speech to practice thoroughly is the introduction, followed by the conclusion, and then the body. The first impression created by a well-practiced introduction lays the foundation for your ultimate success. Rehearse your introduction many times. Your introduction should be delivered enthusiastically. Since introductions are relatively short, put your heart, mind, and energy into it. If you are truly engaged in the introduction, your audience is more likely to become involved in your message.

It is difficult to communicate high energy if you are dependent on notes. Strive to avoid looking at notes during your introduction. Rehearsing your introduction helps you accomplish this.

4. Engage Audience Nonverbally Before You Start

Poise counts! Recall that your speech actually begins as you rise to speak and eyes fall on you. Create a confident, energetic approach to the front. Once there, pause, catch and hold your audience's eye contact for a moment, and take a deep breath. Each of these measures is critical to beginning your speech effectively. You want your audience to know you are interested in the speech and that you want them to be part of the experience. Your nonverbal messages are the first part audiences receive as they form a first impression of you. It may help to picture a favorite speaker or actor whom you admire for their effective posture, poise, and presence. Can you embed these traits in your nonverbal approach?

5. Consider Time Constraints and Mood

When giving a five-minute speech, telling a protracted, dramatic story would be inappropriate. The same is true of showing a one-minute video clip. Alternately, when delivering a 45-minute lecture, such a beginning would be wholly acceptable. The mood you are hoping to create in your audience must be related to the tone you adopt as a speaker. The introduction is your best chance to establish your tone and alter the mood of your audience. Carefully consider what effects different introductions might have on mood. Capture the nonverbal elements of voice and body that reflect the best tone for you to deliver your message in.

Common Pitfalls of Introductions

Excuse the cliché, but as they say, you never get a second chance at a first impression. Here is a list of problematic approaches to avoid during your introduction.

1. **Beginning with an apology.** Do not use your introduction to apologize for mistakes you are likely to make, for inadequate visual aids, being ill prepared, or even just plain ill. Apologies set a negative tone that is hard to overcome.

2. **Being too brief or too long.** Do not jump into the body of the speech or spend too much time setting up the speech. Your introduction should take between 10 and 20 percent of your total allotted speaking time. Not adhering to this guideline means violating an audience expectation and potentially annoying them.

❸ **Giving too much away.** While the introduction should provide a road map for your speech, you do not want to give the substance of your speech in your preview. Instead, use general terms to tell your audience what you intend to cover.

❹ **Reading.** We have advised you to rehearse your introduction thoroughly. Do not read your introductory remarks to your audience. Your script becomes a barrier between you and your audience. Worse yet, you will likely sound more like a reader than a public speaker. Avoid reading extensively in the introduction (or anywhere else).

❺ **Relying on shock tactics.** Your victory will be short lived if you capture audience attention by screaming at the top of your lungs, pounding the table, telling a bawdy joke, or using material that has nothing to do with your speech. Your audience will trust you less because of the way you manipulated their attention. Using an innovative approach can be effective as long as it is tied directly to the topic of your speech and is not over-the-top.

❻ **Promising too much.** Some speakers, fearful that their speech says too little, promise more than they can deliver, in the hope that the promise alone will satisfy their listeners. It rarely does. Once you set expectations in the introduction, the body of your speech has to deliver or you lose credibility.

❼ **Using unnecessary prefatory remarks.** Resist the urge to begin with "I'm so nervous," "I can't believe I have to do this speech," or "Okay, deep breath, here we go." Even if you feel these things, such verbal adaptors are likely to make you even more nervous and hurt your credibility. Instead, begin with your planned opening statement.

❽ **Using long-winded poems, quotations, and prose.** We understand that for full effect, an entire piece of prose or poetry should be read. We also know that editing a poem or piece of prose may not be easy. However, it is possible to find an appropriate nugget embedded within the piece that is perfect for your speech. Consider paraphrasing or moving longer passages to the body of your speech.

❾ **Becoming someone else.** Because your initial credibility is being established in the introduction, avoid histrionics and melodrama. Being true to yourself will earn the respect of your listeners.

❿ **Overusing some techniques.** Often overused are simple questions, rhetorical questions, and startling, catastrophic stories. This is made worse by relying on trite phrases. Spend some time thinking about how to begin your speech. Think about what might be most effective with your particular audience. Seek originality and creativity.

Conclusions

Think of your **conclusion** as the pinnacle of your speech—the words you want your listeners to remember as they leave the room. Too often, speakers waste the opportunity with endings like "That's it," "I guess I'm finished now," or "I'm through. Any questions?" Or they simply stop talking, giving the audience no indication that they have finished their speech. Just as an introduction sets a first impression, a well-delivered conclusion leaves a lasting imprint on your audience.

A conclusion should not be viewed as an afterthought. Understand that the conclusion is your last opportunity to have an impact. Just as the introduction should be clear and flow smoothly to the body of the speech, the body should flow smoothly to the conclusion. Following are three functions of conclusions to consider as you think about the transition from the body to the conclusion and determine how to create the greatest effect on your audience.

> **Glossary**
>
> **Conclusion** Supports the body of your speech, reinforces your message and brings your speech to a close.

Functions of Conclusions

Strong endings to speeches summarize important information, motivate listeners, and create a sense of closure. President George W. Bush addressed the nation in the evening following the tragic events in New York City on what has become known simply as 9/11. After talking about the terror that so many Americans experienced, he explained how the rescuers responded, and what the government planned to do to prevent another attack. His conclusion was designed to touch the emotions of all Americans, and he provided closure at the end by stating the following:

> Tonight, I ask for your prayers for all those who grieve, for the children whose worlds have been shattered, for all whose sense of safety and security has been threatened. And I pray they will be comforted by a Power greater than any of us, spoken through the ages in Psalm 23:
>
> *Even though I walk through the valley of the shadow of death, I fear no evil for you are with me.*
>
> This is a day when all Americans from every walk of life unite in our resolve for justice and peace. America has stood down enemies before, and we will do so this time. None of us will ever forget this day, yet we go forward to defend freedom and all that is good and just in our world. Thank you. Good night. And God bless America.

Summarizing Important Information

The transition from the body to the conclusion is pivotal in signaling the impending end of your speech. Your instructor and your own personal preference may help you decide how to tell your audience you are ending. Whether you use a formal "In conclusion …" or prefer something less formal, such as "Now, to wrap this up today …," you want your audience to be clear that you are about to finish. Audiences know that when you give them that signal, they are about to get an important recap of your key ideas.

According to speech communication professor John Baird Jr. (1974), "Summaries may be effective when presented at the conclusion of a speech [because] they provide the audience with a general structure under which to subsume the more specific points of the speech" (pp. 119–127). Research indicates that in some instances summaries are not essential, but if your audience is unfamiliar with the content of your speech, or if the speech is long or complex, a summary reinforces your main points.

Iceland's Prime Minister, Johanna Sigurdardottir, spoke at official ceremonies on June 17, 2011 in honor of National Day, the celebration of the nation's independence. Her speech is a patriotic one that highlights the country's progress, and specifically identifies Jon Siguardsson's contributions in the struggle for independence. She concluded her speech by saying:

> Fellow Icelanders: Energy, thrift, foresight and persistence, were the words Jon Sigurdsson chose to rally his nation in the early nineteenth century. His rallying cry is no less appropriate today, and we should honor the memory of this great campaigner by making them our watchwords. Let us be energetic and thrifty, show foresight and persistence, and work together in unity to build a healthy and robust society. The summer awaits us, and there are definitely brighter times ahead for the Icelandic nation. May all of you enjoy this National Day and bicentennial year.

In the process of ending, an effective conclusion reinforces the main idea of the speech. The Prime Minister's speech summarizes the main points of her speech, so the audience has one more opportunity to process her main ideas (Learn more about Iceland's Prime Minister in **BTW: Who Is Johanna Sigurdardottir?**).

BTW!

Who Is Johanna Sigurdardottir?

From flight attendant to office worker to politician to Prime Minister in 2009, Johanna Sigurdardottir's life has been anything but dull. After serving on the Board of the Icelandic Cabin Crew Association, she was a member of the Board of the Commercial Workers' Union, and her political aspirations where ultimately, she was head of her political party. Shortly after Iceland passed a law allowing gay marriage in 2010, she married her long-term partner, making her the world's first national leader with a same-sex spouse.

Motivating Listeners

Great speakers do more than summarize in their conclusions; they motivate their audiences. In motivating your audience, you might accomplish three things: relate your topic to your listeners, communicate a feeling, and broaden the message.

❶ **Relate your topic to your listeners.** Your speech will achieve the greatest success if your listeners feel you have helped them in some concrete way. Consider making this connection in your conclusion. At the Virginia Statewide Housing Conference in November 2010, U.S. Secretary of Housing and Urban Development Shaun Donovan drew his speech to end with the following remarks:

> For me, for President Obama, and for Senator Sanders, all this work comes down to a very simple belief: That no matter where you live, when you choose a home, you don't just choose a home. You also choose schools for your children and transportation to work. You choose a community—and the choices available in that community. A belief that our children's futures should never be determined—or their choices limited—by the zip code they grow up in.
>
> Like our President, I know change is never easy—that revitalizing our nation's communities, rural, urban, and suburban won't happen overnight. Nor will it happen because of any one policy or the work of any one agency or one party. But working together, in common purpose—in partnership—we can tackle our toughest challenges. We can push back on this crisis. We can build upon the remarkable change and sense of possibility you're catalyzing in communities across the state.
>
> And most important of all, we can create a geography of opportunity for every American—and every family. Ensuring we do is our goal today. Let us rise to meet it.

In this brief passage, Donovan uses the word *community* four times. His use of the inclusive "we" is yet another way to establish a group identity and a sense of community. Donovan's conclusion clearly serves to motivate listeners to continue to work to improve living conditions in the United States.

❷ **Communicate a feeling.** The conclusion sets the psychological mood listeners carry with them from the hall. A student speaking against aspartame noted at the beginning of her speech that she believed aspartame contributed to her previous depression and weight gain. She ended her speech by noting that eliminating aspartame from her diet lifted her depression and led to significant weight loss. Her passion about the topic and the relief she feels were clearly communicated.

③ Broaden your message. Finally, the conclusion can be used to connect your topic to a broader context. If in your speech you talk about the responsibility of every adult to vote on election day, you can use your conclusion to tie the vote to the continuation of our democratic system. If your speech focuses on caring for aging parents, you can conclude with a plea to value rather than discard the wisdom of the elderly.

Creating Closure

Good conclusions create a sense of closure for the speech. The audience feels a sense of satisfaction that you have completed and accomplished something important. If you are having dinner with others, the dessert often completes the dining experience. So, when speaking, it is not enough to simply stop with a comment: "Well, that's it, I guess I can see if anyone has a question," thus leaving the audience without a sense of closure. An effective conclusion tells your listeners your speech has ended. Next we offer four techniques speakers use to create a memorable closing.

Developing Memorable Conclusions

Thanking as Transition

Although saying thank you at the end of the speech indicates you are finished, it is no substitute for a statement that brings your discussion to a close. You can, however, use the "thank you" statement as a transition into your concluding remarks. For example, Oprah Winfrey received the first Bob Hope Humanitarian Award at the 54th Emmy Awards in September, 2002.

After saying thank you, Winfrey explained why she was thanking people. Rather than ending by saying thank you to several individuals, she gave the speech more impact by quoting Maya Angelou and leaving the audience with a final thought by asserting that she planned to make herself worthy of the honor by continuing to give to the world.

Call to Action

As you wrap up your speech, you can make a direct appeal to your listeners by urging them to take a specific action or to change their attitudes. In a persuasive speech, the conclusion is the most forcible and memorable place to position your final appeal.

Living in an age of mass media, Americans hear calls to action every time we turn on the television. Advertisers plead with us to drop everything and buy their products NOW! We see 1-800 numbers flash across the screen, urging us to order knives or DVDs or diet aids. Televangelists urge us to contribute to their mission. Internet sites and service station pumps now force us to tune in to the sales pitch of the day. As annoying as these pleas can be, the fact that we are accustomed to calls to action makes them a natural conclusion to a speech.

In a speech designed to persuade her audience that industrial hemp should be grown in the United States, Mary, a public speaking student, ended her speech with a call to action:

> It is easy to get excited about this crop. What other plant can give you so many products? Industrial hemp can make jeans and milk and just about everything in between. And what plant has such a rich and diverse history?
>
> I've only given you a small amount of information, and I'm sure you will be hearing more about industrial hemp in the future. States have stopped waiting for the federal government to legalize it and have begun passing their own bills. Industrial hemp won't save the world, but it will make a big difference. The possibilities are endless, so call your representative today. Tell him or her that the time has come for American to again grow Hemp for Victory.

Mary makes her last persuasive appeal, and then asks the audience to do something about it. Her call could have been stronger and more specific if, for example, she had prepared letters for her colleagues to sign and mail in an addressed, stamped envelope. More letters would be sent because Mary would not be relying on her audience to remember to create and mail their letters later.

Here is how a professor of Political Science might conclude a lecture:

> I have explained my thoughts on the implications of the changes that are now taking place in the Middle East. As you review them, keep this in mind: What we are witnessing is nothing less than a change in world politics. In the days ahead, think about these changes and about how it will affect each and every one of us in the Western democracies.

The call to action, in this case, involves mental activity—reflection, rather than some physical action. This is a perfectly acceptable final statement.

Use a Dramatic Illustration

Ending your speech with a dramatic story connected to your speech's thesis reinforces the theme in your listeners' minds. It is the last message of your speech the audience will hear and, as a story, it is the most likely to be remembered.

German Chancellor Angela Merkel spoke to the U.S. Congress on the 20th anniversary of the falling of the Berlin Wall on November 2009. In her speech, she thanked Americans for their support and for their role in helping to end the Cold War. She also reminded U.S. politicians that the world will be looking to America and Europe for leadership in forging a global climate change agreement. She ended her speech with the following:

> I am convinced that, just as we found the strength in the 20th century to tear down a wall made of barbed wire and concrete, today we have the strength to overcome the walls of the 21st century, walls in our minds, walls of short-sighted self-interest, walls between the present and the future.
>
> Ladies and gentlemen, my confidence is inspired by a very special sound—that of the Freedom Bell in the Schöneberg Town Hall in Berlin. Since 1950 a copy of the original American Liberty Bell has hung there. A gift from American citizens, it is a symbol of the promise of freedom, a promise that has been fulfilled. On October 3, 1990 the Freedom Bell rang to mark the reunification of Germany, the greatest moment of joy for the German people. On September 13, 2001, two days after 9/11, it tolled again, to mark America's darkest hour.
>
> The Freedom Bell in Berlin is, like the Liberty Bell in Philadelphia, a symbol which reminds us that freedom does not come about of itself. It must be struggled for and then defended anew every day of our lives. In this endeavor Germany and Europe will also in future remain strong and dependable partners for America. That I promise you.

A dramatic story reinforced German Chancellor Angela Merkel's message on the anniversary of the falling of the Berlin Wall.

© Jörg Carstensen/dpa/Corbis

Conclude with a Quotation

Closing a speech with the words of others is an effective and memorable way to end your presentation. The Nobel Peace Prize for 2010 was awarded to then-imprisoned Liu Xiaobo of China for his long and nonviolent struggle for human rights in his country. Thorbjorn Jagland, president of the Norwegian Nobel Committee, used a quotation in his concluding remarks.

> Isaac Newton once said, "If I have seen further, it is by standing on the shoulders of giants."
>
> When we are able to look ahead today, it is because we are standing on the shoulders of the many men and women who over the years—often at great risk—have stood up for what they believed in and thus made our freedom possible.
>
> Therefore, while others at this time are counting their money, focusing exclusively on their short-term national interests, or remaining indifferent, the Norwegian Nobel Committee has once again chosen to support those who fight—for us all.

> We congratulate Liu Xiaobo on the Nobel Peace Prize for 2010. His views will in the long run strengthen China. We extend to him and to China our very best wishes for the years ahead. © The Nobel Foundation 2010.

The quote serves as a reference point for and transition to the comments that follow. Notice that the quote does not have to be the last words the speaker utters, but the conclusion either leads up to the quote or is structured by the quote.

One of the most famous moments in presidential oratory was the conclusion of President Ronald Reagan's address to the nation from the Oval Office on the Challenger disaster, January 29, 1986:

> The crew of the space shuttle *Challenger* honored us by the manner in which they lived their lives. We will never forget them, nor the last time we saw them—this morning, as they prepared for their journey, and waved good-bye, and "slipped the surly bonds of earth" to "touch the face of God."

As in this example, quotations can be interwoven into the fabric of the speech without telling your listeners that you are speaking the words of others, in this case *High Flight*, by American poet John Magee. If you use this technique, and you are not the president, we recommend that you use the quotation's words exactly and attribute it to the writer.

Conclude with a Metaphor That Broadens the Meaning of Your Speech

You may want to broaden the meaning of your speech through the use of an appropriate metaphor—a symbol that tells your listeners that you are saying more. Mao Tse-Tung, also known as Chairman Mao and identified by *Time* magazine as one of the 100 most influential individuals of the 20th century, spoke at the opening of the Party School of the Central Committee of the Communist Party of China on February 1, 1942. He used a medical metaphor in his closing statement:

> But our aim in exposing errors and criticizing shortcomings, like that of a doctor curing a sickness, is solely to save the patient and not to doctor him to death. A person with appendicitis is saved when the surgeon removes his appendix.

> So long as a person who has made mistakes does not hide his sickness for fear of treatment or persist in his mistakes until he is beyond cure, so long as he honestly and sincerely wishes to be cured and to mend his ways, we should welcome him and cure his sickness so that he can become a good comrade.

> We can never succeed if we just let ourselves go, and lash out at him. In treating an ideological or a political malady, one must never be rough and rash but must adopt the approach of "curing the sickness to save the patient," which is the only correct and effective method.
>
> I have taken this occasion of the opening of the Party School to speak at length, and I hope comrades will think over what I have said.

Without saying it directly, his use of figurative analogy implied that disagreement with the government is a sickness, a disease, and is separate from the afflicted patient. His conclusion was that government must offer a gentle cure for a willing patient. His speech was not about one person being sick, but about a larger context: how China and its citizens grapple with global politics and ideological dissention. His metaphor helps his audience find a new way to conceive of these broader issues by relating them to something basic and familiar.

Conclude with Humor

If you leave your listeners with a humorous story, you will leave them laughing and with a reservoir of good feelings about you and your speech. To be effective, of course, the humor must be tied to your core idea.

A Hollywood screenwriter, invited to speak to students in a college writing course about the job of transforming a successful novel into a screenplay, concluded her speech with the following story:

> Two goats who often visited the set of a movie company found some discarded film next to where a camera crew was working. One of the goats began munching on the film.
>
> "How's it taste?" asked the other goat, trying to decide whether to start chomping himself.
>
> "Not so great," said the first goat. "I liked the book better."

The audience laughed in appreciation of the humor. When the room settled down, the speaker concluded her speech:

> I hope in my case the goat isn't right and that you've enjoyed the films I've written even more than the books on which they were based.
>
> Thank you for inviting me to speak.

(For a summary of humor techniques you might quickly master, see **BTW: Say Things Funny!**)

Say Things Funny

When once asked how comedy works, Bill Cosby noted that comedians don't say funny things, they say things funny. Following his advice, here are some dependable stage techniques of the master comedians (Harrell, 1997):

○ **Stand closer to your audience.** Comedy is an intimate relationship. Notice that in most comedy clubs the stage is small and close to the audience.

○ **Use as much vocal variety as possible.** The wilder your vocal changes, the better you can set off a punch line or make a line funny.

○ **Develop a good sense of timing.** Often story jokes build in momentum and then pause before the punch line. One-liners are often quickly slipped in, as if by accident.

○ **Move and gesture energetically.** Comedians who are "dead pan" are the exception. Most move in an animated manner to increase the audience's sense of silliness and involvement.

○ **Make faces.** Facial expressions hold your audience's attention and cue them as to different characters, sarcasm, and the "mood" of a story or joke. Additionally, comedians use their facial expressions to tell the listeners when and how to react to a joke.

Encourage Thought with a Rhetorical Question

Rhetorical questions encourage thought. At the end of a speech, they leave listeners with a responsibility to think about the questions raised after your speech is over. Your question can be as simple as "Can our community afford to take the step of hiring 50 new police officers? Perhaps a better question is, Can we afford not to?" Rhetorical questions have the power to sway an audience with their emotional impact.

Refer to Your Introduction

In your conclusion, you can refer to an opening story or quotation or answer the rhetorical questions you raised. Here is how Shannon closed her speech on seat belt safety:

> One thing I didn't tell you at the beginning of my speech about my accident was that for years I resisted wearing my belt. I used to fight with my parents. I felt it was such a personal decision. How could they—or the state government, for that matter—dare tell me what to do?

> Thank goodness I had the sense to buckle up that day. And you can be sure that I will never get into a car without wrapping myself securely with my belt of life. I hope that my experience will be enough to convince you to buckle up, too.

Like matching bookends, closing your speech with a reference to your introduction provides intellectual and emotional symmetry to your remarks.

How to conclude the same speech in different ways

Just as many topics lend themselves to different types of introductions, they also lend themselves to various methods of conclusion. Here three techniques are used to conclude a speech on learning to deal more compassionately with the elderly:

Example 1: A quotation that personalizes your message.

In 1878, in a poem entitled *Somebody's Mother,* poet Mary Dow Brine wrote these words:

She's somebody's mother, boys, you know, For all she's aged and poor and slow.

Most of us are likely to be somebody's mother—or father—before we die. And further down the road, we're likely to be grandparents, sitting in lonely places, hoping that our children have figured out a more humane way to treat us than we have treated our elderly relatives.

Example 2: A dramatic story that also serves as a metaphor.

Not too long ago, I had a conversation with a doctor who had recently hospitalized an 82-year-old woman with pneumonia. A widow and the mother of three grown children, the woman had spent the last seven years of her life in a nursing home.

The doctor was called three times a day by these children. At first their calls seemed appropriate. They wanted to be sure their mother was getting the best possible medical care. Then, their tone changed. Their requests became demands; they were pushy and intrusive.

After several days of this, the doctor asked one of the children—a son—when he had last visited his mother before she was admitted to the hospital. He hesitated for a moment and then admitted that he had not seen her for two years.

I'm telling you this story to demonstrate that we can't act like these grown children and throw our elderly away, only to feel guilty about them when they are in crisis.

Somehow we have to achieve a balance between our own needs and the needs of our frail and needy parents—one that places reasonable demands on ourselves and on the system that supports the elderly.

Example 3: Rhetorical questions.

> Imagine yourself old and sick, worried that your money will run out and that your family will no longer want you. You feel a pain in your chest. What could it be? You ask yourself whether your daughter will be able to leave work to take you to the hospital—whether your grandchildren will visit you there—whether your medical insurance will cover your bills—whether anyone will care if you live or die.
>
> Imagine asking yourself these questions and then imagine the pain of not knowing the answers. We owe our elderly better than that.

By providing these three examples, we note that each has a different feel that surely influences the final mood of the audience. It takes time and effort to create an effective conclusion, just as with an introduction. Both activities are centered on discovering how to best reach your audience.

Common pitfalls of Conclusions

Knowing what *not* to do is almost as important as knowing what *to* do. Here is a list of approaches to avoid during your conclusion.

1. **Don't use your conclusion to introduce a new topic.** Develop your main and subordinate points in the body of your speech, not in the conclusion.

2. **Don't apologize.** Even if you are unhappy with your performance, do not apologize for your shortcomings when you reach the conclusion. Remarks like, "Well, I guess I didn't have that much to say," or "I'm sorry for taking so much of your time" are unnecessary and usually turn off the audience.

3. **Don't end abruptly.** Just because you have made all your points does not mean that your speech is over. Your audience has no way of knowing you are finished unless you provide closure. A one-sentence conclusion is not sufficient closure.

4. **Don't change the mood or tone.** If your speech was serious, do not shift moods at the end. A humorous conclusion would be inappropriate and lessen the impact of your speech.

5. **Don't use the phrases "in summary" or "in conclusion" except when you are actually at the end of your speech.** Some speakers use these phrases at various points in their speech, confusing listeners who expect an ending rather than a transition to another point.

⑥ **Don't ask for questions.** Never risk asking, "Any questions?" Think about it, if there are no questions, you will be creating an awkward silence—hardly the climactic conclusion you were hoping for. Also, most speech days in class are designed to have a number of speakers fill the class period. Answering questions or taking comments may interfere with the instructor's schedule.

If there is to be a question-and-answer session, consider it as a separate event from the speech. Complete your entire conclusion, receive your well-earned applause, and *then* field any questions.

⑦ **Don't ignore applause.** Graciously accept the praise of your audience by looking around the room and saying, "thank you."

⑧ **Don't forget to thank your audience and host.** Part of your lasting positive impression will come from a sincere thanks offered to both your audience for their attention and your host for allowing you the opportunity to speak. This is true in many speaking situations, but does not apply to the general public speaking class.

⑨ **Don't run away.** Remember to keep your poise as you confidently make your retreat from the speaking platform. Being in too big a rush to sit down gives the appearance that you are glad it is over. You may be ready to leave, but stifle the urge to flee abruptly from the podium.

⑩ **Don't read it.** Just as with the introduction, the delivery of the conclusion is important. Practice it enough that you are not dependent on your speaker's notes. Eye contact with your audience as you wrap up your message will reinforce your perceived credibility as well as your message's importance. Having to rely heavily on notes, or worst of all, reading your conclusion makes the ending of your message less satisfying to your audience.

Summary

The primacy/recency effect, which suggests that people attend to either the first information they receive or the last information they receive, underscores the importance of strong introductions and conclusions. Introductions serve several functions: they focus attention, provide a motive for the audience to listen, build speaker credibility, and preview the topic of your speech.

Several techniques can be used to capture audience attention in the introduction. Among these are startling statements, dramatic stories, quotations and/or literature references, humor, rhetorical questions, illustrations, examples, anecdotes, audience involvement, personal experience, visual aids, and making reference to your speaking situation.

Your introduction will be successful if you follow established guidelines including preparing it after the body of the speech, making it clear and easy to follow, communicating high energy by practicing it as many times as needed, engaging the audience nonverbally before you start, and considering time constraints and mood. Your introduction will be more effective if you avoid 10 common pitfalls.

The conclusion of your speech should summarize, motivate, and communicate closure. An effective conclusion reinforces your message, acts as a summary, relates your message to your listeners' lives, and connects your message to a broader context.

Among the techniques you can use to conclude your speech are a call to action, a dramatic story, a closing quotation, a metaphor that broadens meaning, humor, rhetorical questions, and a reference to the introduction. Your conclusion will benefit from avoiding 10 common pitfalls such as poor eye contact and apologies.

Discussion Starters

1. What alternatives are available for capturing audience attention in an introduction? What alternatives are available for bringing closure to a speech?

2. What is the relationship between the effectiveness of a speech's introduction and conclusion and speaker credibility?

3. What mistakes do speakers commonly make in preparing the introduction and conclusion of a speech?

4. How do effective introductions and conclusions meet the psychological needs of the audience?

5. What makes some of us funnier than others? Is it genetic or learned? Can it work for you in speeches or is it too dangerous?

References

Baird, John E., Jr. (1974). The Effects of Speech Summaries upon Audience Comprehension of Expository Speeches of Varying Quality and Complexity. *Central States Speech Journal, Summer,* 119–127.

Bush, George W. (2001). *Speech to the Nation on 9/11.* Retrieved September 8, 2011 from www.americanrhetoric.com/speeches/gwbush911addresstothenationon.htm.

Childhood Overweight and Obesity Prevention Program: Fact Sheet. (2011). Retrieved September 7, 2011 from www.surgeongeneral.gov/obesityprevention/factsheet/index.html

Corbett, E., & Connor, R. (1999). *Classical Rhetoric for the Modern Student,* 4th Ed. London: Oxford University Press.

Donovan, Shaun. (2010, November 18). *Speech Given at the Virginia Housing Conference.* Retrieved September 8, 2011 from portal.hud.gov/hudportal/HUD/press/speeches_remarks.2010.htm.

Emanuel, Rahm. (2009). *Commencement Speech at George Washington University*. Retrieved September 8, 2011 from www.blogs.gwhatchet.com/newsroom/2009/05/17/transcript-of-rahm-emanuels-commencement-address/.

Firth, Colin. (2011). *Oscar Acceptance Speech 2011*. Retrieved September 8, 2011 from www.nowpublic.com/colin-firth-oscar-acceptance-speech-2011-video-transcript.2761763.html.

Jagland, Thorbjorn. (2010). *Nobel Peace Prize Speech*. Retrieved September 8, 2011 from www.nobelprize.org/prizes_peace/presentation-speech.html.

Kamkwamba, William. (2009). How I Harnessed the Wind. *TED: Ideas Worth Spreading*. Retrieved July 28, 2011 from www.ted.com/talks/william_kamkwamba_how_i_harnessed_the_wind.html.

Lady Gaga. (2010, September). *The Prime Rib of America* (Speech). Retrieved September 8, 2011 from www.mtv.com/news/articles/1648304/lady-gagas-don't-ask-don't-tell-speech-full-transcript.jhtml.

Merkel, Angela. (2009, November 3). *We Have No Time to Lose* (Speech). Retrieved March 2, 2011 from www.spiegel.de/international/europe.

Notable Quotes from HealthCare Summit. (2010, February 25). Retrieved September 7, 2011 from www.msnbc.msn.com/id/35585513/ns/politics/t/notable-quotes-health-care-summit/.

Reagan, Ronald. (1986). *Challenger* (Speech). Retrieved September 8, 2011 from www.americanrhetoric.com/speeches/ronaldreaganchallenger.htm.

Shapiro, L. (1990, February 26). The Zap Generation. *Newsweek*, 56.

Sigurdardottir, J. Address of the Prime Minister of Iceland at official ceremonies on the parliament square Austurvollur, 17 June 2011. Retrieved on Februrary 2, 2012 on http://www.forsaetisraduneyti.is/.

Tse-tung. Mao. (1942, February 1). *Rectify the Party's Style of Work* (Speech). Retrieved March 2, 2011 from www.marxists.com.

Weiner, Edith. (1989, October 10). Personal interview.

Winfrey, Oprah. (2002, September 22). *Speech*. Retrieved September 8, 2011 from www.famousquotes.me.uk/speeches/Oprah-Winfrey/.

Zucker, Jerry. (2003). *Commencement* (Speech). Retrieved September 8, 2011 from www.news.wisc.edu.8682.

Part

III

TYPES OF PRESENTATION SPEAKING

Image © Helga Esteb, 2013. Used under license from Shutterstock, Inc.

Chapter 9

© *Lee Jin-man/AP/Corbis*

"*Think twice before you speak, because your words and influence will plant the seed of either success or failure in the mind of another.*"

Napoleon Hill

Chapter 9: Informative Speaking

The intent of an informative speech is to communicate information and ideas in a way that your audience will understand and remember. The different types of informative speeches are identified, and goals and strategies for informative speaking are presented. This chapter explores the ethics of informative speaking.

Student Learning Objectives:

○ Students will be able to differentiate between the three genres or classification of speeches, informative, persuasive, and commemorative (special occasion)

○ Students will be able to select and practice the different types of informative speaking

○ Students will be able to describe and explain five goals of informative speeches

○ Students will be able to identify goals, guidelines and strategies for effective informative speaking

○ Students will be able to apply the ethics of informative speaking

INFORMATIVE SPEAKING

Key Terms

abstract topics

calculated ambiguity

informative speech

speech of
demonstration

speech of description

speech of explanation

Whether you are a nurse conducting CPR training for new parents at the local community center, a museum curator delivering a speech on Impressionist art, or an auto repair shop manager lecturing to workers about the implications of a recent manufacturer's recall notice, your informative speech goal is to communicate information and ideas in a way that your audience will understand and remember. In your job, community activities, and in this public speaking class, remember that the audience should hear *new* knowledge, not facts they already know. For example, the nurse conducting CPR training for new parents would approach the topic differently if the audience comprised individuals from various fields working on their yearly recertification. New parents most likely are also new to CPR training, whereas professionals receive training at least once a year.

In this chapter, we first distinguish informative speaking from persuasive or commemorative speaking. We identify different types of informative speeches, and guidelines for informative speaking are presented. Last, the issue of ethics and informative speaking is examined.

Glossary

Informative speech
Communicates information and ideas in a way that your audience will understand and remember..

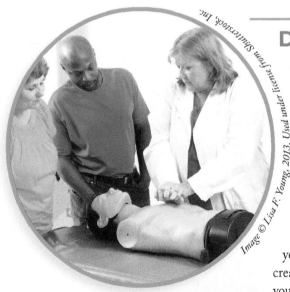

Your informative speech goal is to communicate information and ideas in a way that your audience will understand and remember.

Differentiating Informative, Persuasive, and Entertainment Purposes

The situation or context often suggests what type of speech that is expected. Commencement speeches are motivational, as are keynote speeches at conventions. Speakers deliver commemorative speeches on Veteran's Day, presidents' birthdays, and other occasions that recognize individuals or groups of individuals. Speeches can be classified into three major categories—informative, persuasive, and entertaining (commemorative or inspirational). The next few paragraphs distinguish among these categories.

When you deliver an informative speech, your intent is to enlighten your audience—to increase understanding or awareness and, perhaps, to create a new perspective. In contrast, when you deliver a persuasive speech, your intent is to influence your audience to agree with your point of view—to change attitudes or beliefs or to bring about a specific, desired action. And when you deliver a speech as part of some special occasion, your intent is to entertain, commemorate, inspire, or humor your listeners. In theory, these three forms are different. In practice, these distinctions are much less obvious.

For example, if you developed an informative speech on the consequences of calling off a marriage, your main points might include relationship damage (friends and family), emotional trauma, and financial difficulties. These are acceptable informative topic areas. If, however, you go beyond identifying these issues to suggesting that the engaged couples in your audience implement safeguards to prevent emotional or financial damage, you are being implicitly persuasive. When you tell the men in your audience that they should obtain a written statement from their fiancées pledging the return of the engagement ring if the relationship ends, you are asking for explicit action, and you have blurred the line between information and persuasion. Similarly, if you devote large portions of your speech to a humorous rant about the institution of marriage and why no one should be institutionalized, you have crossed the line toward entertainment.

The key to informative speaking is *intent*. If your goal is to expand understanding, your speech is informational. If, in the process, you want your audience to share or agree with your point of view, you may also be persuasive. And if you want them to pay attention and recall key points later, a little humor and entertaining storytelling always help. After a speech describing the types of assault rifles available to criminals, some of your audience may be moved to write to Congress in support of stricter gun control while others may send contributions to lobbying organizations that promote stricter gun control legislation. Although your speech brought about these actions, it is still informational because your intent was educational. Objective facts can be persuasive even when presented with an informational intent.

A critical place where we often see the intent lines blur is in the conclusion of an informative speech. Take care to avoid providing them with an action plan. Avoid ending a speech with something like "So now that I've explained the history and sociopsychological benefits and drawbacks of tattoos, I hope that you will consider getting one." This final "tag" line changes the nature of the speech from informative to persuasive.

To make sure your speech is informational rather than persuasive or entertaining, start with a clear, specific purpose signifying your intent. Compare the following specific purpose statements:

Specific purpose statement #1 (SPS#1). To inform my listeners how the military has responded historically to minorities in the military, including Japanese Americans, African Americans, women, and gays, bisexuals, transgendered individuals, and lesbians

Specific purpose statement #2 (SPS#2). To inform my listeners how the military has responded poorly and in an untimely fashion to minorities in the military, including Japanese Americans, African Americans, women, and gays, bisexuals, transgendered individuals, and lesbians

Specific purpose statement #3 (SPS#3). To pay tribute to my listeners from minority groups who have suffered under Don't Ask, Don't Tell policies simply to provide invaluable service to our country

While the intent of the first statement is informational, the intent of the second is persuasive, and the third, entertaining. The speaker in SPS#1 is likely to discuss how and where Japanese Americans and African Americans served during WWII, the evolution of women from support positions to combat positions, and the development of the Don't Ask, Don't Tell policy. The speaker in SPS#2 uses subjective words such as "poorly and in an untimely fashion." Most likely this speech would focus more on the negative impact military policy had on minority groups, including being victims of segregation, being placed in high-risk combat situations, and allowing the harassment of women and homosexuals. SPS#3 clearly sets out to commemorate a group of people at a special event, perhaps honoring fallen minority soldiers at a Memorial Day celebration.

Types of Informative Speaking

Although all informative speeches seek to help audiences understand, there are three distinct types of informative speeches. A **speech of description** helps an audience understand *what* something is. When the speaker wants to help us understand *why* something is so, they are offering a **speech of explanation**. Finally, when the focus is on *how* something is done, it is a **speech of demonstration**. Each of these is discussed in detail.

Speeches of Description

Describing the safety features of a typical nuclear power plant, describing the effects of an earthquake, and describing the buying habits of teenagers are all examples of informative speeches of description. These speeches paint a clear picture of an event, person, object, place, situation, or concept. The goal is to create images in the minds of listeners about your topic or to describe a concept in concrete detail. Here, for example, is a section of a speech describing a poetry slam. We begin with a brief, specific purpose and thesis statement:

General purpose: To inform

Specific purpose: To describe to my audience how poetry slams moved the performance of poetry to a competitive event

Thesis statement: To understand the poetry slam, one must understand its history, the performance, and the judging process.

> Imagine reading a piece of poetry in a quaint bookstore with bongo drums playing in the background as a mellow audience snaps their fingers in appreciation. This is how some perceive the traditional poetry reading. Imagine instead, a smoke-filled

Glossary

Speech of description
Helps an audience understand *what* something is.

Speech of explanation
Helps an audience understand *why* something is so.

Speech of demonstration
When the focus is on *how* something is done.

bar, filled with rowdy individuals, many inebriated, anticipating being entertained in three-minute intervals by young poets yearning for the adrenaline rush found in fierce competition. This is how poetry reading becomes the poetry slam.

According to slampapi.com, slam poetry is a competitive event founded by Chicago author Marc Smith in 1987. Individuals perform original poetry designed to elicit an emotional response, and then are judged by experts in the poetry community. Venues across the U.S. include the Bowery Street Poetry Club in New York, Green Mill in Chicago, and the national slam competition hosted in a different city each year.

In this excerpt, the speaker describes a competitive outlet for poets. Audience members learn that this event takes place in bars and clubs, and audience members respond fully. One gets a feeling for the setting through vivid language use. Following is a short list of some possible speech topics for the informative speech of description:

- ○ To describe the important aspects of the Cinco de Mayo celebration
- ○ To describe the life and philosophy of Franz Kafka
- ○ To describe the causes and symptoms of Chronic Fatigue Syndrome (CFT)

Speeches of Explanation

Speeches of explanation deal with more **abstract topics** (ideas, theories, principles, and beliefs) than speeches of description or demonstration. They also involve attempts to simplify complex topics. The goal of these speeches is audience understanding, such as a psychologist addressing parents about the moral development of children or a cabinet official explaining U.S. farm policy.

To be effective, speeches of explanation must be designed specifically to achieve audience understanding of the theory or principle. Avoid abstractions, too much jargon, or technical terms by using verbal pictures that define and explain. Here, for example, a speaker demonstrates the error of using unfamiliar terms to define spiritualism:

General purpose: To inform

Specific purpose: To explain to my audience how the connection between physical and spiritual elements is a basic foundation of Spiritualism

Thesis statement: Spiritualism is a belief system grounded in the idea that each being has both physical and spiritual elements.

According to the National Spiritualist Association of Churches (2011), spiritualism consists of Prophecy, Clairvoyance, Clairaudience, Laying on of Hands, Healing, Visions, Trance,

> **Glossary**
>
> **Abstract topics** Ideas, theories, principles, and beliefs.

> Apports, Levitation, Raps, and Automatic and Independent Writings and Paintings, Voice, Materialization, Photography, Psychometry, and any other manifestation proving the continuity of life as demonstrated through the Physical and Spiritual senses and faculties of man.

While the previous description identifies phenomena associated with spiritualism, too many terms are used to process at one time, and some are not familiar terms. Imagine the speaker saying the following, instead:

> According to Alan Kaslev, developer of the website Kheper. net (meaning transformation), the philosophy known as Spiritualism is based on the premise that man is a dual being; consisting of a physical and spiritual component. The physical element (the body) disintegrates at death, but the spiritual (the "soul") continues exactly as it was, only in another form of existence, the "Spirit-world" or heaven. Spiritualists further claim that communication between the living and those in the spirit-world is possible through a medium.

If the first description is presented alone, listeners are limited in their ability to anchor the concept to something they understand. The second explanation is more effective, and listeners have a clearer idea where the speaker will lead them.

Speeches of explanation may involve policies; statements of intent or purpose that guide or drive future decisions. The president may announce a new arms control policy. A school superintendent may implement a new inclusion policy. The director of human resources of a major corporation may discuss the firm's new flextime policy.

A speech that explains a policy should focus on the questions likely to arise from an audience. For example, prior to a speech to teachers and parents before school starts, the superintendent of a school district implementing a new inclusion policy should anticipate what the listeners will probably want to know—when the policy change will be implemented, to what extent it will be implemented, when it will be evaluated, and how problems will be monitored, among other issues. When organized logically, these and other questions form the basis of the presentation. As in all informative speeches, your purpose is not to persuade your listeners to support the policy, but to inform them about the policy.

To reiterate, strive to keep focused on the informative intent. For example, a group of university employees gathered to hear about the changes in insurance benefits. One particular insurance plan would cost the state less but cost employees more. The speaker, who represented the state, described each option, but made several references to the plan that cost employees more and the state less. After several such references, audience members started making side comments about how the speaker was trying to persuade individuals into the state's preferred plan. The intent was advertised as an informative one, but the speaker's message had strong persuasive undertones.

Following are some sample topics that could be developed into speeches of explanation:

○ To explain the five principles of Hinduism

○ To explain the effect of colonization on African cultures

○ To explain popular superstitions in American culture

○ To explain how different cultures perceive beauty

○ To explain why Japanese internment occurred in the United States during World War II

Speeches of Demonstration

Speeches of demonstration focus on a process by describing the gradual changes that lead to a particular result. These speeches often involve two approaches, one is "how" and the other is a "how to" approach. Here are examples of specific purposes for speeches of demonstration:

○ To inform my audience *how* college admissions committees choose the most qualified applicants

○ To inform my audience *how* diabetes threatens health

○ To inform my audience *how to* sell an item on eBay

○ To inform my audience *how to* play the Facebook game FarmVille by Zygna

Speeches that take a "how" approach have audience understanding as their goal. They create understanding by explaining how a process functions without teaching the specific skills needed to complete a task. After listening to a speech on college admissions, for example, you may understand the process but may not be prepared to take a seat on an admissions committee.

Let's look more closely at a small section of a "how" speech about election judges.

> "You're going to be one of those old ladies at the polling place?" was my daughter's response when I told her I would be an election judge for midterm elections. When she followed up with, "What *is* an election judge?" I realized that many people don't know how election judges are selected. Voters should be aware that the people who check off your name and give you a ballot on election day represent both parties and complete training so that a fair voting procedure exists and is executed in accordance to the law. According to a brochure published by the Illinois government, election judges are selected by the board of elections commissioners, based on lists furnished by the chairs of the county central committees.

Although this excerpt begins to explain how election judges are selected, its primary goal is understanding, not application. In contrast, "how to" speeches communicate specific skills, such as selling an item on eBay, changing a tire, or making a lemon shake-up. Compare the previous "how" example discussing election judges with the following "how to" presentation, How to Buy a New Home.

> According to the U.S. Department of Housing and Urban Development, when it comes time to buying a home, there are seven steps to follow. Given the housing market crisis that exists, the very first step is to figure out how much you can afford. What you can afford depends on your income, credit rating, current monthly expenses, down payment, and the interest rate. Your monthly expenses are not only what it costs to live in an apartment or a rental home, but how much you pay each month for a car as well as any ongoing loan payments. Will you need a newer car soon? Is your job secure? Will you have money left over after paying housing expenses? Do you want to be mortgage free in 15 years? 30 years? All of these are questions you need to answer before you determine how much you can spend on a new home.
>
> The second step in buying a new home is to know your rights. There are several legal documents you must sign. You have rights as a borrower, and you should also be aware of predatory lending.

Notice that the "how to" speech has several steps. These are generally in chronological order, and once learned, should result in "mastery" of a particular ability or skill. In the above example, one should know how to engage in the house-buying process.

One clear difference between the speech of demonstration and speeches of presentation and explanation is that the *speech of demonstration benefits from presentational aids*. When your goal is to demonstrate a process, you may choose to complete the entire process—or a part of it—in front of your audience. The nature of your demonstration and time constraints determine your choice. If you are giving CPR training, a partial demonstration will not give your listeners the information they need to save a life. If you are demonstrating how to cook a stew, however, your audience does not need to watch you chop onions; prepare in advance to maintain audience interest and save time.

Following are several topics that could be developed into demonstration speeches:

- How to make flower arrangements
- How grapes are processed into wine
- How to pick a bottle of wine
- How to swing a golf club
- How to make a website

- How to organize a closet
- How to find cheap airline tickets
- How to determine if you have sleep apnea

Five Goals of Informative Speaking

Although the overarching goal of an informative speech is to communicate information and ideas so the audience will understand, there are other goals as well. Whether you are giving a speech to explain, describe, or demonstrate, the following five goals are relevant: be accurate, objective, clear, meaningful, and memorable. After each goal, we present two specific strategies for achieving that goal.

1. Accurate

Informative speakers strive to present the truth. They understand the importance of careful research for verifying information they present. Facts must be correct and current. Research is crucial. Do not rely solely on your own opinion; find support from other sources. For example, in a speech talking about financing college, you may want to discuss how much debt college students have. After talking with your friends, you may believe that students are deeply in debt. After doing research, you find a source from the Huffington Post in February 2010 that states recent college graduates are carrying an average of $23,200 of debt. This provides specific support.

However, if you looked at a publication from the National Center for Education Statistics in 2000, you would find that in 1997, 46 percent of undergraduates had no debt from college, and the average loan debt was $10,100. Information that is not current may be inaccurate or misleading. Offering an incorrect fact may hurt speaker credibility and cause people to stop listening. The following two strategies will help you present accurate information.

Question the source of information. Is the source a nationally recognized magazine or reputable newspaper, or is it from someone's post on a random blog? Source verification is important. Virtually anyone can post to the Internet. Check to see if your source has appropriate credentials, such as education, work experience, or verifiable personal experience. For example, how valid do you think information is from the Huffington Post?

Consider the timeliness of the information. Information becomes dated. If you want to inform the class about the heart transplant process, relying on sources more than a few years old would mislead your audience because science and technology change rapidly. Your instructor may require sources within a five- or 10-year span. If not, check the date your source was published (online or print), and determine whether it will be helpful or harmful to the overall effectiveness of your speech.

2. Objective

Present information fairly and in an unbiased manner. Purposely leaving out critical information or "stacking the facts" to create a misleading picture violates the rule of objectivity. The following two strategies should help you maintain objectivity.

Take into account all perspectives. Combining perspectives creates a more complete picture. Avoiding other perspectives creates bias, and may turn an informative speech into a persuasive one. The chief negotiator for a union may have a completely different perspective than the administration's chief negotiator on how current contract negotiations are proceeding. They may use the same facts and statistics, but interpret them differently. An impartial third party trying to determine how the process is progressing needs to speak with both sides and attempt to remove obvious bias.

Show trends. Trends put individual facts in perspective as they clarify ideas within a larger context. The whole—the connection among ideas—gives each detail greater meaning. If a speaker tries to explain how the stock market works, it makes sense to talk about the stock market in relation to what it was a year ago, five years ago, 10 years ago, or even longer, rather than focus on today or last week. Trends also suggest what the future will look like.

3. Clear

To be successful, your informative speech must communicate your ideas without confusion. When a message is not organized clearly, audiences become frustrated and confused and, ultimately, they miss your ideas. Conducting careful audience analysis helps you understand what your audience already knows about your topic and allows you to offer a distinct, targeted message at their level of understanding. Choosing the best organizational pattern will also help your listeners understand your message. The following two strategies are designed to increase the clarity of your speech.

Define unfamiliar words and concepts. Unfamiliar words, especially technical jargon, can defeat your informative purpose. When introducing a new word, define it in a way your listeners can understand. Because you are so close to your material, knowing what to define can be one of your hardest tasks. Put yourself in the position of a listener who knows less about your topic than you do or ask a friend or colleague's opinion.

In addition to explaining the dictionary definition of a concept or term, a speaker may rely on two common forms of definitions: operational and through example.

Operational definitions specify procedures for observing and measuring concepts. For example, in the United States an IQ test (Intelligence Quotient) is used to define how "smart" we are. According to Gregory (2004), someone who scores 95–100 is of average intelligence, a score of 120 or higher is above average, and a score of 155 or higher is considered "genius." The government tells us who is "poor" based on a specified income level, and communication researchers can determine if a person has high communication apprehension based on his or her score on McCroskey's Personal Report of Communication Apprehension.

Definition through example helps the audience understand a complex concept by giving the audience a "for instance." In an effort to explain what is meant by the term "white-collar criminal," a speaker could provide several examples, such as Jeff Skilling (former Enron executive convicted on federal felony charges relating to the company's financial collapse), Rod Blagojevich (former Illinois governor found guilty of several charges related to his trying to sell President Obama's Illinois Senate seat), and Wesley Snipes (actor convicted of tax evasion and jailed for three years in December 2010).

Carefully organize your message. Find an organizational pattern that makes the most sense for your specific purpose. Descriptive speeches, speeches of demonstration, and speeches of explanation have different goals. Therefore, you must consider the most effective way to organize your message. *Descriptive speeches* are often arranged in spatial, topical, and chronological patterns. For example, if a speaker chose to talk about Oktoberfest in Munich, a topical speech might talk about the beer tents, food possibilities, entertainment, and tourist activities. A speech following a chronological pattern might talk about when to start planning for the festival, when the festival begins, and what events occur on particular days. The topic is still Oktoberfest, but based on the organizational pattern, the speech focuses differently and contains different information.

Speeches of demonstration often use spatial, chronological, and cause-and-effect or problem–solution patterns. For example, in a speech on how to buy a home, a few organizational patterns are possible, depending on what aspect of the topic you chose as your focus. It would make sense to organize spatially if your focus is on what to examine as you search for homes. You might want to start with the roof and work down toward the basement (or vice versa) or you might look at the lot and outside features and then move inside. The lot could be divided into small parts, such as how big the lot is, how close neighbors are, what the view is all around the house, how much maintenance is needed on the lot, and so on. As you move inside, you could talk about the number of rooms, electricity, plumbing, access (stairs, attic, or crawl space), and so on.

A chronological pattern for how to buy a house would be more appropriate when talking about getting a real estate agent, finding a house, setting up financing, getting an appraisal, making an offer, getting the house appraised, and accepting an offer. As you can see, the speech that is set up to follow a spatial pattern is significantly different than the speech that uses a chronological pattern.

Speeches of explanation are frequently arranged chronologically, or topically, or according to cause-and-effect or problem–solution. For example, for several years, the Asian carp has made headlines in the Great Lakes area because of its potential to harm the habitat of the Great Lakes. Using the Asian carp as a topic, a speech arranged chronologically could discuss how this threat has developed over the last decade, and what the future projection is. A problem–solution speech, on the other hand, could talk about the dangers related to the fish invasion of the Great Lakes and possible solutions to the problem. Important with the second organizational pattern is that the speech be kept as informative as possible, and not identify the "best" solution.

4. Meaningful

A meaningful, informative message focuses on what matters to the audience as well as to the speaker. Relate your material to the interests, needs, and concerns of your audience. A speech explaining the differences between public and private schools delivered to the parents of students in elementary and secondary schools would not be as meaningful in a small town where no choice exists. Here are two strategies to help you develop a meaningful speech:

Consider the setting. The setting may tell you about audience goals. Informative speeches are given in many places, including classrooms, community seminars, and business forums. Audiences may attend these speeches because of an interest in the topic or because attendance is required. Settings tell you the specific reasons your audience has gathered. A group of middle-aged women attending a lifesaving lecture at a local YMCA may be concerned about saving their husbands' lives in the event of a heart attack, while a group of nursing students listening to the same lecture in a college classroom may be fulfilling a graduation requirement.

Avoid information overload. When you are excited about your subject and you want your audience to know about it, you can find yourself trying to say too much in too short a time. You throw fact after fact at your listeners until you literally force them to stop listening. Saying too much is like touring London in a day—it cannot be done if you expect to remember anything.

Information overload can be frustrating and annoying because the listener experiences difficulty in processing so much information. Your job as an informative speaker is to know how much to say and, just as important, what to say. Long lists of statistics are mind-numbing. Be conscious of the relationship among time, purpose, and your audience's ability to absorb information. Tie key points to stories, examples, anecdotes, and humor. Your goal is not to get it all in but to communicate your message as effectively as possible.

BTW!

A Personal Story

A public speaking instructor has some personal advice when it comes to using humor in a speech. She recalls how, in a college speech class, she decided to weave humor into her speech. Little did she realize at the time that if you don't use humor appropriately, not only is it not funny for the audience, but it also undermines your credibility with the rest of your speech.

The speech went downhill fast when she was the only one laughing. She was, needless to say, terribly embarrassed. Now, years later, having the benefit of that experience, she always encourages students to give their funny story or amusing anecdote a trial run in front of family and friends in the context of the speech to gauge its effectiveness. She wants her students to avoid the embarrassment she still feels when she remembers that speech!

5. Memorable

Speakers who are enthusiastic, genuine, and creative and who can communicate their excitement to their listeners deliver memorable speeches. Engaging examples, dramatic stories, and tasteful humor applied to your key ideas in a genuine manner will make a long-lasting impact.

Use examples and humor. Nothing elicits interest more than a good example, and humorous stories are effective in helping the audience remember the material. When Sarah Weddington, winning attorney in the Roe v. Wade Supreme Court case, talks about the history of discriminatory practices in this country, she provides a personal example of how a bank required her husband's signature on a loan even though she was working and he was in school. She also mentions playing "girls" basketball in school and being limited to three dribbles (boys could dribble the ball as many times as they wanted). While these stories stimulate interest and make the audience laugh, they also communicate the message that sex discrimination was pervasive when Weddington was younger (Reaves, 2003). (See **BTW: A Personal Story** to hear an instructor talking about her experience using humor ineffectively.)

© Sergei Bachlakov, 2012. Under license from Shutterstock, Inc.

Enthusiastic speakers deliver memorable speeches.

Physically involve your audience. Many occasions lend themselves to some type of audience participation. Consider asking for audience response to a observation: "Raise your hand if you have ever seen a tornado." Seek help with your demonstration. If you are demonstrating how to make a cake, for example, you could ask someone to stir the batter. Ask some audience members to take part in an experiment that you conduct to prove a point. For example, hand out several headsets to volunteers and ask them to set the volume level where they usually listen to music. Then show how volume can affect hearing.

Guidelines for Effective Informative Speeches

Regardless of the type of informative speech you plan to give, characteristics of effective informative speeches cross all categories. As you research, develop, and present your speech, keep the following 10 guidelines in mind.

Consider your audience's needs and goals

Concern for your audience is the theme of the book and applies here. The best informative speakers know what their listeners want to learn from their speech. A group of Weight Watchers members may be motivated to attend a lecture on dieting to learn how to lose weight, while nutritionists drawn to the same speech may need the information to help clients. Audience goals are also linked to knowledge. Those who lack knowledge about a topic may be more motivated to listen and learn than those who feel they already know the topic. However, it is possible that technology has changed, new information has surfaced, or new ways to think about or do something have emerged. The speaker needs to find a way to engage those who are less motivated.

Make connections between your subject and your audience's daily needs, desires, and interests. For example, some audience members might have no interest in a speech on the effectiveness of halfway houses until you tell them how much money is being spent on prisons locally, or better yet, how much each listener is spending per year. Now the topic is more relevant. People care about money, safety, prestige, family and friends, community, and their own growth and progress, among other things. Show how your topic influences one or more of these and you will have an audience motivated to listen.

Consider your audience's knowledge level

If you want to describe how to use eSnipe when participating in eBay auctions, you may be speaking to students who have never heard of it. To be safe, however, you might develop a brief pre-speech questionnaire to pass out to your class. Or you can select several individuals at random and ask what they know. You do not want to bore the class with mundane minutia, but you do not want to confuse them with information that is too advanced for their knowledge level. Consider this golf example:

> As the golf champion of your district, you decide to give your informative speech on the game. You begin by holding up a golf club and saying, "This is a golf club. They come in many sizes and styles." Then you hold up a golf ball. "This is a golf ball. Golf balls are all the same size, but they come in many

colors. Most golf balls are white. When you first start playing golf, you need a lot of golf balls. So, you need a golf club and a golf ball to play golf."

Expect your listeners to yawn in this situation. They do not want to hear what they already know. Although your presentation may be effective for an audience of children who have never seen a golf club or ball, your presentation is too simplistic for adults.

Capture attention and interest immediately

As an informative speaker, your goal is to communicate information about a specific topic in a way that is understandable to your listeners. In your introduction, you must first convince your audience that your topic is interesting and relevant. For example, if you are delivering a speech on white-collar crime, you might begin like this:

> Imagine taking part of your paycheck and handing it to a criminal. In an indirect way, that's what we all do to pay for white-collar crime. Part of the tax dollars you give the federal government goes into the hands of unscrupulous business executives who pad their expenses and overcharge the government by millions of dollars. For example, General Dynamics, the third-largest military supplier, tacked on at least $75 million to the government's bill for such "overhead" expenses as country-club fees and personal travel for corporate executives.

This approach is more likely to capture audience attention than a list of white-collar crimes or criminals.

Sustain audience attention and interest by being creative, vivid, and enthusiastic

Try something different. Change your pace to bring attention or emphasis to a point. Aloud, say the following phrase at a regular rate, and then slow down and emphasize each word: "We must work together!" Slowing down to emphasize each word gives the sentence greater impact. Varying rate of speech is an effective way to sustain audience attention.

Show some excitement! Talking about accounting principles, water filters, or changes in planet designations with spirit and energy may keep people listening. Delivery can make a difference. Enthusiasm is infectious, even to those who have no particular interest in your subject. It is no accident that advertising campaigns are built around slogans, jingles, and other memorable language that people are likely to remember after a commercial is over. We are more likely to remember vivid language than dull language.

Cite your oral sources accurately

Citing sources accurately means putting in the work ahead of time to understand the source. Anytime you offer facts, statistics, opinions, and ideas that you found in research, you should provide your audience with the source. In doing this, you enhance your own credibility. Your audience appreciates your depth of research on the topic, and you avoid accusations of plagiarism.

Accurate source representation comes from having a well-rounded understanding of the source. Critical thinking is necessary when assessing the source you intend to use. Among other information, it makes sense to check out who the author is or what the source is, what bias, if any exists, what the intention of the author or source is, and what its intended use was.

Your audience needs enough information to judge the credibility of your sources. If you are describing how the HBO show *True Blood* became HBO's most popular show in recent years, it is not sufficient to say, "Jessica Gelt states …" because Jessica Gelt's qualification to comment on this show may be based on the fact that she watches television regularly. However, by adding, "Jessica Gelt, reporter for the *LA Times*, states …," we know she has more credibility.

Signpost main ideas

Your audience may need help keeping track of the information in your speech. Separating one idea from another may be difficult for listeners when trying to learn all the information at once. You can help your audience understand the structure of your speech by creating oral lists. Simple "First, second, third, fourth …" or "one, two, three, four …" helps the audience focus on your sequence of points. Here is an example of signposting:

> Having a motorized scooter in college instead of a car is preferred for two reasons. The first reason is financial. A scooter gets at least 80 miles per gallon. Over a period of four years, significant savings occur. The second reason a scooter is preferred in college is convenience. Parking problems are virtually eliminated. No longer do you have to worry about being late to class, because you can park in the motorcycle parking area. They're all around us.

Signposting at the beginning of a speech tells the audience how many points you have or how many ideas you intend to support. Signposting during the speech acts as a transition because it keeps the audience informed as to where you are in the speech.

Relate the new with the familiar

Informative speeches should introduce new information in terms of what the audience already knows. Using metaphors, analogies, similes, and other forms of speech is useful. Here is an example of an analogy:

> A cooling-off period in labor–management negotiations is like a parentally imposed time-out. When we were children, our parents would send us to our rooms to think over what we had done. We were forbidden to come out for some time in the hope that by the time we were released, our tempers had cooled. Similarly, by law, the President can impose an 80-day cooling-off period if a strike threatens to imperil the nation's health or safety.

Most of us can relate to the "time-out" concept referred to in this example, so providing the analogy helps us understand the cooling-off period if a strike is possible. References to the familiar help listeners assimilate new information. Following is a metaphor for the recent economic crisis.

> The economy is a train wreck. The conductor saw the other train coming toward it, and thought the switchman would set the oncoming train onto the sidetrack and save the day. It didn't happen. The train completely derailed, leaving total destruction in its path.

This metaphor is a way to express visually the idea that banks hoped the regulators would cover their losses and stabilize the economy. Everyone is familiar with the concept of a train wreck, but understanding an economic crisis is not so easy. Using various language devices can help with the explanation. (See **BTW: *The Wizard of Oz*** for information about an allegory, which at its basic level, can be considered an extended metaphor.)

BTW!

The Wizard of Oz

Frank Baum's book *The Wizard of Oz* written in 1900, has been interpreted by economists as an allegory (extended metaphor) on the Populist Movement of the late 1800s. The tornado that sweeps Dorothy away is compared to the Free Silver movement in Baum's time. The Yellow Brick Road represents the gold standard and the Silver Shoes (what became the ruby slippers in the movie) symbolize the Populist Party's desire to construct a bimetallic standard of both gold and silver in place of the gold standard. Dorothy travels to the Emerald City (Washington, D.C.) to speak to the Wizard (the president of the United States). The scarecrow symbolizes a farmer, the tin man represents a worker dehumanized by industrialization, and cowardly lion denotes William Jennings Bryan, a prominent leader of the American Bimetallic League. The Wicked Witch of the West and the Wicked Witch of the East correspond to the wealthy railroad and oil barons of the American West and the financial and banking interests of the eastern U.S., respectively. For more information, check out "Money and Politics in the Land of Oz," at www.usagold.com and "The 'Wizard of Oz' as a Monetary Allegory" by Hugh Rockoff in the edited book *Historical Perspectives on the American Economy* by Whaples and Betts (1995).

Use Repetition

Repetition is important when presenting new facts and ideas. You help your listeners by reinforcing your main points through summaries and paraphrasing. For example, if you were trying to persuade your classmates to purchase a scooter instead of a car, you might have three points: (1) a scooter is cheaper than a car; (2) a scooter gets better gas mileage than a car; and (3) you can always find a nearby parking spot for your scooter. For your first point, you mention purchase price, insurance, and maintenance costs. As you finish your first point, you could say, "So a scooter is cheaper than a car in at least three ways, purchase price, insurance, and maintenance." You have already mentioned these three subpoints, but noting them as an internal summary before your second main point helps reinforce the idea that scooters are cheaper than cars.

Offer Interesting Visuals

As Cyphert (2007) states, "There is no doubt that good visual design can make information clearer and more interesting" (p. 170). He elaborates:

> Audience expectations have changed, not merely in terms of technical bells and whistles available in the creation of visual aids, but with respect to the culture's understanding of what it means to deliver an eloquent public address (p. 170).

Your audience expects you to put effort into your presentation. This means more than practicing. Using pictures, charts, models, PowerPoint slides, and other presentational aids helps maintain audience interest. Use humorous visuals to display statistics, if appropriate. Demonstrate the physics of air travel by throwing paper airplanes across the room. With ever-increasing computer accessibility and Wi-Fi in the classroom, using computer-generated graphics to enhance and underscore your main points and illustrations is a convenient and valuable way to inform your audience effectively.

Consider How to Respond to Audience Questions and Distractions

In an informative speech, your audience may have the opportunity to ask questions. Before you give your speech, decide whether you want questions during your presentation or at the end. If you prefer they wait, tell your audience early in your speech or at the first hand raised. Perhaps try, "I ask that you hold all questions to the end of this presentation, where I have built in some time for them."

When fielding questions, develop the habit of doing four things in this order: *thank* the questioner, *paraphrase* the question (put it in your own words), *answer* the question briefly, and then *ask* the questioner if you answered his/her question. Paraphrasing allows the speaker to stay in control of the situation by pointing questions in desirable directions or away from areas you are not willing to address.

For any question, you have five options: (1) answer it (Remember, "I do not know" is an answer), (2) bounce it back to the questioner ("Well, that is interesting. How might you answer that question?"), (3) bounce it to the audience ("I see, does anyone have any helpful thoughts about this?"), (4) defer the question until later ("Now you and I would find this interesting, but it is outside the scope of my message today. I'd love to chat with you individually about this in a moment"), and (5) promise more answers later ("I would really like to look further into that. May I get back to you later?"). Effective speakers know and use all five as strategies to keep their question-and-answer period productive and on track.

While questions may be expected, distractions are not. When random interruptions occur, do not ignore them. Call attention to the distraction. This allows your audience to get it out and then return their attention to you. One speaker was interrupted when a window washer suspended outside the building dropped into view, ropes and all. The speaker paused, looked at the dangling distraction and announced, "Spiderman!" Everyone laughed, and he then returned to his speech. At a banquet, a speaker was interrupted by the crash of shattering dishes from the direction of the kitchen. She quipped, "Sounds like someone lost a contact lens." Whether humorous or not, calling attention to distractions is key to maintaining control.

What five things should you do when fielding questions?

Ethics of Informative Speaking

Think about the advertising you see on TV and the warning labels on certain products you purchase. After listening to a commercial about a new weight-loss tablet, you believe you have found a solution to get rid of those extra 20 pounds you carry with you. Several happy people testify about how wonderful the drug is, and how it worked miracles for them. At the end of the commercial, you hear a speaker say, "This drug is not for children under 16. It may cause diarrhea, restlessness, sleeplessness, nausea, and stomach cramps. It can lead to strokes and heart attacks. Those with high blood pressure, epilepsy, diabetes, or heart disease should not take this medicine ..." After listening to the warnings, the drug may not sound so miraculous. We have government regulations to make sure consumers make informed choices.

As an individual speaker, *you regulate yourself*. A speaker has ethical responsibilities, no matter what type of speech he or she prepares and delivers. The informative speeches you deliver in class and those you listen to on campus are not nearly as likely to affect the course of history as those delivered by high-ranking public officials in a time of war or national political campaigns. Even so, *the principles of ethical responsibility are similar for every speaker.*

Glossary

Calculated ambiguity
A speaker's planned effort
to be vague, sketchy, and
considerably abstract.

The president of the United States, the president of your school, and the president of any organization to which you belong all have an obligation to inform their constituencies (audiences) in nonmanipulative ways and to provide them with information they need and have a right to know. Professors, doctors, police officers, and others engaged in informative speaking ought to tell the truth as they know it, and not withhold information to serve personal gain. You, like others, should always rely on credible sources and avoid what political scientists label as "calculated ambiguity." **Calculated ambiguity** is a speaker's planned effort to be vague, sketchy, and considerably abstract.

You have many choices to make as you prepare for an informative speech. Applying reasonable ethical standards will help with your decision-making. An informative speech requires you to assemble accurate, sound, and pertinent information that will enable you to tell your audience what you believe to be the truth. Relying on outdated information, not giving the audience enough information about your sources, omitting relevant information, being vague intentionally, and taking information out of context are all violations of ethical principles.

Summary

A blurry line exists between informative, persuasive, and special-occasion speaking. Remember that in an informative speech your goal is to communicate information and ideas in a way that your audience will understand and remember. In a persuasive speech, your intent is to influence your audience in some way—to change attitudes or beliefs or to bring about a specific, desired action. In a special occasion speech, your goal is to entertain or commemorate. The key determinant in whether a speech is informative, persuasive, or entertaining is speaker intent.

Informative speeches fall into three categories. Speeches of description paint a picture of an event, person, object, place, situation, or concept; speeches of explanation deal with such abstractions as ideas, theories, principles, and beliefs; and speeches of demonstration focus on a process, describing the gradual changes that lead to a particular result.

Informative speakers should strive to be accurate, objective, clear, meaningful, and memorable. Preparing and delivering an effective informative speech involves applying the strategies identified in this chapter. To increase accuracy, make sure you question the source of information, consider the timeliness, and accurately cite your sources orally. Being objective includes taking into account all perspectives and showing trends. Crucial to any speech is clarity. To aid your audience, carefully organize your message, define unfamiliar words and concepts, signpost main ideas, relate the new with the familiar, and use repetition.

Audiences gather for different reasons. You want your speech to be meaningful to all listeners. In doing so, consider the setting, your audience's needs, goals and knowledge level, and avoid information overload. An informative speaker wants people to remember his or her speech. To meet that goal, capture attention and interest immediately, sustain audience attention and interest by being creative, vivid, and enthusiastic, use examples and humor, offer interesting visuals, and physically involve your audience.

As you prepare your informative speech, make sure the choices you make are based on a reasonable ethical standard. You have an obligation to be truthful as you prepare your speech and when you deliver it.

Discussion Starters

1. How does speaker intent differentiate informative, persuasive, and special-occasion speaking?
2. How do the three types of informative speeches differ?
3. What are the characteristics of an effective informative speech?
4. How can effective visuals enhance an informative speech?
5. What role does ethics play in informative speaking?

References

Cyphert, D. (2007). Presentation Technology in the Age of Electronic Eloquence: From Visual Aid to Visual Rhetoric. *Communication Education, 56*(2), 168–192.

Gregory, R. J. (2004). *Psychological Testing: History, Principles, and Application.* Needham, MA: Allyn & Bacon.

National Spiritualist Association of Churches. (2011). *Spiritualism. Definitions.* Retrieved June 16, 2011 from www.nsac.org/Definitions. aspx?id=3.0.

Official Slam Poetry History and Beliefs. Retrieved June 16, 2011 from slampapi.com.

Reaves, J. (2003). Interview: Sarah Weddington. *Time* (January 16). Retrieved September 1, 2011 from www.time.com/time/nation/article/0,8599,409103,00.html.

Rockoff, H. (1995). The 'Wizard of Oz' as a Monetary Allegory. In R. Whaples & D. C. Betts (Eds.), *Historical Perspective on the American Economy.* New York: Cambridge University Press.

Spiritualism. Retrieved June 16, 2011 from Kheper.net.

U.S. Department of Housing and Urban Development. *Buying a Home.* Retrieved June 17, 2011 from portal.hud.org.

Chapter

10

> *"I join you, the people of this rainbow nation, to celebrate a life of one of Africa's unique leaders who gallantly fought for freedom and peace for this great country and the world."*
>
> President Joyce Banda

Chapter 10: Special Occasion Speaking

Beginning with general guidelines for special occasion speeches, this chapter discusses how to present effectively in the most common situations wherein a brief speech is appropriate. The chapter also addresses topics such as speeches of introduction, speeches of presentation, speeches of acceptance, commemorative speeches, the keynote speech, and after-dinner speeches.

Student Learning Objectives:

- ○ Students will be able to identify and explain the seven general guidelines for special-occasion speeches
- ○ Students will be able to list and describe specific guidelines for speeches of introduction, presentation and acceptance
- ○ Students will be able to select, develop and deliver commemorative speeches
- ○ Students will be able to select, develop and deliver keynote speeches
- ○ Students will be able to specify guidelines for speeches of presentation
- ○ Students will be able to specify guidelines for speeches of acceptance

SPECIAL-OCCASION SPEAKING

Special-Occasion Speeches

As with other forms of public speaking, a speech delivered on a special occasion can rise to the level of the extraordinary. Certainly as a college student, few ceremonies are likely to be more important than your commencement ceremony. In the following excerpt from his 2010 commencement address at Syracuse University, CEO of JPMorgan Chase Jamie Dimon acknowledged the mixed feelings individuals have about Wall Street executives by setting up the speech in the following manner:

© Haraz N. Ghanbari/AP/Corbis

> Graduating today means you are through with final exams, through with submitting term papers, all that nervousness, the cold sweat of sleepless nights preparing to answer seemingly impossible questions. Well, that's a feeling we banking executives know pretty well these days—we call it "testifying before Congress."

> I am honored to be here today, but I also know that some of your fellow students have raised questions about me being your commencement speaker... Today I will talk about what it takes to be accountable, in the hope that it might be valuable to you in years to come.

Like all good ceremonial speeches, Dimon expressed sincere feelings about the event and his audience. As his method for setting the tone, he chose humor—but only briefly. He quickly moved on to address the banking controversy head-on, and his interest in accountability is relevant to an audience of college graduates.

To parents and students alike, commencement is, indeed, a special occasion. Other special occasions, to name a few, include marriages, anniversaries, deaths, retirements, award ceremonies, special events, and important dates in history. Some speeches may include a little humor or even a great deal of humor; others do not. An overriding principle to remember is that, no matter how short or long, a special-occasion speech has a specific purpose; it should be designed to achieve some objective.

Seven General Guidelines for Special-Occasion Speeches

Most likely, you will be called on to give a special-occasion speech at least once in your lifetime. Many occur within the high school environment. Perhaps you were chosen to speak at your high school graduation ceremony. Maybe you were asked to respond briefly after receiving an award such as "Athlete of the Year." Or maybe, as president of a high school organization, you introduced a featured speaker or an award winner.

Special-occasion speeches, while aptly named, are given every day. To prepare you to provide an impromptu toast or say a few words of praise or thanks, this chapter provides some general suggestions for the special-occasion presentation, and then offers guidelines for several of the most common speaking situations.

Whether you are introducing a guest speaker at your church, presenting an award honoring the volunteer of the year, or toasting the marriage of your sister, the following seven guidelines will help you decide what to say and how best to say it. Although differences exist among the types of special-occasion speeches, as addressed later in this chapter, these guidelines apply in most cases.

1. Make Sure Your Speech Meets Expectations

Ceremonies and the speeches that mark them are surrounded by sets of expectations. Mourners listening to a eulogy, graduates listening to a commencement address, and members of a wedding party toasting the new couple expect certain words, gestures, and acts. Do not disappoint them. The words you choose to mark the occasion should remind people of the event they are commemorating. Even if you are sure everyone realizes the reason for your speech, explain it anyway. Following are a few brief examples of special-occasion speeches and some corresponding expectations:

- **Presenting an award.** Audiences expect the speaker to mention the background and purpose of the award and reasons the recipient was chosen.

- **A speech of acceptance.** Audiences expect the speaker to acknowledge the people who deliberated on the award, and to say thank you to individuals who bestowed the award and people who helped the recipient reach this level.

- **An Eulogy.** Audiences expect to hear some background information on the deceased, a few stories about the person's life, and acknowledgment of the mourners' grief.

- **Toast.** Audiences expect the speech to be brief, to identify the purpose of the toast, and to provide some memorable comment that reflects well on the occasion or individuals involved.

2. Tailor Your Remarks to the Audience/Occasion

Saying what people expect is not the same as delivering a generic speech that could be given before any audience on a similar occasion. It is not enough to change a few facts here and there and give the same speech of introduction no matter who the audience is. For example, introducing a candidate at a fundraiser comprised of close friends and colleagues is different than introducing that same candidate before a group of citizens gathered for a candidates' forum. In the first situation, the audience knows the candidate and supports his or her positions on issues. In the second situation, the audience may not know the candidate, and may be unclear as to his or her stance on various positions.

3. Use Personal Anecdotes and Appropriate Humor

The more you say about the people gathered and the occasion, the more intimate and fitting your speech becomes. Personal anecdotes—especially sentimental or humorous ones—create the feeling that the speech was written for that event and no other.

Actress Lisa Kudrow gave the 2010 commencement address at Vassar College, her alma mater. She begins the speech by saying:

> Thank you, President Hill, for inviting me to speak, and thank you to the Class of 2010 for not protesting ... seriously. I was wondering what I should say to you—there are so many possibilities, you know? So I asked some of you—and by "some" I mean two—who I happened to see in passing (It was convenient for me). Well I couldn't ask every one of you. It's not like there's some kind of social network wherein I could communicate with such a large number of people at once ...

After including some humor in her introductory remarks, Kudrow connects with the audience further by describing her graduation from Vassar in 1985. She provides a personal anecdote, with humor, that describes the quick transformation from biology major to actress.

Not every occasion is one in which humor is anticipated or expected, but as Lisa Kudrow illustrates, it can draw the audience in, and personal anecdotes keep listeners interested.

4. Avoid Clichés

Although speeches for special occasions should follow a predictable form, they should not be trite. To avoid delivering yet another tired introductory, presentation, acceptance, or commemorative speech, dodge the clichés that seem to be part of every speaker's vocabulary. The fact that clichés are overused makes them fairly meaningless, and certainly shows a lack of creativity. These include:

"And now ladies and gentlemen …"

Use this line only if you are introducing Conan O'Brien or David Letterman. Simply avoid saying "ladies and gentlemen." Try saying something like, "And now I am honored to introduce …," or make reference to the occasion. Other meaningless, annoying, and overworked phrases to avoid include:

"Without further ado …"

How many times have you heard this expression in ordinary conversation? We do not use the word "ado," so try "Finally" or "And now."

"I don't know what to say."

An alternative might be to express a statement of feeling, such as "I'm stunned!" or "How *wonderful* this is."

"My friends, we are truly honored tonight."

Is the audience filled with personal friends? Instead, it makes more sense to say, "I'm very honored tonight …"

"Ladies and gentlemen, here is a speaker who needs no introduction."

Then why bother speaking? Just eliminate the phrase. Everyone needs an introduction. Find something else to say about the speaker, occasion, or award. Try "Our speaker is well known for …"

(See **BTW: More About Clichés**.)

More About Clichés

Michael Kaye, travel writer and founder of Costa Rica Expeditions, implores, "Avoid clichés like the plague." What makes the use of clichés so irresistible is that everybody uses them. Most of us have a natural desire to fit in, so we cannot resist using them as well. One reason why clichés are as common as dirt is that even though we know we should not use them, we often do not recognize them.

One way to recognize a cliché is that if you find you can't resist writing it, it is probably a cliché. The reason you have to resist no matter how hard it is, is that clichés are "weak, tiresome, stale," etc. Weak, tiresome, stale writing loses readers—and sales.

For example, rather than "as common as dirt," in the paragraph above, just write "common." Or better yet, consider something fresh that fits, such as, "Common as hype in travel brochures." If you cannot come up with anything else, just remember that, "Avoid clichés," is always more powerful than, "Avoid clichés like the plague."

If you absolutely cannot resist writing "lush" before "forest," "hearty" before "breakfast," or "cascading" before "waterfall," keep practicing until you can resist. If the forest is particularly "lush" or the breakfast particularly "hearty" and you are sure that is important for the reader to know that, take the time and the trouble to write lively, fresh descriptions. For more hints on writing, see the rest of the article at www.huffingtonppost/ richard-bangs/avoidclichesliketheplague. More information on clichés can be found in section 2.5: Word choice at owl.english.purdue.edu.

5. Be Aware That You Are Speaking for Others as Well

Whether you are presenting a gold watch to commemorate a vice-president's 25th year of employment or toasting the conference championship of your college football team, you are speaking as a representative of the group. Although your words are your own, your purpose is to echo the sentiments of those who have asked you to speak. In this capacity, you are the group spokesperson. It is acceptable to make "we" statements when you are referencing events and experiences shared by the audience and honoree. Remember, for the most part, it is not about you.

6. Be Sincere but Humble

You cannot fake sincerity. If you have been asked to give an award or to introduce a person you have never met, do not pretend an intimate relationship. You can make reference to the person's accomplishments that are well known, or you can ask others about the person you will introduce and use that information. Instead of saying "I've seen what Jim can do when he puts his mind to it," tell your listeners "I've spoken to the people who know Jim best—his supervisors and coworkers. They told me how, single-handedly, he helped two dozen of his coworkers escape a fire-filled office and how he refused medical attention until he was certain everyone was safe. I'm proud to honor Jim as our Employee of the Year." Generally speaking, using real information from people the speaker knows creates greater impact.

Being humble is also important. Even when you are accepting an award or being honored as Person of the Year, resist the temptation to tell everyone how great you are. It is in poor taste. Be appropriately humble, remembering that your audience is aware of your accomplishments. When Philip Seymour Hoffman won Best Actor in a Leading Role for his portrayal of Truman Capote in *Capote* at the March 2005 Academy Awards, he started his acceptance speech with these words:

> Wow, I'm in a category with some great, great, great actors. Fantastic actors, and I'm overwhelmed. I'm really overwhelmed. I'd like to thank Bill Vince and Caroline Baron. And Danny Rosett. The film wouldn't have happened without them. I'd like to thank Sarah Fargo, I'd like to thank Sara Murphy. I'd like to thank Emily Ziff, my friends, my friends, my friends. I'd like to thank Bennett Miller and Danny Futterman, who I love, I love, I love, I love. You know, the Van Morrison song, I love, I love, I love, and he keeps repeating it like that. And I'd like to thank Tom Bernard and Michael Barker. Thank you so much. And my mom's name is Marilyn O'Connor, and she's here tonight. And I'd like if you see her tonight to congratulate her, because she brought up four kids alone, and she deserves a congratulations for that.

It was not necessary to attend the ceremony to experience Seymour Hoffman's enthusiasm and gratitude. It may not be the most eloquent acceptance speech, but he avoids bragging, and even requests that his mother be congratulated.

7. Be Accurate

Avoid embarrassing yourself with factual mistakes. If you are introducing a guest speaker, find out everything you need to know before the presentation by talking with the person or reading his or her résumé. If you are giving a commencement address, learn the names of the people who must be acknowledged at the start of your talk as well as the correct pronunciation of the names. If you are toasting an employee for years of dedicated service, make sure you get the number of years right! You do not want to give people higher or lower rank (captain/lieutenant, CEO/CFO), or state incorrect marital status (Ms./Mrs./Miss), or give incorrect information about children, current and past employment, or education.

The guidelines we provided above fit almost any special-occasion speech. As we have mentioned throughout the book, the speech should be audience centered. While all special-occasion speeches should follow general guidelines, we now turn to some of the specific types of special-occasion speeches to see how these general guidelines apply and how other, more specific rules define these speech forms. Several types of special-occasion speeches are not covered here. At the end of the chapter we identify other special-occasion speeches and provide brief outlines to help you plan for most occasions you may encounter.

Speeches of Introduction

The purpose of a speech of introduction is to introduce the person who will give an important address. Keynote speakers are introduced, as are commencement speakers and speakers delivering inaugural remarks. When you deliver this type of speech, think of yourself as the conduit through which the audience learns something about the speaker. This speech is important because it has the potential to enhance the introduced speaker's credibility.

A **speech of introduction** can be viewed as a creative minispeech. Even the speech of introduction has an introduction, body, and conclusion. It is your job to heighten anticipation and prepare your audience for a positive experience. You can accomplish these goals by describing the speaker's accomplishments appropriately. Tell your listeners about the speaker's background and why he or she was invited to address the gathering. This can be accomplished briefly but effectively, as is demonstrated in the following speech of introduction found at Buzzle.com:

> Eight years in office, businessman, environmental activist, Nobel Prize winner, recipient of a Grammy and an Emmy, and runner up for *Time*'s Person of the Year; a pretty mean task for one person to achieve. But our chief guest for today is

no ordinary person. A politician and a keen environmentalist, what most people do not know about him is that he has politics in his genes; his father was also the senator of Tennessee for 18 years. He studied at Harvard, graduating in 1969. He volunteered to go to Vietnam as reporter for the Army, after deciding not to find a way to dodge the draft, and forcing someone with lesser privileges to go to war.

After the war, he attended Vanderbilt University but won a seat in Congress before he got a degree. This started his political life, which we are all familiar with. Without delay, here he is, former vice president of the United States, Mr. Al Gore.

Specific Guidelines for Speeches of Introduction

The following four guidelines will help you prepare appropriate introductory remarks:

Set the Tone and Be Brief but Personal

The tone for the speech of introduction should match the tone of the speech to follow. If a comedian is going to do his/her act following the speech of introduction, then a humorous tone is warranted. If the main speaker will discuss something serious, then the speech of introduction should set that tone.

If you are going to err in an introductory speech, err on the side of brevity and personalization. In other words, an introductory speech should be relatively short, set the appropriate tone, and be specifically designed for the individual being introduced.

Recently, we heard a speech introducing a member of congress at a U.S. Naval retirement ceremony. The speaker went into great detail introducing the man, detailing his education, military service, activities in community service organizations, campaigns for Congress, and so on. This introductory speech was too long, it was not personal, and the speaker failed to set the appropriate tone for the featured speaker. As a result of this information overload, members of the audience shifted restlessly, coughed, yawned, and may have even dozed off. The main speaker began his speech at a big disadvantage.

As part of your preparation, it is helpful to talk with the featured speaker. Doing so may give you important information for the speech as well as some indication of the person's expectations for the introduction. Oftentimes, professional or experienced speakers will have prepared a short introduction for you to weave into your remarks.

Create Realistic Expectations

By telling the audience, "This is the funniest speech you'll ever hear" or "This woman is known as a brilliant communicator," you are making it difficult for the speaker to succeed. Few speakers can match these expectations. Instead, the audience may "appreciate the wisdom" of someone's remarks, or "be inspired" or "be entertained fully" by the speaker. Identify what you hope the audience will experience without creating a bar too high for anyone to clear.

When you read the "A" and then the "B" statements that follow; reflect on how the audience might feel if the speaker did not achieve what is indicated in the "A" statement.

At a gathering of salespeople who are about to listen to a motivational speaker:

> A: "Starting tonight, he will change how you think forever."

> B: "He will challenge you to think in ways you haven't considered before."

In an auditorium where individuals are gathered who are experiencing significant credit card and loan debt:

> A: "Her understanding of personal finance is truly amazing. She will solve all your financial problems."

> B: "Her background and experience give her insight into many aspects of personal finance. She will give you the tools to begin your climb to financial success."

Avoid Summarizing the Speaker's Intended Remarks

Your job is to provide an enticement to listen, not a summary of the remarks to follow. You might tell an audience of college students that you brought a well-known financial advisor to your college to help you make wise financial decisions. Avoid saying, "This speaker will tell you to reduce your spending, save a little money each month, distinguish between wants and needs, and pay your credit card balance on time." This is clearly interfering with the speaker's plan. Teasing a message means providing your audience with a hint of what is to come by mentioning something specific they will want to learn from the speaker. If you have any questions about how much to include in the introduction, share your proposed comments with the main speaker before your presentation.

Recognize the Potential for Spontaneity

Spontaneous introductions are sometimes appropriate. An unexpected guest whom you want to acknowledge may be in the audience. Something may have happened to the speaker, to the audience, or in the world just before the introductory speech, making the planned introduction less effective. For example, when actor Dustin Hoffman was taking his curtain calls after completing a performance of a Shakespeare play on Broadway, he noticed that

Arthur Miller, well-known playwright, was seated in the audience. Hoffman raised his hands, asked for quiet, and said:

> When we were doing the play in London, we had the pleasure of playing one night to an audience that included Dame Peggy Ashcroft, who was introduced from the stage. We do not have knights in America, but there is someone special in the audience tonight. He is one of the greatest voices and influences in the American theater—Mr. Arthur Miller (Heller Anderson, 1990).

Hoffman's impromptu introduction demonstrated that brevity and grace are the hallmarks of an effective introduction.

Speeches of Presentation

The presentation speech is delivered as part of a ceremony to recognize an individual or group chosen for special honors. Our personal and professional lives are marked, in part, by attendance and participation in award ceremonies to recognize personal achievement. Some occasions for presentation speeches include commencements (high school, college, and graduate school), where special presentations are made to students with exceptional academic and community service records, and corporate awards ceremonies, where employees are honored for their years of service or exemplary performance. Televised ceremonies involve award presentations such as the Academy Awards, the Emmy Awards, and Country Music Awards. Other ceremonies recognize achievement in a sport, such as the Heisman Memorial Trophy, presented each year to the nation's most outstanding college football player. Each of these ceremonies includes one or more presentation speeches.

The presentation speech recognizes an individual or group chosen for special honors.

Specific Guidelines for Speeches of Presentation

Every **speech of presentation** should accomplish several goals. Using an example of a speech marking the presentation of the "Reporter of the Year" award for a student newspaper we will illustrate our four guidelines for speeches of presentation.

State the Importance of the Award

Many departmental scholarships and awards are available in college to qualified students. A scholarship may be significant because the selection criteria include finding the individual with the most outstanding academic achievement. Other scholarships may have been established to help single mothers, residents of the town, or students who engage in significant community service. Some awards are established in the names of people living and deceased or companies and organizations.

Glossary

Speech of presentation
Delivered as part of a ceremony to recognize an individual or group chosen for special honors.

The award may be worth $100 or it may be $5,000. Regardless of the monetary value, the audience wishes to understand why the award is important. You may need to describe the achievements of the individual or individuals for whom the award has been established.

Here is the beginning of a speech of presentation, as Tom speaks about his fellow reporter, Kathryn Remm.

> I am pleased to have been asked by our editorial staff to present the Reporter of the Year award—the college's highest journalistic honor. This award was established six years ago by a group of alumni who place great value on maintaining our newspaper's high standard of journalism.

In this example, Tom clearly states the importance of the award when he mentions that it is the college's highest journalistic honor. Further, he clarifies how the award came to be by mentioning who began the award and why.

Explain the Selection Process

The selection process may involve peers, students, teachers, or a standard committee. The audience needs to know that the award was not given arbitrarily or based on random criteria. Explaining the criteria and selection process helps establish the significance of the award. If the award is competitive, you might mention the nature of the competition, but do not overemphasize the struggle for victory at the expense of the other candidates.

The following passage illustrates how this guideline can be followed effectively. Tom continues:

> The award selection process is long and arduous. It starts when the paper's editorial staff calls for nominations and then reviews and evaluates dozens of writing samples. The staff sends its recommendations to a selection committee made up of two alumni sponsors and two local journalists. It is this group of four who determines the winner.

Note the Honoree's Qualifications

Many organizations honor their members and employees for specific accomplishments. For example, the Midas Auto Service "South Central Regional Dealer of the Year" award honors an employee for excellence in regional retail sales, overall retail image, and customer satisfaction. The Edward Jones Investing firm chooses employees for the "Partner's Award" based on sales and service efforts over the past year. The nature of the award suggests what to say about the honoree. The following example shows why the reporter is being recognized.

This year's honoree is Kathryn Remm, the community affairs reporter for the paper. Almost single-handedly, Kathryn reached out to noncollege community residents and established channels of communication that have never been open. In a series of articles, she told students about the need for literacy volunteers at the community library and for Big Brothers/Big Sisters at our local youth club.

Be Brief

Like speeches of introduction, the key to a successful presentation speech is brevity. Choose your words with care so that the power of your message is not diminished by unnecessary detail. Within this limited context, try to humanize the award recipient through a personal—perhaps humorous—anecdote.

As a final note about speeches of presentation, occasionally it is appropriate to ask past recipients of the award to stand up and receive applause. This decision should be based, in part, on your conviction that this acknowledgment will magnify the value of the award to the current recipient as well as to the audience.

Here is how Tom finishes his speech:

> Kathryn was a bit surprised when she learned that student volunteerism for Big Brothers/Big Sisters rose 150 percent after her outreach and articles. This makes her the biggest sister in our community. Please help me acknowledge Kathryn Remm as our reporter of the year.

Speeches of Acceptance

Glossary

Acceptance speech A speech given to express gratitude for an award.

The main purpose of an acceptance speech is to express gratitude for an award. It is personal, gracious, and sincere. Most speakers begin with something like "I am genuinely grateful for this award, and I want to express my sincere thanks to everyone here."

Most acceptance speeches are brief. In many instances, such as an awards night in high school and departmental recognition in college, several individuals are honored for their achievements. If acceptance speeches are long, the event will seem interminable. However, in some cases, such as the Nobel Peace Prize ceremony, recipients are asked to do more than express gratitude. These speeches fit within the category of "keynote speeches," which are discussed later in this chapter. Following are four guidelines for the successful speech of acceptance.

Specific Guidelines for Speeches of Acceptance

© Lucy Nicholson/Reuters/Corbis

Restate Importance of the Award

Restating the importance of the award shows the audience as well as those involved in the award that the recipient values and acknowledges the importance of the award. For example, scholarships are generally established by an individual, an organization, or a group of individuals who have contributed financially. Representatives of the scholarship, along with the scholarship committee, appreciate hearing that the scholarship is viewed as important. Along with this, communicate to your audience what receiving the award means to you.

Be Sincere

An acceptance speech is built around the theme of "thank you." You thank the person, group, or organization bestowing the award. You recognize the people who helped you gain it. Your acceptance should be sincere and heart-felt. The audience wants to feel that the individuals bestowing the award have made the right choice.

So if you know you will be asked to give a brief acceptance speech, think about who deserves recognition. It is not necessary to give a long list of all the individuals who have influenced you in your lifetime, but you want to acknowledge those who have had an impact on you in some way that relates to your accomplishing this goal. A well-developed and appropriately-delivered acceptance speech allows the listeners to be part of the moment and share the recipient's joy or amazement.

Describe How You Reached This Point of Achievement

As you thank people, you can mention in a humble tone how you reached this point of recognition. If you are a gymnast, you can talk about your train-ing and gymnastic meets. If you are a pianist, you can talk about practice and recitals. The audience wants to know that you worked for this award, that you deserve it, but that you are gracious and humble, too.

Use Anecdotes

As you express gratitude and explain how you have reached this point of achievement, select with care the events you want to mention in order to avoid an endless chronology of your life. Stories about your life, or personal anecdotes, give people a lasting impression of your achievements. Instead of simply telling your listeners "I am grateful to everyone who supported me in this project," provide your audience with a personal anecdote. For example, when Joanne received an award for being the Most Valuable Player on her soccer team, she provided this story as part of her acceptance speech:

Three events contributed to my success on the soccer field. The first occurred on Christmas four years ago when I found a soccer ball under the tree and a completed registration form to a soccer camp held in my hometown.

The second event was our final game during my senior year in high school when we won the city championship, and I was fortunate enough to score the winning goal. I cannot tell you the great sense of satisfaction and relief I felt when that kick took the ball past the goaltender and into the net.

The third event was the call I received from our coach inviting me to be part of this great college team with its winning tradition and offering me an athletic scholarship. I hope I can live up to your expectations, coach.

Anecdotes engage the audience and help them understand more clearly why this person was a good choice for the award. Be careful not to be arrogant with the anecdotes you select, or you may leave the audience with regrets. If Joanne had, instead, talked about how she "single-handedly" pulled the team up from a losing record," or how her "teammates stood in awe" as she kicked the winning goal, the acceptance speech would be less effective. (For more explanation, see **BTW: Anecdotes.**)

Watch Colin Firth's 2011 Oscar acceptance speech for Best Actor. Do you think his speech is effective? Certainly, the bulk of the speech corresponds to the basic "thank you" theme. Does he meet all four guidelines? If yes, how? If no, does he compensate for any omissions in other ways?

I have a feeling my career has just peaked. My deepest thanks to the Academy. I'm afraid I have to warn you that I'm experiencing stirrings. Somewhere in the upper abdominals which are threatening to form themselves into dance moves (www.nowpublic.com).

Commemorative Speeches

When we commemorate an event, we mark it through observation and ceremony. Public or private, these ceremonies are often punctuated by speeches appropriate for the occasion. Commencement speeches at college graduation, eulogies at the funeral of a loved one, speeches to celebrate the spirit of a special event or a national holiday like the Fourth of July, toasts at a wedding or the birth of a baby or a business deal, inaugural speeches, and farewell addresses all fit into this category.

Although **commemorative speeches** may inform, their specific purpose is not informational. Although they may persuade, their primary purpose is not persuasive. They are inspirational messages designed to stir emotions. These speeches make listeners reflect on the message through the

Glossary

Anecdote A short account of an interesting or humorous incident.

Glossary

Commemorative speech An inspirational message designed to stir emotions.

Anecdotes

An *anecdote* is a short account of an interesting or humorous incident. Anecdotes likely originated in classical Greece, and have been used throughout the centuries. Ralph Waldo Emerson is quoted as saying "Ballads, bons mots, and anecdotes give us better insights into the depths of past centuries than grave and voluminous chronicles." And Friedrich Nietzsche pointed out the importance of anecdotes when he wrote, "Three anecdotes may suffice to paint a picture of a man."

Not until the 20th century did humor become a key anecdotal characteristic. Mark Twain once attended a meeting at which one of the speakers was raising money. Twain, deeming the cause to be a worthy one, decided to donate $100. As the speaker droned on, however, he decided to cut his contribution in half.

With no end in sight, Twain cut his intended offer again, to $10. At last, the speaker finished and the collection basket was passed around. Twain's contribution? When the basket finally reached him, he removed a dollar and passed it along!

To find the source of the BTW and read over 200 anecdotes, check out www.anecdotage.com.

use of rich language that lifts them to a higher emotional plain. More than in any other special-occasion speech, your choice of words in the commemorative address will determine your success.

Many commemorative speeches express the speaker's most profound thoughts. As you talk about what it means to graduate from college, be inaugurated to office, or lose a family member, your goal is to leave a lasting impression on your audience. Although many commemorative speeches are short, they often contain memorable quotations that add strength and validity to the speaker's own emotion-filled message.

Commemorative speeches can vary significantly, but what they have in common is that they are inspirational. The next section covers three common forms of commemorative speeches: toasts, commencement speeches, and eulogies.

Toasts

Some credit the custom of toasting to the Norsemen, Vikings, and Greeks who lifted their glasses in honor of the gods. But the newer "toast" derives from the 17th-century British custom of placing toasted bits of bread in glasses to improve the taste of the drink. As the concept of the **toast** evolved, so did the customs surrounding it. In England, those proposing the toast knelt on "bended" knee. In France, elaborate bows were required. In Scotland, the toast maker stood with one foot on a chair, the other on a table. Today, Western tradition dictates the clinking of glasses while making strong eye contact (Bayless, 1988).

You are more likely to be asked to deliver a toast than any other form of commemorative speech. Toasts are given at engagements, weddings,

Glossary

Toast Brief message of good will and congratulations.

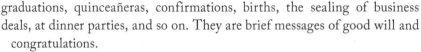

graduations, quinceañeras, confirmations, births, the sealing of business deals, at dinner parties, and so on. They are brief messages of good will and congratulations.

Humor is a part of many occasions where toasts occur. However, it is imperative that boundaries on humor be observed. Tasteful humor is preferable to humor that can end up truly embarrassing or hurting individuals involved in the toast. We turn to the Irish for several examples of brief toasts; some which include humor.

> May those that love us, love us; and those that don't love us, may God turn their hearts; if he can't turn their hearts, then may he turn their ankles, so we'll know them by their limp.

> May the saddest day of your future be no worse than the happiest day of your past.

> May the roof above us never fall in, and may the friends gathered below it never fall out.

> May God be with you and bless you. May you see your children's children. May you be poor in misfortune, rich in blessings. May you know nothing but happiness from this day forward. (www.lollysmith.com)

Following are three guidelines to help you deliver a memorable toast:

1. **Prepare a short, inspirational message and memorize it.** If you are the best man at your brother's wedding, the mother of the new college graduate at his graduation dinner, a close associate of an executive just promoted to company president, you may be asked in advance to prepare a toast to celebrate the occasion. Even though most toasts are generally no more than a few sentences long, do not assume that you will be able to think of something appropriate to say when the glasses are raised. To avoid drawing a blank, write—and memorize—the toast in advance.

2. **Choose words with care that address the audience and occasion.** There is a time to be frivolous and a time to be serious. The audience and the occasion indicate whether it is appropriate to be humorous or serious, inspirational or practical. Here is an example of an appropriate toast to a new law partner:

> Ken has been a portrait of strength for all of us. When four partners were sick with the flu at the same time last year, Ken worked tirelessly, seven days a week, to meet our deadlines. Here's to Ken—the best lawyer in town and the newest partner of our law firm.

❸ **Be positive and avoid clichés.** A toast is upbeat. Look to the future with hope. It is inappropriate to toast a college graduate saying, "If John does as poorly at work as he did at college, we may all be asked to help pay his rent," or at a wedding to say, "After all those other women you brought home, your bride looks pretty good." Such comments will bring a big laugh, but will also wound, and therefore should not be used.

Remember that public speaking is a creative activity. Clichés such as "Down the hatch," "Here's mud in your eye," and "Cheers" waste an ideal creative moment. Instead, you can say something simple like, as is noted in the previous example, "Here's to Ken—the best lawyer in town and the newest partner of our law firm." If the tone is lighter, you might opt for something more creative.

Commencement Speeches

Most of us believe we will not be asked to give a commencement speech. However, colleges and universities have students and guests give commencement speeches every year. Either they are voted on by the student body or they are asked to speak because they were elected to a position, such as student senate president. A speaker may be a distinguished alumnus or may have achieved celebrity status.

No other speech offers greater potential to achieve the aims of a ceremonial speech than the commencement address delivered by an honored guest. Following are several guidelines for developing a commencement speech.

Author John Grisham began his May 9, 2010 commencement speech at the University of North Carolina, Chapel Hill with a brief *expression of honor*, giving thanks for the invitation to speak. Later in his speech, he makes tribute to the college as a place of excellence, saying how proud he is to be a Tar Heel.

Later in his speech, he makes *tribute to the college as a place of excellence*.

Traditional commencement speeches *offer counsel to the graduating members of the audience*.

All commencement speakers *should impart some memorable message*. Grisham moves on to the main point of his speech, which is the importance of finding and using one's "voice."

He concludes on a *congratulatory* note by telling the audience that their future has arrived and they should remember what they want to be right now, wishing them good luck.

Although Grisham's speech lasted only 17 minutes, the strength of its message endures, and it is a model commencement speech. (See **BTW: Best Commencement Speeches** for more speeches.)

BTW!

Best Commencement Speeches

The Huffington Post identified the 10 most-watched commencement speeches in the history of YouTube. The following videos can be viewed on huffingtonpost.com, "The Most Viewed Commencement Speeches in the History of YouTube":

1. Steve Jobs, CEO and cofounder of Apple Computer and of Pixar Animation Studios, spoke at Stanford in June 2005.

2. Professor Randy Pausch made a surprise return to Carnegie Mellon University to deliver an inspirational speech to the Class of 2008.

3. Oprah Winfrey, global media leader and philanthropist, spoke to the Class of 2008 at Stanford.

4. Lisa Kudrow delivered the commencement address to the graduating class of 2010 at Vassar.

5. President Obama spoke at the 2010 University of Michigan commencement ceremony in Ann Arbor.

6. Meryl Streep was the 2010 Barnard commencement speaker at Columbia University.

7. Ellen DeGeneres was the keynote speaker at Tulane University's commencement in 2009.

8. Bill Cosby delivered the keynote address at Carnegie Mellon University's 2007 commencement ceremony.

9. Dolly Parton delivered the commencement address for the University of Tennessee College of Arts and Sciences class of 2009.

10. Anthony Corvino, a bachelor's degree candidate in political science chosen to deliver the undergraduate student commencement remarks, gave a humorous speech entitled "Average Is the New Exceptional."

Eulogies

Glossary

Eulogy A commemorative speech that involves paying tribute to a family member, friend, colleague, or community member who died.

Eulogies are perhaps the most difficult commemorative speeches to make, since they involve paying tribute to a family member, friend, colleague, or community member who died. It is a difficult time for the speaker as well as the audience. A eulogy focuses on *universal themes* such as the preciousness and fragility of life, the importance of family and friends at times of great loss, and the continuity of life, while avoiding impersonal clichés. Here are five guidelines to help you develop and present a eulogy:

Acknowledge the loss and refer to the occasion. Your first words should focus on the family and/or significant others of the deceased. Talk directly to them, taking care to acknowledge by name the spouse, children, parents, and special friends of the deceased. It is safe to assume that all members of the audience feel loss. People come together to mourn because they want to be part of a community; they want to share their grief with others. By using "we" statements of some kind, you acknowledge the community of mourners. For example, you might say, "We all know how much Andrew loved his family" or "I am sure we all agree that Andrew's determination and spirit left their mark."

Celebrate life rather than focusing on loss. Some deaths are anticipated, such as dying from ailments related to old age or after a lengthy illness. Others are shocking and tragic, and those left behind may have unresolved issues. Although it is appropriate to acknowledge shared feelings of sadness and even anger, the eulogy should focus on the unique gifts and lasting legacy the person brought to their world.

Use quotes, anecdotes, and even humor. Nothing is better than a good story to celebrate the spirit of the deceased. A well-chosen anecdote can comfort as it helps people focus on the memory of the person's life. Fitting anecdotes need not be humorless. Rather than using ambiguous phrases such as he was "a loving husband," "a loving father," or "a wonderful person," it would mean more to provide a brief story or a humorous account of some incident in the person's life. Saying something like "Getting an ice cream cone was a reward from Dad, even in my 30s" or "He was a great teacher who liked to experiment with new ideas, such as teaching class outdoors, until the day a bird pooped on his head." Stories and humor help mourners get through the experience of attending the memorial as they recall pleasant memories and laugh along with the speakers.

Quote others. You may choose to turn to the remarks of noted public figures such as Winston Churchill, John F. Kennedy, and Mark Twain, whose words are fitting for your speech. Know that you do not need to always rely on quotations from writers, poets, famous actors, or politicians. You may choose to include the words of friends and family members of the deceased. As part of her eulogy at her mother's funeral, a daughter said the following:

> After reading the cards sent by her many friends, it made sense to include some of what others thought of her. I'd like to share a few of these: "She was so full of enthusiasm and curiosity about everything. Whatever project she took on, she did it with a flair that no one else could match." "A gentle person who really did make a difference in each life she touched." "A warm, vibrant personality and so much courage." "I doubt that anyone has left more happy memories."

The person and occasion of the individual's death should provide guidance in terms of what qualities to highlight and stories to tell. Remember also, a eulogy can include input from others, so do not hesitate to seek advice from others close to the person being eulogized.

Control your emotions. Composure is crucial. If you have any questions about your ability to control your grief, suggest that someone else be chosen. As you offer comfort to others, try not to call undue attention to your own grief. While an expression of loss and its attending emotions is appropriate, uncontrolled crying will prevent you from providing the needed healing your eulogy offers. If you do not think you can make it through without falling apart, have someone else do it or bring someone up to the podium with you who can take over, if necessary.

Be sincere and be brief. Speak from the heart. Avoid "Words cannot express our sorrow," "The family's loss is too much to bear," and "She's in a far better place now." Rely instead on personal memories, anecdotes, and feelings. Eulogies need not be lengthy to be effective. The following is an excerpt from a eulogy a woman gave for her father that indicates how she felt about him.

> Throughout the years, he has been there for my failures and successes, providing me with meaningful advice. His opinion has always been very important to me. My father was a warm and loving man, a man of integrity, a great teacher. I miss him and I love him.

Depending on the wishes of the family, several individuals may be called on to eulogize the deceased. A brief, sincere speech will be greatly appreciated by those attending the memorial service.

Keynote Speeches

Glossary

Keynote speaker Featured speaker at an event.

A keynote speaker is the featured speaker at an event. There may be several people who speak briefly, but the keynote speaker has the top billing of the event. Whatever the setting, whether it is a gathering of members of the American Society of Journalists and Authors or the annual convention of the American Bar Association, the keynote address is usually anticipated as a highlight that has the potential to compel the audience to thought and action. Unlike many special-occasion speeches, the keynote speech is not brief. You may be called on to give a keynote speech at some point. We offer the following guidelines.

Remember That Your Speech Sets the Tone for the Event

Think of keynote speakers as cheerleaders and their speeches as the cheers that set the tone for an event. The purpose of the gathering may be to celebrate the group's achievements, to share information with each other, or to give individuals the opportunity to interact with people who are in similar positions or situations. The keynote speaker is there to excite people, and to stimulate thought and action.

Keynote addresses at political conventions are known for their hard-hitting approach and language. When he was a candidate for the U.S. Senate in Illinois, Barack Obama delivered the keynote address at the Democratic National Convention in Boston in July 2004. Following is an excerpt from that speech:

> Tonight, we gather to affirm the greatness of our nation not because of the height of our skyscrapers, or the power of our military, or the size of our economy; our pride is based on a very simple premise, summed up in a declaration made over two hundred years ago: "We hold these truths to be self-evident, that all men are created equal ... that they are endowed by their Creator with certain inalienable rights, that among these are life, liberty, and the pursuit of happiness."

Obama's speech makes patriotic references that stirred many Americans' sense of pride in their country. But he also suggested that things could be better. His words clearly set the tone for Democrats at that convention.

Select Your Topic and Language *After* Analyzing the Audience and Occasion

There is a reason you were asked to be the keynote speaker. It may be fame, fortune, or simply achievement based on hard work. You may be provided with some basic guidelines for your speech, such as "motivate them," or "talk about success." How you develop the content of your speech and the words you choose to express yourself should be made after reflecting on the audience and occasion. As one of the keynote speakers at the Microsoft India, NGO (nongovernmental organization) Connection workshop in April 2010 in Jaipur, India, Rajendra Joshi, one of the organization's trustees, started her speech by making a specific connection between technology and governance.

> The most powerful weapon on the earth is public opinion [Paul Crouser]. *Governance* encompasses not just government, but also the civil society and the corporate sector.

Joshi asserts the importance of public opinion at the very beginning. Since her speech was presented to individuals connected with Microsoft and/or nongovernmental organizations, she tied technology together with governance to highlight an important aspect of nongovernmental organizations trying to improve the world.

Time Is Still a Factor

Yes, people are gathered to hear you. You are the focus of attention. Say what you need to say, but do not waste their time. Think about what has happened in the time before your speech, and what will happen after your speech. Even if you have what seems to be an unlimited amount of time, realize that your audience may have other things to do.

Consider the audience's attention span. Have they been in the same room for the last four hours? An audience can be enthralled for some period of time, but there is a limit as to how long they can pay attention. One of your authors attended a ceremony celebrating the university's 100-year anniversary, and slipped out of the room after 45 minutes of listening to the keynote speaker. (The speech lasted another 20 minutes!) Time is a factor. You do not want to have your audience dreaming of an escape plan.

After-Dinner Speeches

If the keynote address is the meat-and-potatoes speech of a conference, the after-dinner speech is the dessert. It is a speech delivered, literally, after the meal is over and after all other substantive business is complete. Its purpose is to entertain, often with humor, although it may also convey a thoughtful message. Keep in mind, a more accurate description of this speech would be "after-meal" as an after-dinner speech can occur after any meal. Following are two suggestions for after-dinner speaking.

Focus on the Specific Purpose: To Entertain

Do not make the mistake of delivering a ponderous speech filled with statistics and complex data. Talking about the national debt would probably be inappropriate, as would a speech on what to do with the tons of garbage Americans produce each day. You can discuss these topics in a humorous way, however, relating, for example, how handling the national debt has become a growth industry for economists or how families are trying to cope with community rules to separate garbage into various recycling categories.

Use the Opportunity to Inspire

As is noted in the definition of the after-dinner speech, you do not have to rely solely on humor. You can also be inspirational, filling your speech with stories from personal experiences that have changed your life. This approach is especially effective if you are well known or if the events you relate have meaning to others.

Outlines for Other Special-Occasion Speeches

Following are 14 outlines for you to consider. Each commemorates an event you will probably encounter in the future. These outlines spell out both what is expected and the traditional order we expect to hear them in.

Speech of Introduction

1. Greeting and reference to the occasion
2. Statement of the name of the person to be introduced
3. Brief description of the person's speech topic/company position/role in the organization, etc.
4. Details about the person's qualifications
5. Enthusiastic closing statement
6. Inviting a warm reception for the next speaker

Speech of Welcome

1. Expression of honor this person's visit brings to the group
2. Description of the person's background and special achievements
3. Statement of the reason for the visit
4. Greeting and welcome to the person

Speech of Dedication

1. Statement of reason for assembling
2. Brief history of efforts that have led to this event
3. Prediction for the future success of the company, organization, group, or person

Anniversary Speech

1. Statement of reason for assembling
2. Sentimental significance of the event
3. Explanation of how this sentiment can be maintained
4. Appeal for encouraging the sentiment to continue in future years

Speech of Presentation

1. Greeting and reference to the occasion
2. History and importance of the award
3. Brief description of the qualifications for the award
4. Reasons for this person receiving the award
5. Announcement of the recipient's name
6. Presentation of the award

Speech of Acceptance

1. Expression of gratitude for the award
2. Brief praise of the appropriate people
3. Statement of appreciation to those giving the award
4. Closing of pleasure and thanks

Speech of Farewell

1. Expression of sorrow about the person's departure
2. Statement of enjoyment for the association with this person
3. Brief description of how the person will be missed
4. Announcement of friendship and best wishes for the future
5. Invitation to return again soon

Speech of Tribute (if honoree is alive) or the Eulogy (if deceased)

1. Expression of respect and love for the honoree
2. Reasons for paying tribute to this person
3. Review of the person's accomplishments and contributions
4. Clarification of how this person has touched the lives of others
5. Closing appeal to emulate the good qualities of this person

Speech of Installation

1. Orientation of the audience to the occasion and the theme of this installation
2. Introduction of the current officers
3. Praise of the current officers for the work they have accomplished
4. Announcement for the new officers to come forward
5. Explanation of the responsibilities for each office
6. Recitation of the organization's installation of officers pledge
7. Declaration of the installation of the new officers

Speech of Inauguration

1. Expression of appreciation for being elected or placed in office
2. Declaration of the theme or problem focus while in office
3. Explanation of policy intentions
4. Announcement of goals to achieve while in office
5. Closing appeal for confidence in a successful future

Keynote Address

1. Orientation of the audience to the mood and theme of the convention
2. Reference to the goals of the organization and their importance
3. Brief description of the convention's major events
4. Closing invitation for active participation in the convention

Commencement Address

1. Greeting to the graduates and the audience
2. Review of the graduates' successful accomplishments
3. Praise to the graduates for reflecting respected values
4. Prediction and discussion of future challenges
5. Closing inspiration for the graduates to meet these new challenges successfully

After-Dinner Speech

1. Statement of reference to the audience and the occasion
2. Humorous transition into the central idea or thesis
3. Presentation of major points developed with humorous supporting materials
4. Closing that is witty and memorable

Humorous Speech

1. Humorous attention-getter
2. Preview of the comic theme and intent of the speech
3. Presentation of humorous points and supporting materials that are typical of the audience in terms of events, feelings, experiences, or thoughts
4. Closing that presents a strong punch line (Harrell 1997)

Summary

At some point in your life, chances are you will give a special-occasion speech. You may be called on to toast a member of your family, a colleague, or a good friend. Perhaps you will introduce a guest speaker, or your alma mater may invite you to address the graduating class. All special-occasion speeches have certain characteristics in common. When delivering a speech for a special occasion, make sure it meets audience expectations. Tailor your speech to the honoree and the occasion, use personal anecdotes and appropriate humor, and avoid clichés. Be aware that you are speaking for others as well as yourself, be sincere, be humble, and be accurate.

The purpose of a speech of introduction is to introduce the person who will deliver an important address. Your role is to heighten audience anticipation of the speaker through a brief, personal description of why he or she has been chosen to speak. Speeches of presentation are delivered as part of special recognition ceremonies. These speeches tell the audience why the award is being given and state the importance of the award. Marked by grace and sincerity, speeches of acceptance express gratitude for an award. Commemorative speeches include toasts, commencement speeches, and eulogies. Commemorative speeches are inspirational messages designed to stir emotions and cause listeners to reflect. Keynote speeches often set the tone for an event through the use of direct language. After-dinner speeches are speeches of entertainment and inspiration, generally delivered at the conclusion of substantive business. Special occasion audiences have expectations concerning the ideas a speaker should address as well as the order in which they are presented. Guidelines for 14 special-occasions speeches will help you deliver what is expected in the many occasions you may face.

Discussion Starters

1. What is memorable from the speeches you heard when you graduated from high school? If you were giving that speech, what could you have included to personalize it and make it more memorable?

2. When is it appropriate to use humor? Should speakers tell jokes? When/Why/Why not? Can there be too much of a good thing with humor for a speaker? Can humor hurt credibility?

3. Do you know any good toasts? What are the elements of an effective toast? How can you tell the difference between a good one and a bad one?

4. Have you seen someone introduce someone else in a formal speech setting? How did they do? What are the elements of an effective speech of introduction? Did the speech you are recalling satisfy these elements? What should speakers avoid?

⑤ Why are brevity and gratitude key elements of an effective acceptance speech? Is it appropriate for recipients to use the platform of their acceptance speech to further a cause they care about? What causes or issues are out of bounds? If there are some, why are they not appropriate?

References

Averbuch, Yael. *Speech*. Retrieved January 20, 2010 from potomacsoccerwire.com.

Bangs, M. (2010, December 13). *Avoid Clichés Like the Plague*. Retrieved June 19, 2011 from www.huffingtonpost.com

Bayless, J. (1988). *Are You a Master of the Toast? The Toastmaster*, *November*, 11.

Dimon, Jamie. (2010, May 16). *Commencement Remarks*. Retrieved December 11, 2010 from syr.edu.

Firth, Colin. (2011). *Oscar Acceptance Speech*. Retrieved September 6, 2011 from www.nowpublic.com/culture/colin-firth-oscar-acceptance-speech-2011-video-transcript-2761763.html.

Grisham, John. (2010, May 9). *Commencement Speech*. Retrieved from Forbes.com.

Harrell, A. (1997). *Speaking Beyond the Podium: A Public Speaking Handbook*, 2nd Ed. Fort Worth: Harcourt Brace College Publishing.

Heller Anderson, S. (1990). Chronicle: Interview with Professor Melvin Helitzer. *New York Times*, (January 18), B6.

Henmueller, P. (1989, June 11). Diamonds of Hope: The Value of a Person (Speech). Reprinted in *Vital Speeches of the Day, September 1, 1989*, 680–681.

Irish Weddings Toasts, Blessings, Proverbs, Traditions. Retrieved September 6, 2011 from www.lollysmith.com/irwedtoasble.html.

Joshi, R. (2010, April 15–16). *Keynote Speech.* Retrieved from saath. wordpress.com.

Kudrow, Lisa. (2010, May 23). *Commencement Address.* Retrieved from commencement.vassar.edu/2010.

Nair, T. (2011). *Introduction Speech Examples.* Retrieved September 6, 2011 from www.buzzle.com/articles/introduction-speech-examples.html.

Obama, Barack. (2004). *Keynote Speech.* Retrieved September 6, 2011 from americanrhetoric.com/speeches/convention2004/ barackobama2004dnc.htm.

Praetorius, D. (2011, May 23). *The Most Viewed Commencement Speeches in the History of YouTube* (VIDEOS). Retrieved June 19, 2011 from www. huffingtonpost.com.

Swanger, J. (2010, May 8). *The Tyranny of Certainty* (Baccalaureate Address).

Wells, J. (2009). *Word Choice.* Retrieved June 19, 2011 from www.owl. english.purdue/engagement.

Chapter

11

Image © Ron Foster Sharif, 2013. Used under license from Shutterstock, Inc.

"Using informational gathering and employment interviewing skills will ultimately lead to your future success."

Caffie J. Risher

Chapter 11: Successful Interviewing Techniques

This chapter examines the practical application of two kinds of communication situations that are widely used, information gathering and employment interviews, and invites you to be an active participant in the process.

Student Learning Objectives:

○ Students will be able to explain the various types of open and closed ended questions that are used in interviews

○ Students will be able to describe and explain how interviews are structured

○ Students will be able to prepare, plan, participate in a structured interview

○ Students will be able to conduct an information-gathering interview

SUCCESSFUL INTERVIEWING TECHNIQUES

SUCCESSFUL INTERVIEWING TECHNIQUES

Learning Objectives

After reading this chapter, you should understand the following concepts:

1 Interviewing differs from general conversation in that there is an interviewer and an interviewee, specifically asking and answering questions to further specific goals.

2 Open questions are useful for exploring topics in depth, while closed questions limit the answers to allow the interviewer to gather more specific information.

3 Biased questions, double-barreled questions, open-to-closed questions, and unreliable questions are all potential hazards when conducting an interview.

4 To prepare for an interview, you should have a clear goal and an interview plan for achieving that goal.

5 Interviews have an opening, a body, and a closing, which are designed to set the foundation for the interview, accomplish the goals of the interview, and end the interview on a good note.

Introduction

It's about 3 a.m. on a Wednesday morning and you decide that you should probably try to do a little homework before going to bed. It seems especially important to you, because your calendar says that you have a physics exam at 11 a.m. So you open up your physics notebook and you are faced with "fractals." What the heck is a fractal?

Feeling relaxed, you immediately begin to scan the bold print in the chapter you thought you were covering this week. No fractals. There are plenty of bold-print items talking about "photons," "electromagnetic radiation," and something called "Plank's constant." But there is not a fractal to be found!

Not quite in a panic, and instead of looking in the book's table of contents or subject index, you make up your mind that the only reasonable response to this emergency is to "Google it" and see what you can find. You stumble on "Fractal's World," but you are pretty sure that a fractal is not a cartoon character. Upon further examination, you discover plenty of pictures and illustrations of fractals, including a "fractal of the day," but you don't find an explanation of fractals that you can understand.

Now nearing panic, but before dropping physics and giving up your childhood dream of being the first scientist to master cold fusion, you come up with a sound strategy for solving the problem: You sleep on it! At 10:00 a.m. you wake up, put on a hat, and trek off to visit your physics professor. After all, the test is not until 11:00 a.m. There is still plenty of time!

You arrive at your professor's office, knock on the door, and request a few minutes because you have a quick question. You say that you couldn't find the term fractal in your textbook, and you wonder if you could get a brief definition. After the laughter dies down, the professor gives you the fast answer you asked for, and you go on your way, confident in your ability to "ace" the physics test.

When you return home after the test, you get on the phone and complain to your parents that college is hard and that you just pulled an "all-nighter" to prepare for your physics test. While the parents are feeling sorry for you, you ask if they could send a few dollars to cover some expenses. Recognizing that you are working so hard, they agree to send you as much money as you want.

What do fractals, photons, and cold fusion have to do with interviewing? Probably not much. But during that visit to your professor's office, whether you know it or not, *you conducted an information gathering interview!* When you asked your parents for cash, you conducted a persuasive interview. In both cases, you had a specific goal to accomplish. To help achieve those goals, in both cases, you asked questions, and you received answers. A goal orientation and the asking and answering of questions are essential components of an interview.

You probably take part in many interviews every day without really thinking about it. Because interviewing is such a common activity, and because it is central to accomplishing a wide range of goals in our lives, it is important to approach it in a systematic and organized way. Understanding and organizing interviews is the focus of this chapter.

Interviewing is the key to success.

Image © alexskopje, 2013. Used under license from Shutterstock, Inc.

Interviewing

We begin the discussion of **interviewing** with a definition or description of the concept. There will be plenty of information to put on tests, so there is no reason to include a definition just for that purpose. In this case, however, articulating a definition should make the subsequent discussion of the interview much more clear if we all begin at the same place.

The examples in the previous section give a reasonable idea of what an interview looks like. In addition, most of us have participated in interviews in either a casual or formal setting, so you probably have a decent idea of what is and what is not an interview. You probably know already that an interview is a *form of interpersonal communication* or conversation, so let's begin there.

Although it is true that all interviews are conversations, you should recognize that *all conversations are not interviews!* The ways in which conversations and interviews differ will help us get a handle on exactly how we should view an interview.

Two Parties

All interviews have two parties: interviewer and an interviewee. More than two people could be participating in the event, but there will still be those two parties. For example, a group of reporters could be questioning the producers of the latest reality show, *Excessive and Unnecessary Ear Alteration*, about the rumor that the program could be turned into a full-length feature film. The group of curious reporters makes up one of the parties: the interviewer. The group of *EUEA* producers is the second party: the interviewee. Keep your fingers crossed that *this* movie never makes it to the theaters!

When you think of an interview, does a group of pushy reporters automatically come to mind?

Questions and Answers

The primary structure of this kind of conversation centers on asking and answering questions. The kind of questions and sequence of questions that are asked are largely determined by the type of interview and goals for that interview. Types of questions and organization of questions will be discussed shortly.

Goals

Both parties in an interview have deliberate and specific goals they wish to accomplish with this event. Typical interview goals include gathering information, giving information, seeking employment, seeking employees, making a sale or creating an impression, helping self or others, evaluating employee performance, and assessment of self or another. The more precise or detailed you can be in determining your goals for an interview, the more clearly you can plan and organize your role in the process. Interview goals provide the purpose of the interview, determine the kinds of questions that will be asked, and, to some extent, affect the structure of the inter-action.[1] If the goals of the interview are ambiguous or not well thought out, one or both of the parties will leave the interview unsatisfied.[2]

Clear and precise goals are as important for a successful interview as they are in other situations.

Awareness

All the people involved should know that they are participating in an interview. They should understand that this is not a casual conversation and that they are guided by their own goals for the interview.

Exchange of Roles

While roles of the parties remain constant, each participant engages in a brisk exchange of speaking and listening roles. Both parties in an interview ask as well as answer questions. There is no formula for determining who talks more in a particular context, but it depends on the type of interview

© Zero Creatives/Image Source/Corbis

In a screening interview, the employer attempts to determine the applicant's qualifications.

(see following section), the goals of the individual parties for the interview, and the conversational styles of the participants.

A common view of an employment interview, for example, is that the employer (interviewer) asks all or most of the questions and the applicant (interviewee) provides all or most of the answers. This might be true in a **screening interview**, in which the employer is attempting to determine the qualifications of the applicant for the specific job being offered. However, in later interviews, the interviewee could be asking more questions to better understand the nature of the specific position and the nature of the company. The applicant wants to know if he or she would like to work for this particular company. In this situation, the interviewer (employer) will likely do more talking to provide the necessary information to the applicant.

In a **counseling** or **helping interview**, a psychologist (interviewer) might ask some questions of the interviewee to determine the kind of problem he or she is experiencing, but then the counselor might do more of the talking to give advice to the interviewee about how to try to solve the problem. In other kinds of counseling interviews, the psychologist could determine that the best way to provide help is to ask questions for the purpose of gently guiding the interviewee to talk about his or her problems. In this case, the interviewer would ask a few questions while the interviewee does all or most of the talking.

Types of Questions Used in Interviews

As you already know, all interviews are structured around the asking and answering of questions. Although questions and answers might be viewed as a limitation on the interaction in an interview, there is a wide variety of question types that allow considerable flexibility in the kinds of conversations that you can hold. This section will explore a variety of types of questions and their uses.

Primary and Secondary Questions

A **primary question** is used to introduce topics or new areas of discussion. A primary question is easy to identify because it can stand alone, out of any kind of context, and yet it can still make perfect sense. Here are some examples of primary questions:

○ Where did you attend high school?

○ What is your opinion of the "designated hitter" rule in baseball?

○ For what company have you been working the past two years?

A **secondary question** (or probing question) usually does not make much sense if asked outside of a particular context. This question is used to encourage an interviewee to keep talking, to provide additional or more focused information, or to clarify an answer. If an interviewee doesn't answer a question to the satisfaction of the interviewer, the interviewer can follow up the primary question with a secondary question. Secondary questions can be preplanned and written into your interview plan, or they can just spontaneously emerge during the course of the interview. Some examples of secondary questions that might be used to expand or probe responses to primary questions include the following:

- What classes did you think were the most interesting? (preplanned follow-up)

- Why? What was interesting to you about biology? (spontaneous follow-up)

- Do you think every player should play both offense and defense? (preplanned)

- What's so special about pitchers? (spontaneous)

- Which of those jobs did you like best? (preplanned)

- What was so unusual about that job? (spontaneous)

- Is there anything else that you would like to say?

To avoid possibly influencing the interviewee's response, make an effort to keep your probing questions as nondirective or neutral as possible. Try not to say (with a shocked or surprised look on your face), "*Why* would you do *that*?" Instead, Willis suggests "Tell me more about that."[3]

In addition to asking an actual question as a secondary or probing question, the interviewer could also simply pause and wait for further response. The pause, combined with a posture and/or facial expression that indicates listening or curiosity can "nudge" an interviewee to provide additional information. It's probably a good idea to list possible probing questions on your interview guide, especially if you anticipate that a question will require some probing to accomplish the information-gathering goals of the interview.

Finally, be careful not to lead the interviewee with your probing questions or suggest an answer. Be as neutral as possible. See the section about biased questions that follows shortly.

Why are open questions useful for exploring a topic in depth?

Image © 2008, JupiterImages Corporation.

Open and Closed Questions

Open Questions

When using an **open question**, the interviewee has a great deal of freedom in how to respond to the question. An open question can request very general or nonspecific information, and there is usually very little direction provided by the interviewer as to the direction of the desired response. Here are some examples of open questions:

○ Tell me what happened.

○ How do you feel about smart videogames?

○ What do you know about internet telephones?

Open questions can be very useful for exploring a topic in depth because the interviewee can talk about nearly any related topic for as long as he or she wants. Open questions also allow the interviewer to discover facts concerning a topic about which he or she knows very little. So this kind of question is good for exploring and investigation of new areas of interest. They can also be used to learn more about an interviewee's perspectives, priorities, and depth of knowledge of a particular topic.

The use of open questions requires that the interviewer be very skilled. The questions can take time to answer and therefore demand excellent listening skills. In addition, because the interviewer provides little direction for the desired response, the interviewee is free to go off in any direction with the answer. Consider this question asked by the interviewer: "What are your feelings about cable TV?" The purpose of the interview might be to discover the opinions of a community about programming on the local cable TV system. But because the question is so broad, the interviewee might seize that opportunity to complain about how the cable installer scared his dog or dug up his yard when laying the cable. It takes a good deal of interviewer skill to acknowledge that undesirable response and then to gently direct the interviewee to discuss programming. Consequently, in addition to discovering information consistent with the goals of the interview, the interview must also *manage* the interaction to keep the conversation on topic.

Finally, open questions are rarely useful for covering a wide range of topics because of the amount of time necessary for the interviewee to respond to each question. If the goal of the interview is not coverage of a small number of topics in depth, but a larger number of topics, a more closed type of question should be used.

Closed Questions

In sharp contrast to an open question, a closed question attempts to limit or restrict the response and focus the interviewee on providing only the desired information. Closed questions allow the interviewer to better control the topics covered by the interviewee by requiring more precise and specific answers. Examples of closed questions include the following:

○ What is your favorite summertime sport?

○ What mode of transportation do you use to commute to work every day?

○ In what city would you like to live?

Interviewers can use different types of closed questions to accomplish specific interview goals. In addition to the less restrictive questions, you can also use multiple-choice and dichotomous questions.

Multiple Choice Questions

Which one of the following U.S. presidents took office immediately after John F. Kennedy?

a. Dwight D. Eisenhower
b. William J. Clinton
c. Gerald R. Ford
d. Lyndon B. Johnson
e. Harry S. Truman

How many vacation days do you get every year?

a. None
b. Five or less
c. Six to ten
d. Eleven to twenty
e. Twenty one or more

Would you rather live in Dayton, Ohio; Blacksburg, Virginia; or Norwalk, California?

Multiple-choice questions restrict the interviewee's response options. Public opinion polls and other types of surveys often use this kind of question. Multiple choice is an example of extremely closed questions. They are more common in survey kinds of interviews, but they are occasionally used in more mainstream types of interviews, especially if several people are being interviewed.

Using multiple-choice questions, interviewers are able to collect very specific pieces of information in a relatively short time. The information collected is fairly uncomplicated and easy to summarize, and the responses from many interviewees can be compared because all the collected data are in the same form. In addition, because the responses are restricted and predetermined, the level of interviewer skill and training does not have to be nearly as high as when using open questions. Interviewees are forced to choose the option provided by the interviewer that best describes their responses to the questions.

Even though the interviewers do not need the highest level of skill to use closed questions, the questions themselves must be written with great care. The questions themselves must be clearly worded, and the response lists should be exhaustive and mutually exclusive.

To be *exhaustive*, a list of responses must include all possible answers that could be given by interviewees. For example, in an interview conducted by an automobile manufacturer to gather customer reactions to a new model, the interviewer asked how long the interviewee had owned the car. The possible answers were 3 months, 6 months, 9 months, or 1 year. What if the interviewee had owned the car for only 5 weeks? What is that person to answer? To make this list exhaustive, the responses could be changed to 3 months or less, 4 to 6 months, 7 to 9 months, 10 to 12 months, and more than 12 months. With this change, all interviewees could find a response appropriate to themselves.

Another strategy for achieving exhaustiveness is to include an "other" response. For example, the question you asked is, "With what political party do you affiliate yourself?" Given the variety of existing political parties, the list of responses could be quite long. And even with a long list, you might not cover all the possibilities. However, to make your list exhaustive, you could include several of the more popular parties, and then include an "other" to provide all interviewees with a response.

The responses for multiple choice questions must also be *mutually exclusive*. That is, an interviewee should be able to find only one applicable choice. When constructing this kind of question, you should examine the list and ask if an individual might realistically choose more than one response. Responding to the political party question, it seems unreasonable to expect that anybody would select more than one of those response categories.

Dichotomous questions restrict responses to one of two possible choices. The responses can be a yes/no answer or various two-option answers.

Multiple Choice Questions

With what political party do you affiliate yourself?

a. Democrat
b. Republican
c. Green
d. Independent
e. Other

_____

(please specify)

Dichotomous Questions

○ Are you satisfied or dissatisfied with the course you are taking?

○ Did you complete the assignment for today's class?

○ Do you agree or disagree with the designated hitter rule in baseball?

The kinds of questions you use depend on the goals you have for the interview.

Although this kind of question is easy to ask, easy to answer, and provides results that are easy to summarize, they provide little depth of understanding or insight because they reveal little information beyond what is specifically asked by the interviewer.

As you have likely concluded, closed questions have strengths and weaknesses. On the strength side, they are easy to write, easy to administer, and easy to analyze and compare. Also, they require a lesser level of skill and training to conduct an interview. They also provide the opportunity to precisely direct the flow of an interview and to gather information about a variety of topics in a fairly short time. On the weakness side, closed questions limit the depth of potential responses because of the restrictive format of the question and possible answers.

The kinds of questions that you use really depend on the goals you have for the interview and how you intend to use the information collected in the interview. If you would like to understand the "soul" of the interviewee and find out what makes him or her tick, then more open questions will allow freedom to follow unexpected directions and to explore in depth. However, if you want to collect a variety of information from a large and diverse group of people, perhaps the more closed questions would work better for you. Of course, it's always possible to mix the kinds of questions to achieve your specific interview goals.

Question Hazards and Other Dangers

Biased Questions

Questions phrased in such a way that they would be likely to influence the interviewees' responses are called **biased questions**. You should make every attempt to avoid biased questions, because the responses given do not necessarily represent the true thoughts of the interviewee. Biased questions come in at least two forms: leading questions and loaded questions.

Leading Questions

- Isn't this a great car?

- Everyone knows that fuels burned by cars and trucks harm the environment and contribute to global warming. Are you in favor of restricting vehicle emissions?

- Aren't golden retrievers fabulous dogs?

- You *actually* listen to talk radio everyday?

- Most people agree that the governor of the state is doing a great job and should be re-elected. Using the following scale, how would you rate the governor's work in education?

Great Job　　Good Job　　Neutral　　Poor Job　　Very Poor Job

A leading question guides the interviewee in the direction of the response preferred by the interviewer or otherwise requires the interviewee to give the socially correct or acceptable response. Leading questions are often used by sales people to persuade customers to buy a product or service.

Similar to a leading question, a **loaded question** can incite emotional responses, give equally disagreeable response alternatives, or place the interviewee in a paradox where any answer is inappropriate. Loaded questions almost always create a defensive reaction from the interviewee and seldom yield usable information. Fortunately, these questions are rarely used, so be careful that you avoid them.

Loaded Questions

○ Have you stopped beating your cat?

○ Did you get caught cheating on your girlfriend again?

To fix leading or loaded questions, make sure that your questions are *neutral*. That is, the wording of your questions should suggest no particular response. Remember that you are trying to *discover* information by asking questions. You are not merely trying to get interviewees to say something you want them to say. If you can't decide by proofreading them yourself if your questions are neutral, then you can ask others to read them for you. You can also pretest your questions on a very small number of interviewees. In either case, you can ask the readers if they spotted any biased questions. Here's a rewrite of one of the examples:

Fix: Unbiased Question

Which one of the following best represents you opinion of the governor's work in education

Great Job   Good Job   Neutral   Poor Job   Very Poor Job

Double-Barreled Questions

It's pretty easy to place two questions into one question, so you have to be careful to proofread your questions before you include them in your interview plan. With a double-barreled question, you would be asking for a single answer to what might be several questions.

For example, a question might ask: "Are you in favor of increases in cable TV and electricity rates for this community?" The question asks for a yes or no response. However, if you say yes, what exactly is it that you are in favor of? Are you in favor of a rate increase for electricity? Are you in favor of a rate increase for cable TV? Or are you in favor of a rate increase for both electricity and cable TV? If you say no, what do you oppose? What if you support the increase in cable rates but oppose the increase in electricity rates? How can this attitude be expressed with a single yes or no answer? Here are other examples:

Double-Barreled Questions

The United States should get out of the post office business and spend the money on preparing for natural disasters or other emergencies.   YES   NO

Do you support the president's position on the hurricane clean-up and tax relief?   YES   NO

To fix double-barreled questions, carefully proofread your questions with a sharp eye out for two-pronged questions. If you spot one, the best fix is to break it down into separate questions, assuming that your interview goals include all the concepts covered in the original question. Keep the issues separate and clear. Looking at the previous example, you could rewrite the question as two new questions:

Fix: Individual Questions

Do you support the president's position on the hurricane clean-up?   YES   NO

Do you support the president's position on tax reform?   YES   NO

Open-to-Closed Questions

With this question hazard, the interviewer begins with a question, but then follows up very quickly with a much more narrow, closed question. Although the question is originally designed to allow the interviewee some depth and flexibility in the response, the follow-up question severely limits the response, and often reduces it to a simple yes or no. Here's an example of an open-to-closed question.

Open-to-Closed Questions

Tell me what it's like to be married. (*then, immediately follow with*) Do you guys fight a lot? (or) Do you guys go out a lot? (or) Do you enjoy being married?

Can you please describe the position that you have available? Would I get a vacation? (or) Are there educational benefits? (or) Would I get my own office?

In each case, attempting to take advantage of the benefits of open questions, the interviewer begins by looking for some depth in the response. The goal is to allow the interviewee to provide some personal insight. But before the response can be expressed, the interviewer changes the question and limits the interviewee to a very simple answer.

The cure in this case is less a matter of careful proofreading (that is still very important!) but more a matter of careful timing and listening to the interviewee's response. Make sure you give the interviewee enough time to fully answer your original open question. Then, if you still would like more information, use your follow-up or probing questions. Be patient!

Question Reliability

Somebody bright and famous *should* have said, "Whatever *can* be misinterpreted *will* be misinterpreted!" Can an interviewee find a meaning for your question other than the one that you intended? Can a group of interviewees find *multiple* meanings for your questions or statements? The answer to these questions should always be, "No!"

Being concerned with reliability means that you are concerned with the *consistency* with which other people interpret or give meaning to your questions or statements. You want to make sure that all (or most) of the people who read or hear your questions give the same meaning to them. If you ask, "What color was the mouse?" you would like the interviewees to assume that "mouse" means the furry little creature that somehow got into your house and is living under your bed. You do not want interviewees to assume other meanings for the term, like, for instance, the peripheral accessory that allows you to operate your computer.

If interviewees give different or inconsistent meanings to questions in an interview, the interviewer doesn't really know for certain what question is being answered. Is it the question that I meant to ask? Or is it the question that the interviewee heard? What question am I hearing the response to?

Here's an example. This question was part of a Web-based interview that was trying to measure "vanity" in the interviewees.

Unreliable Question

"If you could significantly improve your body, but that improvement would take ten years off your life, would you do it?"

The question was asking if people would trade ten years of life to significantly improve their looks. As it turns out, people taking the survey gave meaning to the term improve in several ways:

○ *Improve* means to look better.
○ *Improve* means to be more healthy or fit.

○ *Improve* means to cure some ailment or deformity.

○ *Improve* means to develop big muscles.

○ *Improve* means to develop superior athletic abilities.

○ *Improve* means to gain or lose weight, or to become shorter or taller.

○ *Improve* also meant the enhancement of a variety of body parts!

You can see the problem! Look back at the original question. When you read it, what question did you think was being asked? Did you think *improve* meant to "look better?" Many people did not! What meaning did *you* give to the question?

If you are the interviewer, and you asked that same question to 150 interviewees, how can you possibly summarize the responses to that question? You don't even know what question the people are responding to!

The original question was intended to measure vanity. A simple pretest of the question on a small group of interviewees probably would have identified the reliability problem and allowed the interviewer to make the question more clear. That is, the interviewer can rewrite the question to make it less likely to be interpreted in unintended ways. The rewrite might look like this:

Fix: Reliable Question

"If you could significantly improve your looks, but the improvement would take ten years off your life, would you do it?"

Remember that meanings exist in people, and not in the terms that you use. As a result, any term you use can be interpreted in ways that you did not intend. To prevent this from happening, word your questions very carefully. Proofread every question. For some extra peace of mind, try out or pretest your questions on a small group of people and ask them what meaning they give to the questions.

In addition, try to be as specific as possible when choosing words. Choose words for their clarity and their lack of ambiguity. Try to avoid jargon or specialized words unless your preinterview analysis suggests that the interviewees will clearly understand them.

Open questions often have inherent reliability problems. Because an interview using open questions can follow many different paths with many interviewees, it's nearly impossible to determine if every interviewee is responding to exactly the same question. However, if you carefully plan, word, and test your questions, you can avoid many problems with reliability.

How to Prepare for an Interview

To prepare for an interview, you should have firmly determined what you want to gain from the interview. In addition, you should have a strategy for reaching your objective.

Goals

As you saw in the definition of an interview, at least one of the parties comes into the situation with a specific goal in mind. So before you begin any kind of interview, you need to pause and reflect on your **goals** for the interaction. Just what do you want to get form this interview? Are you looking for advice, information, employment, attitude change, directions, instructions, motivation, or solutions to a problem?

When you have made a general determination of your goals, try to narrow the focus and decide what you want to take with you from this specific conversation. Do you want advice on a career choice? Do you need help with a particular problem in your life or career? Do you want to make the "short list" for an employment position? Are you trying to select a major? The more specific your goals, the better you can plan for the interview.

Interview Plan

When you have arrived at a decision about what goals you would like to accomplish in your interview, you should develop an interview plan. The **interview plan** outlines your strategy for goal achievement and it includes the topics that should be discussed as well as the sequence and wording of specific questions. The exact format of the plan is directly tied to your interview goals. The format of your plan can range on a continuum from directed to nondirected.

In a *directed* interview, the interviewer controls the areas of discussion and the pace and flow of the conversation. Questions used in this plan are usually more closed, restricting the focus of the interviewee. If you use a *nondirected* plan, you would include more open questions that allow the interviewee some flexibility of response. As a result, in this type of interview, the interviewee tends to exert more control over the flow of the conversation and, to some extent, the topic areas covered.

As mentioned earlier, the specific plan that you choose depends on your goals for the interview. If you don't know a great deal about the topic, and if you would like to explore that topic in depth with a relatively small number of interviewees, then you should select a more nondirected interview plan. With this plan, the interviewer begins by asking open questions to start the conversation and establish a focus. Because the questions and potential subject areas are broad, the interviewee must be prepared to probe responses and to more completely investigate different content areas. The interviewer therefore has to be very skilled to not only *follow* the flow of the conversation

Image © 2008, JupiterImages Corporation.

What do you want to accomplish in the interview? Determine what you want to gain before you participate.

but to *adapt* to the different directions the conversation might take. Here are some examples of questions appropriate to this type of interview plan:

- Tell me about yourself.
- What happened?
- How do you feel about life as a college student?

If a completely nondirected question is not necessary, that is, if you would like to guide the interviewee more toward a specific topic area, you can use a more restrictive question. The question supplies a little more direction about the desired response. Take a look at these examples:

- What is the biggest challenge you see to attending college part time while raising a family?
- What is your biggest concern about life after college?

If this form of the question doesn't bring the amount of focus that you want, you can follow up your open question with probing questions to move the interviewee to the topics you wish to discuss:

What is your biggest concern about life after college?

- Probe: getting a job? (getting a better job?)
- Probe: raising a family?
- Probe: finding a satisfying career?
- Probe: making a meaningful contribution to society?

What specific questions could you ask a student about her concerns about life after college?

Directed Interview Questions

- Which member of the City Council do you think should be the next mayor of the city?

- If you could only make one improvement to this proposal, what would it be?

- If you want to completely control the range of possible responses, you can use a multiple choice or standardized response question:

- The County should construct four new recreation centers in the next 3 to 5 years.

  Strongly Agree   Agree   Neutral   Disagree   Strongly Disagree

- Which one of the following is your favorite Simpson's character?

  a. Marge
  b. Homer
  c. Bart
  d. Lisa
  e. Maggie
  f. Other

Using a more directed question form allows the interviewer not only to keep the interviewee focused on appropriate topics, but also to restrict the duration of the responses. Pace is important! You do not want to run out of time or energy before you accomplish your interview goals!

The directed interview plan allows the interviewer to exercise more control over responses and the topics covered. If you are interested in gathering a broad range of information about a topic from a fairly large number of interviewees, then the directed interview is the plan you should choose. Common applications for the directed plan include market surveys and opinion polls which typically interview large numbers of people. In addition, employers who conduct screening interviews of large groups of applicants often use a more directed approach. Each interviewee responds to questions that are usually more closed, worded the same way to improve reliability, and asked in the same order. Here are some examples of questions that might be used in a directed interview plan:

How Interviews are Structured

An interview has a recognizable structure much like the structure of a public speech or other messages. There are three main parts to an interview: the opening, the body, and the closing.

Opening

The **opening** or introduction is a critical part of the interview, yet it is often neglected during the planning stages. The opening serves at least three functions critical to the success of the interview. The opening should *set the foundation* of the relationship between the parties that will be further developed during the course of the interview. Some interviewing professionals suggest some small talk or even some self disclosure at this point, but that should be decided case-by-case based on the specific individuals involved and the goals of the interview.[4]

The opening should motivate the other party to participate fully in the interaction. You can offer a reward, stress the importance of the interview goals, show respect for the other, or use some other motivational strategy. The important idea is to let the other party know that you hope for and would appreciate full participation.

Finally, the opening should *provide an orientation* to the interviewee about what will take place in the interview. The interviewer should talk about the goals of the interview, what procedures will be followed as the interview progresses, approximately how long the interaction might take, and provide details about what is expected of the interviewee. If appropriate to the type of interview, the interviewer should let the interviewee know how the information collected will be used after the interview.

When the opening is complete, you should try to move smoothly into the body of the interview. This transition might be best achieved by asking an open question.[5] This first question should be nonthreatening and fairly easy to answer. The open question should get the interviewee talking and allow an easy movement into the body.

Body

The **body** is the central part of the interview. It is in this section that much of the information is exchanged and all or most of the interview goals are accomplished. Regardless of the type of interview you are conducting, you will have to arrange the topics covered in the body in a logical and coherent way. This coherent arrangement allows the most efficient use of your time, prevents both parties from being confused or distracted, and dramatically improves the likelihood that the goals of the interview will be realized.

Planning the body of the interview requires choosing the organizational structure or pattern that will best help you realize your goals. Take a look at the following examples and try to decide which one will best suit the goals of your next interview.

Common Organizational Patterns

Spatial

In this organizational pattern, question topics move in a sequence related to physical location. For example, if you are a reporter gathering information about the National Museum of the United States Air Force, you could begin by asking about the Early Flight gallery, then ask about the Modern Flight gallery, and conclude with questions about the gallery containing presidential aircraft.

Topical

Questions in a topical sequence are arranged according to the interests and priorities of the interviewer. A journalist might follow a sequence of who, what, when, where, and why to cover a story. Or the coverage of the Air Force Museum would follow this sequence:

- Propeller-driven aircraft
- Jet-powered aircraft
- Experimental aircraft
- Rockets and missiles

Chronological

Questions are ordered in a time sequence. If you are questioning someone about a work history, you would begin at the first job, and then move through each job until you reach the present. Let's go back to the Air Force Museum for another example:

○ Military aircraft from WWI and WWII

○ Military aircraft from the Korean War

○ Military aircraft from the Vietnam War

○ Military aircraft from the Gulf conflicts

Cause-Effect

This sequence is arranged according to the causes of a situation and their effects. For example, if you are interviewing a school board member about the degree of absenteeism in the high schools, you could ask about its causes such as economic conditions, motivation to attend class, or family issues. Then you could ask about some possible effects, such as poor test scores, a rising crime rate, or high unemployment. Some other examples:

○ A parent might discuss a student's poor test grades (effect) and then explore the possible causes of those grades.

○ A physician could discuss a child's exercise habits (cause) and then discuss the possible effects of a sedentary lifestyle.

Problem-Solution

This sequence moves from the examination of a problem to the solution of the problem. For example, an appraisal or counseling interview might first focus on the interviewee's problem and then turn to a discussion of solutions. Other examples include the following:

○ A school counselor and a student might talk about the student's poor attendance in class and then discuss how the attendance might be improved.

○ A professor could discuss problems that students have been experiencing in a particular class at mid-semester, and then have an exchange concerning what could be done to improve the class for the rest of the term.

○ A job counselor could discuss why a person seeking employment has had many interviews but has not yet been offered a job. The counselor might discuss with the interviewee how to improve his or her interviewing skills.

Structure and Function

This progression of ideas begins with how something is structured and then turns to a discussion of its function. If you're asking questions about an organization, you might begin with questions about how a particular department or unit is organized or structured. Then you ask questions about what exactly the department does. If you're trying to understand the structure and

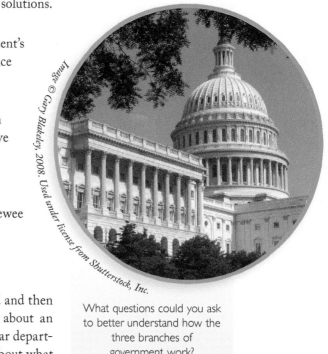

© Gary Blakeley, 2008. Used under license from Shutterstock, Inc.

What questions could you ask to better understand how the three branches of government work?

function of the U.S. government, you could ask about the three branches of the government and how they are organized, and then you could ask about what each branch does.

Build the Relationship

Relationships between people in interviewing situations develop in much the same way as relationships between people in other contexts. In cases where the parties do not know each other, the communication that occurs initially is fundamentally superficial because it is based on broad generalizations and assumptions made by each party about the other. Miller assumes that all initial interactions are impersonal or noninterpersonal, and that relationships become more interpersonal as they develop.[6]

Miller and Steinberg explain that individuals relate to each other on three levels: cultural, sociological, and psychological.[7] The relationship begins on the cultural level, and progresses through the sociological toward the psychological level. A brief look at these levels should help you understand how relationships can grow and be maintained during an interview.

On the *cultural* level, individuals do not relate to each other as persons, but only as role occupants or generalized members of a culture. The communicators only know as much about each other as they know about any other member of the culture, so uncertainty is high. Communication takes place on a superficial and somewhat formal level and is often made up of small talk. There is little or no disclosure of personal information. When the relationship gets to the *sociological* level, individuals relate to each other as stereotyped members of groups. One person interprets the behavior of the other based on what is known about the group to which that other is believed to belong. Finally, on the *psychological* level, individuals begin to relate to each other not only as members of a culture or group, but also as unique individuals. This level of relationship can be reached after the communicators have experienced one another's behaviors and have exchanged more personal types of information. They get to know each other!

In an interview, the initial relationship is likely to exist at the cultural level, or at best, if you have done a reasonable amount of research on the other party or organization, at the sociological level. Regardless, uncertainty at either level is high, and each party is trying to feel out the other to find out if he or she can be trusted with more personal information. As the parties interact, and if they begin to build trust, then more and more personal disclosure will take place and the relationship can move toward the psychological level. As a relationship moves through these levels toward the psychological, the relationship becomes more interpersonal.

The more interpersonal the relationship between the parties, the more freely information will be exchanged. If you can move the relationship toward the interpersonal end of the relationship continuum, you will more likely be able to achieve your goals for the interview. The bad news is that it

Make a plan for your interview that includes specific goals.

Image © Bacho, 2013. Used under license from Shutterstock, Inc.

will not always be possible to move into a trusting interpersonal relationship within the course of just one interview. Even so, you should make the effort to make the relationship as interpersonal as the situation permits!

While there are many ways to build relationships in an interview, here are three suggestions:

1 *Take a little risk*! Volunteer some personal information. Allow the other party to get to know you more on a more interpersonal level. You would prefer the interviewer remember you as "Sam from Dayton who has applied for the drafting position," rather than "applicant 356-C." If the employment interviewer gets to know something about you as a person, he or she will be more able to remember you and differentiate you from the rest of the candidates.

2 *Try to create a supportive climate*! A supportive climate is one in which neither party feels threatened by the other. A perception of threat creates an atmosphere of defensiveness in which both parties begin to question each others' intentions and suspect manipulation by the other. The result of this is inaccurate interpretation of meanings and intentions, and information will not be freely exchanged in this atmosphere. You will probably never make it to the psychological level!

3 *Be engaged*! It could be that the most significant thing you do to build and maintain a relationship with an interview (or conversational) partner is to be involved in the interaction. Involvement means

Tips for Creating a Supportive Climate

To avoid the formation of a defensive climate, follow Gibb's advice:[8]

○   Try to use descriptive statements.

○   Try not to use evaluative statements.

○   Try to remain focused on solving the problem.

○   Try not to give the impression that you want to exert control over the situation.

○   Try to maintain a natural, spontaneous, and engaged point of view.

○   Try not to give others the impression that you are using a strategy to control the situation or to get whatever you want.

○   Try to show a sincere concern and interest in the other.

○   Try not to appear detached and neutral.

○   Try to establish and maintain an atmosphere of equality.

○   Try not to make the other feel inferior.

○   Try to keep an open mind!

full participation in the "here and now" of the interaction without being distracted by factors not connected to the communication. This involvement will not only help you achieve your goals for the interview, but it also communicates an interest in the other participants in the conversation. As the other participants discover that you are genuinely interested and involved in what is happening, they will become more motivated and involved as well. So the outcome of your engagement is the increased commitment to the free exchange of information and to the success of the interview! It's all good!

Transition

When you complete the body of the interview, you should make this very clear to the interviewee. You can do this in a straightforward way by simply saying that the time for the interview is over or that you have no more questions. Be sure that interviewee understands that the questioning is completed.

Closing

How can you tell that this interview is finished?

Much like the opening, the **closing** of an interview is often overlooked while planning, and it often results in the interviewer attempting to simply "wing it." Because they think that there is nothing left to accomplish when the questioning is over, interviewers have a tendency to rush this phase. If the interviewer's only goal is to collect information, once that information is received, he or she might think that the interview is over. Many times the interviewer will just say "thanks!" and leave, giving no consideration to the interviewee or properly closing the interaction. This kind of "nonclosing" leaves interviewees with a poor impression and would not motivate them to cooperate again should the interviewer require more information.

The closing needs to be carefully considered because it also plays a critical role in the interview process: It provides closure, helps to maintain the relationship that was developed during the interview, and can help motivate the interviewee if further cooperation is needed.

As mentioned before, the interviewee should not have to wonder if the interview is over. The interviewer should *provide closure* by being very clear that the conversation is completed. This can be done by summarizing the content of the interview, letting the interviewee know if there is a next step in the interviewing process (such as multiple employment interviews), reminding the interviewee what will be done with the information collected from the conversation, or even through exhibiting some simple verbal or nonverbal leave-taking behavior.

The interviewer should make a strong effort to *maintain the relationship* that has been created and developed during the interview. Try to keep the relationship upbeat and positive, especially if you will be working together with the interviewee after the interview or if you will need further cooperation at a later time. The effort you make to treat the interviewee with respect and maintain that relationship will motivate him or her to cooperate further if needed. The motivation that you provide will also give the interviewee a sense of satisfaction by knowing that the effort and time in the interview was well spent.

Participating in an Interview

The previous section describes the nature of interviewing, the structure of interviews, and typical types of questions. You are now ready to test your wings and move on to some specific applications of interviewing! Congratulations!

This part will help you prepare for two kinds of actual interviewing experiences: the information-gathering interview and the employment interview. In the information gathering interview, our focus will be on organizing the interview, asking questions, listening to responses, and recording information. You will be the interviewer.

For the employment interview, our focus will be on your preparation and participation as an interviewee. You will be asked to complete a self inventory, to get to know yourself better, and prepare to answer common questions asked in a screening interview. You will also be asked to construct a resume, write a cover letter to accompany your resume, and write letters of appreciation for interviews.

What would you do to prepare yourself for an employment interview?

Conducting an Information-gathering Interview

This section will discuss the steps you should take when preparing an **information-gathering interview**. In this type of interview, the focus will be on planning and asking questions, listening to the responses, and recording the information.

Preparation and Planning

To make sure that you have a successful and productive interview, make a plan. A good plan makes it possible that you will get what you want from the interview situation.

The first step in the planning process is to establish your goals for the interview. The more specific your goals, the easier the planning process becomes and the more likely you will have a productive interview. As with any trip you might take, the knowledge of where you are going is enhanced by a detailed plan of how you intend to get there!

Make a plan for your interview that includes specific goals.

The goal in this kind of interview is information. Determine exactly what information you want to gain from the interaction. Are you interested in facts, opinions, descriptions of events or processes, explanations, biographical information, something else? Once you decide on a *general* goal, focus on your *specific* goals. What specific facts or exactly what kind of facts are you looking for?

With this well-articulated goal in mind, next consider *who* should be the subject of your interview. Choose the interviewee according to your goal statement. Who will best help you accomplish this goal?

A clearly thought out and precisely articulated goal will make your questions easier to plan. When your goal is clear, you will know better what to ask. You will also be better able to remain focused on the direction of the interview and keep the interaction on track. In addition, when you communicate your goals to the other party in the interview, he or she will be better able to interpret your questions and help you move toward your goal. Interviewees are willing to help you, or they would not be participating in the first place. Knowledge of what information you are looking for will allow them to help you even more. Also, in the event that your attention span begins to waver or you pull yourself off track by pursuing a false lead, the interviewee can help you find your direction and continue toward your interview goal.

Next, select the type of interview structure and the kind of questions that you will use. The interview structure will, again, depend on your specific goals for the interview. If you are interested in obtaining a description of a small rural town, for example, you could consider using the *spatial* structure. You could begin your questioning by asking about the town's business district, then move to the town square, the neighborhoods, the school, and finally, the parks and recreation facilities. If you are interested in finding out about a process, like how corn is grown, a *chronological* sequence might work best. You could begin by asking about preparation of the fields, then turn to planting procedures, then ask about crop maintenance and irrigation, then harvesting the corn, and finally ask about how corn is used by people. Examine your goal, and then choose your structure.

We suggest that you use questions that are more open that allow the interviewee some measure of flexibility in responding. Because you have goals to accomplish, you want to retain some degree of control over the conversation, so asking completely open questions is not always the best idea. Place a bit of a restriction on your questions so that a specific direction is indicated. Instead of opening your interview with the request to "tell me about corn," try asking, "What is the first step in producing a corn crop?" Or you could be even more specific and directive by asking, "How do you prepare a field for planting corn?"

You should also prepare a series of probing or follow-up questions that you can use (if necessary) to guide your interviewee in the direction that you want to go. If you asked about field preparation, you probably didn't want an explanation about where to find a field for planting corn or what the real estate market prices are for corn fields these days. If you have probing questions at the ready, you can gently refocus the interviewee to the topic you want to discuss.

Finally, prepare a good opening and closing. It's kind of like the introduction and conclusion of a speech. In this case, however, you should tailor them to the specific person in the interviewee chair and your specific purpose for the interview.

The opening should accomplish the following:

○ Begin to build the relationship that should last throughout and beyond the actual interview session.

○ State your specific goals for the interview.

○ Provide orientation by telling the interviewee how long the session will last, what topics will be covered, and perhaps why he or she was chosen by you to help you accomplish your interview goals.

The closing should do the following:

○ Attempt to maintain or continue the relationship that was built during the conversation. It gives the interviewee some satisfaction for participation and it is especially important if you have to ask for further information or clarification after the interview has been completed.

○ Thank the interviewee, provide a summary, and bring closure to the conversation.

○ Use the opportunity to ask permission to contact interviewee in the future for more information.

Listening and Involvement

Paying close attention and carefully listening for the duration of an extended conversation is challenging to all of us, regardless of how intelligent we are or how important the conversation is to us. There are lots of things going on around us and inside our heads that work together to steal our attention away from the here and now of a conversation. The purpose of this section is to give you a basic understanding of listening and the role of distraction, and to examine a few strategies to help you remain focused on the immediate interview conversation.

Listening is the active process of receiving, constructing meaning from, and responding to spoken and/or nonverbal messages. It involves the ability to retain information as well as to react empathetically and/or appreciatively to spoken and/or nonverbal messages.[9]

Listening is an *active*, psychological activity. Active means that it is voluntary and that it requires effort and motivation on our part.[10] The bad news is that most of us are generally poor listeners who only use about 25 percent of our capacity to listen.[11] In addition, we tend to remember only

© Buero Monaco/zefa/Corbis

How can you stay focused on the interview conversation?

about 50 percent of what we hear immediately after listening to a message and that number drops to 25 percent after two days.[12] In some conversational contexts, we listen even less effectively and remember as little as 10 percent of the content.[13]

So listening is voluntary and active, and many people are passive listeners. When we do listen, we do so with poor efficiency and tend to remember only fairly small percentages of what we hear. If these research findings are true, it appears that we don't have a very high probability of success in information-gathering interviews! If your communication goal in an interview is to gain information, it is important to recognize the general tendency to be inefficient listeners and resolve to become a better listener.

It takes a great deal of energy and self-discipline to keep yourself focused on the here-and-now of your communication, but that is the *goal of good listening*. Berko and others have reported that most of us are able to think much faster than we can talk.[14] As a result, our brains have extra processing capability that does not have to be engaged when we listen to others, and this extra processing capacity can interrupt our concentration on the immediate communication situation. As you listen to others speak, you have the capacity to take what we call **mental road trips** to places beyond the "here and now." You could be thinking about your job, or your house, or your dog, how your favorite baseball team is doing. "Did you turn the iron off this morning?" You are thinking about a zillion topics other than what the other person is saying. *The difference between thinking speed and listening speed can be an obstacle to effective listening when the extra mental capacity causes us to lose focus on the message.*[15]

The challenge is to focus attention on the here and now and to ignore any elements irrelevant to the immediate communication situation. Here are some simple strategies that you can use to keep your head in the game.

Focus on the Content

Focusing on the **content** of the conversation means that you become involved in the communication transaction rather than letting your emotions, environmental factors, or extraneous behaviors interfere with your understanding of what the other person is saying.

Review the Content

Reviewing includes mentally going over the central ideas and summarizing the important information. Focus your attention on the bigger picture because trying to memorize all the small details will distract your attention from the conversation as a whole. Sellnow tells us that it is possible to "listen too hard."[16] It doesn't take much time to get lost in the details. If you are going to remember some elements of a conversation and forget others, you should at least remember the major ideas the other person talked about.[17]

Do you tend to take a mental road trip when you should be paying attention to someone?

© 2/Thomas Barwick/Ocean/Corbis

Repeat the Content

Repeat the content to the other person to find out if you truly understood it. The goal of restatement is to check the extent to which both people share meaning. You are essentially asking the question, "This is the meaning I've given to what you have said. Am I correct?"

- If you think you might not have heard the actual words correctly, you could *repeat the words* to check for accurate hearing.

- If you do not understand the meaning of something that was said, you should *paraphrase the content* in your own words, then check with the other party for accuracy.

- If you think you understand the meaning of the content but you do not understand why the person said it, you can paraphrase the motivation of the content. "This is why I think you said that. Is that correct?" This is the most difficult kind of paraphrasing, but it is a very useful skill that can dramatically improve your understanding of a message.[18]

These strategies not only allow interview parties to determine the level of comprehension, but they are indicators of the interest in the other's point of view. The strategies provide feedback that tells the other if you are giving the right meaning to the message. If your repetition or paraphrase is inaccurate, the other person can state the message in a different way to help you better understand the intended meaning.

Another challenge to good listening comes when we focus on ourselves and what we are doing instead of the ideas being presented by the other person. It's very easy to be more involved with what you are saying (or are planning to say), rather than attending to the whole conversation. One flustered participant returned from an interview and reported that he was very worried that his tie was crooked and that he wouldn't be able to ask the right questions. He didn't follow the conversation very well and could barely remember what the interviewee said. He was so self-focused that he did not attend to all the elements of the interview situation and was unable to understand the other person.

A common mistake that hampers productive listening is preparing or rehearsing your next statement instead of listening to the response of the other person.[19] It's very important to pay attention to your own behavior (i.e., to be a good self-monitor); your best effort should be made to focus on the message and not so much on yourself.

Recording Information

If you are conducting the interview with the goal of gathering information, you will have to find some method of recording what you learn from the interviewee. The most common methods are to just listen, listen and record the notes after the interview, listen and take notes during the interview, or make an audio or video recording of the interview.

Just Listen

Simply listening and participating in the interview is probably the best way to discover the information that you are looking for in the interview. Abel conducted a study in which two groups of people participated in interviews to gather information.[20] One group took notes during the interview, and the second group took no notes, but just listened. When the reports were compared, the reports from the group that did not take notes were more accurate than those from the group that did take notes. Those people not taking notes were not distracted by the act of taking the notes during the conversation.

Listen Now, Write Notes Later

To take advantage of the increased involvement with the conversation that you have while simply listening, you should write your notes as soon as possible after the actual interview. The longer you wait, the less likely that you will clearly remember what was said.

Listen and Take Notes

Image © 2008, JupiterImages Corporation.

Taking notes during an interview may work well if you just jot down main ideas.

As if you weren't going to be busy enough during this interview, now we are telling you to take notes! Taking notes during an interview is a significant challenge: you have to listen, manage the direction and pace of the interview, and you have to take notes. You have to do this all at the same time!

You have certainly tried to take notes during class, so you know how difficult it can be. If you try to write absolutely everything down, you will likely miss important things that were said while you were focused on writing. This is especially true in this kind of interview. In addition, such a focus on writing everything down withdraws you from the "here and now" of the communication situation. If you manage to divide your time and attention well enough between listening and note taking, you should have little trouble. If, however, you begin to spend more time and attention on note taking, the situation could quickly deteriorate. Not only will you miss important details, but after a while, the interviewee picks up on your note taking and begins to speak at the speed at which you are taking notes. Not only is this distracting for the interviewee, but any real conversation that you were having will come to a halt and the interview turns into a dictation session. Not good!

The solution to this problem can be found if you revisit your goals for the interview. If your goal is obtaining meticulous detail, then see the section on audio and video recording. If a high level of detail is not exactly what you are looking for, the best solution might be to take notes on a "big picture" or "conceptual" level. Quickly write down main ideas in just enough detail to jog your memory at a later time. In this case, it's a good idea to revisit your notes as soon as you can after the interview and try to fill in as many gaps as you can. It's also another good reason to build and maintain a good relationship with the interviewee: you might need to call to get assistance to fill in the required details. The interview isn't necessarily over when the conversation ends!

Audio or Video Recording

If your goals for the interview require attention to lots of detail, then you should consider an electronic recording of the conversation. If you use an electronic device, make sure you get the permission of the interviewee, and get it in advance of the interview. In addition, when using an electronic device for recording, make sure you have a "Plan B." Electronic gadgets are cool and do some amazing things, but they still break! If you count on Murphy's law, "Whatever can go wrong will go wrong," you will always have a back-up plan if something doesn't work. Don't let a broken gizmo ruin your interview; carefully consider a practical alternative.

Many people using audio recording devices make transcripts of the conversation after the interview. This is a very labor-intensive under-taking, but it captures everything that was said down to the smallest detail. If detail isn't your goal, then you could skip the transcript step and listen to the recording several times for needed quotes or for the level of detail that your goals require.

If your interview goals require even more detail, you could make a video recording. Video captures not only what was said, but facial expres-sions and gestures that can help you interpret more clearly the meaning of the words. It's especially important that you get permission from the inter-viewee before making a video recording. But before pulling out your smart phone and capturing the event, go back to the goals for this interview to help you decide if a video record is actually needed. If it doesn't help you achieve your goals, then this added step is more likely to become a distraction for you as well as your interviewee.

You might find yourself in an interview situation where an entire committee asks you questions.

Approaching Employment Interviews

It is very likely that you have already experienced several employment inter-views. Even though they are very common and "everybody has to go through it," skill in this type of interview is essential for career success. Our focus with the employment interview will be on interviewee responsibilities: preparation and answering questions. After you get some experience in your chosen career, you will be in more of a position to focus on asking the ques-tions and managing the interview.

Employment interviews come in a variety of different shapes and sizes. The kind of situation that we typically expect is one interviewer to one inter-viewee, but don't count on that always being the case. You could find yourself sitting at a table with a search committee with *everybody* asking questions.

This is becoming more common, so consider it to be a real possibility. You could also be interviewed during a meal, or on the telephone (which *could* be a conference call with a committee), or even over a video link (which *could* include that same committee). Just be aware that you might not be walking into the exact situation that you expect. If you have some flexibility in your expectations, you will be much less distracted by different interview situations.

Questions and Answers for Employment Interviews

The type of employment interview that is our focus in this chapter is generally called a **screening interview**. A screening interview is usually the first contact you will have with most organizations and is often is conducted by a professional in the human resources department. The purpose of the interview is to determine if the interviewee meets the necessary requirements for the available position. If the interviewee appears to meet the company's criteria for the position, he or she will be invited back for more interviews. These subsequent interviews, often called **selection interviews**, are conducted by supervisors or other members of the department that is hiring the position.

The purpose of the information-gathering interview section was for you to expand your skills in planning an interview, asking questions, maintaining involvement with the interviewee and the flow of a conversation, and accurately recording information. However, the purpose of this section is for you to acquire skills at responding to questions asked in the selection interview. The best preparation for this kind of interview is to make a commitment to listening, get to know yourself very well, anticipate (in a general way) the questions you are likely to encounter, and plan some of your responses.

Make a Commitment to Listening

With any conversation, each participant has to make a commitment to listening and focusing on the communication event. This focus is even more central in an interview because both parties come to the situation with serious and specific goals they wish to accomplish.

In the first part of this chapter, in the discussion of information-gathering interviews, we talked about listening to the other person and carefully attending to the conversation as more and more information is revealed to you. In the employment interview, listening to the other *should* be a little easier than in the information gathering interview. After all, you are the interviewee and you are the person who will do much of the talking. However, there are still significant challenges in this kind of interview that require a great deal of effort and energy from the interviewee.

You will be asked a series of questions. It is important that you understand the question being asked. You need to be sure of the actual words spoken by the interviewer and you need to be sure about what the interviewer

During the interview, make sure you accurately interpret the questions.

Image © Kzenon, 2013. Used under license from Shutterstock, Inc.

means. Make sure that you accurately interpret the questions. If you didn't hear what the interviewer said or you are not clear on what he or she means, ask questions! Let the interviewer *help you* to understand what is being asked. Don't try to pretend that you understand and stumble through the response!

Listen to *your own* responses! What? Listen to what *you* say! Keep track of what you are saying and be sure it is responsive to the question that was asked. Pay attention so that you don't repeat yourself unnecessarily and that you say what you actually mean to say. Also pay attention to *how* you give your responses. Are you communicating an appropriate tone for this kind of conversation?

Finally, try to stay focused on this conversation and do not allow yourself to be distracted. You came to this interview prepared, so you should not become preoccupied with planning your answer to he next question while you are still in the middle of this one! Commit yourself to expend the effort necessary to remain in the "here and now" of this conversation, and maintain that commitment throughout the conversation.

Self-Inventory

Following is a list of questions that you should answer about yourself. Write the answers down. Included on the Web site for this course is an electronic form that you can complete that is designed to help you conduct your inventory. Take a look at these questions:

- What are five characteristics that you believe define who you are?

- What are your work-related strengths and weaknesses?

- What are the strengths and weaknesses of your personality?

- What would your say are your greatest achievements? What did you learn from them?

- What would you say are your greatest failures? What did you learn from them?

- Why did you choose the college or university that you are attending?

- Why did you choose your major? Describe the path you took to choosing this major: include any experiences, courses, teachers, mentors, role models or significant insights that helped place you on this path.

- What three college courses have you liked the most? Why?

- What three college courses have you liked the least? Why?

- Why are you interested in a career in _____? Describe your path to this career: Include any experiences, courses, teachers, mentors, role models, significant insights, or anything else that helped place you on this path.

- What contribution do you think you can make to the field of _____?

- What do you believe is the most significant challenge currently facing the field of _____?

- What do you think will be the next "growth area" or major development in the field of _____?

- What would you like to be doing five years from now?

- What are your long-range career goals?

Get to Know Yourself

Of course, you already know yourself. You should know yourself better than anybody else knows you. But how good are you at describing and explaining what you know about yourself to others? Most of us aren't very good at it, yet we still try and try, even at the expense of confusing others and boring their socks off! Remember the last time you tried to introduce yourself to a group of people who didn't know you? Does this scenario sound familiar? "Now we will go around the table, and everybody should state their names, what department they work in, and say a few words about themselves so we can all get to know each other better." This hardly ever goes well!

But why? Who knows more about you than you?

The reason that self-introductions often have unfortunate results is not a lack of information, but the lack of a plan! We stumble over these introductions because we are organizing and editing a lifetime of information that will somehow be reported to a group of strangers in three or four sentences. If only we knew this question was coming, we could have planned something to say!

Guess what? Questions asking you to describe yourself, your education, your talents, your interests, your goals, your skills, and even your hobbies *are coming in this interview!* Because you know this, you can begin now to plan what to say about yourself.

Anticipate the Questions

The questions you are likely to be asked in a screening interview are probably not very different from those in the list we have provided. The questions might be worded differently, but the content areas will be similar. You can bet that there will be some surprises, and you'll have to handle those as they come. Our goal in this course is to help minimize surprises and prepare you to tackle the questions we know are coming.

Probably the most common question in a screening interview sounds very much like, "Tell me about yourself!" Many professional interviewers do not like this question and do not recommend asking it. The reason is that nobody knows how to answer it. Even though many of the specialists don't use it, the reality is that you are very likely to hear this question at your screening interview. So you would be wise to prepare a good-quality answer!

You can do a quick *Google* search for employment interview questions and see quite a variety. Here's a short list of questions that you are likely to encounter.

- Tell me about yourself.
- What is your greatest strength? What are your three greatest strengths?
- What is your greatest personal strength?

Image © Monkey Business Images, 2013. Used under license from Shutterstock, Inc.

Can you anticipate the questions you're likely to hear in a screening interview?

- What is your greatest professional strength?
- What is your greatest weakness?
- What is your greatest personal weakness?
- What is your greatest professional weakness?
- What are your three greatest weaknesses?
- Name one weakness and talk about the steps you have taken to overcome it.
- What is your favorite class (or favorite three classes) in college? Why?
- What is your least favorite class (or three least favorite classes) in college? Why?
- Why did you choose _____ for a major? What got you interested in _____? Describe the path you took to selecting this major.
- What is the last book that you read? (The interviewer might ask you to talk about it. Do *not* say you read a book that you haven't read!)
- Why did you choose _____ as a career? Describe the path you took to choose this career.
- Why did you quit working at _____? (Assumes past employment history)
- What do you like best about your position at _____?
- What do you like least about your position at _____?

This is only a partial list and should not be viewed as exhaustive. However, based on your authors' collective experience, this list contains questions that are frequently used and likely to appear in your screening interview. There will be other questions that you did not anticipate. If you have done your homework, however, you should know yourself well enough to be able to construct a respectable answer for unanticipated topics.

Plan Your Responses

Obviously, you can't anticipate every question, and you will not be able to carefully plan every answer. Perhaps you shouldn't try to plan out every response even if you could. You want to sound relaxed and not over practiced or insincere. You can remain spontaneous and still have general responses prepared to questions that you can anticipate.

"Tell Me about Yourself"

For example, you can probably count on some form of the "tell me about yourself" question to be asked. How will you answer it?

Our suggestion for preparing your response begins with *research*: Examine your self-inventory. Select three or four significant items or characteristics that you believe describe you. Then select, perhaps, the reason(s) you picked your specific career. Make a list; write it down.

How can you best respond to a question about what your weaknesses are?

Step two in crafting this response is *organization*. Think of this response as a two-minute speech. As such, your response should have a very brief introduction, three or four main points, and a very brief summation or conclusion. The main points should correspond with the significant characteristics that you believe describe you the best. Mention each characteristic and provide a brief explanation. The first two or three main points should be descriptive of you. The final main point should provide a connection between your characteristics and the company you are interviewing with. You can use this opportunity to describe what a perfect fit can be made with you and this company or with you and this career opportunity.

Strengths and Weaknesses

Another typical question asks about strengths and weaknesses. Go back to your self-inventory and look at it with a very critical eye. Make a list of three or four characteristics that you consider to be strengths, and make sure that you honestly believe them to be strengths. Look at strengths of character and strengths related to your profession.

Now make a list of three or four characteristics that you believe to be weaknesses. This is not always a pleasant task, but a personal weakness is something that you will eventually have to face and make an effort to improve, so look at it as a personal growth exercise. Besides, the question will very likely come up in the interview.

Strengths are much easier to talk about than weaknesses. Don't be shy about discussing your strengths, but don't brag about them either. If you have ways that you live your life or do your work that you are proud of, mention those and maybe talk a little about how you came to be that way. Don't forget to include any strong skills you have learned that might be useful in your professional life.

When you consider your weaknesses, think about real weaknesses that you have and also think about what you have done or what you could do to overcome them. Even if you don't have it beaten yet, at least you have recognized the weakness and are taking steps to eliminate it. Interviewers are very used to hearing about minor weaknesses that have easy solutions. Even people who believe they are perfect come up with small weaknesses because they know it will come up in an interview. We call these *false weaknesses*. Many of those sound phony to the interviewers (who typically interview a lot of people, so you know they have heard nearly everything!). For example, a typical false weakness is "I'm a perfectionist." This is said to be a weakness because it "takes me longer to do things since I have to do them just right." How many times do you think interviewers hear that one?

A response to the weakness question that we hear a lot is, "I'm a procrastinator." This is a fine response, if you follow up with sincere efforts you have made to overcome it. However, this is often followed up with, "But being a procrastinator is fine because I have found that I work really well under pressure." That kind of response, as well as the attitude toward work that it communicates, should provide some entertainment for the interviewer, but it will *not* land you a job.

A good example of an answer to the weakness question is, "I have been working on my listening skills. I have found myself distracted occasionally when other people talk, and I don't always hear everything they say." Having poor listening skills is certainly a weakness, but you have acknowledged that you have recognized the weakness and that you are trying to improve your skills. You can follow the recognition statement with some specific things you are doing to help you improve. "I now understand that listening is not a passive activity and that it takes a lot of effort to listen well. Now when I talk to other people, I focus much more energy on being involved in the whole conversation and listening carefully. I'm not perfect, but I am certainly improving!" Another possibility is to talk about some specific training in listening that you are taking to help you improve.

Career Choice

Discuss not only the future and where you see your career taking you, but also what effect you could have on the career. How do you think your innovative thinking or skills can influence the field you are entering?

You should also, if appropriate in the interview, talk about the path that brought you to this career. What life experiences or classes or individuals influenced you to be interested in this particular career? What sparked your interest? The answers to these questions can be compelling, and they can be an indication of your dedication and commitment to the career.

Past Employment

Present and past employment is very often discussed in screening interviews. Be able to describe the positions that you have held and what duties you performed. What did you learn from each position? Did you learn any skills, or did you learn something about a work ethic?

You might be asked why you left a particular position. *Never* talk in a negative way about a former employer or position. Maybe the job was temporary, or you didn't plan to be there for the long term. Maybe the position was not challenging enough for you or the company didn't offer the opportunities that you were looking for. There is no reason to "trash" a former employer: Doing so can communicate a characteristic in you that is undesirable to a new employer. So even if you wanted to push your former boss out of a window, take the professional high road and let go of the anger!

These are just a few examples of typical questions and answers. Go through the list of questions in this chapter and critically consider how you would answer each one. Check with friends, teachers, and mentors about other questions that might be asked in this kind of interview. Think about how you can answer the question honestly and in a way that truly describes you and what you think you can contribute to an employer.

The Equal Employment Opportunity Commission (EEOC) Basic Rules Preventing Discrimination in the Workplace

Age

http://www.eeoc.gov/laws/statutes/adea.cfm

The Age Discrimination in Employment Act of 1967 (ADEA) protects individuals who are 40 years of age or older from employment discrimination based on age. These protections apply to both employees and job applicants. It is unlawful to discriminate against a person because of his/her age with respect to any term, condition, or privilege of employment, including hiring, firing, promotion, layoff, compensation, benefits, job assignments, and training.

Gender

http://www.eeoc.gov/laws/statutes/epa.cfm

The Equal Pay Act requires that men and women be given equal pay for equal work in the same establishment. The jobs need not be identical, but they must be substantially equal. Employers may not pay unequal wages to men and women who perform jobs that require substantially equal skill, effort, and responsibility, and that are performed under similar working conditions within the same establishment.

Disability

http://www.eeoc.gov/laws/statutes/ada.cfm

The Americans with Disabilities Act of 1990 prohibits private employers, state and local governments, employment agencies and labor unions from discriminating against qualified individuals with disabilities in job application procedures, hiring, firing, advancement, compensation, job training, and other terms, conditions, and privileges of employment. An individual with a disability is a person who:

○ Has a physical or mental impairment that substantially limits one or more major life activities;

○ Has a record of such an impairment; or

○ Is regarded as having such an impairment.

National Origin

http://www.eeoc.gov/laws/types/nationalorigin.cfm

Whether an employee or job applicant's ancestry is Mexican, Ukrainian, Filipino, Arab, American Indian, or any other nationality, he or she is entitled to the same employment opportunities as anyone else.

Pregnancy

http://www.eeoc.gov/laws/types/pregnancy.cfm

An employer cannot refuse to hire a pregnant woman because of her pregnancy, because of a pregnancy-related condition, or because of the prejudices of co-workers, clients, or customers.

Race

http://www.eeoc.gov/laws/types/race_color.cfm

The Civil Rights Act of 1964 protects individuals against employment discrimination on the bases of race and color, as well as national origin, sex, and religion.

Equal employment opportunity cannot be denied any person because of his/her racial group or perceived racial group, his/her race-linked characteristics (e.g., hair texture, color, facial features), or because of his/her marriage to or association with someone of a particular race or color. The law also prohibits employment decisions based on stereotypes and assumptions about abilities, traits, or the performance of individuals of certain racial groups.

Religion

http://www.eeoc.gov/laws/types/religion.cfm

Employers may not treat employees or applicants more or less favorably because of their religious beliefs or practices—except to the extent a religious accommodation is warranted. For example, an employer may not refuse to hire individuals of a certain religion, may not impose stricter promotion requirements for persons of a certain religion, and may not impose more or different work requirements on an employee because of that employee's religious beliefs or practices.

EEOC Considerations

The United States has federal and state laws designed to prevent discrimination in the workplace and in hiring practices. A worker or recruit cannot be discriminated against on the basis of age, sex, race, national origin, marital status, pregnancy, or religious beliefs. These laws apply to procedures used by companies for interviewing and hiring new employees.

This means that, when considering a potential new employee, a company can't consider these characteristics when making hiring decisions. As a result, they are not permitted to ask questions during the interview process about any of those topics. These are regarded as "inappropriate" or even "illegal" questions. If you are asked such a question, you do not have to respond to it. Topics covered and questions asked in employment interviews should be focused only on *job-related* issues. Please see the following box for a brief description of each characteristic and a link to the EEOC Web site for your further research.

Most companies have strict policies related to asking only appropriate questions during interviews, and the interviewers in those companies are normally well trained. It is unlikely that they will ask you an inappropriate question. These companies usually have guidelines on what to do if you think you have been asked an inappropriate question. So if you think such a question was asked in an interview, a good first step is to contact the company's human resources department. If that contact is not satisfying, you should contact the Equal Employment Opportunity Commission (EEOC).

The simple fact that an interviewer asks you an illegal question like those in the box is not a clear indicator that the company is trying to discriminate against you or that it has some hidden agenda in the interview. Very often, when we get engaged and "taken up" in a conversation, we just follow the topics and we let our interest and curiosity dictate the direction. The bad news is that sometimes this curiosity or interest can take the conversation into illegal or inappropriate territory. The inappropriate question *could* be just an honest mistake. However, the interviewer could be trying to obtain information that would violate the Equal Employment Opportunity Commission guidelines against discrimination.

Regardless of the intention of the interviewer, *you* have to be attentive to the kinds of questions you are being asked. Listen carefully to each question you are asked. If you suspect that a question is not appropriate, don't

Inappropriate Questions in Employment Interviews

Take a look at these examples of questions that are inappropriate for an employment interview. Please note that this is not a complete list of all possible forms of discrimination. Some appropriate alternatives are provided.

Issue: Age
Inappropriate question: How old are you?
Inappropriate question: What is your date of birth?
Inappropriate question: What year did you graduate from high school?
Appropriate question: Are you over the age of 18?

Issue: Marital Status
Inappropriate question: Do you have children to care for?
Inappropriate question: Do you have children?
Inappropriate question: Will you need child care services while you work?
Inappropriate question: Does your husband/wife approve of your travel for business?
Appropriate question: Will you be able to travel for business?

Issue: National Origin
Inappropriate question: Where were you born?
Inappropriate question: Where were your parents born?
Inappropriate question: Do you speak English with your family at home?
Inappropriate question: Is your last name Korean?

Issue: Disabilities
Inappropriate question: Do you have any disabilities?
Inappropriate question: Please respond to the following medical questions.
Appropriate question: Are you able to perform all the functions required of this position?

Issue: Religion
Inappropriate question: Are you Catholic?
Inappropriate question: Do you go to church?

get excited. Plan your response. Your reply to the question does not have to be hostile, and you *do* not have to "hit the interviewer on the head" with the law. However, you do have to call it to the interviewer's attention. You could casually ask, "Why do you want to know that?" Or you could ask how the information requested applies to the requirements of the position you are seeking. There might be a good explanation! If you are satisfied with the explanation, then answer the question. If you are not satisfied with the explanation, politely let the interviewer know, and tell him or her that you are not comfortable with responding to a question that you believe is inappropriate. Let us repeat: It's important to be polite and professional at all times!

It's important to be professional because you (as the interviewee) are walking a thin line in this situation. You certainly have the right, under the law, to refuse to answer a question that is inappropriate. However, what if it does happen to be an honest mistake made by the interviewer, or is a case of your misinterpreting the question? If you immediately get excited, become openly hostile, and threaten legal action, you have only made a bad situation much worse. If you did misinterpret something that was, in fact, an appropriate question, your chances of actually getting the job are pretty small. Few companies will hire somebody that they know has a short fuse. No matter what happens, be determined to remain professional at all times.

Many companies are so concerned about this issue that the company interviewers operate from a script. The script isn't just a list of topics to be covered in an interview, but many contain the exact wording of each question. The questions are carefully scripted to obtain the necessary information for making a hiring decision without violating the spirit or letter of the anti-discrimination laws. The resulting interviews are frequently lacking in spontaneity, but it helps all involved avoid making costly errors. It also helps prevent placing the interviewee in an awkward situation.

You and the interviewer should keep in mind at all times that the main goal of any selection interview is to determine your capability to perform the responsibilities of the position. You share in the responsibility to uphold this goal, so be prepared, be attentive, and be professional.

How to Dress for an Interview

We can't conclude a section on employment interviewing without mentioning **appropriate interview attire**. Even though you worked very hard to prepare for an important job interview, you will still find yourself at a significant disadvantage if you allow your appearance to speak for you. If you are remembered by a potential employer because of your *appearance*, it's very likely because it didn't work!

Image © mitchailings 2013. Used under license from Shutterstock, Inc.

The best advice we have heard on how to dress for professional occasions came from an attorney. When asked about appropriate attire for a courtroom visit, the attorney said, "Dress in such a way as to show respect for the court." An employment interview is not the same thing as visiting a courtroom, but the core of the advice is still relevant. *You should dress in such a way as to show respect for the situation, the company you would like to work for, and the interviewer.*

This means that an employment interview is not the place to make your fashion statement. Stick to a conservative look. For this event, you should focus on simple, clean, and tasteful. Remember that anything you do to distract the interviewer takes away from the message you are trying to deliver. So if you have inappropriate clothes, lots of perfume, body piercings and tattoos, excessive jewelry, or if you smell bad from smoking or lack of personal hygiene, there will be distraction. All the preparation that you do for this interview could be negated if you allow your appearance to take center stage.

Always dress in a professional business attire.

We are not going to try to give specific advice on how men and women should dress for this occasion. There is plenty of expert and specific advice available on how to dress for an interview. Consult your school's career center, look at some of the self-help books like *Dress for Success*.[21]

Summary

This chapter looked at the practical application of two kinds of communication situations: Information Gathering interviews and Employment interviews. While there are many different kinds of interviews, these two are widely used and considered to be the most useful for students taking this kind of college course. However, no matter what kind of interview you participate in, you must play an *active* role. You can't be a passive participant and expect to accomplish your goals for the interview.

The Information Gathering interview invites you to take the part of the interviewer where your primary task is to ask the questions. In that role, you should focus on goal setting, planning the interview, asking good and clear questions, and efficiently recording the information that you gather. A significant challenge in this type of interview is maintaining your focus and keeping yourself in the "here and now" of the interview situation. It is very easy to get distracted and to let your mind wander when the interviewee is answering your questions. The Employment interview, on the other hand, allows you to take the role of the interviewee and answer the questions. In the responding role, you should focus on getting to know yourself (i.e., your history, strengths, weaknesses, short-term goals, and long-term goals).

Endnotes

1. L. Hugenberg, S. Wallace, D. Yoder, and C. Horvath, *Creating Competent Communication*, 4th ed. (Dubuque, IA: Kendall/Hunt, 2005).

2. K. Kacmar, and W. Hochwater, "The Interview as a Communication Event: A Field Examination of Demographic Effects on Interview Outcomes," *Journal of Business Communication* 32 (1995); 207–232; and S. Ralston and R. Brady, "The Relative Influence of Interview Communication Satisfaction on Applicants' Recruitment Interview Decisions," *Journal of Business Communication* 31 (1994); 61–77.

3. G. B. Willis, *Cognitive Interviewing: A Tool for Improving Questionnaire Design* (Thousand Oaks, CA: Sage, 2005).

4. R. Anderson and G. Killenberg, *Interviewing: Speaking, Listening, and Learning for Professional Life* (Mountain View, CA: Mayfield, 1999). Also C. Stewart and W. Cash, *Interviewing: Principles and Practices* (New York: McGraw-Hill, 2003).

5. Stewart and Cash.

6. G. R. Miller, "The Current Status of Theory and Research in Interpersonal Communication," *Human Communication Research,* 4 (1978); 164–178.

7. G. R. Miller and M. Steinberg, "Between People," Palo Alto, CA: SRA (1975).

8. J. Gibb, "Defensive Communication," *Journal of Communication,* 1 (1961), 141–148.

9. "An ILA definition of listening," ILA *Listening Post,* 53 (1) (1995).

10. C. Kelly, "Empathic Listening," in R. S. Cathcart and L. A. Samovar (eds.), *Small Group Communication: A Reader* (Dubuque, IA: Wm. C. Brown, 1970). Also R. Nichols and L. Stevens, *Listening to People* (New York: McGraw-Hill, 1957).

11. Nichols and Stevens. Also L. Steil, L. Barker, and K. Watson, *Effective Listening: Key to Your Success* (Reading, MA: Addison-Wesley, 1983).

12. Nichols and Stevens.

13. A. Sillars, J. Weisberg, C. Burggraf, and P. Zeitlow, "Communication and Understanding Revisited: Married Couples' Understanding and Recall of Conversations," *Communication Research* 17 (1990): 500–522.

14. R. Berko, "Test Your Knowledge Here," *Spectra* 10 (1995): 9–12.

15. L. Hugenberg, D. Yoder, S. Wallace, C. Horvath, *Creating Competent Communication,* 4th ed. (Dubuque, IA: Kendall/Hunt, 2005).

16. D. Sellnow, *Public Speaking: A Process Approach* (Belmont, CA: Wadsworth, 2006).

17. F. Wolff, N. Marsnik, W. Tacey, and R. Nichols, *Perceptive Listening* (New York: Holt, Rinehart & Winston, 1983).

18. L. Hugenberg, D. Yoder, S. Wallace, C. Horvath, *Creating Competent Communication,* 4th ed. (Dubuque, IA: Kendall/Hunt, 2005).

19. S. Wallace, D. Yoder, L. Hugenberg, C. Horvath, *Creating Competent Communication: Interviewing.* (Dubuque, IA: Kendall/Hunt, 2006).

20. F. Abel, "Note Takers vs. Non-note Takers: Who Makes More Errors?" *Journalism Quarterly* 46 (1969): 811–814.

21. J. Molloy, *John T. Molloy's New Dress for Success* (New York: Warner Books, 1988).

Chapter

12

© Kurdzuk, Tony/Star Ledger/Corbis

"He who wants to persuade should put his trust not in the right argument, but in the right word. The power of sound has always been greater than the power of sense."

Joseph Conrad

Chapter 12: Persuasive Speaking

Persuasion is intended to influence choice through appeals to your audience's sense of ethics, reasoning, and emotion. This chapter explores the goals of persuasive speaking and discusses elements, reasoning, appeals, and arguments as well as the ethics of persuasive messages.

Student Learning Objectives:

○ Students will be able to describe how to analyze the audience in persuasive speaking
○ Students will be able to explain how to build the elements of persuasion
○ Students will be able to identify and explain the goals, aims, and claims of a persuasive speech
○ Students will be able to explain types of persuasive claims
○ Students will be able to explain how to organize persuasive speeches
○ Students will be able to explain the ethics of persuasive speaking

PERSUASIVE SPEAKING

You cannot escape attempts at persuasion. Either you are the one trying to convince someone of something, or you are the target of the persuasive act. Without consciously thinking about it, much of your communication is persuasive. Through persuasion, you try to make your life better by influencing those around you. On an *interpersonal level,* you attempt to:

○ Convince your friend to go to dinner with you; thus enjoying time with a friend.

○ Persuade someone to share an apartment with you; thus giving you companionship and saving you money on rent.

On a *professional level,* persuasion can enhance your life. Perhaps you try to:

○ Persuade your supervisor to recommend you for promotion; thus giving you money and/or, perhaps, prestige.

○ Convince your employer to fund your trip to a conference; thus allowing you to make professional contacts and gain more knowledge of your profession.

On the *societal level,* persuasion is used to get people to change attitudes or change behaviors so society can improve. Perhaps you to try to:

○ Convince your legislator to vote in favor of a health bill that will reduce health care costs for all citizens.

○ Persuade your local city council to enact curbside recycling so less household waste goes to the local landfill.

Many times throughout the day, we try to convince people to agree with us about small things ("Xbox is better than Wii") and significant things ("We shouldn't have children"). The reverse is also true. Through emails, IMs, advertisements, commercials, infomercials, and conversations, others attempt to influence you. Persuasion permeates your life, all day, every day. The ability to influence is the cornerstone of our democratic republic.

Learning the tools of persuasion helps you become a stronger advocate for what matters in your life. Everything from your daily interactions and friendships to your career advancements is linked to your persuasive abilities. Those who study persuasion gain a competitive edge.

The Audience in Persuasive Speaking

Imagine the following situations:

○ You speak before your church's congregation, to persuade them to vote to withdraw from your church's national organization because of the church's stance on gay clergy.

○ You talk to a student group on campus about the benefits of spending a semester with the Disney College Program in Orlando, Florida.

○ You speak before your city council, urging them to implement a curbside recycling program.

○ You speak before a group of parents of the high school musical cast to get them to volunteer to help make tickets, sell tickets, sell concessions, monitor students during rehearsal, work on the set, work backstage, sell advertisements, work with costume rental, and design and sell T-shirts.

Your success or failure to get your audience to act in the situations above is determined by a number of factors. Knowing who your listeners are is important, as we discussed in an earlier chapter. But, in a persuasive speech, knowing *the attitude of your audience* is crucial, and trying to *determine the needs* of the audience is important to your success.

In general, we can classify audience attitudes into three categories: (1) they agree, (2) they don't agree, (3) they are undecided. When you are clear on which category your audience rests in, you will be able to craft a more targeted, effective message. Here is a closer examination of each category.

The supportive audience, the audience that agrees with you, poses the least difficulty. This type of audience is friendly; its members like you, and they are interested in hearing what you have to say. Your main objective is to reinforce what they already accept. You want to strengthen their resolve or use it to encourage behavioral change. You also want to keep them enthused about your point of view or action plan. A candidate for state's attorney who has invited a group of friends and colleagues to an ice cream social will use that time to restate his/her strengths and urge attendees to help him/her with the campaign.

The audience that agrees with you will welcome *new* information, but does not need a re-hashing of information already known and accepted. The speaker should work to strengthen the audience's resistance to counter-persuasion. For example, the candidate for state's attorney who is running

Glossary

Supportive audience An audience that agrees with you.

Glossary

Opposed audience This audience does not agree with you, is not friendly or sympathetic, and will search for flaws in your argument.

Uncommitted audience An audience that is neither friendly nor hostile, but most like not sympathetic.

How do you get the members of an indifferent audience to care about your topic?

against an incumbent can talk about how change is necessary, and how his/her experience or background will bring a fresh perspective to the office.

With the opposed audience, the speaker runs the risk of having members in the audience who may be hostile. This audience does not agree with you, it is not friendly or sympathetic, and most likely, will search for flaws in your argument. Your objective in this case is to get a fair hearing. A persuasive speaker facing a group that does not agree with him/her needs to set reasonable goals. Also, developing arguments carefully by using fair and respected evidence may help persuade an audience that disagrees with you.

One thing to consider when facing an audience opposed to you is the nature of their opposition. Is it to you? Your cause? A specific statement you made or information made available to them? If you can determine why they are opposed, your effort can be spent on addressing the nature of the opposition.

Seeking common ground is a good strategy when people do not agree with you. Find a place where you and your audience can stand without disagreeing. For example, hospital employees who smoke may not be willing to quit, but they may recognize the need to have smoking banned on hospital property, so they may still smoke on break if they go off-site.

Acknowledging differences is also a helpful strategy for the opposed audience. Making sure you do not set your attitudes, beliefs, or values to be "right" and the audience's to be "wrong" is essential if any movement toward your point of view is likely. Avoid needless confrontation.

Speaking before an uncommitted audience can be difficult because you don't know whether they are uninformed, indifferent, or are adamantly neutral. This audience is neither friendly nor hostile, but most likely, they are not sympathetic.

The uninformed audience is the easiest to persuade, because they need information. A scholarship committee trying to determine which of the five candidates will receive $2,000 needs sufficient information about the candidates to make an informed choice.

The indifferent audience member doesn't really care about the issue or topic. These audience members can be found in most "mandatory" meetings held at work, school, and sometimes training. In this case, it is important that the speaker gets the attention of the audience members and gives them a reason to care. Making the message relate to their lives is important, and providing audience members with relevant, persuasive material helps move audience members out of the uncommitted category. However, it may be difficult to sway most or all audience members.

Maslow's Hierarchy of Needs

Knowing the audience's disposition toward you helps you structure a more effective persuasive speech. Speakers should also consider the needs of the audience. The persuader can develop lines of reasoning that relate to pertinent needs. Human needs can be described in terms of logic or what makes sense to a listener, but needs are immersed in emotions of the individual as well.

Psychologist Abraham Maslow (1943) classified human needs according to the hierarchy pictured in **Figure 12.1**. Maslow believed that our most basic needs—those at the foundation of the hierarchy—must be satisfied before we can consider those on the next levels. In effect, these higher-level needs are put on "hold," and have little effect on our actions until the lower-level needs are met. Maslow's hierarchy provides a catalog of targets for emotional appeals, including:

Physiological needs. At the foundation of the hierarchy are our biological needs for food, water, oxygen, procreation, and rest. If you were delivering a speech in favor of a proposed new reservoir to a community experiencing problems with its water supply, it would be appropriate to appeal to our very basic need for safe and abundant water, without which, our lives would be in danger.

Safety needs. Safety needs include the need for security, freedom from fear and attack, a home that offers tranquility and comfort, and a means of earning a living. If you are delivering the same speech to a group of unemployed construction workers, you might link the reservoir project to safe, well-paying jobs and a steady family income.

Belongingness and love needs. These needs refer to our drive for affiliation, friendship, and love. When appealing to the need for social belonging, you may choose to emphasize the unity and cohesiveness that will emerge from the community effort to bring the reservoir to completion.

Esteem needs. Esteem needs include the need to be seen as worthy and competent and to have the respect of others. In this case, an effective approach would be to praise community members for their initiative in helping to make the reservoir project a reality.

Self-actualization needs. People who reach the top of the hierarchy seek to fulfill their highest potential through personal growth, creativity, self-awareness and knowledge, social responsibility, and responsiveness to challenge. Addressing this audience, you might emphasize the long-range environmental and ecological implications of the reservoir. Your appeal to your audience's sense of social responsibility would stress the need to safeguard the water supply for future generations.

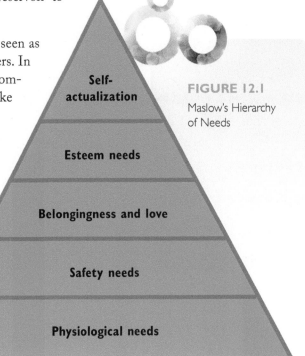

FIGURE 12.1

Maslow's Hierarchy of Needs

Maslow's Hierarchy of Needs can guide you in preparing a persuasive speech. Think about the needs of your audience and how you can reach them. Understanding the basis for Maslow's hierarchy is helpful when developing a persuasive speech, for if you approach your listeners at an inappropriate level of need, you will find them unable or unwilling to respond.

Elements of Persuasion

We define persuasion as attempting to influence others through communication. Critical building blocks of persuasion have been studied by generations of rhetorical scholars, starting with Aristotle. Persuasion is intended to influence choice through what Aristotle termed *ethos*, *pathos*, and *logos*. More recent scholarly work has provided the addition of *mythos*. These four elements provide the underpinnings of our modern study of persuasion. (For more on Aristotle, see **BTW: Aristotle**.)

To illustrate these, let's consider the speech given days after the deadly earthquake, tsunami, and nuclear disaster struck Japan. Here is how Emperor Akihito addressed a stunned nation on March 16, 2011:

> The 9.0 earthquake that struck the Tohoku-Pacific region was an extraordinarily large earthquake. I have been deeply hurt by the miserable situation in the affected areas. The number of deaths from earthquakes and tsunamis has increased day by day, and we do not know yet how many victims we will

BTW!

Aristotle

Aristotle (384–322 BCE), a Greek philosopher, made contributions to many fields, including logic, mathematics, physics, biology, politics, medicine, and theatre. He was a student of Plato, who, in turn, studied under Socrates. Following are a few quotes that illustrate Aristotle's philosophy.

"Knowing yourself is the beginning of all wisdom."

"Happiness depends upon ourselves."

"Hope is a waking dream."

"Wishing to be friends is quick work, but friendship is a slow ripening fruit."

"The educated differ from the uneducated as much as the living differ from the dead."

"Educating the mind without educating the heart is no education at all."

"To avoid criticism say nothing, do nothing, be nothing."

"No great mind has ever existed without a touch of madness."

(www.goodreads.com/author/quotes)

eventually have. I pray for the survival of as many people as possible.

I am also deeply concerned about the situation at the nuclear power plant, as no one can predict what will happen next. It is my deepest hope that, by the effort of people concerned, the current situation can be prevented from becoming any worse.

Currently, a nationwide rescue operation is taking place … (www.americanrhetoric.com)

Emperor Akihito relied heavily on ethos in his speech, as we will see later with other excerpts.

Ethos and the Power of the Speaker's Credibility

As speaker, you must decide not only what to tell your audience, but also what you should avoid saying. In a persuasive speech, you ask listeners to think or act in ways needed to achieve a desired response. Aristotle believed that **ethos**, which refers to speaker credibility, makes speakers worthy of belief. Audiences trust speakers they perceive as honest. Ethics provide standards for conduct that guide us. Persuasive speaking requires asking others to accept and act on ideas we believe to be accurate and true.

We see the Japanese emperor standing on the firm ground of the credibility of his office. In Japanese culture, the emperor has typically been recognized as both statesman-ruler and messenger from God. When the emperor spoke, everyone listened, due in large part to his inherent credibility. Let's take a closer look at what makes up an impression of ethos or speaker credibility.

Dimensions of Speaker Credibility

What your audience knows about you before you speak and what they learn about your position during your speech may influence your ability to persuade them. Credibility can be measured according to three dimensions: competence, trustworthiness, and dynamism.

Competence. In many cases, your audience will decide your message's value based on perceived speaker competence. Your listeners will first ask themselves whether you have the background to speak. If the topic is crime, an audience is more likely to be persuaded by the Atlanta chief of police than by a postal worker delivering her personal opinions. Second, your audience will consider whether the content of your speech has firm support. When it is clear that speakers have not researched their topic, their ability to persuade diminishes. Finally, audiences will determine whether you communicate confidence and control of your subject matter through your delivery.

In our example above, Emperor Akihito makes clear that he is abreast of all the relevant information. He relays the strength of the earthquake, the results of the tsunami, and the seriousness of the nuclear disaster. Listeners quickly understood that he was well informed in this emergency. His display of competence by demonstrating an understanding of the facts increases his credibility even further.

Trustworthiness. When someone is trying to persuade us to think or act a certain way, trusting that person is important. And although competence is important, research has shown that the trustworthy communicator is more influential than the untrustworthy one, regardless of his/her level of expertise (Pornpitakpan, 2004).

Audience perceptions of trustworthiness are based largely on your perceived respect for them, your ethical standards, and your ability to establish common ground. Audiences gauge a speaker's *respect* for them by analyzing the actions a speaker has taken before the speech. If a group is listening to a political candidate running for office in their community, they will have more respect for someone who has demonstrated concern for their community through past actions.

Trustworthiness is also influenced by the audience's perception of your *ethical standards*. Telling the truth is paramount for the persuasive speaker. If your message is biased and you make little attempt to be fair or to concede the strength of your opponent's point of view, your listeners may question your integrity.

Your credibility and your ability to persuade increase if you convince your audience that you share "common ground." In the popular movie *300*, Queen Gorgo addresses a reluctant Spartan Council, pleading with them to send the Spartan army into battle. Rather than appealing to the council as queen, she is made to appeal to common ground in the opening: "Councilmen, I stand before you today not only as your Queen: I come to you as a mother; I come to you as a wife; I come to you as a Spartan woman; I come to you with great humility" (www.americanrhetoric.com).

While few can identify with being a queen, most feel a sense of identification with a humble mother, wife, woman, or citizen. With this common ground appeal in place, the stage is set for the queen to persuade the council to side with her. In this instance, Queen Gorgo establishes common ground by identifying with her audience and provoking them to identify with her.

Dynamism. Your credibility and, therefore, your ability to persuade are influenced by the audience's perception of you as a dynamic spokesperson. Dynamic speakers tend to be vibrant, confident, vigorous, attractive, and skilled in public speaking. Your listeners will make critical decisions about how dynamic you are as they form a first impression. This impression will be reinforced or altered as they listen for an energetic style that communicates commitment to your point of view, and for ideas that build on one another in a convincing, logical way. While charisma plays a part in being dynamic, it is not enough. Dynamic public speakers tend to be well-practiced presenters.

Does credibility make a difference in your ability to persuade? Pornitakpan (2004), who examined five decades of research on the persuasiveness of speaker credibility, found that "a high-credibility source is more persuasive than is a low-credibility source in both changing attitudes and gaining behavioral compliance" (p. 266). Lifelong learning in the art of persuasion involves building and enhancing your speaker competence, trustworthiness, and dynamism.

Pathos and the Power of Emotion

Aristotle argued that **pathos**, which is the "consideration of the emotions of people in the audience" is an integral part of persuasion (Kennedy, 2007, p. 15). Aristotle explained:

> The emotions are those things through which, by undergoing change, people come to differ in their judgments and which are accompanied by pain and pleasure, for example, anger, pity, fear, and other such things and their opposites" (Aristotle, 2007).

Emperor Akihito makes use of emotion in his message. Although stoic by American standards, he acknowledges the suffering of victims:

> [U]nder the severe cold weather, many evacuees have been placed in an unavoidable situation where they are subject to extreme suffering due to the lack of food, drinking water, fuel, and so on. I truly hope that, by making the greatest effort possible to rescue the victims promptly, we can improve their lives as much as possible" (www.americanrhetoric.com).

Akihito's reference to extreme suffering adds an emotional appeal to support the need for continued rescue efforts.

Emotional appeals have the power to elicit happiness, joy, pride, patriotism, fear, hate, anger, guilt, despair, hope, hopelessness, bitterness, and other feelings. Some subjects are more emotionally powerful than others and lend themselves to emotional appeals. Look at the list of topics that follow:

- The homeless
- Abused children
- Cruelty to animals
- Death penalty
- Sex education in school
- Teaching evolution in school
- Gun control
- Terrorist attacks

Many of these topics cause listeners to have emotional responses. Emotional appeals are often the most persuasive type of appeal because they provide the motivation listeners need to change their minds or take action. For example,

Glossary

Pathos Persuading through emotional appeals.

instead of simply listing the reasons high fat foods are unhealthy, a more effective approach is to tie these foods to frightening consequences:

> Jim thought nothing could ever happen to him. He was healthy as an ox—or so he thought. His world fell apart one sunny May morning when he suffered a massive heart attack. He survived, but his doctors told him that his coronary arteries were blocked and that he needed bypass surgery. "Why me?" he asked. "I'm only 42 years old." The answer, he was told, had a lot to do with the high-fat diet he had eaten since childhood.

This illustration appeals to the listener's emotional state, and is ultimately more persuasive than a list of facts.

We must not forget that emotional appeals are powerful, and as such, can be tools of manipulation in the hands of unscrupulous speakers who attempt to arouse audiences through emotion rather than logic. For example, in an effort to lose weight, individuals may buy pills or exercise equipment that may be useless, or worse, a true health risk. Those selling the products accept the emotional message ("lose weight, look beautiful, gain friends, have a great life").

The speaker has an ethical responsibility when using emotional appeals. The ethically responsible speaker does not distort, delete, or exaggerate information for the sole purpose of emotionally charging an audience to manipulate their feelings for self-centered ends.

Logos and the Power of Logical Appeals and Arguments

Logos, or logical appeals and arguments, refer to the "rational, factual basis that supports the speaker's position" (Walker, 2005, p. 3). For example, if a friend tried to convince you *not* to buy a new car by pointing out that you are in college, have no savings account, and are currently unemployed, that friend would be making a logical argument.

Anatomy of an Argument: Claim, Data, Warrant

Logical, critical thinking increases your ability to *assess, analyze,* and *advocate* ideas. Decades ago, Stephen Toulmin (1958), a British philosopher, developed a model of practical reasoning that consists of three basic elements: claim, data, and warrant. To construct a sound, reasonable argument, you need to use three essential parts:

❶ The **claim** is a statement or contention the audience is urged to accept. The claim answers the question, "So what is your point?

   Example: It's your turn to do the dishes; I did them last time.

   Example: You need to call your sister this week; She called you last week.

Glossary

Logos An appeal that is rational and reasonable based on evidence provided.

Claim A statement or contention the audience is urged to accept.

❷ The **data** are evidence in support of an idea you advocate. Data provide the answer to "So what is your proof?" or "Why?"

Example: It looks like rain. Dark clouds are forming.

Example: When I stop at McDonald's on the road, they seem to have clean bathrooms.

❸ The **warrant** is an inference that links the evidence with the claim. It answers the question, "Why does that data mean your claim is true?"

Example: Augie is running a fever. I bet he has an ear infection.

Example: Sarah will be on time. There isn't any traffic right now.

To put the three elements of an argument together, let's consider another example. At a restaurant, you take a bite of a steak sandwich and say, "This is the worst sandwich I have ever tried." With this announcement you are making a *claim* that you *infer* from tasting the meat.

The evidence (*data*) is the food before you. The *warrant* is the link between data and claim is the inference, which may be an *unstated belief* that the food is spoiled, old, or poorly prepared, and will taste bad.

When you reason with your audience it is important to craft claims, warrants, and data your audience will understand and accept. Sound reasoning is especially important when your audience is skeptical. Faced with the task of trying to convince people to change their minds or do something they might not otherwise be inclined to do, your arguments must be impressive.

We persuade others that a claim or conclusion is highly probable by **inductive** and **deductive reasoning**. Strong evidence shows that you have carefully analyzed the support of your points. Only when strong probability is established can you ask your listeners to make *the inductive leap* from specific cases to a general conclusion, or to take the *deductive* move from statements as premises to a conclusion you want them to accept. We now look more closely at inductive and deductive reasoning.

Inductive Reasoning

Through inductive reasoning, we generalize from specific examples to draw conclusions from what we observe. Inductive reasoning moves us from the specific to the general in an orderly, logical fashion. The inference step in the argument holds that what is true of specific cases can be generalized to other cases of the same class, or of the class as a whole. Suppose you are trying to persuade your audience that the decline of downtown merchants in your town is a problem that can be solved with an effective plan you are about to present. You may infer that what has worked to solve a similar problem in a number of similar towns is likely to work in this case as well.

One problem with inductive reasoning is that individual cases do not always add up to a correct conclusion. Sometimes a speaker's list of examples is too small, leading to an incorrect conclusion based on limited information. With inductive reasoning, you can never be sure that your conclusions

Glossary

Data Evidence in support of an idea you advocate.

Warrant An inference that links the evidence with the claim.

Inductive reasoning Generalizing from specific examples and drawing conclusions from what we observe.

Deductive reasoning Drawing conclusions based on the connections between statements that serve as premises.

are absolutely accurate. Because you are only looking at a sample of all the possible cases, you must persuade your audience to accept a conclusion that is probable, or maybe even just possible. The three most common strategies for inductive reasoning involve analogy, cause, and sign.

Reasoning by Analogy

Analogies establish common links between similar and not-so-similar concepts. They are effective tools of persuasion when your audience is convinced that the characteristics of one case are similar enough to the characteristics of the second case that your argument about the first also applies to the second.

As noted in the chapter on language, a *figurative analogy* draws a comparison between things that are distinctly different, such as "Eating fresh marshmallows is like floating on a cloud." Figurative analogies can be used to persuade, but they must be supported with relevant facts, statistics, and testimony that link the dissimilar concepts you are comparing.

Whereas a figurative analogy compares things that are distinctly different and supplies useful illustrations, a *literal analogy* compares things with similar characteristics and, therefore, requires less explanatory support. One speaker compared the addictive power of tobacco products, especially cigarettes, with the power of alcoholic beverages consumed on a regular basis. His line of reasoning was that both are consumed for pleasure, relaxation, and often as relief for stress. While his use of logical argument was obvious, the listener ultimately assesses whether or not these two things—alcohol and tobacco are sufficiently similar.

The distinction between literal and figurative analogies is important because only literal analogies are sufficient to establish logical proof. Your analogy should meet the following characteristics:

○ There are significant points of similarity.

○ Similarities are tied to critical points of the comparison.

○ Differences need to be relatively small.

○ You have a better chance of convincing people if you can point to other successful cases (Freely, 1993, pp. 119–120).

Reasoning from Cause

When you reason from cause, you infer that an event of one kind contributes to or brings about an event of another kind. The presence of a cat in a room when you are allergic to cats is likely to bring about a series of sneezes until the cat is removed. As the following example demonstrates, causal reasoning focuses on the cause-and-effect relationship between ideas.

Cause: An inaccurate and low census count of the homeless in Detroit

Effect: Fewer federal dollars will be sent to Detroit to aid the homeless

An advocate for the homeless delivered the following message to a group of supporters:

> We all know that money is allocated by the federal government, in part, according to the numbers of people in need. The census, conducted every 10 years, is supposed to tell us how many farmers we have, how many urban dwellers, and how many homeless.
>
> Unfortunately, in the 2010 census, many of the homeless were not counted in Detroit. The government told us census takers would go into the streets, into bus and train station waiting rooms, and into the shelters to count every homeless person. As advocates for the homeless, people in my organization know this was not done. Shelters were never visited. Hundreds and maybe thousands of homeless were ignored in this city alone. A serious undercount is inevitable. This undercount will cause fewer federal dollars to be spent aiding those who need our help the most.

When used correctly, causal reasoning can be an effective persuasive tool. You must be sure that the cause-and-effect relationship is sound enough to stand up to scrutiny and criticism. To be valid, your reasoning should exhibit the following characteristics:

- The cause and effect you describe should be connected.
- The cause should be acting alone.
- The effect should not be the effect of another cause.
- The claim and evidence must be accurate (Sprague & Stuart, 1988, pp. 165–166).

To be effective, causal reasoning should never overstate. By using phrases like "This is one of several causes" or "The evidence suggests there is a cause-and-effect link," you are giving your audience a reasonable picture of a complex situation. More often than not, researchers indicate that cause-and-effect relationships are not always clear, and links may not be as simple as they seem.

Reasoning from Sign

With the argument from sign, the inference step is that the presence of an attribute can be taken as the presence of some larger condition or situation of which the attribute is a part. As you step outside in the early morning to begin jogging, the gray clouds and moist air can be interpreted as signs that the weather conditions are likely to result in a rainy day.

Argumentation professor David Vancil (1993) tells us that "arguments from sign are based on our understanding of the way things are associated or related to each other in the world with them, [so] we conclude that the thing is present if its signs are present. The claim of a sign argument is invariably a statement that something is or is not the case" (p. 149).

The public speaker who reasons from sign must do so with caution. Certainly there are signs all around us to interpret in making sense of the world, but signs are easy to misinterpret. For example, saying, "Where there's fire, there's smoke" is a strong sign relationship, but saying, "Where there's smoke, there's fire," is not so strong. Therefore, the responsible speaker must carefully test an argument before using it to persuade an audience.

Deductive Reasoning

Through deductive reasoning, we draw conclusions based on the connections between statements that serve as premises. Rather than introducing new facts, deductions enable us to rearrange the facts we already know, putting them in a form that will make our point. Deductive reasoning is the basis of police work and scientific research, enabling investigators to draw relationships between seemingly unrelated pieces of information.

At the heart of deductive reasoning is the *syllogism*, a pattern of reasoning involving a major premise, a minor premise, and a conclusion. When deductive reasoning is explicitly stated as a complete syllogism, it leads us down an inescapable logical path. The interrelationships in a syllogism can be established in a series of deductive steps:

❶ **Step 1:** Define the relationship between two terms.

Major premise: Plagiarism is a form of ethical abuse.

❷ **Step 2:** Define a condition or special characteristic of one of the terms.

Minor premise: Plagiarism involves using the words of another without quotations or footnotes as well as improper footnoting.

❸ **Step 3:** Show how a conclusion about the other term necessarily follows (Sprague & Stuart, 1988, p. 160).

Conclusion: Students who use the words of another, but fail to use quotations or footnotes to indicate this or who intentionally use incorrect footnotes are guilty of an ethical abuse.

Your ability to convince your listeners depends on their acceptance of your original premises and the conclusion you draw from them. The burden of proof rests with your evidence. You must convince listeners through the strength of your supporting material to accept your premises and, by extension, your conclusion.

Sound and reasonable statements that employ inductive and deductive reasoning are the foundation for effective persuasion. More recently, scholars have recognized the story or narrative as a powerful persuasive appeal they call *mythos*.

Mythos and the Power of Narratives

Humans are storytellers by nature. Long before the written word people used narratives to capture, preserve, and pass on their cultural identity. Within the last several decades, scholars have begun to recognize the power of stories, folklore, anecdotes, legends, and myths to persuade (Osborn, 1990). **Mythos** is the term given when content supports a claim by reminding an audience how the claim is consistent with cultural identity.

The strength of the mythos depends on how accurately it ties into preexisting attitudes, values, histories, norms, and behaviors for a cultural, national, familial, or other collective. For example, when you were a child, you may have been told stories of the boy who cried wolf. Every culture has similar myths and stories that define what is unique and important to that culture. In the case of the boy who cried wolf, the cultural value is honesty and the intent is to teach children that bad things happen when we lie.

When speakers use mythos effectively, they create common ground with their listeners. If you were addressing an American audience and chided them to not listen to "that little boy who cries wolf" when refuting claims of an impending economic crises, your audience will likely be receptive to your position because of the common ground you invoked through their understanding of the myth.

Mythos may not work as well when the argument is inconsistent with other, stronger cultural myths, however. So, if you offered the same retort of the boy crying wolf in response to allegations that you have engaged in illegal, illicit activities, including collusion, embezzlement, and racketeering, the audience will be less likely to agree with your claim of innocence. They are more likely instead to reject the comparison you are drawing to the myth of the boy crying wolf, and instead decide "sometimes cries are warranted, you crook."

Recall the example of Japan's emperor addressing his people following their calamity. Notice how mythos is employed in the following statement that ties the perceived virtues of a disciplined, collectivist orientation to the need for order and calm solidarity:

> I have been informed that there are many people abroad discussing how calm the Japanese have remained—helping one another, and showing disciplined conduct, even though they are in deep grief. I hope from the bottom of my heart that we can continue getting together and helping and being considerate of one another to overcome this unfortunate time.

The extent to which Emperor Akihito's audience embraces these collectivist ideals reflects a cultural value that becomes a reason for pride in their actions that are consistent with these values.

Aristotle offers the advice of employing all available means when crafting persuasive messages. Availing yourself of ethos, pathos, logos, and mythos brings a balanced, well-received message much of the time. Critical thinking is essential for both persuasive speakers and effective listeners if

Glossary

Mythos A term given when content supports a claim by reminding an audience how the claim is consistent with cultural identity. .

strong, reasonable arguments are the goal. Recognizing fallacies is an important aspect of critical thinking and can prevent poor arguments from leading us astray.

Argument Fallacies

Sometimes speakers develop arguments either intentionally or unintentionally that contain faulty logic of some kind. A *fallacy* is traditionally regarded as an argument that seems plausible but turns out on close examination to be misleading (Hample et al., 2009). So whether the speaker intended to misuse evidence or reasoning to complete his/her persuasive goal, the result is that the audience is led to believe something that is not true. Following are six oft-used fallacies. (See **BTW: Logical Fallacies** for more examples.)

Attacking the person. Also known as *ad hominem* ("to the man"), this occurs when a speaker attacks the person rather than the substance of the person's argument. A personal attack is often a cover-up for lack of evidence or solid reasoning. Name calling and labeling are common with this fallacy, and the public is exposed to the ad hominem fallacy regularly through political shenanigans. While fallacies do not meet ethical standards, politicians been elected based on attacks on their opponents rather than refuting stances on issues.

Tina Fey, who won an Emmy award for her spoof of then–vice presidential candidate Sarah Palin, notes that those who dislike her do not identify evidence that she is not funny or original. Instead, she says, "Let's face it,

BTW!

Logical Fallacies

Ryan Weber and Allen Brizee (2011) with the Purdue Online Writing Lab provide additional examples of the fallacies discussed in this chapter as well as the following. For definitions of each of these fallacies, check out www.owl.english.purdue.edu.

Genetic fallacy. The Volkswagen Beetle is an evil car because it was originally designed by Hitler's army.

Begging the claim. Filthy and polluting coal should be banned.

Circular argument. Barack Obama is a good communicator because he speaks effectively.

Either/or argument. We can either stop using cars or destroy the earth.

Ad populum. If you were a true American you would support the rights of people to choose whatever vehicle they want.

Straw man. People who don't support the proposed state minimum wage increase hate the poor.

Moral equivalence. That parking attendant who gave me a ticket is as bad as Hitler.

... there is a certain 50 percent of the population who think we are pinko Commie monsters" (Hirsen, 2011).

Red herring. A **red herring** occurs when a speaker attempts to divert the attention of the audience from the matter at hand. Going off on a tangent, changing the focus of the argument, engaging in personal attacks, or appealing to popular prejudice are all examples of the red herring fallacy.

The red herring fallacy appears regularly in interpersonal communication. A son might be told to "take your shoes off the table," and retort with, "these are boots, not shoes," thus changing the focus of the argument from the issue to the object. In a public speaking environment, red herrings are relatively common. For example, suppose an audience member asks a candidate at a political debate the following: "Do you realize your proposal to bring in a new megastore will result in the loss of livelihood for owners of smaller businesses in town who are active, contributing members to this community? A red herring response might be: "I think everyone likes to shop for bargains!"

Hasty generalization. A **hasty generalization** is a fallacy based on quantity of data. A faulty argument occurs because the sample chosen is too small or is in some way not representative. Therefore, any conclusion based on this information is flawed. Stereotypes about people are common examples of this fallacy. Imagine getting a B on a test, and asking the students on your right and left what grade they received. Finding out they also received a B on the test, you tell your roommates that "everybody received a B on the test."

Suppose you're in a public speaking class that you think is easy. You talk to two friends who share your view. You conclude this class is easy. The problem is, many people find public speaking time-consuming and difficult. Also, it is possible that various public speaking teachers differ in their expectations for students as well as in their grading standards.

False cause. A **false cause** is also known as *post hoc ergo propter hoc* ("after this, therefore, because of this"). The speaker using this fallacy points out that because one event happened before another event, the first event caused the second event. For example, a speaker might say that the reason students are doing better on standardized tests is because teachers are helping them cheat. The school district is facing a budget crisis because teachers are greedy. Or the reason college students leave town on the weekend is because there aren't enough restaurants.

One of our author's mothers (we won't say who, Dr. Mason!) once told her sister, "Elvis Presley is the cause of the loose morals that exist today." Although they both agreed and had a lively conversation regarding "the children today," Elvis Presley would have needed super powers to create such an effect (and, of course, the effect is in question, also).

Superstitions are popular examples of false cause. You have bad luck because you broke a mirror. You get in a wreck because your friend said,

Glossary

Red herring Occurs when a speaker attempts to divert the attention of the audience from the matter at hand.

Hasty generalization A fallacy based on quantity of data

False cause When a speaker uses a fallacy to point out that because one event happened before another event, the first event caused the second event.

"Make sure you don't get in a wreck" before you left. A theatre production is not successful because its actors were wished good luck instead of being told "Break a leg." It is important to recognize that an event is seldom the result of a single cause (such as those provided in the above examples).

False analogy. A **false analogy** compares two things that are not really comparable. You may have heard someone say, "You're comparing apples and oranges," or worse, "You're comparing apples to footballs." In the first case, you may be making a faulty comparison because apples and oranges, while both fruits, are different. In the second case, the listener believes you are comparing two things with nothing in common.

For example, you may argue that online dating is like learning to ride a bicycle. If you fall off (or have a bad dating experience), you get up and try again (date some more). However, when you get on a bicycle, you know whether it is a 10-speed or a one-speed, whether it is built for racing or for rough terrain. Your risk is getting physically hurt. In an online dating situation, you may be deceived by that person, you may be hurt psychologically, and if a face-to-face meeting goes badly, the physical risks are different. Overall, the bicycle–online dating analogy is not appropriate.

Some arguments clearly involve the use of a false analogy, but other arguments may rest on the perspectives or values of the listeners. For example, in the argument about abortion, pro-life individuals generally argue that an adult human being and a fetus are similar, and as such, we cannot violate their human rights. Those who do not see an adult human being and a fetus as being similar do not share that perspective. In this case, the strength or weakness of the analogy is based on values held by the individuals involved in the discussion.

Slippery slope. A speaker using this fallacy claims that if we take even one step onto the **slippery slope**, we will end up sliding all the way to the bottom; that we can't stop. In other words, there will be a chain reaction that will end in some dire consequence.

For example, a booster club ran a concession stand near the gymnasium and the auditorium at the local high school. At a meeting, the president tried to convince the group to maintain control of the room by allowing certain booster club members to have keys to the room, even though many school functions took place in the auditorium, and other groups could raise money through the concession stand.

She suggested that if they give keys to the choir director for the musical, then they'll probably have to give a key to the band director, the speech teacher, and to any groups that meet or perform in the auditorium. She argued that their inventory would be stolen, they'd lose money, their equipment would get vandalized, and the popcorn machine might start a fire that could burn down the whole school. In other words, giving a key to the musical director may lead to the school burning down! Speakers use the

Glossary

False analogy Compares two things that are not really comparable.

Slippery slope This fallacy claims there will be a chain reaction that will end in some dire consequence.

slippery slope argument to play on audience's fears, even though the arguments frequently lack specific evidence.

Focusing Persuasive Messages: Goals, Aims, and Claims

Since Aristotle, some researchers have emphasized the outcomes or the results of persuasion. Researcher Herbert Simons (2001) explains: "Persuasion is a form of attempted influence in the sense that it seeks to alter the way others think, feel or act, but it differs from other forms of influence" (p. 7). We are not talking about coercion, bribes, or pressure to conform. Persuasion is accomplished through ethical communication. Careful consideration of the goals of persuasion, the aims of your speech, and the type of proposition you are making helps focus your persuasive message.

Goals of Persuasion

Critical to the success of any persuasive effort is a clear sense of what you are trying to accomplish. As a speaker, you must define for yourself your overall persuasive goal and the narrower persuasive aim. The two overall goals of persuasion are *to address attitudes* and *to move an audience to action*.

Speeches that focus on attitudes. In this type of speech, your goal is to convince an audience to share your views on a topic (e.g., "The tuition at this college is too high" or "Too few Americans bother to vote"). The way you approach your goal depends on the nature of your audience.

When dealing with a negative audience, you face the challenge of trying to change your listeners' opinions. The more change you hope to achieve, the harder your persuasive task. In other words, asking listeners to agree that U.S. automakers need the support of U.S. consumers to survive in the world market is easier than asking the same audience to agree that every American who buys a foreign car should be penalized through a special tax.

By contrast, when you address an audience that shares your point of view, your job is to reinforce existing attitudes (e.g., "U.S. automakers deserve our support"). When your audience has not yet formed an opinion, your message must be geared to presenting persuasive evidence. You may want to explain to your audience, for example, the economic necessity of buying U.S. products.

Speeches that require action. Here your goal is to bring about actual change. You ask your listeners to make a purchase, sign a petition, attend a rally, write to Congress, attend a lecture, and so on. The effectiveness of your message is defined by the actions your audience takes.

Motivating your listeners to act is perhaps the hardest goal you face as a speaker, since it requires attention to the connection between attitudes and behavior. Studies have shown that what people feel is not necessarily what they do. Ahmad may be favorably inclined to purchase a BMW, but still not buy it. Jill may have a negative attitude toward birth control pills, but still use them.

According to Simons (2001), "some people are highly influenced by what other people they value would have them do; others are more self-reliant" (p. 34). Even if you convince your audience that you are the best candidate for student body president, they may not bother to vote. Similarly, even if you persuade them of the dangers of smoking, confirmed smokers will probably continue to smoke. Researchers have found several explanations for this seeming inconsistency.

First, attitude is likely to predict behavior when the attitude involves a specific intention to change behavior, when specific attitudes and behaviors are involved, and when the listener's attitude is influenced by firsthand experience (Zimbardo, 1988, pp. 618–619). Firsthand experience is a powerful motivator. If you know a sun worshipper dying from melanoma, you are more likely to heed the speaker's advice to wear sun block than if you have no such acquaintance. An experiment by Regan and Fazio (1977) proves the point:

> A field study on the Cornell University campus was conducted after a housing shortage had forced some of the incoming freshmen to sleep on cots in the dorm lounges. All freshmen were asked about their attitudes toward the housing crisis and were then given an opportunity to take some related actions (such as signing a petition or joining a committee of dorm residents). While all of the respondents expressed the same attitude about the crisis, those who had had more direct experience with it (were actually sleeping in a lounge) showed a greater consistency between their expressed attitudes and their subsequent behavioral attempts to alleviate the problem (pp. 28–45).

Therefore, if you were a leader on this campus trying to persuade freshmen to sign a petition or join a protest march, you would have had greater persuasive success with listeners who had been forced to sleep in the dorm lounges. Once you establish your overall persuasive goals you must then decide on your persuasive aim.

Persuasive Aims

Determining your persuasive goal is a critical first step. Next, you must define the narrower persuasive aim or the type and direction of the change you seek. Four persuasive aims define the nature of your overall persuasive goal.

Adoption. When you want your audience to start doing something, your persuasive aim is to urge the audience to adopt a particular idea or plan. As a spokesperson for the American Cancer Society, you may deliver the

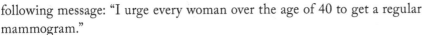

following message: "I urge every woman over the age of 40 to get a regular mammogram."

Continuance. Sometimes your listeners are already doing the thing you want them to do. In this case, your goal is to reinforce this action. For example, the same spokesperson might say:

> I am delighted to be speaking to this organization because of the commitment of every member to stop smoking. I urge all of you to maintain your commitment to be smoke free for the rest of your life.

Speeches that urge continuance are necessary when the group is under pressure to change. In this case, the spokesperson realized that many reformed smokers constantly fight the urge to begin smoking again.

Discontinuance. You attempt to persuade your listeners to stop doing something you disagree with.

> I can tell by looking around that many people in this room spend hours sitting in the sun. I want to share with you a grim fact. The evidence is unmistakable that there is a direct connection between exposure to the sun and the deadliest of all skin cancers—malignant melanoma.

Deterrence. In this case, your goal is avoidance. You want to convince your listeners not to start something, as in the following example:

> We have found that exposure to asbestos can cause cancer 20 or 30 years later. If you have flaking asbestos insulation in your home, don't remove it yourself. Call in experts who have the knowledge and equipment to remove the insulation, protecting themselves as well as you and your family. Be sure you are not going to deal with an unscrupulous contractor who will probably send in unqualified and unprotected workers likely to do a shoddy job.

Speeches that focus on deterrence respond to problems that can be avoided. These messages are delivered when a persuasive speaker determines something is highly threatening or likely to result in disaster. The speaker may try to bring about some sort of effective block or barrier to minimize, if not eliminate, the threat or danger. New homeowners, for example, may find themselves listening to persuasive presentations about the purchase of a home security system. The thrust of such a persuasive speech is the need to prevent burglary through use of an effective and economical security system.

Types of Persuasive Claims

Within the context of these persuasive goals and aims, you must decide the type of persuasive message you want to deliver. Are you dealing with an issue of fact, value, or policy? To decide, look at your thesis statement. In

---

Glossary

Continuance When your listeners are already doing the thing you want them to do.

Discontinuance An attempt to persuade your listeners to stop doing something.

Deterrence Your goal is to convince your listeners not to start something.

persuasive speeches, the thesis statement is phrased as a proposition that must be proved.

For example, if your thesis statement was "All college students should be required to take a one-credit physical education course each year," you would be working with a proposition of policy. If instead, your thesis statement was "Taking a physical education course each year will improve the college experience," this would be a proposition of value.

Propositions are necessary because persuasion always involves more than one point of view. If yours were the only way of thinking, persuasion would be unnecessary. Because your audience is faced with differing opinions, your goal is to present your opinion in the most effective way. The three major types of propositions are those of *fact*, *value*, and *policy*. (Check out **BTW: Arguments of Fact, Value, and Policy** to test your ability to distinguish among them.)

Proposition of fact. A proposition of fact suggests the existence of something. You try to prove or disprove some statement. Because facts, like beauty, are often in the eye of the beholder, you may have to persuade your listeners that your interpretation of a situation, event, or concept is accurate. Like a lawyer in a courtroom, you have to convince people to accept your version of the truth. Here are four examples of facts that would require proof:

❶ Water fluoridation can lead to health problems.

❷ College is not the place for all students.

❸ Hunting is a way to control the deer population.

❹ American corporations are not paying enough in income taxes.

Glossary

Proposition of fact
Persuading your listeners that your interpretation of a situation, event, or concept is accurate.

BTW!

Arguments of Fact, Value, and Policy

1. Picking up groceries from a food bank is wrong if you are not on welfare.

2. Texting while driving causes more accidents than driving while drunk.

3. Cigarette advertisements should be banned from magazines.

4. It is wrong for parents to allow their underage children to drink alcohol at public functions.

5. Universities should not allow credit card companies to hold promotions on campus.

6. Students who work while going to college will have an advantage in the job market over those who don't work.

7. Individuals who are eligible for medical marijuana should be able to purchase it in any state.

8. The higher the speed limit on highways, the greater the number of accidents.

9. It is unacceptable to keep money that you find in public.

Answer key: 1-V; 2-F; 3-P; 4-V; 5-P; 6-F; 7-P; 8-F; 9-V

When dealing with propositions of fact, you must convince your audience that your evaluation is based on widely accepted standards. For example, if you are trying to prove that water fluoridation leads to health problems, you might point to a research article that cites the Environmental Protection Agency (EPA) warning that long-term exposure to excessive fluoridation can lead to joint stiffness, pain, and weak bones. You may also support your proposition by citing another research study that reports that children who are exposed to too much fluoridation may end up having teeth that are pitted and/or permanently stained.

Informative speakers become persuasive speakers when they cross the line from presenting facts to presenting facts within the context of a point of view. The informative speaker lets listeners decide on a position based on their own analysis of the facts. By contrast, the persuasive speaker draws the conclusion for them.

Proposition of value. Values are deep-seated ideals that determine what we consider good or bad, moral or immoral, satisfying or unsatisfying, proper or improper, wise or foolish, valuable or invaluable, and so on. Persuasive speeches that deal with propositions of value are assertions rooted in judgments based on these ideals. The speaker's goal is to prove the worth of an evaluative statement, as in the following examples:

1. It is *wrong* to criminalize recreational or medicinal use of marijuana.

2. Violence in professional sports is *unjustified*.

3. Plagiarizing to complete an assignment is *dishonest*.

When you use words that can be considered judgments or evaluations, such as those italicized above, you are making a proposition of value. When designing a persuasive speech based on a proposition of value, it is important to present facts, statistics, or examples to support your points. Also, using expert opinion and testimony will provide credible support.

Proposition of policy. Propositions of policy propose a course of action. Usually, the speaker is arguing that something should or should not be done. Propositions of policy are easily recognizable by their use of "should," "ought to," "have to," or "must":

1. Campus safety should be reevaluated by the college administration.

2. The same general student academic standards ought to apply to student-athletes, too.

3. Collegiate athletes should be paid.

4. Animals must not be used for product testing in scientific laboratories.

In a policy speech, speakers convince listeners of both the need for change and what that change should be. They also give people reasons to continue listening and, in the end, to agree with their position and, sometimes, to take action.

Glossary

Proposition of value
Persuading your listeners based on deep-seated beliefs.

Proposition of policy Easily recognizable by their use of the word "should."

Propositions of policy have both fact and value aspects to them. Facts need to support the need for the course of action, and values are inherently part of the policy statement. For example, in a speech about using animals for product testing, the person giving the speech against it most likely values animals, and believes in the humane and ethical treatment of animals.

A speaker's persuasive appeal, in summary, derives from the audience's sense of the speaker's credibility as well as from appeals to an audience's emotion and logic. At times, one persuasive element may be more important to one audience than others. Many speakers try to convince audiences based on logical appeals, emotional appeals, myth appeals, and their image and credibility as a speaker. The most effective speakers consider their audience expectations and intended outcomes. Now we turn our attention to common techniques used to organize persuasive messages.

Organizing Persuasive Speeches

Earlier in this text, we presented different ways to organize your speech. Certain organizational patterns are unique to the persuasive speech pattern. In the chapter on organizing and outlining, we presented the **problem–solution pattern**, which involves presenting an audience with a problem and then examining one or more likely solutions. For a persuasive speech, the speaker persuades the audience to accept one particular solution. We also noted the **cause-and-effect pattern**, which entails arranging main points into causes and effects. The persuasive speaker constructs a case for the audience that persuades them to accept the cause–effect connection.

In the following we present three more possible organizational patterns: comparative advantage, criteria satisfaction, and Monroe's Motivated Sequence. Our primary focus is on the latter, since this pattern follows the normal process of human reasoning as it presents a clear way to move through the problem-solving process.

Comparative Advantages

A **comparative-advantages organizational pattern** is useful when the audience already agrees there is a problem that needs a solution. The problem may not be grave, but it is one that may have several potentially acceptable solutions. As a speaker using this pattern, try to convince the audience that your plan is the best. You place alternative solutions or plans side-by-side and discuss the advantages and disadvantages of each. To some extent, this organizational pattern can be viewed as a structured process of elimination.

For example, Lauren, a high school senior, is trying to decide which college to attend. She has prior approval from her parents to look at both in-state and out-of-state schools. Lauren, a minority student who wants to pursue international study and work possibilities, decides that she wants to attend an out-of-state school, and chooses the comparative-advantages approach when persuading her parents to accept her choice.

College 1: Instate U

Advantages: Less expensive, close to home, friends are also attending, small to medium-sized college

Disadvantages: Too close to home (might go home too often), school's reputation is OK, but not great, might not make new friends, lack of diversity

College 2: Outstate U

Advantages: Within four hours of home, diverse population, large university that offers wide range of diverse majors (can major in Folklore), large study abroad program; ability to live in international dorm, many cultural and entertainment possibilities; good scholarship possibilities

Disadvantages: Significantly more expensive, campus is large, possible safety concern

Since Lauren's parents were prepared to pay out-of-state tuition, Lauren can construct a persuasive argument making the comparison between these schools. Although this example is an interpersonal one (persuading her parents, not a large audience), if we switched the scenario to Lauren being a college student at Outstate U speaking to a group of students at her high school, the same pattern could be applied.

Using a comparative-advantages pattern, you can compare two possibilities, or you can compare several possibilities. For example, if you were talking about how to solve the energy crisis, you could compare solar, wind, and nuclear power to convince your audience that one method is superior to the others.

Criteria-Satisfaction

When using the **criteria-satisfaction pattern**, you demonstrate how your idea has the features your audience needs. It is a clear pattern that is useful when you have an audience opposed to your idea. You can help establish a "yes" response from your audience through identification of criteria they find acceptable. You indicate the necessary criteria and show how your solution meets or exceeds the criteria.

Consider a "calendar committee" trying to convince the local school board to change the dates for beginning and ending the school year. The committee might argue that any solution should meet the following criteria:

- acceptable to teachers
- acceptable to parents
- cost effective (not have to turn on air conditioning too soon)
- enhances education or at least does not interfere with learning environment
- includes appropriate start and ending dates for each term
- balances mandatory and optional vacation and teacher institute dates

> **Glossary**
>
> **Criteria-satisfaction pattern** Demonstrating how your idea has the features your audience needs.

Based on these criteria, the committee could present the solution to the school board that meets all these criteria. With the criteria-solution pattern, it is important that you find criteria your audience will accept. For example, if the committee identified one of the criteria as "starts as late as possible and ends as early as possible," that might not have been viewed as an acceptable criterion by the school board. Similarly, criteria may differ, depending on circumstances. In a small college town, having spring break and holiday breaks at the same time the college has them may be an appropriate criterion, but in a large city that has several colleges and universities, this may not be as important.

Monroe's Motivated Sequence

As emphasized throughout this text, effective communication requires connecting with your audience. Audience awareness is particularly important in speeches to persuade, for without taking into account the mental stages your audience passes through, your persuasion may not succeed. The *motivated sequence*, a widely used method for organizing persuasive speeches developed by Monroe (1965), is rooted in traditional rhetoric and shaped by modern psychology.

Monroe's motivated sequence focuses on five steps to motivate your audience that follows the normal pattern of human thought from attention to action. If you want only to persuade the audience there is a problem, then only the first two steps are necessary. If the audience is keenly aware of a problem, then a speaker may focus only on the last three steps. Most of the time, however, all five steps are necessary, and they should be followed in order.

Step 1: Attention. Persuasion is impossible without attention. Your first step is to capture the minds of your listeners and convince them that you have something important to say. Many possibilities were discussed in the chapter on introductions and conclusions. For example, addressing the United Nations regarding prospects for peace in the Middle East, Israeli Prime Minister Benyamin Netanyahu (2009) began his speech by saying:

> ...Netanyahu (2009) began his speech by saying that he was speaking on behalf of the Jewish state. He lashed out against the President of Iran, whom he said was insisting that the Holocaust was a lie.

The prime minister's keen use of irony and strong language surely engaged all listening. His opening also establishes his credibility and introduces his topic. In your attention step, you must catch your audience's attention, introduce and make your topic relevant, and establish your credibility.

Step 2: Need. In the need step, you describe the problem you will address in your speech. You hint at or suggest a need in your introduction, then state it in a way that accurately reflects your specific purpose. You motivate listeners to care about the problem by making clear a problem exists, it is significant, and it affects them. You illustrate need by using examples, intensifying it through the use of carefully selected additional supporting material, and *linking* it directly to the audience. Too often the inexperienced speaker who uses the motivated sequence will pass through the need step in haste to get to the third step, the satisfaction step.

The need step has four parts: (1) it establishes there is a problem, (2) explains the problem, (3) proves that the problem is serious, and (4) connects the problem to specific needs the audience holds dear.

Step 3: Satisfaction. The satisfaction step presents a solution to the problem you have just described. You offer a proposition you want your audience to adopt and act on. A clear explanation as well as statistics, testimony, examples, and other types of support ensure that your audience understands what you propose. Show your audience how your proposal meets the needs you presented earlier in your speech. You may use several forms of support accompanied by visuals or audiovisual aids.

An audience is usually impressed if you can show where and how a similar proposal has worked elsewhere. Before you move to the fourth step, meet objections that you predict some listeners may hold. We are all familiar with the persuader who attempts to sell us a product or service and wants us to believe it is well worth the price and within our budget. In fact, a considerable amount of sales appeal today aims at selling us a payment we can afford as a means to purchasing the product, whether it is an automobile, a vacation, or some other attractive item. If we can afford the monthly payment, a major objection has been met.

Here is how a citizen and mother suggested solving the problem of head injuries in little league baseball:

> Well, "some sort" of protection has been developed. *American Health* reports that Home Safe, Inc. has found an all-star solution. Teams like the Atlee Little Leaguers in Mechanicsville, Virginia, have solved many of their safety problems by wearing face shields like this one [shown].
>
> This molded plastic shield snaps onto the earflaps of the standard batter's helmet. Most youth teams require the use of a batter's helmet, but with this shield they could add complete facial protection, including the eyes, for a cost of under $15 per shield. Some might say that is expensive, but former little leaguer Daniel Schwartz's head injuries have cost his family $23,000 so far.

In sum, a strong satisfaction step involves clearly stating an acceptable solution, offering strong evidence supporting the solution, demonstrating how the solution solves the problem, proving that it is a workable solution, and clarifying how the solution will satisfy the audience's unresolved needs.

Step 4: Visualization. The visualization step compels listeners to picture themselves either benefiting or suffering from adopting or rejecting your proposal. It focuses on powerful imagery to create a vision of the future if your proposal is adopted or, just as important, if it is rejected. It may also contrast these two visions, strengthening the attractiveness of your proposal by showing what will happen if no action is taken.

Positive visualization is specific and concrete. Your goal is to help listeners see themselves under the conditions you describe. You want them to experience enjoyment and satisfaction. In contrast, negative visualization focuses on what will happen without your plan. Here you describe the discomfort with conditions that would exist. Whichever method you choose, make your listeners feel part of the future. For example, here would be an appropriate visualization step:

> Imagine yourself on a quiet and lazy summer afternoon watching your own child, a niece, a nephew, a cousin, or a neighborhood friend up at bat in an exciting youth league baseball game. Think about the comfort you will experience when you see that she or he has the proper safety equipment on so that there is no possibility that a speeding baseball will take his or her life, or result in any permanent disability. See for a moment the face and the form of a child enthusiastically awaiting the pitch and see as well this child effectively shielded from impact that could come from a missed pitch.

The visualization step can be enhanced with powerful visuals. Movie clips, sound tracks, interviews, and memorable photos have all been used successfully to help listeners fully engage their imagination in the future scenario.

Step 5: Action. The action step acts as the conclusion of your speech. Here you tell your listeners what you want them to do or, if action is unnecessary, the point of view you want them to share. You may have to explain the specific actions you want and the timing for these actions. This step is most effective when immediate action is sought.

Many students find the call to action a difficult part of the persuasive speech. They are reluctant to make an explicit request for action. Can you imagine a politician failing to ask people for their vote? Such a candidate would surely lose an election. When sales representatives have difficulty in closing a deal because they are unable to ask consumers to buy their products, they do not last long in sales. Persuasion is more likely to result when direction is clear and action is the goal. Here is how we might conclude our little league example:

> We must realize, however, that it may be awhile before this equipment scores a home run, so now it is your turn up at bat. If you are personally interested in protecting these young ball players, spread the word about these injuries, especially to businesses that sponsor youth teams. Encourage them to

purchase safety equipment for the teams and then to spon-
sor them only on the condition that the equipment be used.
Additionally, I ask for your signature on the petition I am
circulating. This will send a loud message to our representatives in Congress.

To create closure and reinforce the need to act, our final comment
might be:

> Now that we have discovered how children are being seri-
> ously injured and even killed while playing baseball, I know
> you agree that given the children's lack of skill, we need to
> mandate the use of face shields. So take them out to the ball
> game, but make it one that children can play safely, because
> children may be dying to play baseball, but they should never
> die because of it. From *Winning Orations of the Interstate Oratorical
> Association* by C. Spruling. Copyright © 1992 by Interstate Oratorical
> Association. Reprinted by permission.

In review, remember the five-step sequence if you want to lead your audience
from attention to action. The motivated sequence is effective but like all tools
of persuasion, can be misused. The line between use and abuse of persuasive
tools warrants further examination.

Ethics and Persuasive Speaking

The importance of ethics is stressed both implicitly and explicitly throughout
this textbook. Ethics provide standards of conduct that guide us. The ethics
of persuasion call for honesty, care, thoroughness, openness, and a concern
for the audience without manipulative intent. The end does *not* justify the
means at all costs. In a world as complex as ours, one marked in part by
unethical as well as ethical persuaders, the moral imperative is to speak
ethically.

Your authors belong to a professional organization called the National
Communication Association, which publishes a credo for ethical communication that includes the following:

> Ethical communication is fundamental to responsible think-
> ing, decision making, and the development of relationships
> and communities within and across contexts, cultures, chan-
> nels, and media. Moreover, ethical communication enhances
> human worth and dignity by fostering truthfulness, fairness,
> responsibility, personal integrity, and respect for self and oth-
> ers (Pearson et al., 2006, p. 521).

The choice between right and wrong is not simple. Informing people on a
particular topic assumes providing knowledge to an audience that, in turn,
learns more about the topic. In a persuasive speech, however, you are asking
listeners to think or act in ways called for to achieve your specific purpose.

As members of an audience, many of the choices we make are inconsequential, such as which soft drink to buy at a convenience store or which magazine to read in a doctor's waiting room. Far more important however, is the decision to reject our religious, social, or political beliefs in order to embrace new ones. Even the purchase of an expensive automobile is a considerable decision for us when weighed against the selection of a soft drink.

As a speaker, you must decide not only what to tell your audience but what you should avoid saying. Be mindful of your audience's needs and values, and weigh benefits of successful persuasion against possible risks or harms. If a doctor, for example, prescribes a medication for a patient that results in the patient having to fight addiction to the medication, was that an appropriate act on the part of the doctor? Unless the patient was terminally ill, it was probably unethical.

As you prepare for any persuasive speech, respect your audience. Be informed, truthful, and clear about your motives, use various appeals ethically, avoid misleading your audience through faulty argument, and work to create your most effective, honest persuasive message.

Summary

In a persuasive speaking situation, the audience may be supportive, opposed, or uncommitted. The effective speaker develops strategies related to the type of audience as well as the needs of the audience. Understanding Maslow's hierarchy of human needs is helpful to persuasive speakers. The five levels of Maslow's hierarchy form a pyramid; from bottom to top, these needs are physiological, safety, belongingness and love, esteem, and self-actualization. If you approach your listeners at an appropriate level of need, you will find them more able or willing to respond.

Your credibility as a speaker is determined by the way the audience perceives you. Credibility is measured in terms of trustworthiness, competence, and dynamism. A persuasive speaker constructs arguments that have emotional, logical, ethical, or mythic appeal. Emotional appeals (pathos) can be powerful because they provide the motivation for action and attitude change. As a persuasive speaker, you should be conscious of ethical standards (ethos), and what the implications are of the choice you are asking your audience to make. The audience needs to be treated to the truth, without manipulative intent. The newest form of appeal, mythos, recognizes the persuasive power of stories, folklore, and myths.

When making logical arguments (logos), one can take an inductive or deductive approach. Inductive reasoning enables you to generalize from specific instances and draw a conclusion from your observations. Deductive reasoning draws a conclusion based on the connections between statements.

Depending on your purpose for persuasion, you may choose to reason from examples, analogies, causal relations, or with enthymemes. Choose the right amount of support, the most persuasive kind of evidence, and then reason carefully.

Arguments that have faulty reasoning are considered fallacies. Fallacies can distract and mislead listeners as well as pose ethical problems. Fallacies discussed in this chapter are attack on the person, hasty generalization, false cause, slippery slope, and red herring.

The two overall persuasive goals are to address audience attitudes and to move an audience to action. Four specific persuasive aims define the focus of your speech. These aims include adoption, continuance, discontinuance, and deterrence. Your point of view, or thesis statement, is expressed in the form of a proposition that must be proved. Propositions take three basic forms: fact, value, and policy.

Three organizational patterns were discussed: comparative-advantages, criteria-satisfaction, and Monroe's motivated sequence. Monroe's motivated sequence includes five steps designed to motivate the audience to action: attention, need, satisfaction, visualization, and action. The motivated sequence is a widely used method for organizing persuasive speeches that follows the normal pattern of human thought from attention to action.

Discussion Starters

1. What are the dimensions of credibility, and how important is credibility to the overall effectiveness of a persuasive speech? What strategies can improve low credibility?

2. How would you define persuasion, persuasive goals, and persuasive aims? Illustrate your definitions with specific examples.

3. Why is the motivated sequence audience-centered? How does the motivated sequence relate to Maslow's hierarchy of needs?

4. When would comparative-advantages or criteria-satisfaction be more appropriate organizational patterns than Monroe's motivated sequence?

5. What are ethical, logical, emotional, and mythic appeals? How are these appeals distinct, yet interrelated?

6. How important is evidence in a persuasive speech? How important are ethics in persuasive speaking? Does the importance depend on the audience and its shared needs and expectations?

References

300. American Rhetoric Movie Speeches. Retrieved July 8, 2011 from www.americanrhetoric.com/MovieSpeeches/moviespeech300queengorgo.html.

Emperor Akihito. (2011, March 16). *Speech to the Nation on Disaster Relief and Hope*. Retrieved July 8, 2011 from www.americanrhetoric.com/speeches/emperorakitodisasterspeech.htm.

Freeley, A. J. (1993). *Argumentation and Debate: Critical Thinking for Reasonable Decision-Making*, 8th Ed. Belmont, CA: Wadsworth Publishing.

Hample, D., Sells, A., & Valazquez, A. L. I. (2009). The Effects of Topic Type and Personalization of Conflict on Assessments of Fallacies. *Communication Reports*, *22*(2), 74–88.

Hirsen, J. (2011, April 13). Tina Fey Voices Palin Parody Pangs; 'Idol' Voting Needs Reboot. Retrieved July 8, 2011 from www.newsmax.com/Hirsen/Tina-Fay-Palin-Parody/2011/04/13/id/392760.

Kennedy, G. A. (2007). Aristotle's 'On Rhetoric': A Theory of Civic Discourse, 2nd Ed. (G. A. Kennedy, Trans.). New York: Oxford University Press. (Original work published 350 BCE.)

Maslow, A. H. (1943). A Theory of Human Motivation, *Psychological Review*, *50*(4), 370–396.

Monroe, A. H. (1965). *The Psychology of Speech* (Seminar). Purdue University.

Netanyahu, Benjamin. (2009, September 24). *Speech Delivered Before the United Nations*. Retrieved July 8, 2011 from www.washingtontimes.com/news/2009/sep/transcript-Israeli-Prime-Minister-Benjamin-Netanya.

Osborn, M. (1990). In Defense of Broad Mythic Criticism—A Reply to Rowland. *Communication Studies*, *41*, 121–127.

Pearson, J. C., Child, J. T., Mattern, J. L., & Kahl, D. H., Jr. (2006). What Are Students Being Taught About Ethics in Public Speaking Textbooks? *Communication Quarterly*, *54*(4), 507–521.

Pornpitakpan, C. (2004). The Persuasiveness of Source Credibility: A Critical Review of Five Decades' Evidence. *Journal of Applied Social Psychology*, *34*(2), 243–281.

Regan, D. T., & Fazio, R. (1977). On the Consistency Between Attitudes and Behavior: Look to the Method of Attitude Formation. *Journal of Experimental Social Psychology, 13*, 28–45 (Cited in Zimbardo, p. 618.)

Simons, H. (2001). *Persuasion in Society.* Thousand Oaks, CA: Sage Publications.

Sprague, J., & Stuart, D. (1988). *Speaker's Handbook,* 2nd Ed. San Diego: Harcourt Brace Jovanovich.

Spurling, C. (1992). Batter up-Batter down. *Winning orations of the interstate oratorical association.* Mankato State University: The Interstate Oratorical Association.

Toulmin, S. (1958). *The Uses of Argument.* Cambridge, UK: Cambridge University Press.

Vancil, D. L. (1993). *Rhetoric and Argumentation.* Boston: Allyn and Bacon.

Wicker, A. W. (1969). Attitudes versus Actions. The Relationship of Verbal and Overt Behavioral Responses to Attitude Objects. *Journal of Social Sciences, 25*(4), 41–78.

Walker, F. R. (2005). The Rhetoric of Mock Trial Debate: Using Logos, Pathos and Ethos in Undergraduate Competition. *College Student Journal, 39*(2), 277–286.

Zimbardo, P. G. (1988). *Psychology and Life,* 12th Ed. Glenview, IL: Scott, Foresman and Company.

Part

IV

PRESENTING
YOUR SPEECH

Image © Helga Esteb, 2013. Used under license from Shutterstock, Inc.

Chapter

13

© *MARK LENNIHAN/AP/Corbis*

"*It is not enough for language to have clarity and content: it must also have a goal and an imperative.*"

René Daumal

Chapter 13: Language

It is important to remember to consider how words affect your listeners. In this chapter, we identify characteristics of spoken language and provide guidelines for using it more effectively. We also address pitfalls, which are aspects of language that a speaker should avoid. The use of humor is also discussed.

Student Learning Objectives:

○ Students will be able to identify characteristics of spoken language

○ Students will be able to discuss guidelines for language and style

○ Students will be able to describe language pitfalls

LANGUAGE

Language matters. It is so powerful that it can move us to tears. Consider this story attributed to professor, author, and speaker Leo Buscaglia (2007) about a contest he once judged:

> "The purpose of the contest was to find the most caring child. The winner was a four-year-old child whose next door neighbor was an elderly gentleman who had recently lost his wife. Upon seeing the man cry, the little boy went into the old gentleman's yard, climbed onto his lap, and just sat there. When his Mother asked what he had said to the neighbor, the little boy said, "'Nothing, I just helped him cry.'"

Language provokes us. Language can move us to tears, leave us bewildered, make us laugh, or awkwardly blush. More accurately, speakers *using* language influence our emotions and behavior. Your language will in large part determine the success of your speech. Through words, you create the vivid images that remain in the minds of your audience after your speech is over. Moreover, your choice of words and style of language influence your credibility as a speaker. By choosing language that appeals to your audience—by moving your audience intellectually and emotionally through the images of speech—you create a climate that enhances your credibility, encourages continued listening, and ensures retention of key ideas.

The three Cs for public speaking are: Clear, Concise, and Colorful. In this chapter, we explore tools that help your presentations ring clear, concise, and colorful. First, we identify characteristics of spoken language that differentiate it from written language. Then we provide guidelines for using spoken language more effectively. Finally, we end our discussion of language by considering several common pitfalls that detract from the message.

Characteristics of Spoken Language

If you wrote a paper in a Sociology or English class on "Trafficking of Women in Eastern Europe," using it as the basis for an informative speech would be expedient. It would certainly save time and effort, particularly on researching and gathering supporting materials. But be careful. A written report can be used as the foundation for a speech, but it requires major adjustments. The needs of written language and spoken language are different because listeners process information differently than readers. Imagine your instructor speaking for a minute. Then imagine what it would be like if your instructor were reading these comments from a manuscript. It would be remarkably boring. The spoken and written language differ in many ways, including word order, rhythm, and signals. Simply reading a written report would be violating many such spoken language norms.

Word Order

The first characteristic of spoken language is word order, which relates to the order in which ideas should be arranged in a sentence. In general, the last idea presented is the most powerful. Consider this famous line spoken by John F. Kennedy at his inauguration: "Ask not what your country can do for you, ask what you can do for your country." Inverted, the sentence loses its power: "Ask what you can do for your country, ask not what your country can do for you." Because speech is slower than silent reading, individual words take on more importance, especially those appearing at the end of the sentence.

Comedians rely on this technique by making the last word in a punch line the key to the joke. Every "knock knock" joke does the same. Watch for this rule of comedy and see how often the strategy appears and is effective.

Rhythm

The second characteristic of spoken language is rhythm. Rhythm in music and poetry distinguishes these genres from others. The rhythm of a piece of music creates different moods. The rhythm may create a sense of calm and serenity that allows us to listen and reflect, or the rhythm may create the urge to dance like a maniac. Rhythm is important in spoken language, also. It is the speech flow or pattern that is created in many ways, including variations in sentence length, the use of parallel structure, and the expression of images in groups of three.

Read aloud Patrick Henry's famous line, "Give me liberty or give me death," to illustrate the importance of rhythm (Tarver, 1988):

> I know not what course others may take. But as for me, give me liberty or death.

Now read the original, and notice the greater impact:

> I know not what course others may take. But as for me, give me liberty or give me death.

By taking out one of the repetitive "give me" phrases, the rhythm—and impact—of the sentence changes. As you develop your speech, consider the following ways you can use rhythm to reinforce your ideas and to maintain audience attention.

Vary sentence length. First, create rhythm by varying sentence length. The rhythm of speech is affected by how well you combine sentences of varying lengths. Long sentences can be confusing and short sentences might be dull and simple, but a combination of long and short sentences adds rhythmic interest. On June 1, 1997, Mary Schmich, columnist for the *Chicago Tribune*, wrote an essay she described as a commencement speech called "Wear Sunscreen." In addition to imploring graduates to wear sunscreen, Schmich provides several words of advice, including the following:

> Sing.
>
> Don't be reckless with other people's hearts. Don't put up with people who are reckless with yours.
>
> Floss.
>
> Don't waste your time on jealousy.

Schmich's commencement speech is filled with humor and advice, but its impact is due, in part, to the variation in sentence structure. Rhythm is a critical element. The rhythm of this speech is so engaging, it captured the attention of musical artists who developed their own version of Schmich's advice, including Baz Luhrmann's *Everybody's Free (to Wear Sunscreen)* and John Safran's *Not the Sunscreen Song*.

Use parallel structure. Second, create rhythm by using parallel structure. Parallelism involves the arrangement of a series of words, phrases, or sentences in a similar form. Classically, this is done in two ways: anaphora and epistrophe.

Anaphora is the repetition of the same word or phrase at the *beginning* of successive clauses or sentences, as in these two examples:

> In his first inaugural speech, President Richard M. Nixon stated, "Where peace is unknown, make it welcome; where peace is fragile, make it strong; where peace is temporary, make it permanent" (Detz, 1984, p. 69).
>
> Barack Obama's 2009 inaugural address also made effective use of parallel structure in many places, including anaphora in the memorable: "We will harness the sun and the winds and the soil to fuel our cars and run our factories. And we will transform our schools and colleges and universities to meet the demands of a new age" (Phillips, 2009).

A non-inaugural example of parallel structure can be seen when Tina Fey accepted the Mark Twain Prize for American humor at the Kennedy Center in November 2010. Her repetition of "I am proud" gives rhythm to her speech and allows her to make important points succinctly.

> I'm so proud to represent American humor, I am proud to be an American, and I am proud to make my home in the "'not real'" America. And I am most proud that during trying times,

like an orange [terror] alert, a bad economy, or a contentious election that we, as a nation, retain our sense of humor." (Farhi, 2010)

Epistrophe is the repetition of a word or expression at the *end* of phrases, clauses, or sentences. Lincoln used this device in the phrase, "of the people, by the people, for the people." It is an effective technique for emphasis. On January 8, 2008 in his presidential bid, then–Senator Barack Obama delivered an inspired "Yes, We Can" speech. Obama's audience was so captivated by his use of the tag line "Yes, we can" at the end of key sentences that they called back the phrase with him each time he repeated it. Parallel structure emphasizes the rhythm of speech. When used effectively, it adds a harmony and balance to a speech that can verge on the poetic.

Use three as a magic number. Third (yes, we intentionally provided three points!), rhythm can be created by referring to ideas in groups of three. Winston Churchill once said, "If you have an important point to make, don't try to be subtle or clever. Use a pile driver. Hit the point once. Then come back and hit it again. Then hit it a third time—a tremendous whack." Experienced speakers know that saying things three times gets their point across in a way saying it once cannot—not simply because of repetition, but because of the rhythmic effect of the repetition. Many presidents use this device during important speeches. You can hear the emotional impact of Abraham Lincoln's words in his Gettysburg address when he said, "We cannot dedicate, we cannot consecrate, we cannot hallow this ground (Detz, 1984, pp. 68–69).

Re-examine the words quoted above from Barack Obama and Tina Fey, and you will note they freely use the rule of three. Try this in your speeches. For example, in a speech of tribute, you might say, "I am here to honor, to praise, and to congratulate the members of the volunteer fire department."

Signals

A third specific characteristic of spoken language involves using signals. You may reread an important passage in a book to appreciate its meaning, but your audience hears your message only once—a fact that may make it necessary to signal critical passages in your speech. The following signals tell your listeners to pay close attention:

- This cannot be overemphasized …
- Let me get to the heart of the matter …
- I want to summarize …
- My three biggest concerns are …

Although all speakers hope to capture and hold listeners' attention throughout their speech, wise speakers draw people back to their message at critical points. Signals are more necessary in spoken language than in print.

> **Glossary**
>
> **Epistrophe** The repetition of a word or expression at the *end* of phrases, clauses,

Guidelines for Language and Style

As you strive to be precise, clear, and understandable, keep in mind the difference between denotative and connotative definitions. A dictionary provides the literal, objective, denotative definition of the word. Connotation is the meaning we ascribe to words as framed by our personal experiences. These often lie in the realm of our subjective, emotional responses. For example, the American flag can be described denotatively by its color and design, but connotatively, the meaning varies around the world. Americans, in general, see the flag as a symbol of freedom and democracy, whereas some from other cultures may view our flag as a symbol of Western imperialism or immorality. Whether the audience favors or disfavors your view, ensure they understand what you mean and what you believe to be the facts that support your ideas. This next section provides six guidelines for effective use of language.

Glossary

Denotative Literal, objective definition provided by a dictionary.

Connotation The meaning we ascribe to words as framed by our personal experience.

Be Concrete

On a continuum, words range from the most concrete to the most abstract. Concrete language is rooted in real-life experience—things we see, hear, taste, touch, and feel—while abstract language tells us little about what we experience, relying instead on more symbolic references. Compare the following:

TABLE 13.1

Abstract	Concrete
Bad weather	Hail the size of golf balls
Nervousness	Trembling hands; knocking knees
An interesting professor	When she started throwing paper airplanes around the room to teach us how air currents affect lift, I knew she was a winner.

Concrete words and phrases create pictures in listeners' minds and can turn a ho-hum speech into one that captures listener attention. Winston Churchill understood this premise when he said, during World War II, "We shall fight them on the beaches," instead of "Hostilities will be engaged on the coastal perimeter" (Kleinfeld, 1990). Consider the differences between these two paragraphs:

Version 1:

> On-the-job accidents take thousands of lives a year. Particularly hard hit are agricultural workers who suffer

approximately 1,500 deaths and 140,000 disabling injuries a year. One-fifth of all agricultural fatalities are children. These statistics make us wonder how safe farms are.

Version 2:

Farmers who want to get their children interested in agriculture often take them on tractors for a ride. About 150 children are killed each year when they fall off tractors and are crushed underneath. These children represent about half the children killed in farm accidents each year—a statistic that tells us farms can be deadly. About 1,500 people die each year on farms, and an additional 140,000 are injured seriously enough that they can no longer work.

In Version 2 the images and language are more concrete. Instead of wondering "how safe farms are," Version 2 declares that "farms can be deadly." Instead of talking about "disabling injuries," we are told that workers "are injured seriously enough that they can no longer work." Concrete language produces an emotional response in listeners because it paints a more vivid picture, allowing the audience to imagine the situation on a more emotional level.

Complete Your Thoughts and Sentences

Focus on completing every sentence you start. This may seem like common sense, but many people do not follow this advice when speaking before groups. Although we accept the fact that many sentences trail off in conversational speech, we are more likely to lose confidence when a speaker continually does this. From the mouth of a public speaker, this language is disconcerting:

In many states, your signature on your driver's license makes you a potential organ donor. If you are killed ... According to the laws in these states, if you are killed in an auto accident, the state has the right ... Your organs can be used to help people in need of organ transplants. There are sick people out there who need the kidneys, corneas, and even the hearts of people killed. Think about it. When you are dead, you can still give the gift of life.

On the other hand, we encourage you to *violate* this rule by incorporating sentence fragments, where relevant. Keep in mind that carefully chosen sentence fragments can contribute to clear communication. Here is an example:

Is Christmas too commercial? Well, maybe. It wasn't that long ago when the holiday season began after Thanksgiving. Now the first Christmas catalogs reach shoppers in September. Before summer is over. Before the temperature has dropped below 90 degrees. Even before Labor Day.

Do not confuse sentence fragments with the incomplete thoughts and sentences we discussed earlier. In the case above, the fragments are intentional and are used effectively to create drama and emphasis.

Use the Active Voice

A direct speaking style involves the use of the active rather than passive voice as often as possible or preferable. The following example demonstrates the difference between the passive and active voice:

Version 1: Passive voice.

> Students in an English class at Long Beach City College were asked by their teacher to stand in line. After a few minutes, the line was broken by a student from Japan who walked a few yards away. The behavior demonstrated by the student shows how cultural differences can affect even the simple act of waiting in line. In this case, the need for greater personal space was felt by the student who considered it impolite to stand so close.

Version 2: Active voice.

> An English teacher at Long Beach City College asked the class to stand in line. After a few minutes, a Japanese student broke the line and walked a few yards away. The student's behavior demonstrated how cultural differences affect even the simple act of waiting in line. In this case, the student felt the need for more personal space because the Japanese culture considers it impolite to stand so close.

In the active voice structure, the subject is identified first and it performs the action implied by the verb (Purdue OWL, 2011). Here are two shorter examples: "The cat scratched the girl" is active because the subject (cat) is identified first in the sentence and is performing the action (scratch). "The speaker explored her subject thoroughly before she crafted her speech" is active because the subject (speaker) comes before, and performs the action of the verb (explored). In addition to using fewer words, the active voice is more direct, easier to follow, and more vigorous.

There are times when you may prefer the passive voice because it has the ability to create a shift the tone in your message and the moods in your audience. For example, in "rules are made to be broken" the rhythm created by a passive structure is so powerful that we would use it over an active version, like "Authorities make rules to be broken (Purdue OWL, 2011). Passive voice is also used when we want the importance of the subject to be deemphasized or omitted. In our "rules are made to be broken" example, the subject (authorities) is left out altogether because the emphasis is really on breaking rules rather than on authorities. To create rhythm or alter emphasis, we sometimes elect to use the passive over the active voice.

Use Language to Create a Theme

A key word or phrase can reappear throughout your speech to reinforce your theme. Each time the image is repeated, it becomes more powerful and is more likely to stay with your listeners. When addressing women's rights in Africa, First Lady Michelle Obama used her husband's now famous "Yes, We Can" speech to conclude her remarks in a powerful way while reinforcing her theme: "And if anyone of you ever doubts that you can build that future, if anyone ever tells you that you shouldn't or you can't, then I want you to say with one voice—the voice of a generation—you tell them, Yes, we can. [Applause] What do you say?" "Yes, we can." [Applause] "What do you say?" "Yes, we can!" (Mooney, 2011).

When something works, the Obama's stick with it! By referring to a key phrase several times in a speech, the message is often more effective and memorable (Berg & Gilman, 1989).

Use Language That Fits Your Personality and Position

If you are delivering a speech on advances in microsurgery, a casual, flippant tone is inappropriate, though it might work for a speech on naming the family dog. Audiences are perceptive. They quickly know whether you are comfortable with your speaking style or whether you are trying to be something or someone you are not. It is hard to fake an emotional presentation if you are a cool, non-emotional person. If you are naturally restrained, it is difficult to appear daring and impulsive.

Some try to be more formal or articulate than they are comfortable with by choosing big, complicated, rarely heard words. While it can have a comedic pay-off, this is rarely the goal of most speakers. The language you choose mirrors who you are, so choose carefully. Let your language reflect what you want others to know about you, and keep it real.

Use Varying Language Techniques to Engage Listeners

A carpenter uses a saw, a hammer, and nails to construct a building. A speaker uses language to construct a speech. Words are literally the tools of a speaker's trade. A speaker has numerous tools to choose from when building a speech.

When constructing your speech, consider using a variety of language techniques to enhance imagery. **Imagery** involves creating a vivid description through the use of one or more of our five senses. Using imagery can create a great impact and lasting memory. Mental images can be created using many devices, including metaphors, similes, and figures of speech.

Glossary

Imagery Creating a vivid description through the use of one or more of our five senses.

Metaphors

Metaphors state that something *is* something else. Through metaphors we can understand and experience one idea in terms of another. For example, if you ask a friend how a test went, and the friend responded, "I scored a home run," you would know that your friend thought the test went well for him. In his "Sinews of Peace" speech to Westminster College in Fulton, Missouri, Prime Minister Winston Churchill used the following metaphor on March 5, 1946: "An iron curtain has descended across the continent." During his inaugural address, President Bill Clinton said, "Our democracy must not only be the envy of the world but also the engine of our own renewal." Metaphors create "idea marriages" that bring new insights to listeners.

Similes

Similes create images as they compare the characteristics of two different things using the words "like" or "as." Here are two examples. "Speed reading Charlie Sheen's autobiography would be like a trip through a sewer in a glass-bottom boat." "Watching presentations at this conference is like watching a WNBA playoff game; you are practically the only one there and the rest of the world does not care." Both metaphors and similes rely on concrete images to create meaning and insights, and both invite the imagination out to play. Although these can enliven your speech, guard against using images that are trite, odd, or too familiar.

Figures of Speech

Figures of speech connect sentences by emphasizing the relationship among ideas and repeating key sounds to establish a pleasing rhythm. Among the most popular figures of speech are alliteration, antithesis, asyndeton, and personification.

Alliteration is the repetition of the initial consonant or initial sounds in series of words. Tongue twisters such as "Peter Piper picked a peck of pickled peppers" are based on alliteration. With "Peter Piper" the P sound is repeated multiple times. Alliteration can be used effectively in speeches, such as in Martin Luther King's 1963 "I have a dream" speech, when he said, "We have come to our nation's capital to cash a check." Alliteration occurs with the repetition of C in "capital to cash a check."

Antithesis is the use of contrast, within a parallel grammatical structure, to make a rhetorical point. Jesse Jackson told an audience of young African Americans: "We cannot be what we ought to be if we push dope in our veins, rather than hope in our brains" (Gustainis 1987, p. 218). During a press conference in November 2008, President Obama used antithesis when he said, "If we are going to make the *investments we need*, we also have to be willing to shed the *spending that we don't need*" (*New York Times*, 2008). Antithesis is powerful because it is interesting; it is the analogy turned on its head to reveal insights by the pairing of two opposite things.

Asyndeton is the deliberate omission of conjunctions between a series of related clauses. Saying "I came, I saw, I conquered" rather than "I came, then I saw, and finally I conquered" is a good choice and excellent use of this figure of speech.

Personification is investing human qualities in abstractions or inanimate objects either through metaphor, simile, or analogy. General Douglas MacArthur, addressing West Point cadets confessed: "In my dreams I hear again the crash of guns, the rattle of musketry, the strange, mournful mutter of the battlefield." The general personifies the inanimate battlefield by ascribing to it human mournful mutters. This personification creates a much stronger emotional appeal.

Many other linguistic and stylistic devices are available to you. Because ancient Greek and Roman rhetoricians delighted in identifying and naming them, a rich heritage of figures of speech is waiting for you to come and explore. (For a good place to start, see **BTW: Figures of Speech**.)

Use Humor with Care

Nothing brings you closer to your audience than well-placed humor. Humor reveals your human side. It relaxes listeners and makes them respond positively. Through a properly placed anecdote, you let your audience know that you are not taking yourself—or your subject—too seriously. Even in a serious speech, humor can be an effective tool to emphasize an important point.

Research has shown the favorable impact humor has on an audience. In particular, humor accomplishes two things. First, when appropriate humor is used in informative speaking, the humor enhances the speaker's image by improving the audience's perception of the speaker's character (Gruner, 1985). Second, humor can make a speech more memorable over a longer time. In a research study, two groups of subjects were asked to recall lectures they heard six weeks earlier. The group who heard the lecture presented humorously had higher recall than the group who heard the same lecture delivered without humor (Kaplan & Pascoe, 1977).

In another experiment, students who took a statistics course given by an instructor who used humor in class lectures scored 15 percent higher on objective exams than did students who were taught the same material by an instructor who did not (Ziv, 1982).

Glossary

Asyndeton The deliberate omission of conjunctions between a series of related clauses.

Personification Investing human qualities in abstractions or inanimate objects either through metaphor, simile, or analogy.

Figures of Speech

BTW!

A fairly exhaustive list of 64 figures of speech can be found in the Latin text *Rhetorica ad Herennium, Book IV*. One scholar, Dr. Gideon O. Burton of Brigham Young University, has paired these with their definitions and brief examples to help clarify each (Burton, n.d.). His interactive Web resource, titled *Silva Rhetoricae* (translates to "the forest of rhetoric") is available at rhetoric.byu.edu/.

Humor works only if it is carefully used and is connected to the thesis of your speech, the occasion, audience, or yourself in a meaningful way. Here are five guidelines for using humor in a speech.

1. Use Humor Only If You Can Be Funny

Some speakers do not know how to be funny in front of an audience. On a one-on-one basis they may be funny, but in front of a group, their humor vanishes. They stumble over punch lines and their timing is bad. These people should limit themselves to serious speeches or "safe" humor. For example, former Maine senator Ed Muskie made his audience laugh by describing the shortest will in Maine legal history—a will that was only 10 words long: "Being of sound mind and memory, I spent it all" (Rackleff, 1987, p. 313). If you are not sure you can make your planned humor work, have a short practice session among friends and see if they laugh. Not naturally very funny? This is a skill, like any other. (For tips on using humor, see **BTW: Very Funny!**)

2. Laugh at Yourself, Not at Others

In his humble acceptance speech for Best Actor at the 2011 Academy Awards, Colin Firth's humorous comments included a few jabs at himself.

BTW!   Very Funny!

Speech professor Ann Harrell suggests that supporting materials in speeches can be "tweaked" to be more humorous through comic techniques (Harrell, 1997). Here are five examples:

1. **Levity.** Treating something serious in an absurd manner, or something absurd in a serious manner. David Letterman's Top Ten List cites an absurd concern with seemingly serious attention or explores a serious issue with ridiculous observations.

2. **Appropriateness.** Localizing material with names, dates, places, or other specific references familiar to the audience can create an "inside joke."

3. **Understatement.** Making less of something than is true. In Monty Python's "The Holy Grail," when a man has all his limbs dismembered in a sword fight, he replies that it is merely a flesh wound.

4. **Wordplay.** Double meanings for words that lead to new or twisted meanings (puns, malapropisms, or spoonerisms).

5. **Satire.** Exposing someone's weaknesses or follies through comic means. Poking fun at someone who has just put their foot in their mouth is an example of this.

Harrell notes that combining several of these comic devices will make your material even more funny.

Research has shown that speakers who make themselves the object of their own humor often endear themselves to their listeners. In one study, students heard brief speeches from a "psychologist" and an "economist," both of whom explained the benefits of their professions. While half the speeches were read with mildly self-deprecating humor directed at the profession being discussed, the other half were read without humor. Students rated the speakers with the self-deprecating humor higher on a scale of "wittiness" and "sense of humor," and no damage was done to the perceived character or authoritativeness of the speaker (Chang & Gruner, 1981).

Jokes at one's own expense can be effective but telling a joke at the expense of others is in poor taste. Racial, ethnic, or sexist jokes are rarely acceptable, nor are jokes that poke fun at the personal characteristics of others. Although stand-up comics like Dane Cook, Jeff Foxworthy, and Chris Rock may get away with such humor, public speakers typically cannot.

3. Understated Anecdotes Can Be Effective

An economist speaking before a group of peers starts with the following anecdote:

> I am constantly reminded by those who use our services that we often turn out a ton of material on the subject but we do not always give our clients something of value. A balloonist high above the earth found his balloon leaking and managed to land on the edge of a green pasture. He saw a man in a business suit approaching and very happily said: "How good it is to see you. Could you tell me where I am?"
>
> The well-dressed man replied: "You are standing in a wicker basket in the middle of a pasture." "Well," said the balloonist, "You must be an economist." The man was startled. "Yes, I am, but how did you know that?"
>
> "That's easy," said the balloonist, "because the information you gave me was very accurate—and absolutely useless" (Valenti, 1982, pp. 80–81).

This anecdote is funny in an understated way. It works because it is relevant to the audience of fellow economists. Its humor comes from the recognition that the speaker knows—and shares—the foibles of the audience.

4. Find Humor in Your Own Experiences

The best humor comes from your own experiences. Humor is all around you. You might want to start now to record humorous stories for your speeches so that you will have material when the need arises. If you decide to use someone else's material, you have the ethical responsibility to give the source credit. You might start with, "As Jerry Seinfeld would say …" This gives appropriate source citation and makes clear that line or story is meant as a joke. Usually you will get bigger laughs by citing their names than if you tried to convince your audience that the humor was original.

5. Avoid Being *Not* Funny

We chose the double negative to make a point. When humor works and the audience responds with a spontaneous burst of applause or laughter, there is little that will make you feel better—or more relaxed—as a speaker. Its effect is almost magical. However, when the humor is distasteful to the audience or highly inappropriate, a speaker may find no one is laughing.

Ricky Gervais hosted the 2010 Golden Globe awards, and his humor received mixed reviews. Without making specific reference to Mel Gibson's 2006 drunk driving arrest, Gervais quipped, "I like a drink as much as the next man ... unless the next man is Mel Gibson" (www.dailymail.co.uk).

Just before introducing Colin Farrell, Gervais remarked, "One stereotype I hate is that all Irishmen are just drunk, swearing hell raisers. Please welcome Colin Farrell" (www.dailymail.co.uk). He also made reference to Paul McCartney's expensive divorce and Hugh Hefner's marriage to a woman 60 years younger than he. While some jokes were well-received, some felt that he stepped over the line, even for a comedian, because the tone of special occasions should be kept positive.

Often humor is based on direct or implied criticism though. We laugh at things people do, what they say, how they react, and so on. In fulfilling our ethical responsibilities, however, while someone or some event is being mocked, the speaker needs to do so with taste and appropriateness.

So, to avoid being *not* funny, audience analysis is vital. As a beginning public speaker, we urge you to err on the side of caution. It is better to avoid humor than to fail at it. While most humor is risky, there are certain things you can be fairly sure your audience will find funny. Stick with those, and try riskier humor as you gain confidence and experience. You might also check with a friend or classmate if you have any question about the humor of a line or story.

Language Pitfalls

Although your speaking style—the distinctive manner in which you speak to produce the effect you desire—like your style of dress, is a personal choice, some aspects of style enhance communication while others detract. You may have a great sense of humor, but used too much and some may be put off by your lack of seriousness. You may be very bright and reflective, but your overly quiet tone may tire many in your audience. You have read several language guidelines for creating an effective speech. Following are five language pitfalls to avoid.

Long and Unnecessary Words

Using long and unnecessary words violates the first principle of language usage, which is to be simple and concrete. When you read, you have the opportunity to reread something or to look up a word you do not understand. In a speech, you do not have the rewind option, and if the audience does not understand, they lose interest.

When Mark Twain wrote popular fiction, he was often paid by the word, a fee schedule that led him to this humorous observation:

> By hard, honest labor, I've dug all the large words out of my vocabulary ... I never write *metropolis* for seven cents because I can get the same price for *city*. I never write *policeman* because I can get the same price for *cop*.

The best speakers realize that attempting to impress an audience by using four- or five-syllable words usually backfires. We prefer "row, row, row your boat" to "maneuver, maneuver, maneuver your craft" most days of the week. The IRS has been called out to simplify its tax language so it is more readable to the common taxpayer. Translation: Lose the legalese. The Plain Language Act of 2009 (H.R. 946) requires the IRS to write tax documents in "plain writing." Gina Jones, president of the National Association of Enrolled Agents said, "The regulations are not in plain language. For example, the definition of a qualifying child: You almost have to be an attorney to understand where all of the instances apply. If they could make it a little simpler, it would be a tremendous benefit for taxpayers and tax professionals" (Duarte, 2011). It might be wise to audit your use of long and unnecessary words in your presentations.

Here are a few multisyllabic words and their simpler alternatives.

TABLE 13.2

Words to Impress	Words to Communicate
Periodical	Magazine
Utilize	Use
Reiterate	Repeat
Commence	Start
Discourse	Talk

Unnecessary words are as problematic as long words. Spoken language requires some redundancy, but when people are forced to listen to strings of unnecessary words, they may find comprehension difficult. When the listening process becomes too difficult, they stop paying attention. Here is an example of unfocused rambling:

> Let me tell you what I did on my summer vacation. I drove down to Memphis in my car to take part in the dozens of memorial ceremonies marking the anniversary of the death of Elvis Presley. There were about 40,000 or 50,000 other people at the ceremony along with me.
>
> I took a tour of the mansion Elvis lived in before his death, known as Graceland, and I visited the new museum dedicated solely to his cars. The museum holds 20 different vehicles, including the favorite of Elvis's mother: a pink 1955 Cadillac Fleetwood.

Here is a simpler version:

> During summer vacation, I drove to Memphis to celebrate the anniversary of Elvis Presley's death. With about 40,000 or 50,000 other people, I toured Graceland, Elvis' home, and visited the museum dedicated to his 20 vehicles, including his mother's favorite, a pink 1955 Cadillac Fleetwood.

Not only does the second version eliminate almost half of the words, it also sharpens the message and helps listeners focus on the important points.

Using Euphemisms: Language That Masks or Muddles

As a speaker, be clear and provide something meaningful for your audience. Avoid sentences that lack content, mask meaning, or include euphemisms because they can do damage to your credibility. Using a euphemism involves substituting a mild, vague, or indirect word or phrase for a more harsh, blunt, or inciting, yet more accurate, word or phrase. Rather than use the word "war" when the U.S. had troops fighting in Vietnam, government officials used the word "conflict" (a term some still maintain is technically correct). Also, "collateral damage" is a euphemism for civilian deaths that occur during a military action. When someone dies, we hear euphemisms such as "passed," "passed away," "gone," as well as "she is no longer with us." A medical procedure may involve "harvesting" an organ instead of "removing" an organ.

While most of us use euphemisms in our everyday speech, we generally do so to avoid offending our listeners or making them uncomfortable. As a speaker, though, it is important that we do not confuse our listeners. Language that masks or muddies rather than clarifies meaning can confuse listeners. Former President George W. Bush comes to mind here. While he is a capable and intelligent man, he became known for, among many other things, his public muddlings. Here are four noteworthy examples (Kurtzman, n.d.) where the language of the military is combined with the language of diplomacy.

> "Too many good docs are getting out of the business. Too many ob-gyns aren't able to practice their love with women all across this country." —Poplar Bluff, Missouri, September 6, 2004

> "They misunderestimated me." —Bentonville, Arkansas, November 6, 2000

> "Rarely is the question asked: Is our children learning?" —Florence, South Carolina, January 11, 2000

> "Our enemies are innovative and resourceful, and so are we. They never stop thinking about new ways to harm our country and our people, and neither do we." —Washington, D.C., August 5, 2004

An effective speaker avoids using language that is unclear, makes an audience uncomfortable, or confuses the listeners. Using euphemisms is not recommended.

Jargon, Slang, and Profanity

Jargon is the host of technical terms used by special groups. For example, the jargon of the publishing business includes such terms as "specs," "page proofs," "dummy stage," and "halftones." Although these terms are not five syllables long, they may be difficult to understand if you are unfamiliar with publishing.

A special kind of jargon involves the use of acronyms—the alphabet soup of an organization or profession. Instead of saturating your speech with references to the FDA, PACs, or ACLI on the assumption that everyone knows what the acronyms mean, define these abbreviations the first time they are used. Tell your listeners that the FDA refers to the Food and Drug Administration; PACs, political action committees; and the ACLI, the American Council of Life Insurance.

Jargon can be used effectively when you are *sure* that everyone in your audience understands the reference. Therefore, if you are the editor-in-chief of a publishing company addressing your editorial and production staffs, publishing jargon requires no definition. However, if you deliver a speech about the publishing business to a group of college seniors, definitions are needed.

Slang is the use of informal words and expressions that are not considered standard in the speaker's language. For example, instead of saying "marijuana," one might hear slang terms such as "weed," "dope," "pot," and "ganja" (among others). Some words endure over decades (cool) whereas other words or phrases have a shorter life-span (bee's knees). Slang is generally

Glossary

Jargon Technical terminology unique to a special activity or group.

Slang Use of informal words and expressions that are not considered standard in the speaker's language.

spoken by the young, but this is not true in all cases. It may be news to you that your parents grew up when "thongs" were the name for "flip-flops," and "peddle-pushers" were what is now known as "capris."

Slang helps individuals identify with their peers, but it is not often appropriate within the formal speaking environment. Grammatical structures such as "ain't" and "you guys" should be used *only* for specific effect. In public discourse, slang used in any way can violate an audience's sense of appropriateness—or propriety

Profanity is seldom appropriate within the public speaking context. Listeners almost always expect a degree of decorum in a formal speech, requiring that certain language be avoided. Even celebrities are expected to avoid certain profanity in public situations. For example, Melissa Leo dropped the f-bomb during her acceptance speech for Best Supporting Actress at the 2011 Academy Awards ceremony. She quickly apologized for her error during backstage interviews.

Robert Pattinson, while presenting a career achievement award at the MTV Movie Awards in 2011 to actress Reese Witherspoon, his co-star in the film *Water for Elephants*, dropped the f-bomb. This gaffe slipped through the censors. While many individuals use profanity with their peers, when we listen to speakers in a public setting, we have a different set of expectations.

© Patrizia Tilly, 2012. Under license from Shutterstock, Inc.

Slang helps individuals identify with their peers, but it is not often appropriate in formal speaking.

Exaggeration and Clichés

Exaggerations are statements made to impress at the expense of accuracy. Instead of telling your classmates that you "always" exercise an hour a day, tell them that you exercise an hour a day "as often" as you can. Some of your classmates may know you well enough to realize that "always" is stretching the truth. Instead of saying that you would "never" consider double parking, tell your listeners that you would consider it "only as a last resort in an emergency." Obvious exaggerations diminish your credibility as a speaker.

Clichés, according to communication professors Eugene Ehrlich and Gene R. Hawes (1984), are the "enemies of lively speech." They explain:

> They are deadwood: the shiny suits of your word wardrobe, the torn sandals, the frayed collars, the scuffed shoes, the bobby socks, the fur pieces, the Nehru jackets, the miniskirts—yesterday's chewing gum (p. 48).

Clichés can lull your listeners into a state of boredom because they suggest that both your vocabulary and imagination are limited. Here is a section of a speech purposefully altered with slang and clichés:

> Two years ago, the real estate market was weak. *At that point in time* I would *guesstimate* that there were 400 more houses on the market than there are today. For us, it was time to *put our noses to the grindstone. We toughed it out and kept our eyes on the prize.* The winning *game plan* we should follow from

now on is to convince potential buyers that we *have a good thing going* in this community—good schools, good libraries, a good transportation system. We should also convince them that we're a *community with a heart*. We're here to help each other when we're *down and out*. It's a *win-win* relationship we're after today, as…

Imagine listening to this entire speech. Even if the speaker has something valuable to say, it is virtually impossible to hear it through the clichés. Clichés are unimaginative and add unnecessary words to your speech.

Phrases That Communicate Uncertainty

Speakers should avoid phrases that communicate uncertainty. Language can communicate a sense of mastery of your subject or it can communicate uncertainty. Compare the following paragraphs:

Version 1:

Sometimes I think that too many students choose a career solely on the basis of how much they are likely to earn. It seems to me, they forget that they also have to somewhat enjoy what they are probably going to spend the rest of their work lives doing, in my estimation.

Version 2:

Too many students choose a career based solely on how much they would earn. They forget that enjoying what they spend the rest of their work lives doing is important, too.

Version 1 contains weakening phrases: "sometimes I think", "likely", "it seems to me", "somewhat", "probably", and "in my estimation," adding nothing but

BTW!

Business Meeting Bingo!

Company meetings are often rife with worn out catch phrases and overworked analogies. One creative way to help heighten awareness of business cliché's while adding entertainment value is to play Meeting Bingo! Developed by Derose (2011). Simply create a bingo card with the following one word or phrase on it, and let the laughs begin: win-win, leverage, milestones and objectives, out of the loop, knowledge base, high-level approach, fast-track, work smarter, on the same page, vision statement, think outside the box, game plan, incent, facilitate and lead, proactive, the truth is, information-based, air cover, client focus(ed), identify potential, drill down, empower(ment), synergy, result-driven.

Check off each word or phrase when you hear it. When you get a whole row, column, or major diagonal, shout or otherwise signal that you've won!

uncertainty to the speaker's message. At least it is phrased in an active voice, which does communicate confidence. If you have a position, state it directly without crutch words that signal your timidity to the audience.

Summary

Spoken language differs from written language in several important ways. In many cases, spoken language requires redundancy; it affects the order of ideas, and requires that the speaker pay attention to rhythm. Spoken language may also require that you signal your audience before you present important material.

The most effective language is simple, clear, and direct. Use short, common words instead of long, unusual ones; avoid euphemisms and jargon; eliminate unnecessary words that pad your speech; be direct and concrete, and avoid exaggeration.

Engage the imagination of your listeners through the use of metaphors, similes, and other figures of speech that paint memorable word pictures. Use language to create a theme. Regardless of the choices you make, be certain your language fits your personality, position, and the needs of your audience. The effective use of humor requires that you have confidence in your ability to make people laugh. Be cautious with humor, particularly if you are not typically a funny person. Laugh at yourself, not others. Use understated anecdotes. And remember, humor is everywhere. Find humor in your own experiences.

To improve your speaking style, avoid long and unnecessary words, clichés, inappropriate euphemisms. Edit out profanity, slang, and jargon, drop exaggeration and clichés, as well as sentences that say nothing or communicate uncertainty. Removing these common pitfalls will enhance your language prowess.

Discussion Starters

1. In your opinion, is spoken language significantly different from written language? How can language contribute to or detract from the effectiveness of your speech?

2. Why must language fit the needs of the speaker, audience, occasion, and message? What do you need to consider when choosing proper language in a speech?

3. What are some of the language pitfalls that you have witnessed while watching a speech? What effect did these have on the overall message for you?

④ How does humor affect the speaker–audience relationship? What impact might it have on speaker ethos? Generally, do you believe humor is correlated with higher intelligence? If so, when might this generalization not hold true?

References

Berg, K., & Gilman, A. (1989). *Get to the Point: How to Say What You Mean and Get What You Want.* New York: Random House.

Buscaglia, Leo. (2007). *I Helped Him Cry.* Children's Thoughts on Love. Utah Government Document. Retrieved July 28, 2011 from www.schools.utah.gov/cte/documents/.../6_8ChildrensThoughtsOnLove.

Burton, G. O. (n.d.). Silva Rhetoricae: *The Trees of Rhetoric* (Online resource). Brigham Young University. Retrieved September 1, 2011 from rhetoric.byu.edu/.

Chang, M., & Gruner, C. R. (1981). Audience Reaction to Self-Disparaging Humor. *Southern Speech Communication Journal, 46,* 419–426.

Colin Firth Oscar Acceptance Speech 2011: Video, Transcript. Retrieved September 3, 2011 from www.nowpublic.com/culture/colin-firth-oscar-acceptance-speech-2011-video-transcript-2761763.html.

Derose, S. (2011). *Business Meeting Bingo.* Retrieved August 1, 2011 from www.derose.net/steve/resources/papers/Bingo.html.

Detz, J. (1984). *How to Write and Give a Speech.* New York: St. Martin's Press.

Dosomething.org. (2011). *Tips and Tools, 11 Facts About the BP Oil Spill.* Retrieved August 1, 2011 from www.dosomething.org/tipsandtools/11-facts-about-bp-oil-spill.

Duarte, N. (2011). *Congress, Preparers Urge IRS to Clarify Publications by Using Plain Language.* Retrieved July 28, 2011 from www.tax.com/taxcom/features.nsf/Articles/054E880A97191EFF852576E3006878C5?OpenDocument.

Ehrlich, E., & Hawes, G. R. (1984). *Speak for Success.* New York: Bantam Books.

Farhi, P. (2010, November 15). PBS Edits Tina Fey's Remarks from Twain Event. *The Washington Post Online.* Retrieved September 3, 2011 from www.voices.washingtonpost.com/arts-posts/2010/11/by_paul_farhi_tina_fey.html.

Gruner, C. R. (1985, April). Advice to the Beginning Speaker on Using Humor—What the Research Tells Us. *Communication Education, 34*, 142.

Gustainis, J. J. (1987). Jesse Louis Jackson. In B. K. Duffy & H. R. Ryan (Eds.), *American Orators of the Twentieth Century: Critical Studies and Sources*. New York: Greenwood Press.

Harrell, A. (1997). *Speaking Beyond the Podium: A Public Speaking Handbook, 2nd Ed.* Harcourt Brace College Publishing: Fort Worth.

Kaplan, R. M., & Pascoe, G. C. (1977). Humorous Lectures and Humorous Examples: Some Effects upon Comprehension and Retentions. *Journal of Educational Psychology, 69*, 61–65.

Kleinfeld, N. R. (1990). Teaching the 'Sir Winston' Method. *New York Times, March 11*, 7.

Knowlton, B. (2008). Obama Vows to Cut Budget Waste. *New York Times. November 25*. Retrieved September 3, 2011 from www.newyorktime/2008/11/26/us/politics/25-cnd-transition/html.

Kurtzman, D. (n.d.). *Political Humor, Top 10 Bushisms*, About.com. Retrieved July 29, 2011 from politicalhumor.about.com/cs/georgewbush/a/top10bushisms.htm.

Mooney, A. (2011, June 22). Michelle Obama Brings 'Yes, We Can' to Africa. *CNN Politics, The 1600 Report*. Retrieved July 29, 2011 from whitehouse.blogs.cnn.com/2011/06/22/michelle-obama-brings-yes-we-can-to-africa/.

Phillips, M. (2009, January 21). President Barack Obama's Inaugural Address. *The White House Blog*. Retrieved July 29, 2011 from www.whitehouse.gov/blog/inaugural-address/.

Purdue OWL. (2011). *Active and Passive Voice*. Purdue Online Writing Lab, Purdue University. Retrieved July 29, 2011 from owl.english.purdue.edu/owl/resource/539/4/.

Rackleff, R. B. (1987, September 26). The Art of Speech Writing: A Dramatic Event (Speech). Reprinted in *Vital Speeches of the Day*, March 1, 1988.

Schmich, M. (1997). Advice, Like Youth, Probably Just Wasted on the Young. *Chicago Tribune, June 1*. Retrieved June 10, 2007 from www.chicagotribune.com.

Tarver, J. (1988, March 2). Words in Time: Some Reflections on the Language of Speech. Reprinted in *Vital Speeches of the Day*, April 15, 410–412.

Valenti, J. (1982). *Speak Up with Confidence*. New York: William Morrow and Company, Inc.

Ziv, A. (1982). Cognitive Results of Using Humor in Teaching. Paper presented at the *Third International Conference on Humor*, Washington, DC. (Cited in Gruner, Advice to the Beginning Speaker, p. 144).

Chapter

14

> *"Nothing gives one person so much advantage over another as to remain always cool and unruffled under all circumstances."*
>
> Thomas Jefferson

Chapter 14: Delivery and Communication Apprehension

Your ability to communicate information, persuade, and entertain is influenced by the manner in which you present yourself to your audience. This chapter discusses methods of delivery and offers specific strategies for vocal delivery and physical delivery so your message is favorably enhanced by the way you convey it, with a focuses on communication apprehension and strategies you can use to control it.

Student Learning Objectives:

○ Students will be able to list the four methods of delivery

○ Students will be able to describe the aspects of vocal delivery

○ Students will be able to explain the aspects of physical delivery

○ Students will be able to recognize communication apprehension and learn strategies to avoid it

DELIVERY AND COMMUNICATION APPREHENSION

What do you remember after a speaker is finished? Although you may walk away with the speaker's ideas buzzing through your mind, it is often the quality of the performance that remains with you long after you have forgotten the content of the message. That is to say, the *how* of public speaking—the speaker's style of delivery—often makes the most lasting impression.

Imagine being one of the graduates at Stanford University in 2005 listening to Steve Jobs, co-founder of Apple who battled pancreatic cancer for many years, as he said the following during his commencement address:

> When I was 17, I read a quote that went something like: "If you live each day as if it was your last, someday you'll most certainly be right." It made an impression on me, and since then, for the past 33 years, I have looked in the mirror every morning and asked myself: "If today were the last day of my life, would I want to do what I am about to do today?" And whenever the answer has been "No" for too many days in a row, I know I need to change something. (www.stanford.edu).

BTW!

Steve Jobs

Steve Jobs was the co-founder and CEO of Apple, Inc. In addition to working at the helm of Apple Computers, Jobs served as chief executive of Pixar Animation Studios and was a member of the board of directors of The Walt Disney Company.

As a result of his technical expertise, motivation, and creativity, Jobs was listed as either primary inventor or co-inventor in over 230 awarded patents or patent applications related to a range of technologies.

In 2004 Steve Jobs announced he had pancreatic cancer. Although still involved with major strategic decisions at Apple, Jobs' health had been the source of much speculation for several years. Despite this, he made appearances in 2011 to help launch both the iPad2 and iCloud before resigning as CEO due to poor health. He died in October 2011.

To learn more about his life and to hear his speech, "You've Got to Find What You Love," go to YouTube and search "Steve Jobs 2005 Commencement Address."

Those listening to Jobs' speech were motivated by his business success, and the section above was particularly poignant because of his health issues. Words alone are not enough to make audiences want to listen to a speech. Many brilliant people—scientists, lawyers, politicians, engineers, environmentalists—never connect with their listeners, not for lack of trying, but for problems with the delivery of their speech. Maybe they are too stiff or appear uninvolved. Worse, they may try to imitate other speakers, and it just doesn't work.

Delivery affects your credibility as a speaker. Your ability to communicate information, persuade, and entertain is influenced by the manner in which you present yourself to your audience. An effective delivery works *for* you, an ineffective delivery against you—even when the content of your message is strong. (You decide whether you think Steve Jobs' speech is effective or not by clicking on the link provided in **BTW: Steve Jobs**.)

Methods of Delivery

Speeches can be delivered in one of four ways. You may find comfort in one style more than the other, but hopefully, you will have an opportunity to explore different methods of delivery during your public speaking course. Each of the four methods is appropriate in certain situations. Analyze your audience and the occasion when choosing the most appropriate and effective delivery method.

Performance guidelines accompany each method of delivery. Consider these as you plan your delivery. Methods of delivery include impromptu—a speech that frequently involves no preparation time; extemporaneous—a speech that involves preparation and practice; manuscript—a speech where everything is written out; or memorized—a speech that has been committed to memory. The following section covers these four methods in order of the most to least frequent method of delivery.

Impromptu Speaking

Impromptu speaking involves little to no preparation time. As a result, the speaker uses no notes or only the briefest of notes. You may have several occasions over your lifetime when you are asked to speak briefly without any advance notice. For example, as a principal of a high school attending a local school board meeting, you may be asked to comment on the recent basketball victory or recognize the accomplishments of a retiring teacher. During other occasions, you may be asked to "say a few words" about a newlywed couple, the dearly departed, or a promotion you just received.

In a public speaking class, many instructors include impromptu speaking opportunities throughout the semester to help students get on their feet and face the audience. Instructors generally feel that the more opportunities students have to present, the more comfortable students will feel in the speaking

Glossary

Impromptu speaking
Speaking with little or no preparation time; using no notes or just a few.

environment. You may have an activity in class where you introduce yourself or someone in the class or you may asked to give an impromptu speech on "my proudest moment," or "my favorite vacation spot."

Not everyone has the ability of Marcus Garvey, African American nationalist leader, to speak on the spur of the moment. Dorothy Pennington, an expert in the rhetoric of African Americans, describes Garvey's oratorical style:

> He often spoke impromptu, gleaning his topic and remarks from something that had occurred during the earlier portion of the program. For example, in speaking before the conference of the Universal Negro Improvement Association in August 1937, Garvey showed how his theme emerged: "I came as usual without a subject, to pick the same from the surroundings, the environment, and I got one from the singing of the hymn 'Faith of our Fathers.' I shall talk to you on that as a theme for my discourse." This type of adaptation allowed Garvey to tap into the main artery of what an audience was thinking and feeling (Duffy & Ryan, 1987, p. 170).

Impromptu speaking forces you to think on your feet. With no opportunity to prepare, you must rely on what you know. Following are several suggestions to help you create an effective impromptu speech.

Focus your remarks on the audience and occasion. Remind your listeners of the occasion or purpose of the meeting. For example, "We have assembled to protest the rise in parking fines from $10 to $25." When unexpectedly called to speak, talk about the people who are present and the accomplishments of the group. You can praise the group leader ("Michelle's done so much to solve the campus parking problem"), the preceding speaker, or the group as a whole. You may want to refer to something a previous speaker said, whether you agree or disagree. This gives you a beginning point, and a brief moment to think about and organize your comments.

Keep it simple. Every speech needs an introduction, body, and conclusion. Since time is limited in an impromptu speech, create a brief introduction that is tied to the other parts of speech. For example, if you are giving a toast to the bride and groom, consider mentioning them in the introduction ("I am so honored to be able to toast Allison and Adam, two of my favorite people …"), and in the conclusion ("So raise your glasses high, and join with me in congratulating Allison and Adam, a couple who define happiness and commitment"). The body of your speech should include only one or two main points. Each point should be supported by a reason, and each point should have an example.

Use examples. Be as concrete as possible, such as "I decided to become active in this organization after I heard about a student who was threatened with expulsion from school after accumulating $500 in unpaid parking fines."

Keep in mind that as an impromptu speaker, you are not expected to make a polished, professional speech—everyone knows you have not prepared. But you are expected to deliver your remarks in a clear, cogent manner.

Do not try to say too much, and do not apologize. Instead of jumping from point to point vaguely, focus on your specific purpose. When you complete the mission of your speech, turn the platform over to another speaker. Never apologize. Your audience is already aware it is an impromptu moment; apologizing for the informality of your address is unnecessary. You do not need to say anything that will lessen your audience's expectations of your speech.

Extemporaneous Speaking

Extemporaneous speaking is a method of delivery that involves using carefully prepared notes to guide the presentation. This form of delivery has many advantages. Specifically, speakers can maintain a personal connection with their listeners and respond to their feedback. The most effective public speaking is often described as the speaker's response to the listener's reaction.

The extemporaneous mode of delivery allows the speaker–listener interaction to occur as you adjust your choice of words and decide what to include—or exclude—in your speech. You can shorten a speech or go into greater detail than you originally planned. This mode of speaking provides flexibility.

Speaking extemporaneously means that your word choice is *fresh*. Although you know the intent of your message in advance, and you practice your speech so that key words or phrases remain with you, you choose your exact words as you are delivering your speech. The result is a spontaneous, conversational tone that puts you and your audience at ease.

Consider the following guidelines as you prepare your extemporaneous speech. A disclaimer here may be helpful: Not all speakers need all suggestions listed, nor do instructors of public speaking agree entirely on all advice. (This is true of our suggestions throughout this chapter and textbook.)

Prepare carefully. Use the same care you would use when preparing a written report. Choose your purpose, develop your core idea, research your topic, organize your ideas, and select the language and presentation style that are most appropriate for your audience.

Prepare both a full content and key-word speaker's outline. Develop an outline containing main points and subpoints, then create a key-word outline that can be transferred to index cards of the appropriate size. The full content outline is *not* your speech written out; it represents the major ideas of your speech and supporting material. The key-word outline is brief enough to be transferred to note cards.

Note cards, which can be held or placed on a lectern, should be large enough to accommodate information from your key-word outline, yet small

Glossary

Extemporaneous speaking
A method of delivery that involves using carefully prepared notes to guide the presentation.

To prepare for your extemporaneous speech, develop an outline containing main points and sub-points.

© Alberto Zornetta, 2012. Under license from Shutterstock, Inc.

enough to be unobtrusive. You may include delivery cues, such as using "//" to symbolize where you should pause and look up if you feel cues about eye contact would be helpful. Recently, as a student gave his own eulogy in a special occasion speech, he worked from a very brief outline. His speech was too short, and he seemed to have a lapse of memory. Had he used a more fully developed outline, these problems would have been eliminated.

Place detailed information on separate note cards. Facts, figures, and quotations may be written on separate note cards for easy reference. Always remember your ethical responsibility not to misrepresent facts or opinions that require careful and precise explanations. Rather than take the chance of misquoting people or facts, it may help to have information written on separate cards. You may find that presentational software can help. You may want to put a particularly vivid quote on a slide, or you may have specific facts and figures that might be more appropriately presented on a slide than assuming your audience will remember such information.

Write legibly. Your notes are useless if you cannot read them, so print your words boldly and consider highlighting critical ideas. If typing, use an appropriate font size. Remember, too, as stated above, your visual aids can serve as notes to some extent.

Use your notes as a prompter *not* as a script. Notes enable you to keep your ideas in mind without committing every word to memory. Notes also make it possible to maintain eye contact with your listeners. You can glance around the room, looking occasionally at your note cards, without giving anyone the impression that you are reading your speech.

Using a Manuscript

Manuscript reading involves writing your speech out word for word and then reading it. A manuscript speech may be considered in formal occasions when the speech is distributed beforehand, if it is to be archived, translated, or printed after it is given. Having a manuscript speech minimizes the temptation to add remarks during the speech.

If an issue or occasion is controversial or sensitive, a speaker may choose to rely on a manuscript. Having a carefully crafted statement may help avoid misstating a position. Reading from a manuscript when addressing a hostile audience may be beneficial because your listeners are ready—and waiting—to attack your statement. This is a time when your communication needs to be exact.

For those who are not professional speakers, a manuscript may be troublesome. If the font size is too small, it may be difficult to read. It is possible to lose your place in the manuscript because you must look up and then back down. Some people tend to sound as though they are reading rather than speaking when working from a manuscript. While many speaking situations call for note cards, there are occasions when manuscript speaking is appropriate. If you find yourself involved in one of these occasions, we offer four performance guidelines.

Pay special attention to preparing the written text. If you cannot read what you have written, your delivery will falter. Avoid using a handwritten manuscript. Make sure you choose a large enough font to see without squinting, and have the lines spaced well enough that you do not lose your place.

A big mistake students make is typing the entire speech on the required number of note cards (even though they have been warned not to do this). If a five- to eight-minute speech is typed on three to five note cards, the outcome is not pretty. Students find themselves unable to read the cards—font size is six points, and 12 lines of type are on each note card. They cannot read, they lose their place, they stumble as they try to decipher the words, and even worse, because they are concentrating so hard on reading the notes, they forget about the vocal aspects of delivery! The lesson learned? Use a manuscript only when the occasion suggests it.

Practice. The key to successful manuscript speaking is practice and more practice. One run through is not sufficient. Practice enough that you are not dependent on the manuscript, and you do not need to look down for each sentence. Consider inviting friends, roommates, or relatives to listen to your speech and provide constructive feedback. Try practicing your speech first in sections—introduction, then body, then conclusion. You might find one or more parts of your speech needs more work, or more delivery preparation.

Express yourself naturally and communicate your personality. Think of the speaking occasion as a way to converse with your audience. You want them to have a peek into your personality. If you're an upbeat, energetic individual, work to convey those traits through movement, meaningful gestures, and solid eye contact.

Keep a somewhat conversational tone with your audience. For example, sometimes when reading aloud, speakers will say "a book" but pronounce the "a" as in "hay" rather than "a" as in "spa." Think about what you want to emphasize and vary the pitch of your voice to avoid being monotone. Pronounce words as you would in normal speech and be conscious of speaking too quickly or too slowly. When you are dependent on a manuscript, you need to make sure it does not sound like you are reading to the audience.

Make eye contact with your audience. Glance back and forth between your manuscript and your audience, but take care not to bob your head in the process. Looking up from the manuscript and making eye contact with members of your audience are important aspects of manuscript delivery.

Memorization

Committing your speech to memory may be useful when you know you will be receiving an award or recognition so you make sure you thank the

© Stuart Jenner, 2012. Under license from Shutterstock, Inc.

A memorized speech is a great time to use eye contact and engage the audience.

right people and express appropriate appreciation. Special occasions, such as toasting the bride and groom or delivering a *brief* commencement address, are also opportunities for delivering a memorized speech. Memorization enables you to write the exact words you will speak without being forced to read them. It also makes it easier to establish eye contact with your audience and deliver your speech skillfully.

Memorization is a risky choice for the beginning public speaker. In the middle of a 10-minute speech, you may find you cannot remember the next word. Because you memorized the speech (or so you thought), you have no note cards to help you through the crisis. You pause, hoping the next words will come to mind. Sometimes they do, and sometimes you're out of luck. Even those who spend hours preparing for the presentation may forget everything when facing an audience. If you find yourself in a situation where memorization is necessary, consider the following five performance guidelines.

1 **Start memorizing the speech as soon as possible.** You do not want to delay the process so that you are under a severe time constraint. The night before does *not* work! Make sure you have ample time to work on the memorization aspect of your delivery. Even experienced professional speakers have to work hard to remember their lines.

2 **Memorize small sections of your speech at a time.** Do not allow yourself to become overwhelmed with the task. Memorizing small sections of your speech at a time minimizes the chance that you will forget your speech during the delivery. Remember that some people can memorize speeches more easily than others, so work at your own pace and do not compare yourself to the classmate who memorized her speech in a short time.

3 **Determine where you need pauses, emphasis, and vocal variety.** You want to convey the appropriate tone for your speech— enthusiasm, excitement, anger, bewilderment. You can achieve this by emphasizing certain words, speaking faster or more slowly, and increasing or lowering your volume and/or pitch. More about vocal aspects of delivery is discussed shortly.

4 **Use eye contact effectively.** Avoid looking like you are trying to remember the speech. This takes away from the effectiveness of the message. A memorized speech is a great time to use eye contact and engage the audience. Sustained eye contact can enhance a speaker's credibility, increase the persuasive effect of the speech, and maintain audience interest.

5 **Be calm if you forget.** It is possible to be distracted in a number of ways:

- Audience member has loud coughing fit
- Cell phone goes off
- Someone leaves

- Audience members applaud when you are not expecting it
- Jets fly overhead

One teacher told about being in the audience when the speaker kept backing up two sentences each time the audience applauded. The audience recognized it was memorized, and left feeling it was not as effective as the speaker intended it to be.

If you lose your place, pause. Do not announce it. Do not laugh. Do not curse. Do not apologize. Remember, your job is not to be perfect, it is to communicate something important to your audience. If you were perfect, after all, many would be distracted by your delivery and others might even resent it. Simply plan for it, know how to handle it, and move on!

Overall, delivering a memorized speech can be effective. Some speech instructors include a memorized speech as a required activity, and find success. But it is also a gamble. In addition to the actual task of memorization, work on connecting with the audience through eye contact, vocal variety, and gestures.

Aspects of Verbal Delivery

The speaker should never forget about the needs of the audience, and this applies to vocal delivery also. Many of us mumble, leave off the endings of our words, and fail to pronounce words correctly A German friend of ours once joked, "Americans speak as though they have hot potatoes in their mouths." Poor verbal delivery makes the listeners work hard, and can distract them. When presenting in public, consider the following aspects of vocal delivery: articulation, pronunciation, volume, rate, pitch, pauses, and emphasis.

Articulation

A person who articulates well is someone who speaks clearly and intelligibly. **Articulation** refers to the production of sound and how precisely we form our words. How we place our jaw, tongue, and lips influence our vocal production. The more formal the situation, the more precise our articulation needs to be. The more casual the situation, the more likely we are to relax our speech. In front of most audiences, sloppy or careless pronunciation patterns should be avoided.

Words need to be crisp and clear. The listener should be able to distinguish between sounds and not be confused. The popular phrase, "Da Bears" shows how we mainstream some of our "inarticulation." Leaving off the "g" in going, driving, shopping, etc., is a common language simplification in American culture. Saying "I wanna," "I coulda," and "I hafta" are other examples of sloppy articulation that is acceptable in informal situations, but not within a formal context. We offer the following two guidelines to help with articulation.

Glossary

Articulation The verbalization of distinct sounds and how precisely words are formed.

❶ **Adapt to your audience.** In a formal setting, such as a commencement speech or an awards ceremony, you want to be as articulate as possible. It is *always* important to be understood.

❷ **Eliminate bad habits.** Reflect a moment about how you articulate. Do you speak clearly? Do you mumble? Do you mispronounce certain words? Do you leave the endings off words? Make a conscious effort to think about articulation. Check out how well you do with the following:

- Red leather, yellow leather
- Which witch watched Willy watch Wanda wash windows?
- Thinking, making, stinking, faking.
- My momma made me mash my red M&Ms.
- Betty Botter had some butter, "But," she said, "this butter's bitter. If I bake this bitter butter, it would make my batter bitter. But a bit of better butter—*that* would make my batter better." So she bought a bit of butter, better than her bitter butter, and she baked it in her batter, and the batter was not bitter. So 'twas better Betty Botter bought a bit of better butter.
- A big black bug bit a big black bear, made the big black bear bleed blood.

Pronunciation

Pronunciation is related to articulation, but it involves saying a word correctly as opposed to how you form sounds. Sometimes speakers simply do not know the word and mispronounce it; other times, a word is mispronounced because of dialect differences among speakers. For example, you may have heard President George W. Bush leave off the "g" in "recognize," so the words sounds like "reconize." We hear speakers present "satistics" instead of "statistics," and talk about "I-talians" and the citizens of "I-raq."

Are you someone whose name is always mispronounced? If so, you know it can be annoying. More importantly, however, mispronunciations may hurt your credibility. Listeners may perceive you to be less educated or less culturally aware.

Check pronunciation of unfamiliar words. A speaker's credibility is somewhat dependent on pronunciation. It is a speaker's ethical responsibility to determine how to pronounce the words in his/her speech. The speaker should know how to pronounce all words, including the names of people, places, and foreign terms. Not knowing can convey laziness, lack of concern, or lack of respect, in the case of foreign terms or names. Recently, a student participating in a speech contest lost points when she quoted the German philospher Goethe, and pronounced his name as though it rhymed with

Glossary

Pronunciation Knowing how to say a word and saying it correctly.

"both" as opposed to something that rhymes closely to "Berta" (and apologies to you German speakers).

Do not comment on your pronunciation. Do not say, "or however you pronounce that" or "I cannot pronounce that." While we are likely to forgive regional differences, our credibility will be reduced if our listeners see we have made little or no effort to determine the correct pronunciation.

Practice the pronunciation of difficult words. You do not want to stumble or draw attention away from the point you are making. Just like learning a foreign language, it may take several efforts to pronounce a word correctly. So practice the word several times over a span of time.

Volume

If your audience cannot hear you, your speech serves little purpose. Volume is controlled by how forcefully air is expelled through the trachea onto the vocal folds. This exhalation is controlled by the contraction of the abdominal muscles. The more forcefully you use these muscles to exhale, the greater the force of the air, and the louder your voice. Some individuals are naturally quiet, and must work to be heard. Consider the following suggestions when working on your volume.

Do not mistake shouting for projection. Shouting involves forcing the voice from the vocal folds, which is irritating to the folds, instead of projecting the sound from the abdominal area. Straining your voice will only make you hoarse. Instead, work on your posture and breathing from the diaphragm. Also, some cultures value a lower volume. Speakers need to understand possible cultural differences.

Use volume to add interest and variety to your speech. Maybe you want to add a bit of humor to your introduction of a speaker. Using a "stage whisper," you could say something like, "And if we all clap very loudly, we can coax him on to the stage." On his television show, Dr. Phil uses volume effectively by getting loud when he thinks people should be annoyed by what is happening and speaking softly when he is showing amazement or sharing a startling fact. Increasing volume at certain times during your speech draws attention to your point, and having variety, in general, maintains interest.

Adapt to other variables. If you use a microphone, conduct a volume check before the speech, or if that's not possible, check your volume as you begin your speech. A microphone is not necessary in a small room but may be vital in a larger room. Adapt your volume to the size of the room as well as to distractions that may be occurring within the room (fans whirring, chairs creaking) or outside the room (airplanes, hallway noise, construction).

Glossary

Volume The loudness of your voice, controlled by how forcefully air is expelled through the trachea onto the vocal folds.

Be sure to test the microphone before your speech!

Do not talk to the podium. If you have your notes on the podium and your head is bent, the audience will not be able to hear. Do not talk to your notes, period. Look up, and speak to your audience. Remember also, if you turn to look at your PowerPoint, you will not be heard as well. Avoid giving your speech to the wall behind you.

Rate

On the average, Americans' rate of speech is between 120 and 160 words per minute. Keep in mind, our normal rate of speech may be acceptable within our own region or culture, but when speaking to a culturally diverse audience, we may need to speak more slowly. One of your authors recently took a course in Germany, and met students from many different countries. Several were interested in practicing their English. They thanked her because she spoke slowly and clearly, so they could process her words. Sometimes we forget that others may not understand us at our normal rate.

Nervousness may affect your normal pattern. When practicing alone, you may be relieved when you find that in timing your speech you are just over the minimum time required. However, under the pressure of giving a speech, you may find yourself speeding up ("The faster I talk, the faster I'll finish") or slowing down. Rate is also affected by mode of delivery. If you read a manuscript rather than speak extemporaneously, you may find yourself running a verbal road race.

Choose an appropriate rate. Knowing your audience also influences the rate of your speech. Your rate should be consistent with the ideas being expressed and for the cultural context. For example, it makes sense that a sportscaster announcing a basketball game speaks faster than a sportscaster at a golf match. Also, if you are using several terms that might not be known to your audience, you want to slow down as you mention those terms. One of your authors attended an international conference in Russia that was conducted primarily in English. When presenting in English, it was important for the American speakers to slow down so Russian listeners with various level of English language competency could understand.

Vary your rate of speech. By changing your rate of speech, you can express different thoughts and feelings. You may want to speak slowly to emphasize an important point or to communicate a serious or somber mood. A faster pace is appropriate when you are telling your audience something it already knows (many speeches include background information that sets the scene) or to express surprise, happiness, or fear. If you find yourself racing through your speech, you need to figure out how to slow down. One suggestion is to find a transitional word to emphasize, such as "although," or "yet," or "and so," and then work to achieve a slower rate.

Glossary

Rate The pace at which you speak.

Pitch

Pitch refers to your vocal range or key. Your voice produces a high or low pitch by the tightening and loosening of your vocal folds. The range of most people's voices is less than two octaves. Pitch is a problem when your voice is too high pitched; in men a high-pitched voice may sound immature, and in women it may sound screechy.

Vary your pitch. Variety adds interest to your presentation. Avoid a monotone. When you do not vary the pitch of your voice, you risk putting your listeners to sleep. Giving an illustration, telling a story, or providing startling statistics are all good instances in which one can raise your pitch because it can convey a sense of excitement or urgency.

Use your voice potential. Take advantage of the fact that our voices have incredible range. To add a sense of amazement, disgust, or to share a moment of seriousness with your audience, you can lower the pitch of a word or phrase you want to emphasize. Resist the temptation to raise your voice too much at key points.

Pauses

Some speakers talk nonstop until, literally, they run out of breath. Others pause every three or four words in a kind of nervous verbal chop. Still others, particularly those who read their speeches, pause at the wrong times—perhaps in the middle of an important idea—making it difficult for their listeners to follow.

Pauses serve multiple purposes. First, they communicate self-confidence. Pauses deliver the nonverbal message that you are relaxed enough to stop talking for a moment. Second, they help listeners digest what you are saying and anticipate what you will say next. Third, a significant pause helps you move from one topic to the next without actually telling your listeners what you are doing. Fourth, a pause signals *pay attention*. This is especially true for long pauses lasting two or three seconds.

Pauses add color, expression, and feeling to a speech. They should be used deliberately to achieve a desired effect. If used effectively, pauses add power and control to your speech. According to Don Hewitt, producer of *60 Minutes*, "It's the intonation, the pauses, that tell the story. They are as important to us as commas and periods are to the *New York Times*" (in Fletcher, 1990, p. 15).

In 1993, Nelson Mandela, then president of the African National Congress, received the Nobel Peace Prize. The following is an excerpt from his acceptance speech (Mandela, 1993):

> We speak here of the challenge of the dichotomies of war and peace, violence and nonviolence, racism and human dignity, oppression and repression and liberty and human rights, poverty and freedom from want.

We stand here today as nothing more than a representative of the millions of our people who dared to rise up against a social system whose very essence is war, violence, racism, oppression, repression, and the impoverishment of an entire people.

I am also here today as a representative of the millions of people across the globe, the anti-apartheid movement, the governments and organizations that joined with us, not to fight against South Africa as a country or any of its peoples, but to oppose an inhuman system and sue for a speedy end to the apartheid crime against humanity.

Try reading the excerpt aloud, using pauses where you find commas. Try using pauses of different lengths. While his words are powerful, they gain greater impact as he pauses before or after key words or phrases. (For more information about Nelson Mandela, see **BTW: Nelson Mandela**.)

Tie your pauses to verbal phrasing. To a speaker, a phrase has a different meaning than it does to a writer. It is a unit you speak in one breath to express a single idea. Each pause tells your listeners you are moving from one thought to the next. Pausing when you introduce a new idea or term gives your listeners time to absorb what you are saying.

Use pauses to change the pace and add verbal variety. Pauses can be an effective tool speakers use to keep attention or to draw attention to a particular thought or emotion. Pause just before you speed up or pause just before you slow down. In both cases, the pause indicates to the audience that something is going to happen.

BTW!

Nelson Mandela

Nelson Mandela, who turned 93 in 2011 and who is one of the world's most revered statesmen, led the struggle to replace the apartheid regime of South Africa with a multiracial democracy. In the 1950s, Mandela began his struggle to end apartheid. In 1964, he was imprisoned for trying to overthrow the government, but continued his fight from his prison cell.

Jailed for 27 years, he emerged to become the country's first black president and to play a leading role in the drive for peace in other spheres of conflict. He won the Nobel Peace Prize in 1993. His charisma, self-deprecating sense of humor and lack of bitterness over his harsh treatment in prison, as well as his amazing life story, help to explain his global appeal. For more information, we suggest starting with www.nelsonmandela.org, nobelprize.org, and seque.atlas.uiuc.edu.

Extend pauses when displaying a visual. This tactic enables your audience to read the information on the visual without missing your next thought. It is important to pause after the display, not before it. Try pausing for two or three seconds.

Emphasis

A speaker uses emphasis to draw attention to a specific word or phrase. It involves stressing certain words or phrases. It can add weight to what you say, and make a particular word or phrase more noticeable or prominent. An emotion can be highlighted through the use of emphasis. Emphasis is a nonverbal way of saying, "Listen to this!"

Think about how many ways you can say, "Come in." Depending on how they are said and how they are accented by nonverbal behavior, these words can be:

Glossary

Emphasis Stressing certain words or phrases to draw attention.

TABLE 14.1

A friendly invitation	from one friend to another
A command	from a supervisor to an employee
An angry growl	from a mother with a headache to her teenage son who has already interrupted her five times
A nondescript response	to a knock at your office door

Similarly, read the following sentences and emphasize the word indicated.

> **I** didn't say she stole the money.
>
> I **didn't** say she stole the money.
>
> I didn't say **she** stole the money.
>
> I didn't say she **stole** the money.
>
> I didn't say she stole the **money**.

In all these cases, change of emphasis gives meaning to a word or phrase. By singling out a few words for special attention, you add color to your speech and avoid monotony. Emphasis can be achieved by using different techniques.

Change your volume and pitch. Whether you choose to speak more loudly or more quietly, you draw attention to your speech through contrast. A quieter approach is often a more effective attention-grabber. When you speak in a monotone, you tell your listeners you have nothing to emphasize. When you vary the pitch of your voice, you let them know that what you are saying is important.

Pause when changing your speaking rate. A change of pace—speeding up or slowing down—draws attention to what will come next; pausing can do the same.

Use emotion. Emphasis comes naturally when you speak from the heart. When you have deep feelings about a subject—drug abuse, for example, or the need to protect the environment from pollution—you express your feelings emphatically. Anything other than an impassioned delivery may seem inadequate.

Work with the excerpt of Nelson Mandela's acceptance speech. Read it aloud. The first time, do not emphasize anything. Read it in a monotone, just as you would a telephone book. It is hard to get involved, is it not? Now, underscore the words or phrases that, if emphasized, would add meaning to the speech. Then read it a second time, adding the emphasis and emotion you think appropriate. You may find that the words seem to take a life of their own as they demand attention.

Eliminating Nonfluencies

Nonfluencies, also known as filled pauses or vocal fillers, are meaningless words that interrupt the flow of our speech. We use nonfluencies for a variety of reasons. They may be place-holders as we speak, they may indicate nervousness, or they may be one of our bad habits. We may use them unintentionally, but we need to work consciously to avoid them.

While pauses can work for you, nonfluencies distract your listeners. These include "like," "you know," "uh," "um," "so," and "okay." If your economics professor says "okay" after every concept presented, or your history professor adds "uh" or "um" after every thought, it can cause you to lose focus. Nonfluencies are verbal debris; they add nothing to the content of your speech, and they annoy an audience. Avoid them.

Throw out other types of speaking debris as well: giggling, throat clearing, lip smacking, and sighing. These interrupt the flow of speech and may also distract or annoy the audience. As you give speeches during this term, think about habits you have that may distract your audience. We do not expect you to be perfect, but striving to improve your speaking ability is a realistic goal.

Be aware of your speech patterns. Many people do not realize they use fillers. If you are videotaped, listen for nonfluencies as you watch your speech. You can also try recording your voice or ask friends to identify your nonfluencies.

Train yourself to be silent. Work actively to rid your speech of nonfluencies. Pause for a second or so after completing a phrase or other unit of thought. Because fillers indicate, in part, a discomfort with silence, this approach will help you realize that pauses are an acceptable part of communication.

Hopefully you noticed two central themes throughout this discussion of vocal delivery. The first is to *practice*. It is important to practice your speech so it flows smoothly. Practice pronouncing unfamiliar words so they come easily to you when you give your speech. The second theme is *vocal variety*. Vary pitch, rate, and volume to keep the audience's attention. Create interest in your speech, and stress key words, phrases, and thoughts. You have something relevant to share with your audience. You want to make it easy for them to understand you, and you want to keep them interested from start to finish.

Understanding Verbal Differences Across and Within Cultures

Language shapes how we perceive our world. Since every culture has its own unique features, it makes sense that we respond to situations differently. Verbal behaviors that are perfectly acceptable in one culture may be highly discouraged in another.

Cultures differ linguistically in a number of ways. For example, while English uses the word "you" as both an informal and formal pronoun, many cultures, including French and German, use a different form of "you" based on status and relationship. Variations in vocabulary exist, also. For example, depending on whom you ask, there are from seven to 50 words for snow in the Eskimo language. In Arabic, thousands of words are used to refer to a camel. The Dani of West New Guinea divide all colors into two words that roughly translate to "dark" and "light" (Lustig & Koester, 2010, p. 179).

Volume and directness are also aspects of language that differ across cultures. For example, in France, it is no secret that U.S. executives "are known to offend everyone in a restaurant, meeting, or on the street with their loud voices and braying laughter" (Morrison et al., 2001, p. 148). In Japan, it is important to emphasize and build on points of agreement. A high-pressure, confrontational approach is not compatible with Japanese culture (p. 229). In Mexico, courtesy and tact are valued more than truth. Directness is not considered a virtue (p. 255).

Differences exist within the United States. As a nation of immigrants, our blending of cultures has created a national culture with many subcultures. One of your authors remembers with fondness when she moved from Michigan to Arkansas, and on her first day of teaching was asked, "You're not from around here, are you?" Her accent and rate of speech differentiated her from her students.

As a speaker, it is always important to consider your audience. With a diverse audience, you may need to speak at a slower rate and avoid slang or jargon. You may need to speak more crisply and clearly, avoid dropping the ends of your words or slurring words together. When listening to someone who speaks English as a second language, you may notice differences in accent, rate, and pronunciation. Rather than judge the differences as "bad," recognize that the listener has a role in the communication situation also. Make the effort to attend to the speaker's message.

Aspects of Physical Delivery

Your physical delivery may convey professionalism or lack thereof. It can convey self-confidence or nervousness, enthusiasm or relative boredom. Your gestures, movement, eye contact, and dress say a great deal about you. More importantly, these elements leave a lasting impression that affects the speaker–audience connection. Although mastering the art of nonverbal communication will not guarantee your speaking success, it will help you convince your audience to pay attention.

Gestures

Gestures involve using your arms and hands to illustrate, emphasize, or provide a visual experience that accompanies your thoughts. Before we discuss the importance of gestures, body movement, and eye contact, we have a story about Katie, a nontraditional student who returned to school after five years of working for the loan department of a bank. She gave a speech adapted specifically to her audience, explaining how recent college graduates abuse credit cards and wind up owing thousands of dollars. She began:

> When you receive your first credit card, think of it as a loaded gun. If you don't use it properly you may wind up killing your credit for up to 10 years. That means that no one will loan you money to buy a car, a plasma TV, or a house. You may not get the job you want because your credit is bad (prospective employers check applicants' credit ratings). And you'll go through a lot of torment while this is going on. Take my word for it. I've seen it happen dozens of times to people just like you.

Making a connection between a credit card and a loaded gun is a great attention-getter. Also, college students are usually fairly new to using credit cards, so the message is an important one to the audience. Although Katie's message was effective, her delivery was stiff and uncomfortable. She grasped the lectern for dear life, as if she were afraid to move from her spot. She was a talking statue, and her listeners responded by becoming restless and uncomfortable themselves. During the post speech criticism, one audience member explained what he was feeling: "You looked so wooden that I had trouble listening to what you were saying, which is amazing since I'm already in credit card trouble."

Glossary

Gestures Using your arms and hands to illustrate, emphasize, or provide a visual experience that accompanies your thoughts.

© Golden Pixels LLC, 2012. Under license from Shutterstock, Inc.

How can you use gestures effectively in your speech?

Katie's problem was a lack of gestures and body movement, which her audience could not ignore despite the inherent interest of her speech. Gestures tell an audience that you are comfortable and self-confident. As an outlet for nervous energy, they actually help you feel more at ease. Gestures encourage an enthusiastic presentation. If you put your body into your speech through movement and gestures, it is difficult to present a stilted speech. Gestures also have a positive effect on breathing, helping you relax the muscles that affect the quality of the voice.

Gestures are especially important when you are speaking to a large audience. People in the back rows may not be able to see the changes in your facial expressions, and gestures may be their only way of seeing your involvement with your speech. Think about the following three guidelines as you practice using gestures.

❶ **Use natural gestures.** Your gestures should reinforce both the ideas in the message and your own personality. Stand straight, with your arms bent at the waist and your hands relaxed, so you are ready to gesture. Pay attention to the position of your elbows. If they hang stiffly at your sides, your gestures will look artificial. To move your hands and forearms freely, make sure there is plenty of room between your elbows and your body. Avoid looking as though your upper arms are velcroed to your body.

❷ **Gesture purposefully.** Gestures should not appear random but should be meaningful and enhance your message. For example, if you were trying to persuade people to donate blood, you might want to give your audience three reasons for doing so. When you say, "three reasons," you can hold up three fingers. When you say, "First," hold up one finger, and then when you say, "Second," hold up two fingers. You get the picture. These gestures are meaningful because they serve as an organizational guide. If you were giving an after-dinner speech in which you tried to convince your audience to stop complaining, you could put up one hand in the "stop" position when you say, "Stop complaining," to your audience. This is meaningful because it emphasizes your assertion.

❸ **Gesture appropriately.** Gestures should be timely. You do not want to hold up three fingers before or after you say "three reasons," but *as* you are saying it. You do not want arms flailing around as you speak; they should match what you are saying. Appropriate gestures are timely, and they should make sense within the context of your message. If you are speaking before a large audience, gestures are bigger and, generally, more dramatic. Those same gestures may look awkward and exaggerated in a smaller environment.

Actions That Inhibit Gesturing

The preceding three guidelines are designed to help you gesture effectively. Your authors have over 90 years of combined experience grading student speeches, and we have noticed several actions that reduce the overall effectiveness of a student's speech and/or distract the audience. Various actions may communicate uncertainty, nervousness, and may affect your message as it impacts your ethos. As you deliver your speech, try to avoid the following:

TABLE 14.2

Clasping your hands together	It makes gesturing impossible.
Hugging your body	It makes you look as though you are trying to protect yourself from assault.
Clasping your hands in the "fig leaf" stance	Holding your hands together at your crotch is another protective position, and it may be distracting.
Locking your hands behind your back	This may encourage you to rock back and forth. The "at ease" military stance is not appropriate for the classroom.
Hands on hips	This is a position of power that may distance you from your audience, and it restricts gestures.
Arms folded in front of you	This communicates defensiveness and a need for control; creates a barrier.
Putting your hands in your pockets	This restricts movement and may encourage you to play with change in your pocket or something else that will make a sound and distract your audience.
Grasping and leaning into the lectern	Some students do this for support when they are nervous. You can touch the lectern; just do not hold it in a death grip. Free your hands so you can gesture. Release your energy through your movement.

For your next speech, work to make your gestures appear more natural. Being aware of your gestures or lack thereof is the first step. Ask a friend or colleague to comment on your movement and gestures. Gestures should *not* draw attention to themselves and away from your ideas. Start your speech with your hands at your side or near your waist, ready to gesture. If you find yourself engaging in some inhibiting gesture, release yourself from the position and put your hands back at your side or waist.

Using Note Cards

If you work with note cards, it is important to use them effectively. Many instructors restrict the number and size of the note cards you may use during your speech. Stick to their instructions, and consider the following:

○ View your note cards as an extension of your arm, gesturing as you would without the note cards.

○ Cards should fit into your hand comfortably.

○ Generally, 4"x6" cards are going to be easier to work with than 3"x5" cards.

○ Avoid distracting note cards. Pink cards … really? Pink ink … really?

○ Number your note cards so you are able to keep them in order as you write them, transport them, and use them when you deliver your speech. If you drop them, you can get them back in order quickly.

○ Check to see that they are in sequence before speaking.

○ Never staple your note cards.

Common Problems Using Note Cards

Using note cards effectively is not as easy as it seems. Sometimes, students wait until the last moment to create their note cards. As with every other aspect of speaking, students should practice their speech using note cards and consider the following pitfalls.

Playing with note cards. This is a manifestation of your nervousness. Avoid bending them back and forth. Do not fold them. Do not use them as a fan. Do not hit your head with them. Whatever you do, do not shuffle them mindlessly, or you will (a) lose your place, or (b) drop them, which will lead you to, well, (a).

Holding note cards with both hands. Holding on to note cards with both hands may be distracting to the audience because cards are relatively small pieces of paper that do not need the support of both hands. Holding on with both hands also restricts your physical movement (gestures).

Including too much on the note cards. You only need enough information on your note cards to trigger your thoughts. With enough practice, only a few note cards are necessary. Also, if you have most of your speech on note cards, you may end up sounding like you are reading to the audience.

Having too many note cards. Teachers sometimes swap stories about how many note cards a particular student used. The assignment may call for three note cards, and a student has a quarter-inch pile of note cards—sometimes as many as 20 for a four- to six-minute speech. This is not necessary if you have practiced your speech!

Writing on both sides of the card. Sometimes students misinterpret the "three cards rule" and use three note cards, but write on both sides. It is easy to lose your place when you have written on both sides, and it can be distracting to the audience ("Hey! She used bright pink ink for her notes!"), and it usually means that you are relying too heavily on your notes. Practice!

Using a Legal Pad, Outline, or Electronic Tools

Traditionally, public speaking instructors wince at the notion of allowing students to use something other than note cards. Our professors taught us to use note cards, and we teach our students the same. In reality, not every occasion calls for small note cards. It is certainly not uncommon to see speakers using note pads or legal pads of some kind in the corporate world. Long and detailed presentations may be better served by using a note pad instead.

You may find yourself in a speaking situation outside of class where having a pad of paper makes sense. Once you have your notes on something larger than your hand, it may be more distracting when you gesture. You do not want a pad of paper waving around in the air. It should not be used as an extension of your arm. Hold the pad in one hand, at a distance from your eyes that allows you to see your notes but not covering your face. Gesture with your free hand.

If you find yourself in a room where a podium is used, you may find it helpful to use a brief speech outline on one or two pieces of paper. Having notecards on a podium may result in your squinting to see what is written, but if you have a brief outline on regular paper, you can increase the font size. Keep in mind the distinction between a manuscript speech and an extemporaneous one. Make sure you engage the audience through eye contact and gestures, and do not include so much detail on your outline that you appear to be reading your speech,

You may also find yourself in a situation where it makes sense to have your notes available on a computer. You may have notes in a file you can access, or you have main ideas embedded in a PowerPoint presentation. One of the main complaints listeners have about presentation software is that speakers read slides word for word. Try accessing your notes (in a large font size so they are easily seen) on a computer screen that the audience does not see. If you choose to do this, make sure your slides contain more than the outline of your speech, and you do not spend all your time behind the computer. Also, remember to have a hard copy of your notes in the event of a problem with the technology.

Caution: Holding a piece of paper is different than holding a note card. If you are nervous, the audience is more likely to see a full-sized piece of paper shake than a smaller, sturdier note card.

Physical Movements

Remember the second problem related to Katie's delivery? She appeared glued to the lectern. After a while, her listeners got tired of watching her. Katie's mistake is typical. Like many speakers, she failed to realize that an active speaker can encourage an active response from an audience, but an immobile speaker can leave listeners listless.

When you move from one place to another while you speak, your listeners are more likely to keep their eyes on you. Movement has an additional advantage of helping to release nervous energy. It can work against you, however, if you look like a moving target or if your movement has no purpose. Think about the following three guidelines as you prepare your speech.

1. **Move naturally.** Relax and use movement reasonably. Do not pace back and forth like a caged lion or make small darting movements that return you to the safety of the lectern.

2. **Tie your movements to your use of visual aids.** Walk over to the visual as you are presenting it and point to its relevant parts. Walk back to the lectern when finished. Aim for fluid movement.

3. **Be prepared.** Your instructor and the speaking environment will influence the opportunities for physical movement. Your instructor may allow or prohibit you from speaking behind a lectern or podium. In informal situations, it may be appropriate to walk through the aisles as you talk. In a small room, you can walk around without a microphone and still be heard. In a large room, you may need the help of a wireless microphone. Be prepared to adapt to your instructor's rules and the speaking environment. Remember that movement is a way to connect with the audience, get them involved, and keep their attention.

Facial Expressions

Our face not only provides information about our identity, age, and gender, it is the primary source of emotions. As we speak, our facial expressions change continually and are constantly monitored and interpreted by our listeners.

Research suggests we have *three* faces (Samovar et al., 2007). First is your "assigned" face. This is your face at rest; the face you were born with. As you age, as your health changes, your face changes also. Your second face is the face you can control. You determine to pout, "put on" an angry face, or smirk. It is the second "face" we are most concerned about in the realm of

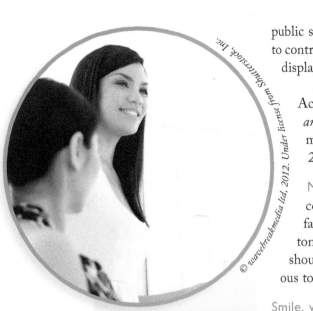

Listeners feel engaged when speakers smile.

© wavebreakmedia ltd, 2012. Under license from Shutterstock, Inc.

public speaking. Third is the face that reacts to stimuli before there is time to control it. If you are surprised, worried, or fearful, it is your third face that displays these emotions.

As an aside, recent research on Botox addresses facial expression. According to a 2011 study published in the *Journal of Social Psychology and Personality Science*, Botox may not only numb facial muscles, but may also numb users' perception of other people's emotions (Babej, 2011).

Match facial expressions with your tone. Admittedly, there is much to consider when giving a speech, but sometimes we do not think about facial expressions. Your facial expression, however, should match the tone or emotion present in your speech. A serious tone in your voice should be accompanied by facial expressions that contribute to the serious tone.

Smile, when appropriate. Listeners also feel engaged when speakers smile. Even if you are nervous, work to demonstrate enthusiasm not only through your vocal qualities but through facial expressions.

Eye Contact

No other aspect of nonverbal behavior is as important as eye contact, which is the connection you form with listeners through your gaze. The speaker engages the audience by drawing them in through eye contact. Sustained eye contact can communicate confidence, openness, and honesty. It suggests you are a person of conviction, you care what your listeners are thinking, and you are eager for their feedback. Making eye contact with your audience is a way for you to express nonverbally, "I want you to understand me."

When your eye contact is poor, you may be sending unintentional messages that the audience interprets as nervousness, hostility, being uncomfortable, or lack of interest. The audience may think you have something to hide or that you are not prepared.

In the process of writing this text, one of the authors attended a recognition ceremony where several honorees gave brief speeches. One speaker began by looking at her notes, then made eye contact with the audience, looked back at her notes, and then appeared to look at something on the wall to her right. She repeated these behaviors throughout her speech. Audience members were observed looking up at the same spot on the wall. The speaker admitted to being nervous before her speech. Clearly, this nervous tic distracted her audience.

Sometimes students only look at the instructor during their speech. Do not do this! It makes teachers uncomfortable and you are excluding the rest of the audience. Also, some student speakers ignore half the class by looking at the right side or the left side of the class only. When a speaker looks away, we sense that something is wrong. We offer the following three performance guidelines for reflection.

❶ **Distribute your gaze evenly.** Work on sustained eye contact with different members in the audience. Avoid darting your eyes around or sweeping the room with your eyes. Instead, maintain eye contact with a single person for a single thought. This may be measured in a phrase or a sentence. It may help to think of your audience as divided into several physical sectors. Focus on a person in each sector, rotating your gaze among the people and the sectors as you speak.

❷ **Glance only briefly and occasionally at your notes.** Do not keep your eyes glued to your notes. You may know your speech well, but when you are nervous, it may feel safer to keep looking at your notes. This is counterproductive.

❸ **Do not look just above the heads of your listeners.** Although this advice is often given to speakers who are nervous, it will be obvious to everyone that you are gazing into the air.

Appearance

Standards for appearance are influenced by culture and context. Americans visiting the Vatican will find that shoulders and knees should be covered in order to gain entry. It is okay for students to wear baseball caps outside, but in some contexts, it may be offensive to keep one on inside.

An effective speaker is aware of the norms and expectations for appearance as he or she moves from one culture to another. In a 1989 summit between Soviet President Mikhail Gorbachev and Chinese leader Deng Xiaoping, Gorbachev made a nearly fatal blunder: He wore a pair of beige loafers with his formal suit, a choice that offended the Chinese who believed that "holiday shoes" should not be worn on such a special occasion. Gorbachev's advisors failed to provide him with such relevant information.

We do not have to move from one country to another to experience differences in perspectives on appearance. Some businesses allow more casual attire; others expect trendy, tailored clothing. As rhetorical theorist Kenneth Burke (1969, p. 119) reminds us, your clothes make a rhetorical statement of their own by contributing to your spoken message.

Your choice of shoes, suits, dresses, jewelry, tattoos, hair style, and body piercings should not isolate you from your listeners. If that occurs, the intent of your speech is lost. We offer the following guidelines for appearance, but the bottom line is, *do nothing to distract from the message.*

Your appearance should be in harmony with your message. Communication professor Leon Fletcher (1990) describes a city council meeting addressed by college students pleading for a clean-up of the local beaches. Although the speeches were clearly organized, well-supported, and effectively presented, the unkempt physical appearance of the speakers conflicted with their message. They wore torn jeans, T-shirts, and sloppy sandals. Their hair looked unkempt. The city council decided to take no action. Several months later, the same issue was brought before the council by a second group of students, all of whom wore ties and sport jackets—symbols of the neatness they wanted for the beaches. This time the proposal was accepted (p. 14).

Although no one would tell you that wearing a certain suit or dress will make your listeners agree with your point of view, the image you create is undoubtedly important. Research on employment interviews suggests that "physical appearance and grooming habits are factors in the hiring process" (Shannon & Stark, 2003, p. 613).

Be clean and appropriately dressed and groomed. In your public speaking class, your shoe choice is not likely to create a stir. However, your audience expects that you will be clean and appropriately groomed. Your instructor may provide you with specific guidelines regarding your appearance on the day you speak. A general guideline is to be modest and dress slightly more formally than your audience.

Avoid clothing that detracts from your message. If the audience focuses on your appearance, your speech loses effectiveness. Wearing a cap is usually frowned on. The audience wants to see your eyes. Do not ignore the possibility that your instructor views caps as outdoor, not indoor, wear.

Avoid shirts that have writing on them. It is probably not wise to give a persuasive speech on the day you wear a T-shirt with "I Make Stuff Up" on it. One of our female students held her poster in front of her, with the word "Hooters" showing on her T-shirt, just above the visual aid. Whether what is written on your T-shirt is witty or offensive, it takes focus off the message.

Some students may need the following gentle reminder: Your instructors, and probably many of your classmates, are not interested in seeing your belly or *any* type of cleavage. And tight clothes should not be tugged or pulled on because the focus switches to you, not your message.

Understanding Nonverbal Differences Across and Within Cultures

Intense, constant eye contact in Mexico can be interpreted as aggressive. Instead, subordinates display respect by looking at the ground (Morrison et al., 2001, p. 254). Germans tend to smile as an indicator of affection. In a business meeting, they rarely smile, and laughter is certainly not considered appropriate (p. 160). Body language is different in India than in the U.S. Indians show agreement by tossing their head from side to side, and toss their heads up and back to show disagreement (p. 172). In a business setting, Nigerians may interpret casual dress as a form of disrespect (p. 279). (See **BTW: Did You Know?** for more information about intercultural differences.)

In Morrison et al.'s (2001) book on doing business around the world, they provide us with the following insight:

○ Conducting business in China takes time. Most of the first meeting will be taken up with a ritual introductory speech that is so basic, it is fairly useless (p. 75).

○ A visiting British poetry professor lecturing in Cairo, unthinkingly displayed the sole of his foot to his audience. In Egypt, as in other Muslim countries, this is a serious insult (p. 137).

○ In Saudi Arabia, eye contact is intense and constant. Saudis speak at much closer quarters than North Americans. In an empty elevator, a Saudi may choose to stand next to you rather than in an opposite corner (p. 333).

The above examples demonstrate that, as with language, nonverbal cues are interpreted differently across cultures. We may wonder why a speaker does not engage in direct eye contact with his/her audience. We might attribute aloofness or lack of interest to a speaker who does not smile when the tone of the speech would seem to warrant it.

Our own repertoire of nonverbal behavior and our interpretation of others' nonverbal cues are culturally based. Our nonverbal communication is also influenced by how we were raised, our level of confidence and self-esteem, and the feedback on our nonverbal communication we've received from others. It may be difficult sometimes to know whether a difference in behavior is cultural or strictly personal.

As speakers and listeners, remember that proper nonverbal behaviors "are those that are appropriate and effective in the context of the culture, setting, and occasion" (Lustig & Koester, 2010, p. 220). If you speak to an audience whose culture differs from yours, it is important to learn what is unacceptable or discouraged. Much can be gained through research and observation. As has been said many times, an effective public speaker is one who adapts to the audience. We do not want you to enact behaviors that are not true to your personality, but it is important to understand the impact your nonverbal communication may have on your listeners.

Communication Apprehension

Students of public speaking may understand how important effective organization, language, and delivery are, but that doesn't stop them from being nervous in front of an audience. Some individuals do not seem to experience much anxiety before or during the speech, but others are overwhelmed. Decades ago comedic entertainer George Jessel quipped, "The human brain is a wonderful organ. It starts to work the moment you are born, and does not stop until you get up to deliver a speech" (brainyquote.com). Maybe you can relate to this. When confronted with an audience ready to listen, perhaps you find yourself lost in a fog.

With a bit of preparation and a few pointers, your nervousness can actually propel you toward a confident, energized delivery style. We take a closer look now at fear responses. Our goal is to help you learn how to listen closely to your body and regain control.

The Nature of Communication Apprehension

For some, speaking in public can be an exciting, adrenalin-producing activity, but for others, it is an experience to be feared. If you are fearful of public speaking, you are not alone. Research has found that "public speaking is the single most commonly feared situation reported in both community and university samples" (Bottella et al., 2010, p. 407). A Gallup poll found that 40 percent of Americans are terrified at the *thought* of talking to an audience (Naistadt, 2004, p. 1), and approximately 70 percent of the people in the United States report experiencing communication apprehension when they have to give a public speech (McCroskey, 2009, p. 164).

Communication apprehension, as defined by McCroskey (1984), the leading researcher in this area, is "an individual's level of fear or anxiety associated with either real or anticipated communication with another person or persons" (p. 13). The intensity of discomfort most feel when giving a speech varies widely, but we can identify symptoms as falling into three categories: physiological, psychological, and behavioral.

Physical manifestations include a rapid pulse, increased metabolism, dry mouth, increased sweating, shallow breathing, shaky hands and knees, stammering, throat constriction, quivering voice, "butterflies" in the stomach, gastrointestinal dysfunction, flushing and heat flashes, dizziness, and loss of concentration, among others. Most of us experience at least one of these symptoms during a public speaking situation. The good news is, a degree of tension is positive because it keeps us alert and energized. Too much, however, can debilitate us, and make it difficult or impossible to continue.

Psychological manifestations of communication apprehension are more difficult to treat, because they are not observable, and they speak to our fears. As we know, whether our fears are real or imagined, they are still a part of us. Naistadt (2004) identifies six obstacles to effective speaking (pp. 52–60):

1. Fear of criticism or being judged negatively
2. Fear of forgetting
3. Fear of embarrassment or humiliation
4. Fear of failure
5. Fear of the unknown
6. Fear of bad (emotional) past experiences

The anxious speaker may need to address one or more of these fears in order to take control from a psychological perspective. Our fears may be the result

Glossary

Communication apprehension An individual's level of fear or anxiety associated with either real or anticipated communication with another person or persons.

of negative messages from our parents, siblings, or peers. Or they may be the result of low self-esteem, lack of self-confidence, poor coping strategies, or other psychological barriers. Regardless, as we know, a negative mind-set will most likely yield a negative result. (To check out your "nervousness profile," see **BTW: Are You One of These?**)

The *behavioral manifestation* of speech anxiety has been researched the least over the past decades. It is defined as "the degree of assumed speaker anxiety perceived by observers on the basis of manifest speaker behavior" (Mulac & Sherman, 1975, p. 276). Unlike physiological and psychological aspects of anxiety, behavioral manifestations are observed by audience members. Audiences receive information from and make judgments about paralanguage (i.e., volume, pitch, rate, pauses, vocal variety, etc.) and physical actions (i.e., eye contact, gestures, body movement, etc.). These observations influence audience members' perceptions of the speaker, including how anxious the speaker is believed to be.

Communication apprehension has been found to exist in virtually every culture in which it has been investigated (Pryor et al., 2005, p. 247). However, while American culture views communication apprehension in a negative light, other cultures—Japanese culture, for example—does not see communication apprehension as having negative implications. Because of its collectivist culture (focus on the group, not on the individual), less value is placed on individual assertiveness (p. 250).

On a related note, speaking English as a second language (as well as living in a different culture with different norms) can cause communication

BTW!

Are You One of These?

Book author and public speaking coach/trainer Ivy Naistadt (2004) identifies "four nervousness profiles":

Avoiders have so much anxiety associated with speaking or communicating in any formal setting that they will go to almost any length to avoid being put in a situation that demands it. May even give up promotions or pass up job opportunities to avoid the spotlight.

Anticipators start getting nervous as soon as they hear a speech, presentation, or job interview is scheduled. The event could be three weeks or three months away, it doesn't matter. They will spend all their waking time until then worrying about what can, may, or will occur.

Adrenalizers become nervous just before the event and are suddenly hit with a surge of energy that must be dealt with, like a track star gearing up for a race who controls the surge of excess energy with focusing techniques as a way of getting ready to meet the challenge ahead.

Improvisers get nervous during the event because they are the last-minute type who either put off preparing or spend no time preparing, then typically run into all kinds of trouble that might easily have been avoided with even just a little preparation. (p. 29)

apprehension. Some research has shown that speaking a second language increases apprehension but other results show that compared to situational factors like years of speaking English or living in the U.S., communication apprehension in a first language has a greater impact on communication apprehension in a second language (Jung & McCroskey, 2004). So, while communication apprehension may be found in other cultures, it is not necessarily interpreted the same as it is in the United States.

McCroskey (2009) summarized effects of high communication apprehension discovered by researchers over the last four decades. Some of these effects are:

○ People with high communication apprehension (CA) prefer occupations that have low oral communication demands.

○ People with high CA are less likely to be turned to as opinion leaders or to be selected as friends than other people.

○ College students with high CA prefer classes where they may sit on the sides or back of the room.

○ College graduates with high CA are more likely to marry immediately upon graduation.

○ Job candidates with high CA have less likelihood of being successful in the job applicant screening process (pp. 167–168).

Overall, the effects of communication apprehension are numerous and varied. Since we value oral communication skills and agree that effective public speaking is a goal, we will turn to strategies one might use to control apprehension.

Strategies for Controlling Public Speaking Apprehension

Coping strategies are numerous and varied, and work for some better than others. One study found some instructors treat apprehensive students during their regular class time by concentrating on a skills-training approach to teach the necessary speaking skills. They create a supportive and positive classroom environment by recognizing students' CA as normal and by teaching techniques that help students handle feelings of apprehension (Robinson, 1989). We agree with this strategy. By now you have begun to pick up valuable skills for presenting, feel safe in class because the climate is supportive and positive, and understand that some CA is normal.

Anxiety and coping processes may start with anticipation of a stressful event, may continue through the stressful event itself, and may extend into the period after the event as individuals await feedback or deal with the consequences of their performance (Sawyer & Behnke, 1999).

The chances are slim of escaping communication apprehension. However, we can provide some help. Recognize that your physiological symptoms actually consist of four stages.

Stage 1: The *anticipatory stage* takes place in the minutes before the speech—heart rates zoom from a normal rate of about 70 beats per minute to between 95 and 140.

Stage 2: The *confrontational stage* is typically at the beginning of the speech, when heart rates jump to between 110 and 190 beats per minute. This stage usually lasts no more than 30 seconds.

Stage 3: *Adaptation stage* is when you begin calm down, typically after you have been speaking for over 30 seconds to a minute

Stage 4: The *release stage* is the final stage and is characterized by the pulse returning to anticipation levels or lower.

The confrontational stage is strong, and speakers may not perceive the increase in pulse rate. Also, as a nervous speaker, you may stop feeling nervous without realizing it (Motley, 1988). For this reason, make sure you have planned and rehearsed a strong beginning for your message. Research on psychological and physiological anxiety claim that anxiety is highest during the minute prior to confrontation with an audience and during the first minute of speaking (Behnke & Sawyer, 2004). So, once you have made it through the first minute, you should feel more relaxed.

You may recall other people's advice about your fear. Suggestions such as imagining your audience in their underwear (guaranteed to make you blush), looking above their heads (guaranteed to make you aloof), and drinking plenty of water (guaranteed to make you wet) don't work, as you have no doubt already discovered. That's because they don't effectively treat the problem, your fear, itself. But researchers over the last several decades have found and refined new strategies and interventions to reduce public speaking apprehension (Dwyer, 2000). We present nine strategies as follows:

1. **Complete a public speaking course.** You are probably not surprised that we included this as a strategy. However, data are consistent with the explanation that "completing a public speaking class systematically reduces speaking anxiety" (Duff et al., 2007, p. 85). A public speaking course gives you the opportunity to learn and practice basic skills. As with anything that is skills based, the more opportunity you have to practice, the less anxiety-producing it should be. Research has also shown that watching a video on coping with the fear of public speaking helped to reduce CA and negative thoughts about public speaking (Ayers et al., 1993).

2. **Focus on your audience, not yourself.** Sometimes we get caught up in thinking about our performance ("What if I forget?" "What if I don't wear the right thing?" "What if they don't like me?"). Research shows that students who reported experiencing lower levels of communication apprehension were those who focused on the *audience*, not the message (Ayers, 1996, p. 229). Create a message with the audience in mind, and decide how best to convey it to that particular audience. Think of your audience as being on your side.

③ Reframe your message. Another technique to help you reduce your anxiety levels is to reframe the way you view the speaking situation. Turn negative thoughts into positive ones. Researchers discovered that, because some of us think of a speech as a "performance," we become obsessed with trying to deliver speeches as a famous speaker or trained actor might. This added pressure increases our anxiety levels even more.

If we can change our ideas about the speaking situation, we can work toward a positive experience. For example, instead of thinking "I don't want to lose my place," which is negative, replace it with "I want to look confident and poised." Then, reframe that even further with the thought "I am confident and poised speaking in front of groups" (Naistadt, 2004, pp. 81–82).

④ Prepare! Preparation sharpens your presentation and builds confidence. Interestingly, how you prepare is important. Research has indicated that individuals with high CA spend more time preparing their speeches but get less return for the efforts than low CAs (Ayers, 1996, p. 234).

Evidently, people who are anxious about speaking in public spend a great deal of time *developing* their speech, but they avoid *practicing* it. So, start with a sound speech plan and then rehearse the speech aloud by yourself. Then practice in front of others to get the feel and response of an audience. You will get a sense for how the words sound and how the material flows when you speak before an audience. When you know how to organize your thoughts for a speech and have an understanding of effective delivery techniques, you will feel more confident.

⑤ Take several deep breaths. What happens when we get nervous as speakers is that we restrict our breathing capacity, which impacts our ability to communicate effectively (Naistadt, 2004, p. 152). Deep breathing has a calming effect on the body and mind. We have used this technique ourselves and find our students have used it with success as well. Learning to breathe properly improves the sound of our voice and protects the health of our vocal instrument. You can work on breathing as you are waiting to speak. It also helps to take a final deep breath after you get in front of the audience and just before you speak. Try it!

⑥ Realize that you may be your own worst critic. Studies have shown that the amount of tension a speaker reports has little relationship to the amount of nervousness an audience detects. Even listeners trained to detect tension often fail to perceive it (Motley, 1988, p. 47). Audience members are relatively forgiving, and do not expect perfection. In a public speaking class, your classmates are generally supportive of your efforts. Also, don't think you're a failure if you experience anxiety after one, two, or three speeches. Listen to feedback and figure out what is most important for the next speaking situation.

7. **Gain skill and confidence by choosing to speak.** Find opportunities to speak. Give "minispeeches" at meetings or speak out in classes when discussion is invited. A colleague of ours conquered his considerable fear of public speaking before an audience and became a successful speaker in large lecture classes by volunteering to speak whenever a situation was convenient and available.

Systematic desensitization is based on the premise that people have learned to associate anxious states with public speaking. To reduce the fear of public speaking, speakers need to learn to associate relaxed states with public speaking (Ayers et al., 1993, p. 133). By doing so, a person with high CA learns to see public speaking as "nonthreatening" rather than "threatening" (Ayers et al., 2000, p. 24). We suggest you find opportunities to speak before an audience so you can reduce anxiety and create a more relaxed state

8. **Visualize your success as a speaker.** Creating powerful mental images of skillful performances and winning competitions is a technique that has been used for years by athletes who use visualization to help them succeed. The athlete may visualize winning a medal, throwing a curveball, playing zone defense, practicing 10 lay-ups, and so on. In addition to improving golf putts and tennis serves, you can use positive visualization to improve your speaking engagements and all the while reduce your fear levels (Ayers et al., 1997). Research has shown that visualization reduces public speaking fears and is effective over time.

Using visualization takes you through the day on which you are to speak, with an emphasis on imagining a positive outcome (Ayers & Hopf, 1992). Visualize yourself speaking with confidence and self-assurance and imagine the sound of applause after your presentation. You might visualize yourself approaching the podium with confidence, speaking clearly, engaging in effective eye contact with audience members, noticing that they are attentive and friendly, stating your main points and providing relevant support, then concluding your speech effectively and on time. Research has found that students who practice performance visualization display fewer nonfluencies, less rigidity, and less inhibition.

9. **Release tension through assertive and animated delivery.** Here is where a nervous speaker may be caught between a rock and a hard place. Being nervous can inhibit your delivery, but assertive and animated delivery can help you release pent-up tension. So, if you are prepared to speak, you have practiced speaking out loud, and you focus on your audience, you will be able to gesture, use eye contact, and move—all means for releasing nervous energy.

Glossary

Systematic desensitization
A premise that people have learned to associate anxious states with public speaking.

Positive visualization
Creating powerful mental images of skillful performances and winning competitions.

Having some level of apprehension before speaking is normal, since most of us have fears about speaking before an audience. We encourage you to try several of these suggestions during your first speech. Research indicates that using several of the above techniques to reduce nervousness works better than relying on only one (Whitworth & Cochran, 2009), so we encourage you to mix and match. You may not overcome your fear of speaking, but you may reduce it, and you may use your nervous energy productively. Remember that nothing substitutes for preparation and practice. Just like getting ready for a piano recital, taking your first driver's test, or taking on a sumo wrestler, the more you practice, the more you learn, and the greater the likelihood of success. Ultimately, your goal is to channel this nervous energy into public speaking with self-confidence.

Summary

The four methods of speech delivery are impromptu speaking, extemporaneous speaking, manuscript speaking, and memorization. Impromptu speaking involves speaking without preparation. Extemporaneous speaking, which is the primary focus of this chapter, requires significant research, preparation, and practice. Generally, extemporaneous speakers use note cards to aid their delivery. Manuscript speaking means reading your prepared speech word for word, whereas memorization involves giving a speech without any notes. Each method is appropriate in varying circumstances. Following the guidelines for the method you choose enhances the effectiveness of your speech.

Nonverbal communication is an important part of delivery. Your vocal and physical delivery influences the effectiveness of your presentation. Aspects of vocal delivery include articulation, pronunciation, volume, rate, pitch, pauses, and emphasis. In addition, an effective speaker has relatively few nonfluencies. Guidelines for your vocal delivery include: remember to adapt to your audience, work to eliminate bad habits, check pronunciation of unfamiliar words, vary your rate and pitch, and use pauses and emphasis for impact.

Aspects of physical delivery include gestures, physical movement, eye contact, and appearance. A good speaker uses nonverbal delivery to capture and maintain the attention of the listeners. Gestures and movement should be natural, appropriate, and purposeful. Note cards should not distract the audience or cause delivery problems for the speaker. Avoid dependence on notes. Eye contact engages the audience. Your appearance should be in harmony with your message.

Public speaking apprehension is difficult to avoid and poses a problem for most speakers. We have both physical and psychological manifestations of apprehension, and it is important to recognize that there are different stages of apprehension, including anticipatory, confrontational, adaptation, and post confrontational. Nine suggestions are offered to help you control your public speaking apprehension, including complete a public speaking course, focus on your audience, not yourself, prepare, take several deep breaths, realize that you may be your own worst critic, gain skill and confidence by choosing to speak, visualize your success as a speaker, and release tension through assertive speaking and animated delivery. Your goal is ultimately to make your nervousness work for you.

Discussion Starters

1. Why is extemporaneous speaking generally the most appropriate form of delivery? When would it be best to use a manuscript? To memorize? To give an impromptu speech?

2. Have you given an impromptu speech? What was its purpose, and do you think you were successful? Why or why not?

3. To what extent do you think effective verbal delivery is necessary to your overall evaluation of a speech? How do your movements, gestures, eye contact, and clothing influence your relationship with your audience and the communication of your message?

4. What is most important to remember when using note cards during your speech? Other than note cards and note pads, how else do people display notes for the speeches?

5. Under what circumstances do you feel communication anxiety? How do you know physically that you're experiencing apprehension? How do you respond psychologically?

6. Six obstacles (fears) to public speaking were presented early in the chapter. Which of those fears do you personally experience in a public speaking situation? Which obstacles do you think would be most common in college students?

7. Although degrees of speech tension vary from speaker to speaker, most inexperienced speakers share common feelings of discomfort. What can you do to minimize your feelings of apprehension and make your nervous energy work *for* you rather than against you?

References

Ayers, J. (1996). Speech Preparation Processes and Speech Apprehension. *Communication Education, 45*(4), 228–234.

Ayers, J., Ayers, F. E., Baker, A. L., Colby, N., DeBlast, C., Dimke, D. et al. (1993). Two Empirical Tests of a Videotape Designed to Reduce Public Speaking Anxiety. *Journal of Applied Communication Research, 21*(2), 132–147.

Ayers, J., & Hopf, T. (1992). Visualization: Reducing Speech Anxiety and Enhancing Performance. *Communication Reports, 5*(1), 1–10.

Ayers, J., Hopf, T., & Myers, D. M. (1997). Visualization and Performance Visualization: Application, Evidence, and Speculation. In J. A. Daly, J. C. McCroskey, J. Ayers, T. Hopf, & D.M. Ayers (Eds.), *Avoiding Communication* (pp. 305–330). Cresskill, NJ: Hampton Press.

Ayers, J., Hopf, T., & Will, A. (2000). Are Reductions in CA an Experimental Artifact? A Solomon Four-Group Answer. *Communication Quarterly, 48*(1), 19–26.

Babej, M. C. (2011). Botox May Deaden Ability to Empathize, New Study Says. *Forbes*, April 23. Retrieved September 1, 2011, from www.forbes.com/sites/marcbabej/2011/04/23/botox-may-deaden-ability-to-empathize-new-study-says/.

BBC. (2011, January 28). *Mandela's Life and Times*. BBC/Mobile/Africa. Retrieved May 29, 2011 at www.bbc.co.uk/news/world-africa-12305154.

Behnke, R. R., & Sawyer, C. R. (2004). Public Speaking Anxiety as a Function of Sensitization and Habituation Processes. *Communication Education, 53*(2), 164–173.

Brainyquote.com. (n.d.). *George Jessel Quotes*. Brainy Quotes. Retrieved August 26, 2011 from www.brainyquote.com/quotes/quotes/g/georgejess392909.html.

Botella, C., Gallego, M. J., Garcia-Palacios, A., Guillen, V., Baños, R. M., Quero, S. et al. (2010). *Cyberpsychology, Behavior, and Social Networking, 13*(4), 407–421. doi:10.1089/cyber.2009.0224.

Burke, K. (1969). *A Rhetoric of Motives*. Berkeley, CA: University of California Press.

Duffy, B., & Ryan, H. (Eds.). (1987). *American Orators of the Twentieth Century: Critical Studies and Sources*. New York: Greenwood Press.

Duff, D. C., Levine, T. R., Beatty, M. J., Woolbright, J., & Park, H. S. (2007). Testing Public Anxiety Treatments Against a Credible Placebo Control. *Communication Education, 56*(1), 72–88.

Dwyer, K. K. (2000). The Multidimensional Model: Teaching Students to Self-Manage High Communication Apprehension by Self-Selecting Treatments. *Communication Education, 49*, 72–81.

Fletcher, L. (1990). Polishing Your Silent Languages. *The Toastmaster* (March), 14.

Hopf, T., & Ayres, D. M. (Eds.). (1997). *Avoiding Communication: Shyness, Reticence, and Communication Apprehension*. Cresskill, NJ: Hampton.

Jung, H. Y., & McCroskey, J. C. (2004). Communication Apprehension in a First Language and Self-Perceived Competence as Predictors of Communication Apprehension in a Second Language: A Study of Speakers of English as a Second Language. *Communication Quarterly, 52*(2), 170–181.

Lustig, M. W., & Koester, J. (2010). *Intercultural Competence*, 6th Ed. Boston: Allyn & Bacon.

Mandela, Nelson. (1993). *Acceptance Speech of the President of the African National Congress*. Retrieved September 1, 2011 from .db. nelsonmandela.org/speeches/pub_view.asp?pg=item&ItemID=NMS161 &txtstr=Nobel%20Peace

McCroskey, J. C. (1984). The Communication Apprehension Perspective. In J. Daly & J. C McCroskey (Eds.), *Avoiding Communication: Shyness, Reticence, and Communication Apprehension*. Beverly Hills, CA: Sage Publications.

McCroskey, J. C. (2009). Communication Apprehension: What Have We Learned in the Last Four Decades? *Human Communication, 12*(2), 157–171.

Motley, T. M. (1988). Taking the Terror Out of Talk. *Psychology Today*, 46–49.

Morrison, T., Conaway, W, A., & Douress, J. J. (2001). *Doing Business Around the World*. Paramus, NJ: Prentice Hall.

Mulac, A., & Sherman, A. R. (1974). Behavioral Assessment of Speech Anxiety. *Quarterly Journal of Speech, 60*(2), 134–143.

Naistadt, I. (2004). *Speak Without Fear*. New York: HarperCollins Publishers Inc.

Pryor, B., Butler, J., & Boehringer, K. (2005). Communication Apprehension and Cultural Context: A Comparison of Communication Apprehension in Japanese and American Students. *North American Journal of Psychology, 7*(2), 247–252.

Robinson, T. E. (1989). Communication Apprehension and the Basic Public Speaking Course: A National Survey of In Class Treatment Techniques. *Communication Education, 46*(3), 1997.

Samovar, L. A., Porter, R. E., & McDaniel, E. R. (2007). *Communication Between Cultures*, 6th Ed. pp. 209–211. Belmont, CA: Thomson Wadsworth.

Sawyer, C. R., & Behnke, R. R. (1999). State Anxiety Patterns for Public Speaking and the Behavior Inhibition System. *Communication Reports, 12*(1), 33–41.

Shannon, M. L., & Stark, C. P. (2003). The Influence of Physical Appearance on Personnel Selection. *Social Behavior and Personality, 31*(6), 613–624.

Whitworth, R. H., & Cochran, C. (2009). Evaluation of Integrated versus Unitary Treatments for Reducing Public Speaking Anxiety. *Communication Education, 45*(4).

Chapter

15

"They say one of a baby's first non-verbal forms of communication is pointing. Clicking must be somewhere just after that."

Anonymous

Chapter 15: Presentational Aids in an Electronic World

Exploring the different types available and offering criteria for their use and display, this chapter focuses on the benefits of using presentation aids. Your decision to include an aid should be based on the extent to which it enhances your audience's interest and understanding. Guidelines are presented for determining what to incorporate and how to use it.

Student Learning Objectives:

○ Students will be able to explain the nature of presentational aids today

○ Students will be able to use the various types of presentational aids with maximum comprehension and clarity

○ Students will be able to describe the types of technology-based presentational aids

○ Students will be able to explain effective use of presentational aids

PRESENTATIONAL AIDS IN AN ELECTRONIC WORLD

Few of us think of speech making in visual terms—or find ways to reach our speaking goals by turning to presentational aids. As technology has become more accessible, expectations have increased. Audiences crave dazzling multimedia presentations. Being tech savvy is clearly an advantage to the public speaker today. Although the tools may have changed, the bottom line has not: Any presentational aids you create must communicate a clear, relevant, direct, and interesting message.

This chapter examines how technology relates to public speaking in general and presentational aids in particular. First, we consider the nature of technology and presentational aids today by describing their pervasiveness and how they function. Then, we catalog the types of presentational aids available and identify ways to include them in your presentations. We end this chapter by offering guidelines for using presentational aids effectively in your speeches.

The Nature of Presentational Aids Today

"We cannot *not* communicate" is a communication axiom developed by Paul Watzlawick (1967). This suggests that in face-to-face communication, even when we choose to *not* speak, we are still communicating a message through our silence and our nonverbal communication. A similar case can be made for communicating through our presentational aids. We cannot not communicate here as well. What message does a poorly designed or displayed aid communicate to an audience about the speaker? Some might draw conclusions regarding the speaker's commitment to the speech, his/her credibility to speak on the subject, or his/her ability to deliver a captivating, well-thought-out message. Worse yet, what might an audience think of a speech that had no accompanying presentational aids at all? We have come to expect the bells, whistles, and pizzazz presentational aids can bring to a speech.

Pervasiveness of Technology

Technology is ubiquitous. We see it everywhere. We use technology for all levels of communication: intrapersonal, interpersonal, group communication, mass communication, and public speaking. As it changes—and it does rapidly—we adapt. As new technology arrives, we consider how it might aid our communication.

Consider the relatively recent advent of the smartphone. People walk, drive, sit, wait, eat, and sleep with their phones. A December 2010 survey reports that 285 million Americans are mobile subscribers (CTIA–The Wireless Association). Research suggests that 91 percent of all Americans use cell phones (arstechnica.com). And it is not only an American phenomenon. In March 2009, Reuters reported that a study by the broadband company Bitkom found that Germans in their 20s are typically more willing to give up their current partners or their cars than their cell phones!

In parallel fashion, technology-based presentational aids have become not only commonplace, but of central importance to many speakers and audiences. Can you imagine a conference today without laptops and PDAs serving up glittering eye-candy: no gumdrop bullets, sweet-tart charts, or pop rocks special effects? Not likely. But has it gone too far? What is center stage, the message or the frosting?

Whether good for the message or not, presentational aids in this electronic age are here to stay. You will benefit from understanding how these technologies may function to help, or hurt, your key message.

Do you ever go anywhere without your phone?

Functions of Presentational Aids

Presentational aids operate in a variety of ways. They can satisfy an ever-escalating thirst for information and entertainment. They promise to enhance, or hinder, our presentations. They are more than afterthoughts, add-ons, or speech class requirements. Your instructor may require you to use presentational aids not only to enhance the effectiveness of your speech, but also to help you learn how to use them comfortably as you speak. But the main reason you may be required to use them is because nearly *everyone else is using them*!

Did you know greater numbers of us have been exposed to PowerPoint than any other presentation software? Today, more people use PowerPoint to accompany presentations than any other type of technology, including YouTube, video clips, and websites. In April 2006, Microsoft estimated that it had 400 million PowerPoint customers worldwide. Why? Microsoft claims that PowerPoint can improve the way "you create, present, and collaborate on presentations" (office.microsoft.com). Chances are good that you "speak" PowerPoint, too, because it is easy to learn and use, and is effective. On the other hand, foolproof systems rarely take into account the ingenuity of fools.

Poorly conceived or executed visuals like PowerPoint can bring trouble. Using presentational software like PowerPoint, Keynote, Prezi, and others is expected by today's audiences, who were largely raised in the media era (Cyphert, 2007). When developing visuals for your audience, Professor Edward Tufte, an expert in the visual representation of technical data, offers a stern warning: "[F]ailure to think clearly about the analysis and the presentation of [visual] evidence opens the door for all sorts of ... mischief to operate in making decisions" (Tufte, 1997, p. 52).

Clearly, paying attention to how a visual message is received by an audience is essential. We must keep the needs of our audience in mind. The speaker–audience connection is strengthened when the speaker judiciously considers potential advantages and disadvantages of each presentational aid before placing them in a speech.

Advantages of Presentational Aids

Availability

As long as one has access to the Internet, a nearly infinite amount of presentational material is available, often without cost. As you prepare for your speech, you can create everything online and transfer it to a flash drive when you're ready. Millions of videoclips, photos and images, and clip art are available, too. Adding music, special effects, timed sequencing, and flash video, for example, may be a little trickier for the novice, but it is being used increasingly in professional and student presentations.

Engaging

Have you ever seen a lotto billboard alongside an interstate? As you approach it, you can see the jackpot amount increasing as the digital numbers change constantly. When a presentational aid is well prepared, little can compete with it to capture—and hold—audience interest. We live in a visual age. Images that surround us in the mass media make us more receptive, on conscious and unconscious levels, to visual presentations of all kinds. We are attuned to these presentations simply because they are visual—a phenomenon you can use to your advantage during a speech.

One student wanted to emphasize how fast the world's population is growing. During her speech, she accessed a website (worldometers.info) that keeps a digital tally of births, and kept the digital counter on the screen for about a minute. Then she made reference to the number of births that had occurred during that minute. This helped keep the interest of the class. A well-placed, professional-looking presentational aid draws attention to the point you are trying to make or to statistics you want your audience to process.

Persuasive

Seeing the devastation a tornado creates is more persuasive than having someone simply talk about it. Watching a video of animals being euthanized is more powerful than talking about the process. Looking at statistics that have been organized in a clear manner through graphs or charts is more persuasive than simply hearing the numbers. Presentation software adds impact to your argument.

Presentational aids have persuasive power. Business speakers, especially those in sales, have long realized that they can close a deal faster if they use visual aids. A study by the University of Minnesota and the 3M Corporation found that speakers who integrate visuals into their talks are 43 percent more likely to persuade their audiences than speakers who rely solely on verbal images (Vogel, Dickson, & Lehman, 1986).

One of the most well-known examples of presentation software images being used to strengthen and elucidate arguments can be seen in former U.S. Vice President Al Gore's 2006 documentary film *An Inconvenient Truth*. Gore's narration is accompanied by graphs, animation, video clips, and other images derived from presentation software (Wright, 2009). An analysis of that film reveals that slides containing text alone are used only 11 times, and bullet points are used only once. Gore links his main points to events with which Americans can relate, and provides a frame of reference for understanding and comparing his statistics. His presentational aids help to create a powerful message that was persuasive to many.

Entertaining

If you are in the mood, it takes only a few minutes to surf for video that makes you laugh. Comedy abounds on the Internet and funny clips are uploaded to countless video-sharing sites continually. Notice that both appropriate, professional clips exist as well as plenty of, well, unsavory ones. If you searched the term "stupid human tricks," you will find all sorts of hijinks, some guaranteed to make you blush. In other words, speakers have a plethora of options when seeking something entertaining to support their point, but not all are appropriate.

Presentational software offers animation and sound effects, so speakers can add entertainment value to their slides. Even something simple like creating a graphic that uses stacked hamburgers to talk about the number of hamburgers sold, or stacked oranges, apples, and pears to talk about the amount of fruit sold will add visual impact and enhance meaning. With a little forethought, technology can enhance the entertainment value of your message.

Memorable

Did you read the newspaper this morning? What do you remember from it? Chances are, if you read the paper, a photo comes to mind—the picture of a fireman rescuing a child from a burning building or the president of your university getting a pie in the face at the end of a fundraiser. You may have read the articles that accompanied these pictures, but the images are likely to have had the greatest impact.

Technology gives you the power to etch permanent images into the minds of attendees. Do you recall a TV commercial asking you to assist starving children or neglected pets? These pitches are persuasive and memorable because of the tragic and compelling pictures they offer us. Using pictures, you can create lasting mental images in the minds of your audience. Moving graphics and sound effects can be catchy and add an entertainment effect so long as they are not overdone. Through video-sharing websites like YouTube, bleekr.com, and Yahoo! video, you can easily find footage of a tornado in full fury, the war in Pakistan, and police attacking civilians in the latest Middle East revolution. Such video clips are available, tend to be vivid, and may be unforgettable.

Speakers are told that the more senses you engage, the more your audience will remember. Research indicates our retention increases significantly when messages are presented both verbally and visually (Mayer, 2001). Kraus (2008) notes other research that concluded that mixed modality presentation (auditory and visual) is superior for recall, regardless of whether the presentation is concurrent or sequential or whether materials are presented once or twice. It is important to keep this in mind: Visuals should rarely stand alone. When an audience is shown the devastating effects of a tornado via video, the prudent speaker might verbally clarify, elaborate, or refer to the visual images to create the most effective message.

After a review of relevant educational psychology, education, and experimental psychology studies, the U.S. Department of Labor concluded that: "[T]hree days after an event, people retain 10 percent of what they heard from an oral presentation, 35 percent from a visual presentation, and 65 percent from a visual and oral presentation" (OSHA, 1996). Using a simple bar graph to display this information makes it easier to understand these significant differences (see Figure 10.1). Researchers did find an exception: When the accompanying visual is primarily text and the speaker simply reads what is projected, memory scores drop (Unnava et al., 1996). Beyond being annoying, there seems to be no memory benefit from a speaker reading bulleted text from a screen to an audience that can read it for themselves. The visuals that supplement, vivify, and contextualize a speaker's words, rather than simply repeating them, are most effective in aiding message retention.

FIGURE 15.1

This chart depicts effectiveness of visuals on audience memory 3 days after an event (osha.gov, 1996).

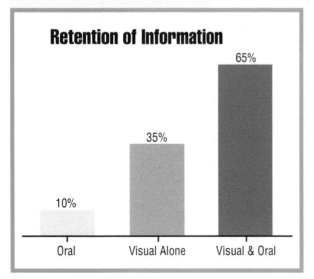

Clarity

A good visual design can make information clearer and more interesting (Cyphert, 2007). It also helps to emphasize key points (Kraus, 2008). Some speeches rely on many facts and statistics, which may be difficult for an audience to process. Using visuals like bar graphs, line graphs, or tables may help. Sometimes technology can lead an audience through complex material by using simple slides that highlight key points. Similarly, if you're talking about a process, such as brewing beer, for example, creating slides that identify the different steps by pairing each with photos will clarify the process.

Presentational software significantly aids teaching and learning (Kraus, 2008). Consider the last school lecture you attended. Did visuals accompany the presentation? Did they help? A study of college students' perceptions found that more than three-fourths agreed that PowerPoint presentations added clarity to an instructor's lecture and made the structure easier to follow (Nicholson, 2002). Anecdotally, they make naps easier, too, when overused.

Presentational aids have the power to clarify complex ideas. They are invaluable tools when explaining mechanical functions such as how a hot air balloon rises or how a computer stores information. They can clarify complex interrelationships involving people, groups, and institutions. They can show, for example, the stages a bill must go through before it becomes a law, and the role Congress and the president play in this process. Visuals may reduce but do not eliminate the need to explain complex details.

Presentational aids take the place of many words and, therefore, may shorten the length of a speech. They do not replace words, and one or two statements are insufficient verbal support for a series of visual displays. But presentational aids and words *in combination* reduce the amount of time you spend creating word pictures.

Makes Abstract Ideas Concrete

Abstract language can hurt your message clarity. If you are delivering a speech on the effects of the estimated 17–39-million-gallon oil spill from the BP Deepwater Horizon explosion in the Gulf of Mexico in spring and summer 2010, it may not be enough to tell your audience that the explosion killed 11 people and injured 17 more. But you can add something specific: Actual pictures of the clean-up effort of oil-saturated, sick animals.

Along with these visuals, you explain:

> But people were not the only victims. Did you know that despite deploying over 5 million feet of floating barrier, the spill was allowed to drift and contaminate 125 miles of Louisiana shoreline? An estimated 30,000 first responders helped to clean up, but over a thousand animals, including endangered birds, turtles, and mammals, died. Of the animals who survived, only an estimated 6 percent have been cleaned, and biologists anticipate most will die too (Dosomething.org, 2011).

The image of the spill's devastating effect on wildlife provides us with specific visual pictures that make the situation more relevant, personal, and easily grasped. We need to see something concrete to process abstract ideas such as large catastrophes.

© corbpics. 2012. Under license from Shutterstock, Inc.

Images of specific visual pictures make the situation more relevant, personal, and easily grasped.

Helps Organize Ideas

As with every other aspect of your speech, presentational aids should be audience-centered. They may be eye-catching and visually stimulating, but they serve a more practical purpose. The flow and connection of a speaker's ideas are not always apparent to an audience, especially if the topic is complicated or involves many steps. Pictures, flow charts, diagrams, graphs, tables, and video clips help listeners follow a speaker's ideas. Additionally, presentational aids help keep the speaker on his/her organizational track. This benefit, however, is only realized when a speaker has rehearsed a number of times with the aids.

Disadvantages of Presentational Aids

What about when technology turns ugly? Poorly conceived or executed visuals can bring trouble. Paying attention to how a visual message is received by an audience is essential. Careful consideration of drawbacks, pitfalls, and caveats ensures the technology you use actually serves you, rather than serves to hurt you.

Access

Consider first, technology may not be available. While many colleges have computers in all classrooms, others may have them available in designated classrooms or by request only. Internet access via LAN (Local Area Network) may be out of service temporarily. What if your flash drive elects to self-destruct moments before your speech begins or you used newer, incompatible software, and the dinosaur computer you are now trying to use does not recognize your materials? Murphy's Law for the speaker who relies on technology is "If anything can go wrong, it will go wrong, during your presentation, in the worst possible way!"

Impersonal

When a speaker uses no presentational aids, the audience must focus on the speaker. One of the speaker's tasks is to create a connection with the audience through content, personality, language, and movement. When technology is used, focus often shifts. A problem exists when slides become the message rather than a means to enrich the message. When this happens we "forego an important opportunity to connect with the audience as human beings" (Alley & Neeley, 2005, p. 418). We risk losing our human connection to our audience by overusing technology.

The concern that computer-generated and projected images may hamper the speaker–audience connection is echoed by Peter Norvig, director of research at Google. He argues that a slide presentation may reduce the speaker's effectiveness, because "it makes it harder to have an open exchange between presenter and audience to convey ideas that do not readily fit into outline format" (Norvig, 2003, p. 343). Newer approaches to presentations allow the speaker to shift seamlessly from frame to frame within a larger visual context, providing more flexibility when feedback from an audience warrants this (c.f., www.prezi.com). Often, technology adds impact and clarity but can also create psychological distance and a perception of rigidity that some audience members will not appreciate.

Time Consuming

Creating slides with a standard background is fairly easy. However, finding the right video clip, creating graphs, incorporating video clips, and synchronizing music are all activities that take time and effort, and may distract you from your primary goal, which is to develop and support your ideas. Surely you have witnessed a presentation that had great visual appeal but little substance. The speaker may have spent too much time with the "bells and whistles" at the expense of developing sound arguments with ample support.

In addition to expending effort to create the slide show, setting up might take too much time before the speech. Once the computer is on and the projection equipment is warmed up (no guarantee of this actually happening when you need it to), the speaker must control volume, launch and operate software, etc. Speech classes sometimes endure lengthy gaps of dullness while an unprepared speaker bumbles with their set-up. The considerate speaker will find ways to minimize this waste of audience time.

Possible Smoke Screen

Similar to magician sleight-of-hand techniques, moving the focus from the speaker to the screen may shift attention away from a speaker's difficulties or lack of preparation. Some speakers rely heavily on 20, 40, or more slides hoping to cover up their deficiencies as a speaker (Alley & Neeley, 2005). Wright (2009) writes that "multimedia presentations can be a prop for weak presenters, but can also detract from messages delivered by competent communicators" (p. 34).

Speakers (and lecturers) who use slides for the purpose of providing the outline to their talk may find themselves less motivated or excited about the presentation. Knowing they don't have to worry about losing their place, they may spend less time practicing their speech. According to Carey (1999), "PowerPoint's reliability has lulled more than a few presenters and planners into creative complacency, resulting in audiovisual presentations that too often are monotonous, static, even boring" (pg. 47). Death by PowerPoint, as it is termed, is a painful way to go. Strike a balance by not overusing slides. One or two per minute you speak is acceptable; 20 in a five-minute speech will surely power us to the point of unconsciousness.

Potential for Reductionism

Some claim that design defaults in presentation software create the potential for reductionism because they oversimplify and fragment the subject matter (Alley & Neeley, 2005, p. 418). Only a limited amount of information can be presented on any one slide or group of slides. Abstract connections may be difficult to make, and sometimes critical assumptions are left out or relationships are not specified. Research indicates that people often begin to prepare presentations by thinking about what should appear on screen, slide by slide, and then constructing their presentations accordingly, rather than by considering what they want to say or how they can make the audience's experience better (Wright, 2009). When we reduce issues to slides of text and little pictures, we risk our audience not getting the big picture.

Messages composed mainly of bullet points and text are not always fully understood (Kalyuga et al., 1991). Furthermore, computer-based presentations can obscure messages or mislead audiences (Tufte, 2006). The focus on creating slides rather than creating arguments is problematic since the speaker's first task is to create effective messages. Relying too heavily on bullet points may reduce the richness of your ideas by limiting the information your audience focuses on, thereby fostering misinformation, misinterpretation, and mistakes in judgment.

Guaranteed Glitches and Gremlins

Having created an excellent set of slides does not guarantee an effective speech. Researchers found that listeners are most annoyed when the speaker reads the slides to his/her audience (Paradi, 2009). Your speech instructor will appreciate it if you reread that last sentence again. Out loud. Also problematic are full sentences that are too small, too long, or accompanied by different font sizes, overuse of animations, and other special effects.

Sometimes students feel compelled or coerced to use computer-based presentational software because an instructor's assignment requires it, but the resulting slides may reflect a lack of effort, conviction, or inspiration. Settling for defaults in font types, design templates, and colors can cause slide presentations to look and feel painfully similar (Alley & Neeley, 2005, p. 418). A lack of creativity often results in listeners' lack of attention, interest, and comprehension. Selecting and using the most appropriate technology for the audience, occasion, and message is the focus of the next section.

Types of Presentational Aids

Presentational aids fall into four classifications: actual objects, three-dimensional models, two-dimensional reproductions, and technology-based aids. Each type has the potential to assist the speaker.

Actual Objects

Actual objects are real objects. Your authors quickly generated this list of inappropriate objects brought to their speech classes: snakes, guns, grenades, margaritas, M-80 firecrackers, marijuana, and so on. Of course, these were all bad choices. Yet good options abound. One student who had been stricken with bone cancer as a child, a condition that required the amputation of her leg, demonstrated to her classmates how her prosthetic leg functioned and how she wore it. Not one of her listeners lost interest in her demonstration.

Another student, concerned about the volumes of disposable diapers lingering in our landfills, brought to class a (heavy) week's worth of dirty diapers from one infant. In addition to visual and olfactory shock value, it left a powerfully strong image to accompany her statistics about the slow decomposition of dirty, disposable diapers.

As these examples demonstrate, objects can be effective visual aids. Because you are showing your audience exactly what you are talking about, objects have the power to inform or convince unlike any other presentational aid.

When bringing an object to class, be concerned with safety. Clear any questionable objects with your instructor. Objects you intend to use must not pose a safety risk to you or your audience. Animals, chemicals, and weapons certainly fall into this category. For example, you may think your pet Madagascar Hissing Cockroaches are snuggly-adorable, but to your instructor and some of your classmates, they may elicit terror and panic.

Three-Dimensional Models

If you decide that an actual object is too risky, a three-dimensional model may be your best choice. Models are commonly used to show the structure of a complex object. For example, a student who watched his father almost die of a heart attack used a model of the heart to demonstrate what physically happened during the attack. Using a three-dimensional replica about five times the size of a human heart, he showed how the major blood vessels leading to his father's heart became clogged and how this blockage precipitated the attack.

Models are useful when explaining steps in a sequence. A scale model of the space shuttle, its booster rockets, and the launch pad would help you describe what happens during the first few minutes after blast-off.

When considering a three-dimensional model, take into account construction time and availability. It is possible you already have the model or you know where you can borrow one, so no construction time is needed. If you need to create the three-dimensional model from a kit or your own imagination, consider how much time it will take to put it together. Here is a general rule: You do not want your presentational aid construction time to take longer than your speech preparation time.

If the three-dimensional model is in your possession, availability is not an issue. If the model is sold at the local Mega-lo-Mart, then availability is not an issue. If it is in your bedroom, attic, or garage in your hometown, you need to take travel time into account. If you have to sign your life away to borrow it, or if you have to plan six weeks or more ahead to access the model, it may not be worth your trouble.

Some replicas are easier to find, build, or buy than others. If you are delivering a speech on antique cars, inexpensive plastic models are available at a hobby shop and take little time to assemble. But if you want to show how proper city planning can untangle the daily downtown traffic snarl, you would have to build your own scaled-down version of downtown roads as they are now, and as you would like them to be. That would be too time consuming and expensive to be feasible. But a two-dimensional representation (like a map or diagram), as we see next, would be effective and affordable.

Two-Dimensional Reproductions

Two-dimensional reproductions are the most common visual aids used by speakers. Among these are photographs, diagrams and drawings, maps, tables, and graphs. Computer-projected presentations, such as Microsoft's PowerPoint, Prezi Inc.'s Prezi, or Apple's iWork Keynote, are also two-dimensional reproductions but are discussed as a separate type because of their reliance on newer, higher technologies.

Photographs

Photographs are realistic two-dimensional choices. They can have great impact. For a speech on animal rights, a photo of a fox struggling to free his leg from a trap will deliver your message more effectively than words. If you are speaking about forest fire prevention, a photo of a forest destroyed by fire is your most persuasive evidence.

Photos must be large enough for your audience to see. If a photo is important to your presentation, consider enlarging it so that the entire audience can see it. Typically, using magazine or newspaper pictures is as clear as photos.

Although photographs are effective aids, overly graphic pictures can yield negative results. If a photograph offends or disgusts your audience, some may tune you out.

Drawings and Diagrams

When you cannot illustrate your point with a photograph—or would rather not use one—a drawing is an alternative. A drawing is your own representation of what you are describing. If you are demonstrating the difference between a kettledrum and a snare drum, a simple drawing may be all you need. If you want to extend your explanation to show how musicians are able to control the pitch of the sound made by a drum, your drawing must include more detail. The location of the screws used to tighten the skin of the drum must be shown as well as the relationship between the size of the drum and the pitch of the sound.

A detailed drawing showing the arrangement and relationship of the parts to the whole is considered a diagram. **Figure 10.2** is a simple diagram of a kettledrum. Labels are often used to pinpoint critical parts.

Do not attempt a complex drawing or diagram if you have little or no artistic ability. Neither should you attempt to produce drawings while your audience is watching. Prepare sketches in advance. Keep your audience's needs and limitations in mind when choosing diagrams. Imagine the audience's eyes as they listen to someone using Figure 10.3 to discuss every dimension of a complex floor design. Too much detail will frustrate your audience as they strain to see the tiniest parts and labels. And when people are frustrated, they often stop listening.

Maps

Weather reports on TV news have made maps a familiar visual aid. Instead of merely talking about the weather, reporters show us the shifting patterns that turn sunshine into storms. The next time you watch a weather report, note the kind of map being used. Notice that details have been omitted because they distract viewers from what the reporter is explaining.

Too much detail will confuse your audience. For example, when talking about Europe's shrinking population, do not include the location of the Acropolis or the Eiffel Tower. Because you must focus on your specific purpose, you may have to draw a map yourself. Start with a broad outline of the geographic area and add to it only those details necessary for your presentation.

On election night, many news programs show a map of the United States divided into "blue states" and "red states." Blue states may be those where the majority of voters voted Democratic, and red states were Republican. Such a map (see Figure 10.4) gives a quick visual of where election results stand. Making a visual distinction between Republicans and Democrats began with the 2004 presidential election between John Kerry and George W. Bush, and has been so successful that the concept of "blue states" and "red states" has become part of our political vernacular.

FIGURE 15.2

A simple diagram can show how the parts of objects such as this drum interact.

FIGURE 15.3

An intricate line drawing may frustrate your audience. Keep illustrations simple.

FIGURE 15.4

This map shows "blue states" and "red states," clarifying where election results stand.

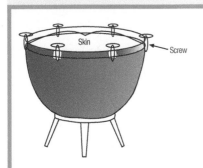

Tables

Tables focus on words and numbers presented in columns and rows. Tables are used most frequently to display statistical data. If you were delivering a speech on the fat content of food and you note the types and percentage of fat in nuts, you could refer to a table similar to that shown in **Figure 10.5**. However, this single table should be divided into two parts because it contains too much information to present in one visual. Keep in mind the audience's *information absorption threshold*—the point at which a visual will cease to be useful because it says too much.

Charts

Charts help the speaker display detailed information quickly and effectively. Charts can summarize data in an easy-to-read format, illustrate a process, and show relationships among parts.

Flow charts are used to display the steps, or stages, in a process. Each step is illustrated by an image or label. If you are an amateur cartoonist, you might give a talk on the steps involved in producing an animated cartoon. **Figure 10.6** displays a simple flowchart of the process a golfer goes through when deciding whether to golf on a particular day. This humorous visual reveals the specific decision-making sequence.

A flow chart can make use of pictures. You might draw the pictures yourself or, if your artistic ability is limited, use selected photographs available online. Flow charts that depend on words alone should use short, simple labels that move the audience through the stages of the process.

Organizational charts reflect our highly structured world. Corporations, government institutions, schools, associations, and religious organizations are organized according to official hierarchies that determine the relationships of people as they work. You may refer to an organizational chart if you are trying to show the positions of people involved in a project. By looking at a chart like that shown in **Figure 10.7**, your audience will know who reports to whom.

Graphs

When referring to statistics or when presenting complex statistical information, a visual representation can be effective because it has the ability to simplify and clarify. Statistics may be presented in numerous ways, including bar graphs, pictographs, line graphs, and pie graphs.

Glossary

Flow chart Used to display the steps, or stages, in a process.

Organizational chart Organized according to official hierarchies that determine the relationships of people as they work.

FIGURE 15.5

The fat content of food is measured in a single table.

	Saturated	Monosaturated	Polyunsaturated	Other
Chestnuts	18%	35%	40%	7%
Brazil Nuts	15%	35%	36%	14%
Cashews	13	59	17	11
Pine Nuts	13	37	41	9
Peanuts	12	49	38	6
Pistachios	12	68	15	5
Walnuts	8	23	63	6
Almonds	8	65	21	6
Pecans	6	62	25	7
Hazelnuts	6	79	9	6

FIGURE 15.6

A simple flow chart of the golfer's decision-making process.

FIGURE 15.7

Almost every large group or company has an organizational chart to illustrate the official hierarchy and lines of access.

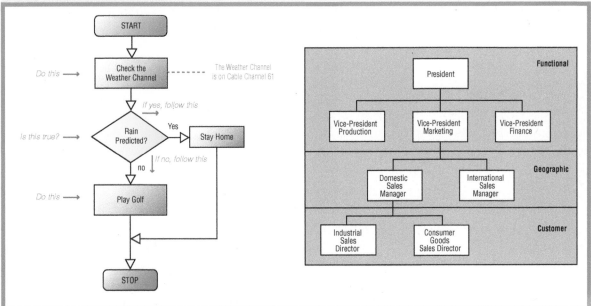

In a speech urging today's college students to consider teaching social sciences or humanities in college, you want to show, graphically, that our universities will face a serious shortfall of liberal arts professors well into the future. As part of your speech, you tell your audience:

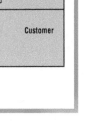

FIGURE 15.8

A speech to outline the projected need for new faculty in the next 30 years would be enhanced by a bar graph such as this.

> There were days back in the 1980s when having a Ph.D. in history, sociology, English literature, or philosophy garnered little professional and monetary opportunities. Indeed, many people who aspired to teach the humanities and social sciences were forced into menial jobs just to survive. So great was the supply of potential faculty over the demand that a new phenomenon was created: the taxi-driving Ph.D. Today, the story is different.

The visual referred to is shown in **Figure 10.8**, a bar graph displaying the history of supply and demand for faculty members. The

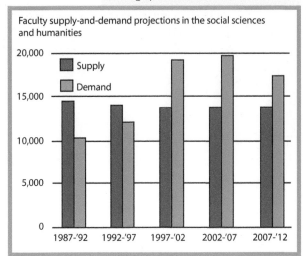

Glossary

Pictograph Most commonly used as a variation of the bar graph. Instead of showing bars of various lengths, comparing items on the graph, the bars are replaced by pictorial representations of the graph's subject.

Line graph Used to show a trend over time.

Pie graph Also known as circle graphs, shows how the parts of an item relate to the whole.

graph compares figures for five-year periods and measures these figures in thousands. This type of graph is especially helpful when you are comparing two or more items. In this case, one bar represents the supply of faculty while the other represents demand. To make the trend even clearer, you may want to color code the bars.

Pictographs are most commonly used as a variation of the bar graph. Instead of showing bars of various lengths comparing items on the graph, the bars are replaced by pictorial representations of the graph's subject. For example, if you are giving a speech on the popularity of ice cream bars, you can use a pictograph like that shown in **Figure 10.9** to demonstrate when the most bars were sold. The pictograph must include a legend explaining what each symbol means. In this case, each ice cream bar represents 100 sold.

When you want to show a trend over time, the **line graph** may be your best choice. When two or more lines are used in one graph, comparisons are possible. **Figure 10.10** is a visual representation of the number of Irish immigrants entering the United States between 1820 and 1990. The tall peak in the graph represents the period of time when the potato famine was affecting the majority of Ireland. This simple graph could be used in a speech about Irish immigration trends.

Pie graphs show your audience how the parts of an item relate to the whole. It is one of the most popular and effective ways to show how something is divided. The most simple and direct way to

FIGURE 15.9

Pictographs provide a twist on the traditional bar graph by using pictures of the items discussed to illustrate the "bar." The pictograph should include a scale that explains what each symbol means, such as each ice cream bar sold.

FIGURE 15.10

This is a graph of the number of Irish immigrants who entered the U.S. from 1820 to 1990. The climax of the migration was in 1851 when 221,253 immigrants entered the U.S. This was around the time when the potato famine seized the majority of Ireland.

FIGURE 15.11

The pie chart effectively illustrates how parts of a whole are divided.

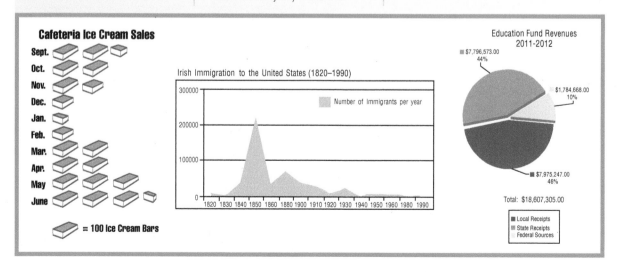

demonstrate percentages graphically is with a pie graph. In a budget presentation to the local school board, the chief financial officer might display a series of pie graphs. She might explain that revenue comes from three levels: federal, state, and local. Figure 10.11 shows that taxes from local communities provide approximately half the revenue generated for the district. The federal government provides only 10 percent, thus illustrating how dependent the school district is on local funding.

No matter what type of two-dimensional aid you choose, clarity is essential. It may happen that you create a two-dimensional aid that makes your audience think, "What does that *mean*?" Any presentational aid you use must clarify rather than confuse. If the aid contains too much information, your audience will be unable to process it easily, and you may lose their attention. If you use graphs, pie charts, maps, or tables, information must be understandable. For example, if you have an x-axis and a y-axis, they should be clearly labeled so your audience knows what you are referring to quickly and easily.

Displaying Two-Dimensional Presentational Aids

When you decide to use a line graph to illustrate the volatility of the market place, your next decision involves how to display the graph. Speakers have numerous options for displaying two-dimensional presentational aids. Time and cost alone are not good predictors of the effectiveness of a presentational aid. Sometimes emphasizing important points on a flip chart or using prepared overhead transparencies are acceptable. This next section focuses on how to display two-dimensional aids. In particular, we discuss the benefits and disadvantages of using erasable boards, large Post-its®, posters, and flip charts.

Chalk or Dry Erase Board

It is a rare classroom that does not have some type of erasable board, be it black, green, or white. These serve as the universal presentational aid. Advantages include: It is already in the classroom, you cannot lose or damage it, and it requires no preparation time (other than the day of presentation). Boards are the easiest visual aid to use and involve the least amount of preparation time.

Using a board requires neat, legible handwriting. Seldom is it acceptable to write on the blackboard *during the speech*, but if you must, write as little as possible. Use key terms only. If possible, arrive early and prepare the board in advance. If the board has a screen above it, you might pull the screen down to hide your work until time for your presentation.

In terms of disadvantages, the blackboard is generally viewed as less professional than other presentational aids. We suggest that chalk or eraser boards should serve as your back-up plan. If your poster is ruined, you cannot find an easel for your flip chart, or the computer is unavailable or malfunctioning, then the blackboard is your backup plan.

Your audience may interpret your use of it as lack of preparation. Also, writing on the blackboard requires a speaker to turn away from the audience. Turning your back on your audience is never a good idea, and writing on the board cuts into your valuable speaking time.

Poster Board

A generation ago, the clarity of a poster depended on the art skills of the students since posters were "designed" by hand. If your college has an instructional materials office of some kind, you can make your own posters using die-cuts (generally, Ellison die-cuts). These allow you to cut out letters and shapes to make the poster look more professional. Even better, a computer lab on campus or a photocopying facility will allow access to poster-sized computer-generated graphics. Another option is to use poster-sized foam board in different colors.

Advantages to using a poster board include its low cost and familiarity, and potential use in classrooms where computer-generated technology is not available or difficult to access. Disadvantages include some speaker's lack of time, talent, or patience to create a professional-looking poster, potential difficulty displaying the poster if there is no easel or the chalkboard lacks chalk tray; and posters may get damaged during transportation. Many have abandoned poster boards for computer-generated graphics in the classroom. Where this is not possible, posters are still a viable way to display two-dimensional information.

What are the advantages of using a flip chart in your presentation?

© AISPIX, 2012. Under license from Shutterstock, Inc.

Flip Chart

Flip charts are still popular way to for displaying two-dimensional information. According to professional speaker and presentation skills expert Lenny Laskowski (2006), since most presentations are delivered before small groups of 35 people or less, the flip chart is the perfect size. Flip charts give speakers the ability to show a sequence of visuals. Studies indicate that listeners are more likely to retain information when the chart is not fully completed ahead of time. Instead, leave out a few key lines or words and fill them in during your speech. This process encourages listeners to perceive the visual as a product of your own expression, and more of an interactive, rather than static presentation.

There are several advantages to using flip charts. The main advantage is that they allow for spontaneity. The speaker may add words or lines based on audience response. A flip chart can be prepared in advance *or* during your speech. Other advantages are that they do not require electricity, they are economical, and one can add color to them easily (Laskowski, 2006).

Disadvantages to using flip charts are they may not be seen by all and they may be distracting. Laskowski (2006) suggests avoiding yellow, pink, or orange markers that are difficult to see, and sticking to one dark color and one lighter color for highlighting. Also, less expensive paper may lead to the marker bleeding through to the following page. Test your markers and paper ahead of time.

Repositional Note Pad

The large repositional note pad, most commonly known as a poster-sized Post-it, is a type of flip chart. These large sticky notes have useful applications in group meetings where members brainstorm and then display the results on multiple pages around the walls. For your speech, you may have some pre-designed Post-its that you stick on the board at different intervals for emphasis. Like posters, these are most useful in rooms lacking more advanced technology.

Two advantages to using poster-sized sticky notes are that you do not have to worry about chalk, tape, push pins, or staples, and you have tremendous flexibility. In addition to being able to stick them just about anywhere, the speaker can write on them before or during the speech. The main disadvantage is that, as they are most likely hand-written, they may not look as professional as some other display techniques. One way to work around it is to use pencil on the pages in advance so the writing is neat and at the same time, so light that only you can see it. Then, during your presentation, go over your work with a marker.

Technology-Based Presentational Aids

Often speakers must clearly communicate statistics, trends, and abstract information. As funds become available and technology costs decrease, more classrooms will be technology-enhanced. This does not mean, however, that older options are now useless. Instances still exist where an audio recording or actual object may make more sense than a computer-generated slide presentation. This next section discusses audio and projected images.

Audio and Projected Images

Rarely is the eraser board your only option for a presentational aid. Depending on the needs of your audience, the content of your speech, the speaking situation, and your own abilities, you may choose a presentational aid requiring the use of other equipment.

Audiotape/CD/iPod

Not all presentational aids are visual, and incorporating some audio clip into your speech is a simple task. If you are trying to describe the messages babies send through their different cries, it would be appropriate and helpful to play an audiotape, CD, iPod, or a smartphone recording of different cries as you explain each. Of course, in a technology-enhanced room, students can access music and many sounds on the computer.

Take care when using an audio clip. Time is an issue, and the clip can overshadow the oral presentation if it consumes too much time. The inexperienced speaker may not have the sound bite or audio clip set up at the right spot or the right volume, and recording quality may be an issue. Getting set up on the computer may take too much time. As always, check the equipment to make sure it is working, the volume is set correctly, and that it is properly queued before the presentation.

Using an overhead projector, object projector, document cameras (for example, ELMO), or smart board allows you to face your listeners and talk as you project images onto a surface. They may be used in normal lighting, which is an important advantage to the speaker. You may face your listeners and use a pointer, just as you would if you were using any other visual. If you choose to remain near the projector instead, you run the risk of talking down to the material you are projecting rather than looking up at your audience. An advantage over PowerPoint is projected images, documents, and transparencies can be altered as you speak, such as underlining a phrase for emphasis or adding a key word.

PowerPoint, Prezi, and Keynote are popular software applications that create visuals to accompany presentations. All have unique features (Prezi lets you create 3-D effects) and common ones (templates, samples, editing, etc.). Using these products as a speech aid is expedient and the finished product looks good and is easy to use, too. For the sake of audiences everywhere, let us offer one plea: Please don't bullet, point, and read us to death. We cannot take it anymore! Keep the presentation centered on you, not the slide show. (See **BTW: PowerPointless** for further illumination on this point.)

Video, DVD, and Online Media Sharing Sites

In certain situations, the most effective way to communicate your message is with a video, DVD, or an online host, such as YouTube. In a speech on tornadoes, showing a video of the damage done by a tornado is likely to be impressive. Showing snippets of a press conference or a movie clip to illustrate or emphasize a particular point can also be interesting and effective.

The novice speaker giving a five-minute speech may not edit the video carefully enough, however. The result may be four minutes of video and one minute of speech. If you choose an audio or video clip, practice with it, plan

PowerPointless

Comedian Don McMillan's YouTube video "Life After Death by PowerPoint" is both informative and entertaining (www.youtube.com/watch?v=IpvgfmEU2Ck). What problems do you relate to? What advice can you give someone who uses too much PowerPoint assistance? What are the software's strengths? Weaknesses?

how to use it, and know how to operate the equipment. Plan for what you will do if the equipment fails.

It is possible to be upstaged by your video clip. Your visual presentation—rather than your speech—may hold center stage. To avoid this, carefully prepare an introduction to support the video clip. Point your listeners to specific parts so they focus on what you want rather than on what happens to catch their interest. After the visual, continue your speech, and build on its content with the impact of your own delivery.

When thinking about using any of the above projected images, allow for sufficient set-up time. Check the equipment to make sure you can operate it and that it is in good working order. Remember also, a darkened room can disrupt your presentation if you need to refer to detailed notes, and if you want people to take notes, the room may be too dark.

Considerations for Technology-Mediated Communication

Speeches have been broadcast via radio and TV for generations. However, these events were coordinated and executed with a team of individuals connected to radio and TV stations. Now, individuals can create and disseminate their own videos over the Internet, and some self-produced work goes viral on YouTube.

While most speeches you will give will involve a live audience, at times you may be required to record your speech. Technology in this respect is the medium, or the channel through which your speech is presented. In this next section, we provide some suggestions for those specific technology-mediated occasions.

Speaking on Camera

You may find yourself facing traditional cameras, including professional cameras associated with TV stations, video cameras, or less traditional cameras, such as built-in or remote webcams, phone cams, or digital cameras with video capabilities. With an audience present, you still need to follow the basic tenets of public speaking and adapt your speech to the particular audience and situation. Without a live audience, your primary focus becomes creating a message that is conveyed effectively to your intended audience through the camera. Adaptation becomes paramount if you are to succeed.

If you have an audience present, give the speech to them and assume those who record you will do a good job. If you do not have a live audience, you should not "play" to the camera unless directed to do so. Treat the camera as another audience member. President Obama has many positive traits as a speaker, but on occasion, he turns his head to audience members on the left and right, and avoids looking forward toward the camera. The result is the at-home viewer may not feel as connected to Obama's message. Eye contact should be direct and sustained, and strong speakers avoid moving their head, eyes, and hands too quickly.

Posture is important, and the camera may not be as forgiving of imperfections as a live audience. Keep your posture erect. Whether your speech is before a live audience or not, do not forget to gesture naturally. Be sincere and conversational. A recorded speech should be similar to a live audience, but those who are not part of the live audience do not share the same context.

When you know your speech will be recorded, consider how your clothes will look on camera. Professional speaker and speaking coach Tom Antion suggests the following and more on his informative web page (www.public-speaking.org).

- ○ Pastels are the best colors to wear (this applies to men, too!).
- ○ Good clothing colors include beige, gray, green, brown, and blue.
- ○ Avoid white, red, and orange clothing.
- ○ Black, or dark browns and blues are fine alone or combined with pastel colors.
- ○ Avoid fine checks, stripes, herringbone, and similar patterns.
- ○ Avoid very glossy, sequined, or metallic clothing. Also avoid clinging attire, or low-cut necklines.

Radio

A speech on radio may be live or taped, and you may have the option to edit your speech. If it is in front of an audience, you cannot rewind and start again. Audience analysis is a critical element of public speaking. Unlike national and international politicians and dignitaries who may be heard on most radio stations, most speeches you give will be heard locally or regionally. Therefore, it is important to have a basic profile of the listeners within that particular programming market. Establishing common ground is important no matter what the medium.

Once on air, focus on speaking clearly and passionately. Being alone in a room with a microphone may be difficult, but work to energize yourself and deliver your speech enthusiastically. Be aware that pauses are powerful tools, although they may seem longer when the listener can't see you. Since your audience is not present, their awareness of your pacing, articulation, and pronunciation becomes even keener. Work to use pauses strategically and avoid nonfluencies such as um, er, uh, well uh, and so on.

As you craft your message for the radio audience, paying special attention to your main points, transitions, and supporting materials helps ensure effectiveness. Generally, radio also requires us to make key points in shorter sentences. Use effective transitions that help your audience track where you are in your message. Phrases like "Now I will turn to my third point" or "To wrap this talk up" help your listeners understand where you are and where you are headed. Further, anticipate audience questions, and structure your support material in a way that addresses these concerns. For example, if you anticipate many listeners might pose an objection to an idea you present, address the objection yourself and then overcome it with additional support.

Often your audience will not have the opportunity to ask for clarification, and lingering questions work against you.

Video Conferencing/Skype/Webinars

Video conferencing can be set up in three ways: computer-based system, desktop system, and studio-based system. A computer-based system is often the least expensive method, but its drawback is a lower degree of quality. In essence, computer-based systems often include a webcam and free software like CUseeMe and NetMeeting. A desktop system has dedicated software installed on the computer and can improve the audio and video quality. The studio-based system offers the best quality, but is also the most expensive and difficult for most to access.

Video conferencing is a "green" technology. By communicating over video, organizations substantially reduce their carbon footprint. With tools that provide a powerful way to enable conferences and other video content to be streamed live or on demand around the world, we can communicate, engage, and interact with others across distances at any time, from wherever they are. The need to hop in a car or jet in, in many cases is now circumvented through these technologies. The effects of videoconferencing are evident within the airline industry. Hewlett Packard, for example, has reduced its global travel by 43 percent (*Travel Weekly*, 2008). Travel management companies predict this trend toward videoconferencing to continue over the next several years.

Yet, because these mediated interactions can be awkward and have the potential for technical problems, sometimes live face-to-face meetings are worth the extra effort, cost, and time. However, *Travel Weekly* notes, "[T]he technology for video and web conferencing has got its act together—no longer does it freeze or crash as soon as you overload the data line, as it did in the early 1990s." Even when all works correctly, as is usually the case, the loss of intimacy, comfort, and ease of communicating as well as the somewhat limited access to immediate nonverbal feedback of those not on camera can impact the effectiveness of the conference.

While videoconferencing is often used for group meetings, the medium is used for public speaking, too. In a video conference speech, we encourage you to look into the camera to create eye contact. Avoid sudden abrupt or sweeping movements to prevent ghosting (motion blur), and in general, move a little more slowly and deliberately than normal to compensate for audio delays. (For information about Skype, see **BTW: Using Skype**.)

You may have an occasion to present at a webinar. Generally, a webinar is announced in advance, and people register for it. A date and time for attending via the Web is provided. Depending on the situation, those who miss the webinar may be able to access a recording of it later. The audience participating in the webinar may have the opportunity to speak or type questions or comments for the speaker. These questions can be monitored by a third

Glossary

Computer-based system Includes a webcam and free software.

Desktop system Dedicated software improves the audio and video quality.

Studio-based system Offers the best quality, but also is most expensive.

BTW!

Skype is one of the fastest-growing Voice over IP (VoIP), IM, and video call applications available today. It promotes the creation of many hardware and software add-on products.

Skype runs on Windows, Mac, Linux, Pocket PC, and many cell phones. In addition there are Wi-Fi phones that do not require a computer at all.

○ Did you know you can use Skype without sitting at your computer?

○ Did you know you can use Skype with the same telephone you use for regular telephone calls?

○ Did you know you can have an answering machine with Skype?

○ Did you know Skype can call almost any cell or telephone in the world?

○ Did you know you can use your cell phone to send messages to a Skype user?

Using Skype is similar to the computer-based system one would use in video conferencing, but the major benefit is, it is free! Skype has over 663 million current users. While many people use Skype to communicate interpersonally, it has a clear public speaking application, and the system provides video conferencing support. For more information, visit SkypeTips.com.

person or by the speaker. This allows the speaker to clarify points, discuss related information, or respond to the audience in some directed manner.

Podcasts and Streaming Audio

Podcasts most generally are audio presentations. Individuals who produce their own podcasts may not edit their speeches. This leads to mixed success. Podcasts connected to organizations are more likely to have equipment and personnel to create a more polished end result. Podcasts such as "Jimmy's No-Lose Sports Picks of the Week," broadcast live from his parent's garage, on the other hand, can be quite low in production value.

As a speaker, remember that your audience may include people who are listening on their iPods, smartphones, and laptops while working out, sitting at their desk, or driving to work. Listeners may be multitasking. They may choose to skim the podcast, and not catch the whole speech. Since they are not listening in real time, listeners may allow for distractions. Keeping in mind your listeners' attention span limitations, it makes sense to remind listeners who you are and what your central idea is more frequently in your podcast than in a traditional speech.

During an interview with Chris Bjorklund, podcast editor for AllBusiness. com who spent 15 years on radio in the San Francisco Bay Area, several suggestions were offered for creating effective podcasts. She emphasizes that the quality of the audio is of utmost importance. Listeners will tune out if the podcast sounds as though it's coming from a hollow room or a tunnel. A bad connection, a hiss, or some other irritating sound "is a deal breaker." She emphasizes the importance of listening to your surroundings while recording (Is the light buzzing or the air conditioner vent whishing?) as well as the quality of sound after you have finished.

Further, Bjorklund stresses the importance of sounding conversational, and to avoid sounding as though you're lecturing. Communicating energy and enthusiasm is necessary, and she encourages speakers not to "overscript." In other words, the message should not be memorized, and the speaker should focus on creating an effective speaker–audience connection that is less formal than a traditional speech.

Striving for a middle ground between an extemporaneous speech and an informal interpersonal conversation can be difficult to get used to at first, but is usually best received by audiences. Bjorklund encourages individuals who podcast regularly to "brand" themselves by using the same, identifiable theme music to "bookend" the beginning and ending of the program. This helps standardize the podcast, enhances listening enjoyment, and creates a sense of closure at the conclusion. Many radio program talk show hosts use this technique and are identified, in part, by the "bumper" music that has become associated with them.

Effective Use of Presentational Aids

Suppose your speech topic is "College Athletes Don't Graduate." You attend a college that graduates a low percentage of its athletes—a guarded scandal gripping your school. Recent articles in the student newspaper have criticized your school's athletic department for emphasizing winning over education. An editorial in last week's paper asked, "How can student-athletes practice 40 hours a week and still go to class, study, and complete their assignments? The answer is they cannot."

As you collect supporting material for your speech, you find statistics about how much money athletes bring to your university, and you discover that not only do they not get a part of the money, they may not be equipped to go professional or be prepared for anything more than menial work. Making things worse yet, great disparity exists between graduation rates of African American student athletes and their white team members. Here is part of the speech your classmates hear:

> According to a 2010 study by the Institute for Diversity and Ethics (TIDES) at the University of Central Florida, of the 64 colleges and universities with Division I-A basketball programs, 44 teams, or 69 percent of the total, graduated at least 50 percent of their basketball student-athletes, 37 teams (58 percent) graduated at least 60 percent, and 29 teams (45 percent) graduated at least 70 percent. Only 12 teams (19 percent) graduated less than 40 percent. In terms of equity in graduation rates, 13 of the 67 Division I-A schools

graduated less than 40 percent of their African American players, whereas only four schools graduated less than 60 percent of their white counterparts. Also, eight schools graduated 80 to 100 percent of their African American players, but 39 Division 1-A schools graduated 100 percent of their white basketball players.

The graduation rates for football players of Division 1-A teams is similar. Of the 67 of the 68 teams providing data, 61, or 91 percent, of the total graduated at least 50 percent of their football student athletes, 43 teams (64 percent) graduated at least 60 percent, and 24 teams (36 percent) graduated at least 70 percent. In terms of equity in graduation rates, seven of the 67 Division 1-A schools graduated less than 40 percent of their African American players, whereas no schools graduated less than 40 percent of their white football players. Also, one school graduated 90 percent of its African American players, but 10 schools graduated 90 percent or more of their white counterparts.

Instead of startling your listeners, these statistics numb them. You may see several people yawning, doodling, whispering, and looking out the window. You have no idea why until your classmates comment during the post-speech evaluation. The complaints are all the same: Your "can't miss" speech was boring and difficult to follow. Instead of stimulating your listeners, your long list of statistics put them to sleep.

In this example, an appropriately constructed visual aid could have helped you avoid saying so much in words. Despite the interest your listeners had in your topic before your speech began, the number and complexity of your statistics made it difficult for them to pay attention. By presenting some of your data in visual form, you would communicate the same message more effectively. Consider the difference when the following speech text is substituted for the text above and combined with Figure 10.12.

According to a 2010 study by the Institute for Diversity and Ethics (TIDES) at the University of Central Florida, graduation rates for Division 1-A football and basketball players have increased somewhat over previous years. For example, less than

FIGURE 15.12

A visual aid is an effective way to present statistics.

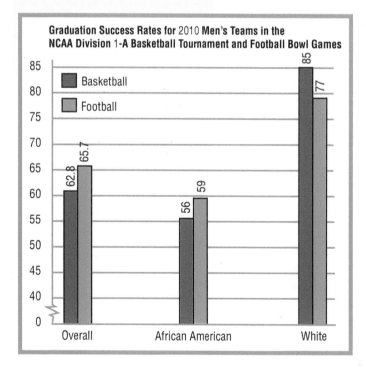

half of the basketball teams graduate at least 60 percent of their athletes, and almost two-thirds of the football teams graduate at least 60 percent of their athletes.

The study discovered a disturbing gap between white and African-American student-athletes, however. Eight schools graduated 80–100 percent of their African American basketball players, while 39 schools graduated 100 percent of their white counterparts. In football, one school graduated 90 percent of their African American players whereas 10 schools graduated 100 percent of their white football players. But the worst news is some schools only graduate about a third of their athletes—and our college is one of them.

Numbers are still used, but not as many. With the presentational aid, the audience gets a visual feel for the information and they can process the information awhile longer than if you just stated the numbers.

Criteria for Presentational Aids

Your decision to include an aid should be based on the extent to which it enhances your audience's interest and understanding. The type of aid you choose should relate directly to the specific purpose of your speech and information you intend to convey. Training documents provided by the U.S. Department of Labor remind speakers that presentational aids "enable you to appeal to more than one sense at the same time, thereby increasing the audience's understanding and retention level" (osha.gov, 1996). As you consider using a presentational aid, consider the following four general criteria.

① Value to presentation. Your instructor may require you to use a presentational aid for one or more of your speeches, but it does not mean that *any* aid is better than no aid. First and foremost, the aid must add value to your presentation. If you are considering a presentational aid just to meet assignment requirements, make sure you select something that adds meaning or impact. For example, if a student is giving a speech about "washing your hands to prevent spread of disease" and brings in a half-used bar of soap, there is not much value added to the presentation. We all know what soap looks like. But if the same student gave a speech on "shower sanitation considerations," he might pass around that half-used bar of soap to his listeners as he says:

Does this bar of soap look clean? Silly question, it's soap, of course it is clean. Let me ask you this: Where is the first part of yourself you wash with a bar like this in the shower? [audience motions towards face and head] That's right, your face. OK, now where is the last place you wash before you get out of the shower? [audience members giggle and indicate buttocks and groin areas] Yes, most people do save the privates for last. Then what do you do? You put the bar of soap back until the next shower when you apply it to your … that's right … face again! As you pick up any bar of soap, including the one I am passing around now, I want you to ask yourself, just where is the last place that bar has been" [those in the audience who handled the bar now frown and look at their hands.

In this example, the student went on to identify diseases such as hepatitis that can be transmitted by contaminated soap. His attention-grabbing visual aid succeeded in helping make his case more real. Although passing around objects is generally distracting, he decided the impact was worth the added chaos, and we agree. So ask yourself, what is the purpose of the aid? To surprise? To entertain? To illustrate? To make some concept concrete? If you think your presentational aid will improve your speech, then it has value. If you think the audience will benefit from the visual aid, then it has value.

❷ **Item safety.** If the item is precious to you, think twice about bringing it to class. It may rain or snow. You might drop it. In the afterglow of your stunning speech, you might leave it behind. Also consider the possible implications of the item not being returned to you if someone in your audience "borrows" it. One of your authors, Mark, passed around a pill bottle containing a homeopathic remedy purported to help reduce nervousness called Gelsemium Sempervirens. The occasion was a corporate presentational skills training session and each member was soon going to be delivering their final presentations. By the time the bottle had made its way around the room and was returned, it was empty. All 30 pills were gone! Fortunately, no one had any ill effects, although the remainder of the workshop had taken a decidedly more laid back tone. Mark should have considered carefully what might happen if someone in his workshop had taken the entire amount.

❸ **Ease of transportation.** Think about what may happen to your object during transportation. Is it a large poster you are trying to carry on a bus or subway? Does it weigh 40 pounds? Do you have to carry it with you all day? Is it bigger than a breadbox? Is it alive? You want to consider how difficult your aid will be to transport, as well as what you are going to do with it before and after your speech.

❹ **Size of object and audience.** Imagine spending hours preparing a series of pictures, graphs, and charts for a speech on U.S. immigration reform. However, no one beyond the third row could see them. This violates the cardinal rule of presentational aids: To be valuable, they must be visible. Whether you use a flip-chart or bring in an object of some kind, people in the back of the room need to see it. If they cannot see what is on the table or cannot read a chart clearly, the aid does not serve its purpose.

Consider both object and audience size. Bringing a rare coin, say the 1944 steel penny, to show the class is not helpful because it is too small. And, even if you bring in enough coins for everyone, you take the risk of losing their attention as they examine the penny, drop it, make friendly wagers, or otherwise play with it during your speech. Students are better served by viewing an enlarged picture of the coin on a slide or poster. Showing an 8"x10" picture of the penny would be appropriate in a small class but not in an auditorium where it would need to be projected onto a large screen. Next we examine principles for *using* aids.

Principles for Using Presentational Aids

1. **Do not let your presentational aid distract your audience.** When you pass things around the room, you compete with them as you speak. Your listeners read your handouts, play with foreign coins, eat cookies you baked, and analyze your models instead of listening to you. If handouts are necessary, distribute them at the end of the speech. When appropriate, invite people to take a close look at your displays after your speech. This first suggestion is provided as a general rule, and as noted earlier, exceptions do exist.

2. **Be aware of timing and pauses.** Timing is important. Display each visual only as you talk about it. Do not force people to choose between paying attention to you and paying attention to your aid. If you prepare your flip chart in advance, leave a blank sheet between each page and turn the page when you are finished with the specific point. Cover your models with a sheet. Turn the projector off. Erase your diagram from the blackboard. Turn your poster board around. These actions tell your audience you want them to look at you again.

Display your presentational aid and then pause two or three seconds before talking. This moment of silence gives your audience time to look at the display. You do not want to compete with your own visual aid. Conversely, try to avoid excessively long pauses as you demonstrate the steps in a process.

To demonstrate to his class how to truss a turkey, a student brought in everything he needed including a turkey, string, and poultry pins. He began by explaining the procedure but stopped talking for about five minutes while he worked. Although many members of the class paid attention to his technique, several lost interest. He would have benefited from preparing some turkey trivia, stories, or humorous anecdotes that he could slide in while working. Without a verbal presentation to accompany the visual, our attention drifts to other things. Because most audiences need help in maintaining their focus, keep talking.

❸ Make sure the equipment is working but be prepared for failure. Set up in advance. Make sure equipment is working *before* class, and know how to operate the it. This includes CDs, DVDs, portable music, white board, and the computer/projector. Instructors are frustrated when time is lost, and students become bored when a speaker wastes valuable class time trying to discover how the equipment works. Similarly, find out in advance if the classroom computer is equipped for the Internet, a jump drive or zip disk, and specific programs you are counting on using.

Be prepared for equipment failure. What is Plan B? How much time are you willing to waste before you acknowledge that you cannot use Plan A? Your audience may be sympathetic to your troubles, but we really do not want to hear you complain about it. Your presentation may be acceptable without the high tech. Perhaps bring in a jump drive *and* a CD *and* email the presentation materials to yourself so you have online access to it as well. Maybe you want to use handouts or, as a back-up plan, write on the blackboard. Be prepared. Having multiple ways to get the visuals across may seem redundant until that one really bad day when Plans A, B, and C do not work and you have a Plan D to go to.

❹ Use multimedia presentations only with careful planning and practice. Multimedia presentations are effective, but they can be challenging. Gracefully moving from a flip chart, to the computer, to a tabletop model requires skill that comes from practice and experience. Mixing media increases your chance that something will go wrong. You can mix media successfully, but careful planning and preparation are essential. Can speakers act with the listener in mind when developing multimedia presentations, just as they do when developing their speeches? Is it possible to have audience-centered advanced technologies accompany a presentation? We believe so, and the following section presents guidelines to help you get there.

Making and Using Computer-Generated Images

You probably learned how to create PowerPoint presentations well before you reached college. By now, you have probably seen hundreds, if not thousands, of PowerPoint presentations. This rise in use is surely because effective computer-generated graphics can have a great impact on listeners. But not always. Many of you can relate to the cartoon shown in Figure 10.13. Too many slides, coupled with a dry, monotonous delivery, spells disaster. "Some of the world's most satisfying naps, deepest day dreams, and most elaborate notebook doodles are inspired by the following phrase, 'I'll just queue up

this PowerPoint presentation,'" states Josh Shaffer (2006), staff writer for the Raleigh, North Carolina *News & Observer*.

Some scholars are concerned that when students give speeches with "poorly designed and poorly performed multimedia," they create ineffective presentations; therefore, students must learn to "distinguish ineptitude from eloquence" in accompanying multimedia (Cyphert, 2007, p. 187). In other words, beginning speakers typically lack skill in public speaking *and* creating presentational aids. For this reason, we include guidance for using presentational software. Although aimed primarily at computer-generated graphics, much of the following applies to all presentational aids.

❶ Choose a presentational aid that fits your purpose, the occasion, and your audience. Develop a clear, specific purpose early in the creative process. If you begin with a specific purpose in mind that fits your goals, the audience's needs, and the requirements of the occasion, you are more likely to find and use relevant technology. Katherine Murray, author of more than 40 computer books, offers the suggestion, "Start with the end in mind" (www.microsoft.com). Knowing what you are trying to accomplish should guide you in designing accompanying multimedia presentations.

Choose aids appropriate for the occasion. Certain situations are more serious, professional, intimate, or formal than others. Displaying a cartoon during a congressional hearing, for example, may diminish the credibility of the speaker.

Consider whether the visual support is right for your listeners, analyzing their ages, socioeconomic backgrounds, knowledge, and attitudes toward your subject. Remember that some listeners are offended by visuals that are too graphic. Pictures of abused children,

FIGURE 15.13

Dilbert causes a PowerPoint tragedy.
© *Scott Adams/Dist. by United Feature Syndicate, Inc.*

for example, can be offensive to an audience not prepared for what they will see. If you have doubts about the appropriateness of a visual, leave it out of your presentation.

Presentation specialist Dave Parodi (2004) urges people to "awaken themselves to the power of a well-designed, well-structured, well-delivered presentation, and work as hard as they can to make it happen." These words have great instructional value.

❷ **Emphasize only relevant points.** Do not be "PowerPointless," according to Barb Jenkins of the South Australia Department of Education, Training and Employment. Avoid "any fancy transitions, sounds, and other effects that have no discernible purpose, use, or benefit" (www.wordspy.com). The bells and whistles may be fun, but they can be annoying or, worse, distracting.

In your desire to create an attractive, professional slide presentation, do not forget the message. It is easy to find tips on general design, the number of words per slide, number of slides, images, transitions, color, and so on. After you select the presentational aid that meets your purpose most effectively, decide what information needs to be on each slide. Link only the most important points in your speech with a presentational aid. Focus on your thesis statement and main points, and decide what words or concepts need to be highlighted graphically.

Our suggestion: Keep your visuals simple: Convey one idea. You may want to use a second visual rather than include more information than your listeners can process. Animations, sound, and visual effects tend to be overused, distracting, and time consuming both in creation and display. Eliminate extraneous material.

❸ **Implement the "Rule of Six."** Use no more than six words per line, and no more than six lines per slide. Avoid using full sentences. This is an outline, not an essay. Make the text easy to read. Words need to be large enough, and do not think that using CAPITALIZED words will help. In addition to being a symbol for yelling when instant messaging, it actually takes more effort to read words that are all capitalized. Try using 24-point type or larger. If the audience cannot read your slide, the message is lost.

Compare Figure 10.14A with Figure 10.14B. Similarities include the title, points covered, and organization. However, Figure 10.14a violates many rules of effective PowerPoint, including too many icons (too busy), full sentences, and small font size. Figure 10.14b is clear, simple, and professional. The template used would be appropriate for all slides used for a presentation on traveling abroad.

FIGURE 15.14A

What features make this
an ineffective PowerPoint
slide?

FIGURE 15.14B

What features make this
an effective PowerPoint
slide?

FIGURE 15.15

Colors opposite each other on this wheel provide the most striking contrast for visual displays. Using an overhead projector during your speech gives you greater flexibility than many other visual aids.

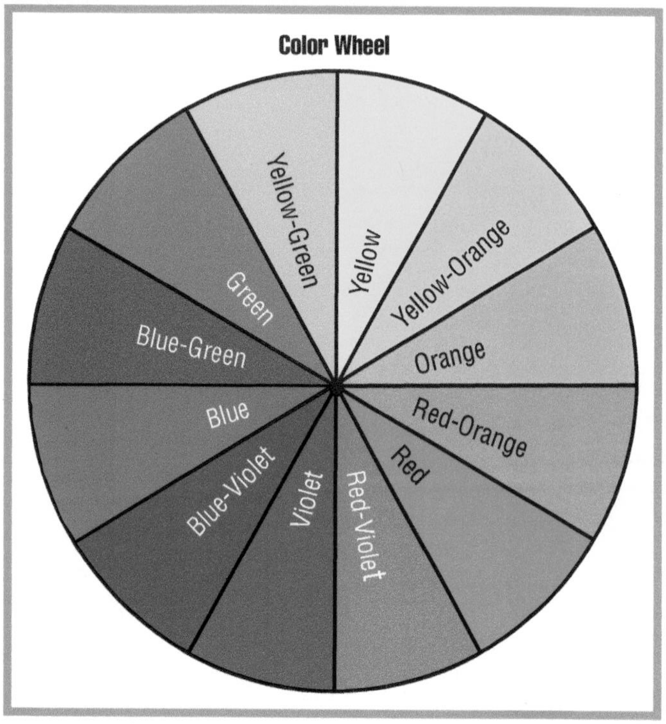

Color Wheel

Yellow-Green
Yellow
Green
Yellow-Orange
Blue-Green
Orange
Blue
Red-Orange
Blue-Violet
Red
Violet
Red-Violet

❹ **Select appropriate design features.** Decisions need to be made regarding template, type of font, and color. The template, which provides color, style, and decorative accents may be distracting to your audience if you change it regularly. Use one template consistently. In general, select a simple font. While font types may look fun, cute, or dramatic, they may be hard to read and distracting. Keep your audience focused on the message; they may be distracted from the text if you have moving animation and slides filled with special effects.

Make sure the font type and font color complement the template. Rely on strong, bold colors that make your message stand out even in a large auditorium. In their article "About Choosing Fonts for Presentations," Microsoft Office Online suggests, "To ensure readability, choose font colors that stand out sharply against the background" (Microsoft Office PowerPoint, 2003). The words you place on the slide should not melt into the background color. Aim for contrast but keep in mind that the contrast you see on your computer screen may not exist on the projected screen.

Research on college students shows that color aids students' ability to organize and recall information and to solve problems (Kraus, 2008). The color wheel in **Figure 10.15** will help you choose contrasting colors. You will achieve the strongest contrasts by using colors opposite one another. Blue and orange make an effective visual combination, as do red and green, and so on. Colors opposite each other on this wheel provide the most striking contrasts for visual displays.

❺ **Avoid allowing your presentational aid to upstage you.** Keep in mind that your audience has come to hear you, not to see your presentational aids. If you create a situation in which the visual support is more important than the speaker or the purpose of the speech, you will have defeated your purpose and disappointed your audience.

Be protective of the beginning and end of your presentation. It is usually prudent to avoid using any presentational aid for the first few moments. After you set the tone of your speech and introduce your main idea, turn to your first aid. Likewise, do not use a presentational aid to end your speech. Doing this risks the person-to-person contact you have built to that point by shifting the focus away from you. These are merely guidelines. Some speakers have both begun and ended speeches effectively with well-selected media.

6 Preview and practice. An inability to navigate smoothly through your slides limits your effectiveness (Howell, 2008). After creating your slides, run through them. Make sure slides are in the correct order, and that font type, font color, and font size are consistent. Proofread and run spell check. Make printouts of your slides. Then practice the speech using your slides. According to a 2009 survey, the most annoying aspect of the PowerPoint presentation is "the speaker read the slides to us" (Paradi, 2009).

One way to avoid sounding as though you are reading to the audience is through practice. Adding some type of presentational aid makes practicing even more important because you do not want to disrupt the flow of your speech. A reflective pause after displaying a slide can be powerful (Howell, 2008).

During your practice session, focus on your audience, not your presentational aid. Many speakers turn their backs on the audience. They talk to the projection screen or poster instead of looking at the audience. To avoid this tendency, become familiar with your aid so that you have little need to look at it during your talk. Use a remote control, if possible, so you can move more freely.

Summary

Presentational aids serve many functions in a speech. For public speakers, choosing a presentational aid that fits the purpose, occasion, and above all, is audience-centered is paramount. Advantages of using aids in a speech include making the message more memorable, available, clear, persuasive, and entertaining. On the other hand, they can be impersonal, time consuming, serve as a smoke screen for ineffective speakers, result in reductionism, and be too predictable.

Presentational aids fall into four general categories, including actual objects, three-dimensional models, two-dimensional reproductions, and technology-based visual aids. Two-dimensional reproductions include photographs, diagrams and drawings, maps, tables, and charts. Two-dimensional visual aids can be mounted on poster board and displayed on an easel or displayed on a flip chart, or on repositional note pads. Technology-based visual aids include slides, videotape and audiotape, projections, and computer-generated images.

To present effective aids, choose the points in your speech that need visual support; set up your presentation in advance; never let your presentational aids upstage you. Use multimedia presentations only if they are well planned and rehearsed. Avoid repeating what your audience sees in the visual and learn to display each aid only when you are talking about it. Focus on your audience, not your visual. Display your visual, then pause before talking, although you need to avoid long pauses during demonstrations. Do not circulate your presentational aids around the room. Presentational technology should be used when it emphasizes relevant points, adheres to the "Rule of Six," offers appropriate design features, does not upstage, and is used comfortably because it has been well rehearsed.

Typically we give a speech before live audiences, but we may also record that speech for later playback. A speech may be given over the radio, during a video conference, or presented as part of a webinar or podcast. Speakers using technology as a medium for their speeches make important adjustments when an audience is not "live" and face-to-face. These include dressing appropriately for the camera, if present, communicating energy, articulating clearly, avoiding meaningless pauses and verbal fillers, and maintaining acceptable audio quality and sound levels.

Discussion Starters

1 Do you think technology is inherently persuasive? When does it add impact beyond the power of the content of a message? When does it distract from the content of a message?

2 What criteria for using presentational aids would you add to the list? If you were Emperor of the World and you had the power, what decrees would you make? Can you provide three laws of the land that you would enforce on all presenters in your world?

3 How might technology augment ethos, pathos, and logos?

4 Is the speaker who uses more technology in a speech more credible than one who uses less or no technology?

5 Has increased technology made people more or less connected? Why?

6 Do students generally rehearse the use of their presentational aids for classroom reports? How about professional speakers; do you think they rehearse? If more students understood the potential payoff for rehearsing with their aids, do you think more would do dress rehearsals, or do you think most already understand this but don't make time for it anyway? Why would that be the case, even for some?

7 What should you keep in mind as you design and develop a PowerPoint presentation? What is death-by-PowerPoint? How can you avoid this epidemic? What is the appropriate level of "PowerPointedness"?

References

Alley, M., & Neeley, K. A. (2005). Rethinking the Design of Presentation Slides: A Case for Sentence Headlines and Visual Evidence. *Technical Communication, 52*(4), 417–426.

Carey, R. (1999). Spice it up. *Successful Meetings, October,* 47–50.

CTIA Semi-Annual Wireless Industry Survey. Retrieved May 17, 2011 from ctia.org/research.

Cyphert, D. (2007). Presentation Technology in the Age of Electronic Eloquence: From Visual Aid to Visual Rhetoric. *Communication Education, 56*(2), 168–192.

Foresman, C. *Wireless Survey: 91% of Americans Use Cell Phones.* Retrieved May 17, 2011 from arstechnica.com.

German Twenty-Somethings Prefer Internet to Partner. Retrieved March 2, 2009 from reuters.com.

Hickey, A. R. (2010, August 2). *Social Networking Dominates U.S. Web Use; Facebook Leads the Way.* Retrieved from www.crn.com.

Howell, D. D. (2008). Four Key Keys to Powerful Presentations in PowerPoint: Take Your Presentation to the Next Level. *TechTrends, 52*(6).

Internet Usage Statistics for the Americas. Retrieved June 30, 2010 from internetworldstats.com.

Kalyuga, P., Chandler, P., & Sweller, J. (1991). When Redundant On-Screen Text in Multimedia Technical Instruction Can Interfere with Learning. *Human Factors, 46*(3), 567–581.

Kraus, R. (2008). Presentation Software: Strong Medicine or Tasty Placebo? *Canadian Journal of Science, Mathematics and Technology Education, 8*(1), 70–81.

Lapchick, R. E., Harrison, K., & Hill, F. *Keeping Score When It Counts: Academic Rates for Teams in the 2009–2010 NCAA Division Bowl Games.* Retrieved from www.tidessports.com.

Lapchick, R. E., Harrison, K., & Hill, F. *Keeping Score When It Counts: Academic Rates for Teams in the 2011 NCAA Division I Men's Basketball Study.* Retrieved from www.tidessports.com.

Mayer, R. E. (2001). *Multimedia Learning.* New York: Cambridge University Press.

Morales, X. Y. Z. G. (2010). *Networks to the Rescue: Tweeting Relief and Aid During Typhoon Ondoy.* Thesis abstract. Retrieved from www.firstsearch.oclc.org.

Nicholson, D. T. (2002, Summer). Lecture Delivery Using MSPowerPoint: Staff and Student Perspectives at MMU. *Learning and Teaching in Action.* Retrieved from www.celt.mmu.ac.uk.

Paradi, D. (2009). *Results from the 2009 Annoying PowerPoint Survey.* Retrieved from thinkoutsidetheslide.com.

A Polycom Fact Sheet. *The Top Five Benefits of Video Conferencing.* Retrieved from polycom.com/telepresence.

Purcell, K., Rainie, L., Rosenstiel, T., & Mitchell, A. (2011, March 14). *How Mobile Devices Are Changing Community Information Environments.* Retrieved from pewinternet.org.

Smith, A. (2011, March 17). *The Internet and Campaign 2010.* Retrieved from pewinternet.org.

Travel Weekly. (2008, October 16). Business Travel: The Rise of Video-Conferencing. Retrieved from travelweekly.com.

Tufte, E. R. (1997). *Visual Explanations: Images and Quantities, Evidence and Narrative.* Cheshire, CT: Graphics Press.

Tufte, E. R. (2006). *The Cognitive Style of PowerPoint: Pitching Out Corrupts Within,* 2nd Ed. Graphics Press: Cheshire CT.

U.S. Department of Education, National Center for Education Statistics. (2008). *Distance Education at Degree-Granting Postsecondary Institutions: 2006–07.* Retrieved May 16, 2011 from nces.ed.gov/fastfacts.

Wazlawick, P., Bevelas, J. B., & Jackson, D. D. (1967). *Pragmatics of Human Communication: A Study of Interactional Patterns, Pathologies, and Paradoxes.* New York: Norton.

Wright, J. (2009). The Role of Computer Software in Presenting Information. *Nursing Management, 16*(4).

Zetter, K. (2011). TED 2011: Wael Ghonim—Voice of Egypt's Revolution. *Wired,* March 5. Retrieved from www.wired.com.

GLOSSARY

A

Abstract topics
Ideas, theories, principles, and beliefs.

Acceptance speech
A speech given to express gratitude for an award.

Accurate
Reliable, current, and error-free.

Adapting
Making your speech fit the audience's needs.

Adoption
When you want your audience to start doing something.

After-dinner speech
Purpose is to entertain, often with humor, although it usually conveys a thoughtful message.

Alliteration
The repetition of the initial consonant or initial sounds in a series of words.

Analogy
Establishes common links between similar and not-so-similar concepts.

Anaphora
The repetition of the same word or phrase at the beginning of successive clauses or sentences.

Anecdote
A short account of an interesting or humorous incident.

Antithesis
The use of contrast, within a parallel grammatical structure, to make a rhetorical point.

Aristotle
Ancient Greek philosopher. Lived 384–322 BCE.

Articulation
The verbalization of distinct sounds and how precisely words are formed.

Asyndeton
The deliberate omission of conjunctions between a series of related clauses.

Attacking
Occurs when a speaker attacks the person rather than the substance of the person's argument

Attitudes
Predispositions to act in a particular way that influences our response to objects, events, and situations.

Audience-centered
Showing your audience you understand their needs and want to help them achieve their goals.

Authority
An individual cited or considered to be an expert; power to influence or command thought; credible.

B

Bandwagoning
Unethical speakers may convince listeners to support their point of view by telling them that "everyone else" is already involved.

Beliefs
Represent a mental and emotional acceptance of information. They are judgments about the truth or the probability that a statement is correct.

Body
Includes your main points and supporting material that reinforces your specific purpose and thesis statement.

Brainstorming
Generating a list of ideas consistent with the goals of your speech.

C

Calculated ambiguity
A speaker's planned effort to be vague, sketchy, and considerably abstract.

Captive audience
Those who are required to attend.

Cause-and-effect pattern
Arranging main points into causes and effects.

Civic responsibility
The duty of citizens in a democracy to participate in governance of their society by voting, debating issues, and volunteering for public office or public service.

Claim
A statement or contention the audience is urged to accept.

Cliché
A trite phrase.

Commemorative speech
An inspirational message designed to stir emotions.

Communication
The creation of shared meaning through symbolic processes.

Communication apprehension
An individual's level of fear or anxiety associated with either real or anticipated communication with another person or persons.

Comparative-advantages organizational pattern
Place alternative solutions to a problem side-by-side and discuss the advantages and disadvantages of each.

Computer-based system
Includes a webcam and free software.

Conclusion
Supports the body of your speech, reinforces your message and brings your speech to a close.

Connotation
The meaning we ascribe to words as framed by our personal experience.

Continuance
When your listeners are already doing the thing you want them to do.

Coverage
The depth and breadth of the material.

Credibility
The extent to which a speaker is perceived as a competent spokesperson.

Criteria-satisfaction pattern
Demonstrating how your idea has the features your audience needs.

Culture
The rules people follow in their relationships with one another; values; the feelings people share about what is right or wrong, good or bad, desirable or undesirable; customs accepted by the community of institutional practices and expressions; institutions; and language.

Currency
The timeliness of the material.

D

Data
Evidence in support of an idea you advocate.

Declamation
A form of public speaking that is forceful and dramatic.

Deductive reasoning
Drawing conclusions based on the connections between statements that serve as premises.

Delayed feedback
Audience response after the speech is performed.

Demographics
Age, gender, race and ethnicity, education/knowledge, group affiliation, occupational group, socioeconomic status, religious background, political affiliation, and geographic identifiers of listeners.

Denotative
Literal, objective definition provided by a dictionary.

Desktop system
Dedicated software improves the audio and video quality.

Deterrence
Your goal is to convince your listeners not to start something.

Dialogic communication
Demonstrates an honest concern for the welfare of the listeners.

Discontinuance
An attempt to persuade your listeners to stop doing something.

Dynamic variables
Those things that are subject to change.

E

Emphasis
Stressing certain words or phrases to draw attention.

Epistrophe
The repetition of a word or expression at the *end* of phrases, clauses, sentences.

Equality pattern
Giving equal time to each point.

Ethics
The rules we use to determine good and evil, right and wrong. These rules may be grounded in religious principles, democratic values, codes of conduct, and bases of values derived from a variety of sources.

Ethnocentrism
The belief that one's own culture is superior to other cultures.

Ethos
Ethical appeal, makes speakers worthy of belief.

Eulogy
A commemorative speech that involves paying tribute to a family member, friend, colleague, or community member who died.

Euphemism
A word or phrase substituted for more direct language.

Evaluation
Assessing the worth of the speaker's ideas and determining their importance to you.

Examples
Support that illustrates a point or claim.

Extemporaneous speaking
A method of delivery that involves using carefully prepared notes to guide the presentation.

Extrinsic ethos
A speaker's image in the mind of the audience.

Eye contact
The connection you form with listeners through your gaze.

F

Facts
Verifiable and irrefutable pieces of information.

Fallacies
Appealing to audience emotions to disguise the deficit of the speaker's logic not holding up under scrutiny.

False analogy
Compares two things that are not really comparable.

False cause
When a speaker uses a fallacy to point out that because one event happened before another event, the first event caused the second event.

Figurative analogy
Drawing comparisons between things that are distinctly different in an attempt to clarify a concept or persuade.

Fixed-alternative questions
Limit responses to several choices, yielding valuable information about such demographic factors as age, education, and income.

Flow chart
Used to display the steps, or stages, in a process.

Forum
Group members respond to audience questions.

G

General encyclopedias
Cover a wide range of topics in a broad manner.

General purpose
There are three general purposes for speeches: to inform, to persuade, and to entertain or inspire.

Gestures
Using your arms and hands to illustrate, emphasize, or provide a visual experience that accompanies your thoughts.

Glittering generalities
Relying on audience's emotional responses to values such as home, country, and freedom.

Group-oriented goals
Center around specific tasks to be performed.

Groupthink
Conformity in thought and behavior among the members of a group.

H

Hasty generalization
A fallacy based on quantity of data.

Hearing
The physical ability to receive sounds.

Hidden agenda
Private motivation for acting in a certain way. This is unethical behavior.

Hypothetical example
A fictional example; the circumstances they describe are often realistic and thus effective.

I

Imagery
Creating a vivid description through the use of one or more of our five senses.

Immediate feedback
Audience response as the speech is performed.

Impromptu speaking
Speaking with little or no preparation time; using no notes or just a few.

Inductive reasoning
Generalizing from specific examples and drawing conclusions from what we observe.

Information literacy
Consuming information wisely and appropriately.

Informative speech
Communicates information and ideas in a way that your audience will understand and remember.

Innuendos
Veiled lies, hints, or remarks that something is what it is not.

Internal previews
Extended transitions that tell the audience, in general terms, what you will say next.

Internal summaries
Follow a main point and act as reminders; useful to clarify or emphasize what you have just said.

Interpreting
Attaching meaning to a speaker's words.

Intrinsic ethos
Ethical appeal found in the actual speech, including such aspects as supporting material, argument flow, and source citation.

Introduction
Supports the body of your speech and should capture your audience's attention and indicate your intent.

J

Jargon
Technical terminology unique to a special activity or group.

K

Keynote speaker
Featured speaker at an event.

Key-word search
A Web search that leads you to a list of records that are weighted in order of amount of user access.

L

Line graph
Used to show a trend over time.

Listener
Perceives through sensory levels and interprets, evaluates, and responds to what he or she hears.

Listening
The attending, receiving, interpreting, and responding to messages presented aurally.

Literal analogy
Compares like things from similar classes, such as a game of professional football with a game of college football.

Logos
An appeal that is rational and reasonable based on evidence provided.

M

Metaphor
A symbol that tells your listeners that you are saying more.

Monologic communication
From this perspective, the audience is viewed as an object to be manipulated and, in the process, the speaker displays such qualities as deception, superiority, exploitation, dogmatism, domination, insincerity, pretense, coercion, distrust, and defensiveness.

Mood
The overall feeling you hope to engender in your audience.

Mythos
A term given when content supports a claim by reminding an audience how the claim is consistent with cultural identity.

N

Name calling
Linking a person or group with a negative symbol.

Nonfluencies
Meaningless words that interrupt the flow of our speech; also known as filled pauses or vocal fillers.

Norms
Often invisible social structures that group members develop that govern behavior.

O

Objectivity
Information that is fair and unbiased.

Open-ended question
Audience members can respond however they wish.

Opinions
Points of view that may or may not be supported in fact.

Opposed audience
This audience does not agree with you, is not friendly or sympathetic, and will search for flaws in your argument.

Oratory
A form of eloquent public speaking.

Organizational chart
Organized according to official hierarchies that determine the relationships of people as they work.

Organization of ideas
The placement of lines of reasoning and supporting materials in a pattern that helps to achieve your specific purpose.

P

Panel discussion
Group members have an informal interchange on the issues in front of an audience.

Pathos
Persuading through emotional appeals.

Personification
Investing human qualities in abstractions or inanimate objects either through metaphor, simile, or analogy.

Persuasive speech
Public speaking meant to influence the way people think about a given subject.

Philosophes
French intellectuals, including philosophers, writers, scientists who wrote about new ideas such as reason, religious tolerance, and natural rights during the Enlightenment Era.

Physical noise
Anything in the environment that distracts the speaker or listeners.

Physiological noise
A result of our senses failing us in some way.

Pictograph
Most commonly used as a variation of the bar graph. Instead of showing bars of various lengths, comparing items on the graph, the bars are replaced by pictorial representations of the graph's subject.

Pie graph
Also known as circle graphs, shows how the parts of an item relate to the whole.

Pitch
Vocal range or key, the highness or lowness of your voice produced by the tightening and loosening of your vocal folds.

Plagiarism
Using another's work, words, or ideas without adequate acknowledgment.

Plain folks
An effort to identify with the audience.

Positive visualization
Creating powerful mental images of skillful performances and winning competitions.

Primacy effect
The belief that it is the first point in your speech that listeners will most likely remember.

Primary group
A group that fills the basic need to associate with others, such as family and best friends.

Primary sources

Firsthand accounts such as diaries, journals, and letters, as well as statistics, speeches, and interviews. They are records of events as they are first described.

Problem–solution pattern

Presenting an audience with a problem and then examining one or more likely solutions.

Progressive pattern

Progression from least important argument to most important argument.

Pronunciation

Knowing how to say a word and saying it correctly.

Proposition of fact

Persuading your listeners that your interpretation of a situation, event, or concept is accurate.

Proposition of policy

Easily recognizable by their use of the word "should."

Proposition of value

Persuading your listeners based on deep-seated beliefs.

Psychographics

The lifestyle choices, attitudes, beliefs, and values of your listeners.

Psychological noise

A distraction that exists in an individual's mind.

R

Rate

The pace at which you speak.

Reacting/responding

Providing feedback to the speaker's message.

Recency effect

The belief that it is the last point in your speech that listeners will most likely remember.

Red herring

Occurs when a speaker attempts to divert the attention of the audience from the matter at hand.

Research

The raw material that forms the foundation of your speech.

Rhetoric

The art of persuasive speech.

S

Scale questions

A type of fixed-alternative question that asks people to respond to questions set up along a continuum.

Secondary group

A group that accomplishes a task or achieves a goal.

Secondary sources

Generally provide an analysis, an explanation, or a restatement of a primary source.

Self-oriented goals

Relate to the individual's personal needs and ambitions.

Semantic noise

The disconnect between the speaker's words and the listener's interpretation.

Sensing

To become aware of or to perceive.

Similes

Create images as they compare the characteristic of two different things using words "like" and "as."

Slang

Use of informal words and expressions that are not considered standard in the speaker's language.

Slippery slope
This fallacy claims there will be a chain reaction that will end in some dire consequence.

Specialized encyclopedias
Focus on particular areas of knowledge in more detail.

Specific purpose
The precise response you want from your audience.

Speech of demonstration
When the focus is on *how* something is done.

Speech of description
Helps an audience understand *what* something is.

Speech of explanation
Helps an audience understand *why* something is so.

Speech of introduction
Introduces the person who will give an important address.

Speech of presentation
Delivered as part of a ceremony to recognize an individual or group chosen for special honors.

Static variables
Those things that remain stable from speaking situation to speaking situation.

Statistics
The collection, analysis, interpretation, and presentation of information in numerical form.

Stereotypes
Related to race, ethnicity, or nationality, even if these groups are not present in your audience.

Strongest point pattern
You spend the most time in your speech on the first point, less time on the second point, and even less time on the last point of your speech.

Studio-based system
Offers the best quality, but also is most expensive.

Supporting material
The information used in a particular way to make your case.

Supportive audience
An audience that agrees with you.

Symposium
Prepared speeches on a specified subject given by group members who have expertise on the subject.

Systematic desensitization
A premise that people have learned to associate anxious states with public speaking.

T

Testimonials
Statements testifying to benefits received; can be both helpful and destructive.

Thesis statement
The core idea; identifies the main ideas of your speech.

Toast
Brief message of good will and congratulations.

Tone
The emotional disposition of the speaker as the speech is being delivered.

Transitions
Verbal bridges between ideas; words; phrases, or sentences that tell your audience how ideas relate.

U

Uncommitted audience
An audience that is neither friendly nor hostile, but most likely not sympathetic.

V

Values

Socially shared ideas about what is good, right, and desirable; deep-seated abstract judgments about what is important to us.

Volume

The loudness of your voice, controlled by how forcefully air is expelled through the trachea onto the vocal folds.

Voluntary audience

Those who choose to attend.

W

Warrant

An inference that links the evidence with the claim.

INDEX